Mental Health Care and Social Policy

EDITED BY PHIL BROWN

BROWN UNIVERSITY

Routledge & Kegan Paul
Boston, London, Melbourne and Henley

First published in 1985
by Routledge & Kegan Paul plc

9 Park Street, Boston, Mass. 02108, USA

14 Leicester Square, London WC2H 7PH, England

464 St Kilda Road, Melbourne,
Victoria 3004, Australia and

Broadway House, Newtown Road,
Henley on Thames, Oxon RG9 1EN, England

Set in Linotron Times, 10/12 pt
by Input Typesetting Ltd, London
and printed in Great Britain
by T. J. Press (Padstow) Ltd,
Padstow, Cornwall

Library of Congress Cataloging in Publication Data

Mental health care and social policy.

   1. Mental health services—United States. 2. Mental
health policy—United States. 3. Psychiatry—United
States—Methodology. I. Brown, Phil.
RA790.6.M397   1985   362.2′0973   84–23796

ISBN 0–7100–9899–5 (c)
     0–7102–0472–8 (p)

Department of Social and Administrative Studies,
Barnett House,
Wellington Square,
Oxford.

*M*ford.

a

BROWN, Phil (editor)

Mental Health Care and
Social Policy

IE 70

In loving memory of my father, William Brown and my father-in-law, Eli A. Littenberg

Contents

Preface

In teaching sociology of mental health and illness courses for many years, I have always been plagued by not having just the right readings, especially for issues of social policy and service delivery. There were no books which presented the material as I wished to teach it. I would send students to the library to read journal articles, but no single library ever has all the necessary ones. So I embarked on a project to write a monograph on the subject of mental health policy and services, (*The Transfer of Care: Psychiatric Deinstitutionalization and its Aftermath*, Routledge & Kegan Paul, 1985), and to produce an anthology which could serve as either a supplement to the book, or as a collection in its own right.

Books always change shape as they are written, and anthology contents change too. The process of writing my other book led me to continually change my selection of articles for this one. Not only has this process improved the contents of this anthology, but it also makes it a more useful companion volume to *The Transfer of Care*.

Two colleagues and friends were very helpful in thinking about this book as it took shape. Peter Conrad and Joseph P. Morrissey spent many hours discussing with me the rationales for sections and articles, commenting on my choices and suggesting others. As this process unfolded it led to many stimulating discussions of the material, a wonderful side-effect of the writing process.

Henry J. Steadman also offered valuable comments on the anthology's contents. Peter Conrad and Carol Baker read the introductions to the book and the sections, and offered comments and criticisms. As my editor at Routledge & Kegan Paul, Carol provided all the support one could wish for. Ronnie Littenberg, my wife, has been for many years my most consistent supporter, avid discussant, and thoughtful critic. Her direct and indirect help have been influential in the creation of this anthology.

INTRODUCTION

This collection of articles is designed to provide a comprehensive overview of the major issues in mental health practices and policy in the United States. Most approaches to this subject are concerned with a variety of programs, providers and institutions, but rarely offer historical background. Nor do they emphasize the underlying social structural forces which affect mental health services. As a result, we are often at a loss to understand the many, seemingly disparate parts of the mental health system. Yet this network of services is a vast, expensive and troubled one which is increasingly in the public light. I have selected these articles for *Mental Health Care and Social Policy* to explain the recurrent problems and themes in mental health care, and to analyze the institutions, providers and treatments which pervade our society.

In the last two decades we have witnessed dramatic changes in the mental health system: the decline of the traditional state hospital, the birth of the community mental health center (CMHC), the expansion of psychiatric services in general hospitals, the creation of a huge nursing home population of chronically mentally ill persons, and the production of a corps of urban 'bag people.'

Compared to earlier times, citizens now have access to a larger number of mental health providers and services, as well as a greater variety of programs. Mental illness no longer need mean that a person will spend the rest of his or her life on the back wards of state hospitals. One need not travel long distances to what used to be the primary location of care – the state hospital. Nor is treatment predominantly inpatient any more.

A few statistics can illuminate some of these shifts. The 1955 peak of 559,000 state hospital inpatients fell to approximately 137,810 in

1980. A person diagnosed psychotic in a state hospital in 1950 would stay there for an average of twenty years, a neurotic for nine years. In 1975, inpatient treatment for psychotics lasted an average of nine months, while the outpatient treatment for neurotics averaged five months. By 1980, average length of stay in state hospitals was slightly over six months. In facilities which treat the majority of inpatients – general hospitals – average length of stay is only 11.6 days (Kiesler and Sibulkin, 1982). Outpatient treatment was rare in the immediate postwar years, but has risen 1,000 percent to the point where five times as many new psychiatric admissions are to outpatient services as to inpatient ones (Redlich and Kellert, 1978; Kiesler, 1982). State hospitals in 1977 accounted for 9 percent, rather than the 1955 figure of 49 percent of all psychiatric episodes[1] (Witkin, 1980). Focusing on inpatient episodes, we notice important changes in the location of mental health care. State hospitals and private asylums in 1979 accounted for only 25 percent of the nation's 3,012,500 inpatient episodes. General hospitals (with and without psychiatric units), however, accounted for 60 percent of total episodes.

These changes in the service delivery system have by no means been largely beneficial. Many errors have been made, and a good number of problems plague us at present. State hospital residents, especially the elderly, were discharged without adequate preparation, often to inappropriate community placements, and lacked continuity of care. Few follow-up studies were conducted to find out where discharged patients went and what happened to them. Deinstitutionalization was not coordinated with the new CMHCs, partly because the centers selected more interesting and less wounded populations. Planning became more chaotic as a multitude of federal, state and local agencies failed to mesh their goals and practices. Reimbursement restrictions favored inpatient care and private institutions, and fiscal crisis brought cutbacks. Practitioners and institutions did not reorient their work to serve the most needy, since that brought neither income nor creative prestige nor challenge. Nursing and boarding homes became the largest single location of mental health treatment, and this primarily profitmaking sector has been widely recognized to be quite often abusive and detrimental to patients' well-being. For the large number of persons falling between the cracks of the mental health system, homeless street life has become a common phenomenon.

These problems in the psychiatric arena have been criticized from many sides. Criticism has come from within the mental health fields, from various parts of state and federal governments, from patients and ex-patients, civil liberties organizations, lay mental health groups, trade unions, media, academia, the public-interest bar, and the judicial bench. Most critiques have been limited in scope, and have not dealt with deeper structural forces in the society as well as in the mental health sector. In *The Transfer of Care* I explained these issues in terms of several types of transfer of care.

There has been a transfer of chronic patient care from the mental health system to other social service systems and to non-system settings. Deinstitutionalization of state hospital patients represents an attempted transfer of financial responsibility from state mental health budgets to federal Medicaid and Social Security Supplemental Security Income (SSI) budgets. The relocation of chronic psychotics to nursing homes, boarding homes, flop houses and the street represents a transfer of social responsibility from professional psychiatric providers to low quality, non-psychiatric facilities. This relocation is a transfer of responsibility from public authority to private control. Even though there is government regulation of nursing homes (but very little regulation of boarding homes), that regulation is weaker than is governmental authority in direct service. Further, it is a transfer of responsibility from state mental health departments to public health and public welfare departments.

This transfer results in less attention to the psychiatric and psychological needs of patients. Patients need a wide range of social services – housing, health care, food assistance, income supports, recreation, rehabilitation, and employment training. Those needs could, hypothetically, be met by health and welfare departments, but rarely are those needs adequately served. For many chronic psychotics, those other social services are often the most important ones, since they involve the basic ability to survive on one's own outside the hospital. Indeed, while the old state hospital provided sparse therapeutic treatment, it did house, feed and otherwise care for the patients, even if poorly. The shift to the welfare sector also contributes to a transformation of the public perception of clients from mental patients to welfare cases, thus demeaning them further. Also, while the shift to nursing and boarding homes involves a shift of location, the new mini-institutions retain traditional forms of personal control and institutional rigidity.

In terms of acute care (and some chronic care) there has been a shift within the mental health system. This has involved the growth of private sector care (especially general hospital psychiatric care) to replace and/or augment public services. Even though this largely centered around a new public-private alliance, it is a transfer of power and authority to a private sector which is less accountable to government and public scrutiny.

The widespread critique mentioned above has not been the exclusive domain of public interest organizations and advocacy groups. Much of the sharp criticism of public mental health care has derived from investigations by the Congress's General Accounting Office, the Inspector-General of the former Department of Health, Education and Welfare, the National Institute of Mental Health, Congressional committees, and other such bodies. But these important investigations have not been able to penetrate deeply enough to understand the social forces directing this flawed mental health policy. A proper analysis requires a historically grounded, political-economic approach that can describe the legacy of early asylum building and reform, and articulate its present relationship to social, political and fiscal forces. Also needed is an emphasis on the role of professionalization, in order to understand practitioners' attitudes toward and treatment of patients, as well as the professionals' organizational development. Another requirement is an examination of institutional change strategy, relations between facilities, and matters of administrative and planning practice. These themes are treated in differing ways in this volume, though they are not always spelled out as such. It is therefore useful to outline these concerns briefly.

A political-economic approach informs us that the general direction of mental health services will reflect underlying social structures. For instance, the centrality of the profit motive in American society leads to a widening role for profit-making enterprise in psychiatric care, most notably in nursing and boarding home placements and in the expansion of the use of psychiatric drugs. The profitability of psychotropic drugs has been clear from the first widespread application of these drugs in the middle and late 1950s, though this profitability has increased with the growing numbers of ex-mental patients now taking drugs. The lucrative nursing and boarding home industry has been a more recent development, resulting from state hospital deinstitutionalization in the 1960s, and from new federal programs (Medicare, Medicaid and Social Security disability) which play such a large role in the homes. An additional aspect is the role of the federal government in the organization, regulation and financing of health services. This is particularly evident with reimbursement mechanisms of SSI, Medicare and Medicaid, and in the role of research and institutional support from a variety of government bodies such as the National Institutes of Health, and the National Institute of Mental Health. Although much power remains in the hands of professionals and institutions, state and federal controls have made important alterations in health care (Navarro, 1976). As will be evident, this governmental role is very central to mental health services. This government involvement may be positive, such as when it expands accessibility to underserved populations and breaks down local and state discrimination (especially racial). But federal health care intervention can have negative effects, such as when it bureaucratizes services or restricts them by fiscal austerity measures.

According to political-economic analyses, health professions and institutions function to reinforce and replicate existing class, gender and race stratification. This may occur due to unequal provision of health services, as well as due to preexisting structural forces which produce differential well-being. Related to the continuation of race, class and gender inequality is the professionalist monopoly of knowledge (which will be treated as a separate but related theme) and the individualist conception of health problems. This individualist ideology blames people for their health status, rather than locating the causes of ill health largely in the society's structural forces (Ryan, 1972; Navarro, 1976). Although most focus on political-economic matters is oriented to the present, the selections in the section on 'Historical and Conceptual Concerns' will demonstrate how these forces have always played fundamental roles in psychiatric care.

The issue of professionals' roles is key to mental health policy and services. As in other areas of medicine, physicians dominate the mental health field, directing the work of others. Professional dominance (Freidson, 1970) involves solidifying and expanding status, power and wealth through a monopoly of knowledge and skills, and through expansion into many new areas. Given the success of doctors in their professional advancement, other professionals have emulated them; in mental health this applies mainly to clinical psychologists. When mental health work is designed largely to benefit the providers, professional gains may detract from patient-oriented goals; this occurs, for instance, when professionals make selective choices of who will receive care and of what type of care will be given.

There is one issue which pertains more to mental health than to medicine – social values and social control. Historically, the mental health field has had a tradition of employing its power to enforce the existing social order. Nineteenth-century psychiatry applied medical concepts to defend slavery, oppose women's rights and attack immigration (Chesler, 1973; Thomas and Sillen, 1972). Such social control was by no means restricted to the last century. In recent times such racism and sexism have continued to play a large role in directing mental health ideologies and practices. Additionally, professional definitions of mental disorder frequently focus solely on the individual, with little regard for social factors.

The institutional framework of mental health care meshes with some of the professionalist factors. This is evident in the psychiatric expansionism of the 1960s and early 1970s, which increased the number and types of treatment locations, as well as expanding the purview of mental health professionals to include many non-psychiatric social problems. With this expansion came problems of bureaucratic management involving a lack of coordination between the multitude of agencies responsible for mental health services. At the state and/or federal planning level, as well as at the individual facilities level, there are always multiple goals (Perrow, 1963) and a multiplicity of purposes (Strauss *et al.*, 1964) which make it difficult to attain a unified policy. Deinstitutionalization and community mental health have been plagued by this disunity, though researchers and planners have not usually understood this complexity.

There are many linkages between political-economic, professional and institutional factors. The selections in this anthology treat these linkages in the mental health care system, and also in matters of mental health policy. A few words on the definition of policy are in order here. Given the above discussion of multiple goals and purposes, it may be unclear whether any overarching policy exists. Despite the lack of a unified program and goals, it does make sense to consider mental health practices to reflect a policy. One rationale for this approach is that mental health planners and government officials in the 1960s clearly considered that they were enbarking on large-scale policy formation. National Institute of Mental Health (NIMH) and other federal planning documents reveal this notion of coherent and rational policy-making. Studies on the policy and history of community mental health (e.g. Connery *et al.*, 1968; Foley, 1975; Bloom, 1975) also emphasize this coherence. Key Community Mental Health Center (CMHC) planners' retrospective analyses of the period likewise argue for a rational, comprehensive policy approach. Stanley Yolles, past NIMH chief, wrote that the establishment of community mental health centers was to be a *national public policy*: 'the first national effort to create a nationwide network of mental health services' (Yolles, 1975). President Kennedy (1963) stated that the goal was a 'national mental health program to assist in the inauguration of a wholly new emphasis and approach to care for the mentally ill.'

A second reason for taking this approach to policy analysis is based on Gil's (1976:3–16) conception of social policy as being the totality of how a society deals with its social and economic relations. According to Gil's framework, there are three mechanisms through which all social policies develop. First, *resource development* involves the basic resources needed for survival. Second, *division of labor* deals with the breakdown of tasks and roles by which society is maintained and reproduced. Third, *rights distribution* includes the allocation of resources and privileges in the society. This macro-level approach is important to mental health services since the new programs developed in the 1960s and 1970s contained elements of social change emphasis which touched upon many fundamental aspects of the social order. For instance, mental health planners hoped to apply community mental health strategies to deal with issues such as racism, poverty, urban decay and other forms of inequality.

A third and final reason for considering the panoply of mental health programs and developments as a policy is found in the definition of policy put forward by DiNitto and Dye (1983: 3–11) They argue against those who demand that a set of specific goals be evident in order to demonstrate the existence of social policy. Such a perspective, they argue, presupposes a well-planned, rational policy based on consensual values. Yet policy making is not so well-planned in reality. Further, policy-making is more political than scientific-rational. This results from the conflicting values of groups in an unequal social structure where there are no consensual values, no common recognition of social problem areas, and thus no agreed-upon solutions. As Dye (1972:2) observes, we can rarely visualize a government goal; we can only witness what a government actually does. Therefore,

> Realistically, our notion of public policy must include *all* actions of
> government – and not just stated intentions of governments or
> government officials. Finally, we must also consider governmental
> inaction – what a government chooses not to do – as public policy.

Applying the above three reasons for considering mental health services as a social policy matter enables us to make sense out of what might be seen by others as a chaotic non-policy. As the selections in this book demonstrate, there are important linkages and similarities between current programs, as well as over time. This anthology provides both descriptive and explanatory readings which permit us to make the important connections in analyzing modern psychiatric services and in seeking necessary improvements.

In order to provide the most current material, the selections – with a few exceptions – are no older than the late 1970s. To introduce these articles and their overall analysis of the mental health system, we begin with a section on 'Historical and conceptual concerns' which offers perspectives on the social conceptions of mental illness and on the ideological background which gave rise to community mental health reforms. These articles also demonstrate the continuity of problems from the early nineteenth century to the present time.

Section II, 'The changing mental health system,' explores the dynamics of institutional and noninstitutional care. These articles examine hospital deinstitutionalization, and the creation of new locations of care, such as CMHs, general hospitals, and nursing and boarding homes. Both the planned and the unintended outcomes are discussed, with reference to financial, professional, institutional, and civil libertarian factors.

Section III, 'Providers and treatments,' explores professional values and practices in psychiatry which shape the directions of mental health practice. This includes material on the education of psychiatrists and the social power which psychiatrists often obtain. There is also emphasis on the important role of psychiatric drugs as a cornerstone of modern mental health care.

The last section, on 'Alternatives' offers glimpses of alternative care in other countries, in somewhat traditional mental health models, and in patient-run and feminist alternative services in the

US. The rich variety of these alternatives demonstrates that despite the many flaws in current mental health services, there are options for progressive change.

Brief introductions to each section place the selections in their appropriate context. While the order of the selections has been carefully designed to provide a logical progression of the material, any one section may be readily understood by itself.

Notes

1 An episode is a period of treatment in any service during the reporting year which is begun by an admission or transfer, and terminated by a discontinuation or transfer. Episodes are counted even if the patient has been treated in the service at a prior time in the same year, and thus represent a duplicated count.

References

Bloom, Bernard L. 1975.
  Community Mental Health: A General Introduction. Monterey, CA: Brooks/Cole.
Chesler, Phyllis 1973.
  Women and Madness. New York: Avon Books.
Connery, Robert H. and associates 1968.
  The Politics of Mental Health: Organizing Community Mental Health in Metropolitan Areas. New York: Columbia University Press.
DiNitto, Diana M. and Thomas R. Dye 1983.
  Social Welfare: Politics and Public Policy. Englewood Cliffs, NJ: Prentice-Hall.
Dye, Thomas R. 1972.
  Understanding Public Policy. Englewood Cliffs, NJ: Prentice-Hall.
Foley, Henry A. 1975.
  Community Mental Health Legislation: The Formative Process. Lexington, MA: Lexington Books.
Freidson, Eliot 1970.
  Profession of Medicine: A Study of the Sociology of Applied Knowledge. New York: Dodd, Mead.
Gil, David G. 1976.
  Unravelling Social Policy. Cambridge: Schenkman.
Kennedy, J. F. 1963.
  Message on mental illness and mental retardation. Feb. 5, 1963, Congressional Record Vol. 88, No. 1, CIX, Part 2, 1744–1749.
Kiesler, Charles A. 1982.
  Public and professional myths about mental hospitalization: An empirical reassessment of policy-related beliefs. *American Psychologist*, 37: 1329–1339.

Kiesler, Charles, A. and Amy E. Sibulkin, 1982.

Episodic length of hospital stay for mental disorders. In G. M. Stephenson and J. H. Davis, eds, *Progress in Applied Social Psychology*, Vol. 2.

Navarro, Vicente 1976.

Medicine Under Capitalism. New York: Prodist.

Perrow, Charles 1963.

Goals and power structures: A historical case study. In Eliot Freidson, ed., *The Hospital in Modern Society*. New York: Free Press, pp. 112–146.

Redlich, Fritz and Stephen R. Kellert 1978.

Trends in American mental health. *American Journal of Psychiatry*, 135: 22–28.

Ryan, William 1972.

Blaming the Victim. New York: Vintage.

Strauss, Anselm, Leonard Schatzman, Rue Bucher, Danta Ehrlich, and Melvin Sabshin 1964.

Psychiatric Ideologies and Institutions. New York: Free Press.

Thomas, Alexander and Samuel Sillen 1972.

Racism and Psychiatry. New York: Brunner/Mazel.

Witkin, Michael J. 1980.

Trends in patient care episodes in mental health facilities, 1955–1977. *NIMH Statistical Note*, No. 154. Rockville, MD: NIMH.

Yolles, Stanley F. 1975.

Community psychiatry: 1963–1974. Paper presented April 25, 1975 at Missouri Institute of Psychiatry Research Seminar, University of Missouri School of Medicine, St Louis.

Part I

*Historical and
conceptual concerns*

INTRODUCTION

In this first part of the book, we are concerned with the social historical background of mental health care, and with a conceptual framework for studying mental health institutions and policy. The three selections here cover a long period of history, and the reader may wonder what can be learned about the present from eighteenth- and nineteenth-century concerns. Unfortunately, most examination of mental health policy has been flawed by ahistoricism. As these readings demonstrate, there is much to learn from the historical record, and these authors have pioneered in extrapolating current methods of examination from the past.

Andrew Scull's 'Madness and segregative control: The rise of the insane asylum' grounds the origins of the asylum in the political and economic system of its environment. Scull shows how emerging capitalist market relations required a more precise identification of able-bodied and non-able-bodied deviants. Relief and other social welfare programs would then be able to prevent the able-bodied from freeloading, and could attempt to inculcate work habits and social discipline into the recipients of relief. Further, these institutions were intended as punitive, restrictive locations where the able-bodied would work for their keep. Yet they became centers for the very non-able-bodied misfits.

The workhouse or almshouse was difficult to run with mentally ill residents, and an increasing differentiation of deviants was necessary. A growing state centralization made possible the centralization of deviant-processing institutions, so that the asylum became a highly structured phenomenon run by a more bureaucratic authority. The huge new madhouses, however, did not in fact operate very rationally in terms of patient care, since their size and changing social composition made moral treatment impossible. Whatever rationality existed was that which could maintain the bare minimum of survival in the easiest, most bureaucratic and most inexpensive way.

Still, rationalist, scientific beliefs held by dominant classes and groups led those social leaders to seek the advice and practices of an expert group of psychiatrists, thus providing a framework for professional development. This demand for a professional group, Scull argues, was a search for scientific legitimation of the developing institutional social control practices. It was also an attempt to classify existing mores and value systems as normal or abnormal. Scull goes beyond a conspiracy approach to labor-force control, however, in demonstrating that institutionalization in the custodial hospitals served the interests of various classes and the psychiatric profession.

The United States of the early nineteenth century saw the declineof informal, local care for the insane as a result of urbanization, industrialization and immigration. Some reformers responded with a naturalistic, optimistic attitude toward mental illness and a crusading theology concerned with mainstream social reform. In such an environment the state hospital boom began.

The first state mental hospitals employed 'moral treatment,' based on Tuke's English approach. This involved much interaction between provider and patient, in an attempt to restore the person's normal social involvement and sense of reality. Early successes of moral treatment were due to a small patient population of persons similar in background to the psychiatrist/superintendent, allowing for intensive therapy grounded in shared values. But within a decade there were more lower-class patients, which, combined with a growing inpatient census, led to a decline of personalized treatment in favor of an administrative psychiatry typified by its main text, Kirkbride's manual of asylum construction and maintenance. At midcentury, hospital directors and boards were openly nativist, alarmed at the many immigrant patients. An increase in the number of patients, and overworked staff led to an increased use of restraints, and a working-class and peasant immigrant clientele contributed to public support for protection and social control since such patients were considered unlikely to adjust to social norms. Psychiatry veered toward a somatic approach and a nihilistic prognosis that replaced the earlier 'cult of curability.' Thus a state hospital system was stripped of its original goals of short-term therapy for a small clientele. Those goals were to be carried out in smaller, elite private asylums, while public facilities faced financial constraints and growing prejudice.

David Rothman's book, *Conscience and Convenience: The Asylum and its Alternatives in Progressive America*, picks up the matter in the late nineteenth and early twentieth centuries. Scull's discussion of Rothman's earlier book, *The Discovery of the Asylum: Social Order and Disorder in the New Republic*, pointed out that Rothman focused too much on value systems and avoided discussion of the state and the economic factors. In 'The enduring asylum,' excerpted from Rothman's *Conscience and Convenience*, we observe greater attention to those factors. Rothman seeks to go beyond the recording of specific reforms, in order to examine the problematic elements of social service reform in general. He emphasizes the increasing power of the state, as well as the erroneous view of Progressive era reformers that the state was solely a benevolent actor.

Mental health reformers failed to consider realistic obstacles to their ideal notions. Failure, therefore, was viewed as due to faulty implementation; underlying assumptions and structures were not to be questioned. Thus the *conscience* of the reformers lost out to the various forms of *convenience*. For example, the new alternative facility, the psychopathic hospital, shortly came to function simply as a processing station along the path to the state hospital. The new hospitals themselves became overcrowded, and a new custodialism developed in the supposed alternative to custodialism.

Institutional self-preservation remained important. For instance, state hospitals did not want to board out or parole those patients who were most suitable for family care in the community, since the labor of those patients would be lost. Professionalist practices played their part too – psychiatrists largely opposed the development of outpatient care by hospitals for fear of incursions on private practice.

Joseph Morrissey, Howard Goldman and Lorraine Klerman's 'Cycles of institutional reform' provides an excellent synthesis of the last two centuries of mental health care, showing the continuity of problems. The authors show how the same issues constantly arose. Both the nineteenth-century project and the current community mental health and deinstitutionalization programs were flawed, since 'each movement was launched with little or nor appreciation of the practical limits to which the core ideas could be pushed.' For example, the cult of the asylum perpetuated faith in the state hospitals even when they were clearly unable to deal with a growing and more chronic population. In this century new techniques such as milieu therapy and psychoactive drugs were applauded, but there was sparse research on their use in chronic care or on the need for community support systems.

Both nineteenth- and twentieth-century mental health reforms were 'initially stimulated by therapeutic innovation but were ultimately accelerated by political-economic considerations.' In the former case, according to Morrissey *et al.*, concern shifted from moral treatment to custodial care at the cheapest cost. In the present,

fiscal conservatism was joined to the ideals of community mental
health advocates and civil libertarian reformers, but with little documentation of the cost-benefit virtues of deinstitutionalization and
no analysis of the social costs of dumping patients. Even now, as
deinstitutionalization is being reversed, there is still a paucity of clear
research knowledge.

Theoretically and analytically, Morrissey *et al.*'s sophisticated
effort builds on three themes. First, a social institutional perspective
examines manifest and latent functions of state hospitals. Second,
an organizational perspective explores changes in the institutional
arrangements of mental health care. Third, a social policy analysis
points to the scope of necessary changes. Throughout their work,
Morrissey *et al.* point to how a two-class system of care was
developed and perpetuated. Like Rothman, these authors show how
professionalist and economic concerns defeated many fine ideas.
Thus, despite many changes within the mental health system, the
overall framework remained very much the same.

CHAPTER 1

Madness and Segregative Control: The Rise of the Insane Asylum*†

Andrew T. Scull

In recent years sociologists have rightly come to see deviance and control as essentially symbiotic rather than antagonistic phenomena. Unfortunately much of the work done pursuant to this basic insight has been marred by its narrow, ahistorical and non-structural focus. While the immediate interaction between deviants and control agencies and the etiological significance of deviance-processing have received considerable attention, the historical and structural contexts within which this processing occurs have been largely ignored. We have thus been forced to make do with 'an analysis which lacks a sense of history, a sensitivity to institutional patterns, and a range which is wider than a narrow focus upon encounters between deviants and officials' (Rock 1974: 145). Adequate theoretical work in this area clearly demands that we develop an historically informed, macro-sociological perspective on the inter-relationships between deviance, control structures, and the wider social systems of which they are a part. More specifically, we need to clarify the developing relationships between the nature of deviance and its control, and the increasing rationalization of the social order which has been the

* Revised version of a paper presented at the 70th Annual Meeting of the American Sociological Association, August 25–29, 1975. I am very grateful indeed to Steven Spitzer for his advice and criticism. I should also like to thank Magali Sarfatti Larson and two anonymous *Social Problems* readers for their comments on an earlier draft.

† Reprinted from *Social Problems*, vol. 24, pp. 337–51, 1977, with permission of the Society for the Study of Social Problems and the author.

dominant feature of Western social development since the Middle Ages.

I

Three key features distinguish deviance and its control in modern society from the shapes such phenomena assume elsewhere: (1) the substantial involvement of the state, and the emergence of a highly rationalized, centrally administered and directed social control apparatus; (2) the treatment of many types of deviance in institutions providing a large measure of segregation from the surrounding community; and (3) the careful differentiation of different sorts of deviance, and the subsequent consignment of each variety to the ministrations of experts – which last development entails, as an important corollary, the emergence of professional and semi-professional 'helping occupations.' Throughout much of Europe, England, and the United States, all these features of the modern social control apparatus are a comparatively recent development.

Prior to the eighteenth century, and in many places as late as the early nineteenth century, the control of deviants of all sorts had been an essentially communal and family affair. The amorphous class of the morally disreputable, the indigent and the powerless – including such elements as vagrants, minor criminals, the insane, and the physically handicapped – was managed in essentially similar ways. Characteristically, little effort was made to segregate such 'problem populations' into separate receptacles designed to keep them apart from the rest of society. Instead, they were dealt with in ways which left them at large in the community. Most of the time families were held liable to provide for their own, if necessary with the aid of temporary assistance or a more permanent subsidy from the community. Lunatics were generally treated no differently from other deviants: only a few of the most violent or troublesome cases might find themselves confined – in a specially constructed cell or as part of the heterogeneous population of the local gaol (Fessler 1956).

The transformation of traditional arrangements into what we know today as systems of social control is clearly a subject with a profound sociological significance. I shall comment on some aspects of this transition with respect to one major variety of deviance, by examining nineteenth century efforts to 'reform' the treatment of the mentally ill. More specifically, I shall try to provide an account of the reasons for the emergence of the asylum as the primary, almost the sole, response to the problems posed by insanity.

This explanation will radically challenge David Rothman's (1971) provocative account of the American 'discovery of the asylum,' probably the study of the history of mental institutions most familiar to American sociologists working in the field of deviance. The account Rothman provides in his book is essentially, despite occasional backsliding, an idealistic one. The rise of the asylum is pictured as the product of a peculiarly Jacksonian *angst* about the stability of the social order – anxiety mixed with a naive and uniquely American utopianism about the value of the well-ordered asylum. This was to be an institution which would at one and the same time eliminate the scourge of insanity, and by correcting 'within its restricted domain the faults of the community . . . through the power of example spark a general reform movement' (Rothman 1971: 133). But while Rothman persuasively *describes* this anxiety, he almost entirely neglects to *explain* it – to give us any understanding of why these persons became anxious about these things at this time. The structural sources of the concern with the imminent breakdown of the social order remain unexplored and unperceived. Similarly, Rothman's account places heavy emphasis on the uniqueness of American developments. Yet the rise of the asylum is *not* a uniquely American phenomenon. For example, its emergence is also characteristic of English society in this period, presenting obvious problems for a culture-specific theory.

Despite these weaknesses, Rothman's account has appealed to sociologists: partly because of the resonance its implicitly anti-institutional message has for an audience reared on Goffman's *Asylums*; partly because of how easily the model may be assimilated to the way most sociologists of deviance already 'explain' transformations of control structures – by reference to the nefarious activities of 'moral entrepreneurs' (Becker 1963). Equally important, its allure reflects the absence on either Rothman's or his readers' part of a comparative perspective on American developments; and the crudeness and implausibility of alternative explanations. My intent in this paper is to make use of some of these neglected comparative materials (those dealing with the parallel and almost contemporaneous lunacy reform movement in England) to develop a *structurally based* explanation of the rise of segregative means of managing

the mad. In doing so, I hope to avoid the mechanistic and historically
dubious assumptions plaguing earlier interpretations of this sort.

II

At the very outset of this book Rothman engages in a polemic against
a portrait of the asylum as 'the automatic and inevitable response of
an industrial and urban society [to insanity]' (Rothman 1971: xi–xii).
The weaknesses of the position he criticizes are so patent that one
is tempted to dismiss it as a straw man, erected to lend an air of
greater plausibility to his interpretation. Yet any such notion is not
only uncharitable, but unfair. For 'explanations' of this sort are
indeed to be found, nowhere more prominently than in the brief
forays of sociologists into these areas. David Mechanic (1969: 54)
succinctly outlines this position:

> Industrial and technological change . . . coupled with increasing
> urbanization, brought decreasing tolerance for bizarre and disruptive
> behavior and less ability to contain deviant behavior within the existing
> social structure.

The increased mobility of the population and the anonymity of existence in the urban slums were combined with the destruction of
the old paternal relationships that went with a stable, hierarchically
organized rural society. Huddled together in the grossly overcrowded
conditions accompanying the explosive, unplanned growth of urban-
industrial centers, the situation of the poor and dependent classes
became simultaneously more visible and more desperate. There
emerged the new phenomenon of urban poverty 'among concentrated masses of wage earners without natural protectors to turn to
in distress' (Perkin 1969: 162).

All of this is consistent with the view that the structural preconditions for a system of parochial relief were fast disappearing. The
new class of entrepreneurs could not wholly avoid making some
provision for the 'undeserving poor,' if only because of the revolutionary threat they posed to the social order. The asylum, and
analogous institutions such as the workhouse, allegedly constituted
the bourgeoisie's response to this situation.

But there are serious problems with this argument; it rests on a systematic misreading and distortion of the historical record. For, even in England, when pressures developed to differentiate and institutionalize the deviant population, the process of urbanization was simply not as advanced as this line of reasoning would lead us to expect. In the early stages of the Industrial Revolution,

> cotton was the pace-maker of industrial change, and the basis of the first regions which could not have existed but for industrialization, and which expressed a new form of society, industrial capitalism (Hobsbawm 1968: 56).

Though technical innovations introduced into the manufacturing process in the latter half of the eighteenth century and the application of steam power soon resulted in factory production, the technology of cotton production remained comparatively simple; and much of the industry remained decentralized and scattered in a variety of local factories, as likely to be located in 'industrial villages' as concentrated in large urban centers (Hobsbawm 1968: 58–65). Consequently, although large towns absorbed an increasing proportion of the English population, city dwellers remained a distinct minority during the first decades of the nineteenth century, when pressures to establish public lunatic asylums on a compulsory basis were at their strongest (cf. Weber 1899). The lack of parallelism in these events casts doubt on the notion that it was *urban* poverty as such which forced the adoption of an institutional response to deviance; a conclusion strengthened when one notes the marked enthusiasm of many rural areas for the asylum solution, an enthusiasm manifested at a comparatively early date (cf. Scull 1974: Chs. 3 and 4; Rothman 1971 *passim*, esp. 130).

Instead, I would contend that many of the transformations underlying the move toward asylums can be more plausibly tied to the growth of the capitalist market system and to its impact on economic and social relationships. Prior to the emergence of a capitalist system, economic relationships did not manifest themselves as purely market relationships. Economic domination or subordination was overlaid and fused with personal ties between individuals. But the market destroyed the traditional connections between rich and poor, the reciprocal notions of paternalism, deference, and dependence characterizing the old order, producing profound shifts in the

relationships between superordinate and subordinate classes, and of
upper class perceptions of responsibilities toward the less fortunate.

Indeed, one of the earliest casualties of the developing capitalist
system was the old sense of social obligation toward the poor (Townsend 1786; Hobsbawm 1968: 88; Hobsbawm and Rudé 1969: 26;
Mantoux 1928: 428). At the same time, the increasing 'proletarianiz-
ation' of labor – that is, the loss of alternatives to wage work as a
means of providing for subsistence – went together with the tendency
of the primitive capitalist economy to oscillate unpredictably between
conditions of boom and slump. Obviously, these transformations
greatly increased the strains on a family-based system of relief
(Polanyi 1944: 92ff.; Hobsbawm 1968: Chs. 3 and 4; Furniss 1965:
211–221). There is, despite its simplification and rhetorical flourish,
a profound and bitter truth to Marx's comment that the advent of a
full-blown market system:

> has pitilessly torn asunder the motley feudal ties that bound man to his
> 'natural superiors,' and has left no other nexus between man and man
> than naked self interest, than callous 'cash payment'. . . . In one word,
> for exploitation veiled by religious and political illusions, it has substituted
> naked, shameless, direct, brutal exploitation (Marx and Engels 1968:
> 37–38).

And while the impact of urbanization and industrialization was at
this stage geographically limited in scope, by the latter part of the
eighteenth century almost all regions of England had been drawn
into a single national market economy (Mantoux 1928: 74;
Hobsbawm 1968: 27–28). The impact of the universal market of
capitalism was felt everywhere, forcing 'the transformation of the
relations between the rural rich and the rural poor, the farmers and
their labor force, into a purely market relationship between employer
and proletarian' (Hobsbawm and Rudé 1969: Ch. 2).

The changes in structures, perceptions, and outlook marking the
transition from the old paternalist order to a capitalist social system
triggered a search for an alternative to traditional, noninstitutional
methods of managing the indigent. The development of an industrial
economy also precipitated a sizable expansion in the number of those
receiving temporary or permanent poor relief. This expansion took
place at precisely the time when the newly powerful bourgeoisie was
least inclined to tolerate it. The industrial capitalists readily

convinced themselves that laxly administered systems of household relief promoted poverty rather than relieved it – a position they found well-justified ideologically in the writings of Malthus and others (cf. Malthus 1798, esp. Ch. V.; MacFarlan 1782: 34–36; Temple 1770: 258; Rimlinger 1966: 562–563). Increasingly, therefore, the bourgeoisie were attracted to an institutionally-based response to the indigent. Institutional management would, at least in theory, permit close oversight of who received relief, and, by establishing a regime sufficiently harsh to deter all but the most deserving from applying, would render the whole system efficient and economical (Furniss 1965: 107; Temple 1770: 151–269; Poor Law Report 1834).

Moreover, just as the vagrancy laws of the sixteenth century had begun to produce the 'discipline necessary for the wage labour system' (Marx 1967 Vol. I: 737; also Chambliss 1964), so too the conditions in the new institutions mimicked the discipline necessary for the factory system. The quasi-military authority structure of the total institution seemed ideally suited to the inculcation of 'proper' work habits among those marginal elements of the workforce most resistant to the monotony, routine, and regularity of industrialized labor. As William Temple (1770: 266ff.) put it,

> by these means, we hope that the rising generation will be so habituated to constant employment that it would at length prove agreeable and entertaining to them.

Bentham's (1791) Panopticon, which fascinated many of the lunacy reformers (cf. Stark 1810; Wakefield 1812), was, in his own words, 'a mill to grind rogues honest and idle men industrious . . .' (Bentham to Brissot in Bentham 1843 Vol. X: 226), an engine of reformation which would employ 'convicts instead of steam, and thus combine philanthropy with business' (Stephen 1900 Vol. I: 203). And, undoubtedly, one of the attractions of the asylum as a method of dealing with the insane was its promise of instilling the virtues of bourgeois rationality into that segment of the population least amenable to them.

There were, of course, other factors behind the move toward an institutionally focused, centrally regulated system of social control. For the moment, however, I will leave further analysis of these factors to one side and turn to the question of how and why insanity came to be identified and managed as a unique problem requiring specialized treatment in an institution of its own, the asylum. For it should be obvious that before the asylum could emerge as a specialized institution devoted to the problems of insanity, the latter had to be distinguished as a separate variety of deviant behavior not found only among a few upper-class families or confined to cases of furious mania; but existing more pervasively among the lower classes of the community as a distinct species of pathology – a pathology unclassifiable as just one more case of poverty and dependency.[1]

The establishment of a market economy, and, more particularly, the emergence of a market in labor, provided the initial incentive to distinguish far more carefully than heretofore between different categories of deviance. Under these conditions, it was important to distinguish the able-bodied from the non-able-bodied poor. A precondition for the development of a capitalist system, as both Marx (1967 Vol. I: 578, 717–733) and Weber (1930: 22; 1961: 172–173) have emphasized, was the existence of a large mass of wage laborers who were not 'free' to dispose of their labor power on the open market, but who were actually forced to do so. But to provide aid to the able-bodied, as frequently occurred under the old relief arrangements, was to undermine the whole notion of a labor market.

Parochial relief for the able-bodied interfered with labor mobility (MacFarlan 1782: 176ff.; Smith 1776: 135–140). In particular, it encouraged the retention of a 'vast inert mass of redundant labor,' a stagnant pool of under-employed laboring men in rural areas, where the demand for labor was subject to wide seasonal fluctuations (Redford, cited in Polanyi 1944: 301; cf. also Polanyi 1944: 77–102; Webb and Webb 1927, *passim*; Hobsbawm 1968: 99–100). Social protection of those who *could* work distorted the operations of the labor market and, thereby, of all other markets, because of its tendency 'to create cost differentials as between the various parts of the country' (Polanyi 1944: 301; MacFarlan 1782: 178; Poor Law Report 1834: 43; Mantoux 1928: 450). Finally, by its removal of the threat of individual starvation, such relief had a pernicious effect on labor discipline and productivity (MacFarlan 1782: 169ff.), an outcome accentuated by the fact that the 'early laborer . . . abhorred the factory, where he felt degraded and tortured . . .' (Polanyi 1944: 164–165; cf. also Thompson 1963).

Instead of organizing poor relief in a way which failed to take motivation or compliance into account, it was felt that want ought to be the stimulus to the capable, who must therefore be distinguished from the helpless. Such a distinction is deceptively simple; but in a wider perspective, this development can be seen as a crucial phase in the growing rationalization of the Western social order and the associated transformation of *extensive* structures of domination into the ever more *intensive* forms characteristic of the modern world. In the pre-capitalist era, domestic populations were generally viewed as an unchangeable given, from which to squeeze as large a surplus as possible. But with the emergence of capitalism and the need for greater exploitation of labor resources, the labor pool came to be viewed as manipulable human material whose yield could be steadily enlarged through careful management and through improvements in use and organization, rationally designed to transform its value as an economic resource. As Moffett (1971: 187 *et passim*) has shown, during this process:

> the domestic population came increasingly to be regarded as an industrial labor force – not simply a tax reservoir as formerly – and state policies came increasingly to be oriented to forcing the entire working population into remunerative employment.

The significance of the distinction between the able-bodied poor thus increases *pari passu* with the rise of the wage labor system.

The beginnings of such a separation are evident even in the early phases of English capitalism. The great Elizabethan Poor Law (43 Eliz. c. 2, 1601), for example, classified the poor into the aged and impotent, children, and the able but unemployed (Marshall 1926: 23); and a number of historians have been tempted to see in this and in the Statute of Artificers (1563) a primitive labor code of the period, dealing respectively with what we would call the unemployed and unemployable, and the employed. But, as Polanyi suggests, in large measure 'the neat distinction between the employed, unemployed, and unemployable is, of course, anachronistic, since it implies the existence of a modern wage system which was absent [at that time]' (Polanyi 1944: 86). Until much later, the boundaries between these categories remained more fluid and ill-defined than the modern reader is apt to realize. Moreover, though it is plain that the Tudors and Stuarts did not scruple to invoke harsh legal penalties in an effort to compel the poor to work (cf. Dobb 1963: 233ff.), these measures were undertaken at least as much 'for the sake of political security' as for more directly economic motives (Marshall 1926: 17; Mantoux 1928: 443).

Gradually, however, economic considerations became increasingly dominant. As they did, it became evident that 'no treatment of this matter was adequate which failed to distinguish between the able-bodied unemployed on the one hand, the aged, infirm, and children on the other' (Polanyi 1944: 94). The former were to be compelled to work, at first through the direct legal compulsion inherited from an earlier period (Marshall 1926: 37ff.; Furniss 1965: *passim*). However, the upper classes came to despair of the notion 'that they may be compelled [by statute] to work according to their abilities' (MacFarlan 1782: 105); they became increasingly attracted by an alternative method according to which, in the picturesque language of John Bellers (1696: 1), 'The Sluggard shall be cloathed in Raggs. He that will not work shall not eat.' The superiority of this approach was put most bluntly by Joseph Townsend (1786):

> Hunger will tame the fiercest animals, it will teach decency and civility, obedience and subjection to the most perverse. In general, it is only hunger which can spur and goad [the poor] on to labour; yet our laws have said they shall never hunger. The laws, it must be confessed, have likewise said, they shall be compelled to work. But then legal constraint is attended with much trouble, violence, and noise; creates ill-will, and can never be productive of good and acceptable service: whereas hunger is not only peaceable, silent, unremitting pressure, but, as the most natural motive to industry and labour, it calls forth the most violent exertions.

Or, in the words of his fellow clergyman, T. R. Malthus,

> When nature will govern and punish for us, it is a very miserable ambition to wish to snatch the rod from her hands and draw upon ourselves the odium of the executioner (Malthus 1826 II: 339).

Thus the functional requirements of a market system promoted a relatively simple, if crucial, distinction between two broad classes of the indigent. Workhouses and the like were to be an important *practical* means of making this vital theoretical separation, and thereby of making the whole system efficient and economical. But even though workhouses were initially intended to remove the able-bodied poor from the community in order to teach them the wholesome discipline of labor (Bailey 1758: 1), they swiftly found themselves depositories for the decaying, the decrepit, and the unemployable. And an unintended consequence of this concentration of deviants in an institutional environment was that it exacerbated the problems of managing at least some of them (MacFarlan 1782: 97ff.). More specifically, it rendered problematic the whole question of what was to be done with those who could not or would not abide by the rules of the house – among the most important of whom were the acutely disturbed and refractory insane.

A single mad or distracted person in the community produced problems of a wholly different sort than those the same person would have produced if placed with other deviants within the walls of an institution. The order and discipline of the whole workhouse was threatened by the presence of a madman who, even by threats and punishment, could neither be persuaded nor induced to conform to the regulations. By its very nature, a workhouse was ill-suited to provide safe-keeping for those who might pose a threat to life or property. In the words of a contemporary appeal for funds to set up a charity asylum:

> The law has made no particular provision for lunaticks and it must be allowed that the common parish workhouse (the inhabitants of which are mostly aged and infirm people) are very unfit places for the Reception of such ungovernable and mischievous persons, who necessarily require separate apartments (St. Luke's Considerations 1750: 1).

The local gaol, a common substitute in such cases, proved scarcely more satisfactory; the dislocations produced by the presence of lunatics provoked widespread complaints from prisoners and gaolers alike. General hospitals of the period, facing similar problems, began to respond by refusing to accept lunatic inmates 'on Account of the safety of other Patients' (St. Luke's Considerations 1750: 2). Clearly, then, the adoption of an institutional response to all sorts of 'problem populations' greatly increased the pressures to elaborate the distinctions amongst and between the deviant and dependent.[2]

Initially, with respect to the insane, this situation provided no more than an opportunity for financial speculation and pecuniary profit for those who established private madhouses and asylums. Such, indeed, was the general character of the eighteenth-century 'trade in lunacy,' a frequently lucrative business dealing with the most acutely disturbed and refractory cases, those who in the general mixed workhouse caused trouble out of all proportion to their numbers. While claims to provide cures as well as care were periodically used as a means of drumming up custom, the fundamental orientation of the system (besides profit) was toward an economical restraint of those posing a direct threat to the social order (cf. Parry-Jones 1972). In the long run, however, such a differentiation of deviants provided the essential social preconditions for the establishment of a new organized profession, claiming to possess a specific expertise in the management of insanity, and oriented toward a rehabilitative ideal.

On the most general level, the English elite was receptive to the notion that a particular occupational group possessed a scientifically based expertise in dealing with lunacy. This receptivity reflected the growing secular rationalization of Western society at this time; a development which, following Weber, I would argue took place under the dominant, though not the sole, impetus of the development of a capitalist market system. More specifically, it reflected the penetration of this realm of social existence by the values of science, the idea that 'there are no mysterious incalculable forces that come into play, but rather that one can, in principle, master all things by calculation' (Weber 1946: 139). Linked to this change in perspective was a fundamental shift in the underlying paradigm of insanity, away from an emphasis on its demonological, non-human, animalistic qualities toward a naturalistic position which viewed the madman as exhibiting a defective *human* mechanism, and which therefore saw this condition as at least potentially remediable.

How the 'mad-doctors' of the period were able to exploit this favorable cultural environment to secure for themselves the status of a profession is a question dealt with elsewhere.[3] Here I am concerned with one important consequence of the fact that they were able to do so. The growing power and influence of what was to become the psychiatric profession helped to complete and to lend scientific legitimacy to the classification of deviance; transforming the vague cultural view of madness into what now purported to be a formally coherent, scientifically distinguishable entity reflecting and caused by a single underlying pathology.

In a sense, then, one had here a self-reinforcing system. For while the key to the emerging profession's claims to expertise, the new system of moral treatment,[4] did reflect a fundamental transformation in the basic paradigm or perception of insanity, it was not based on a more *scientific understanding* of the subject (cf. Foucault 1965; Scull 1974: Chs. 5 and 8) Rather, it represented, from one perspective at least, a novel administrative technique, a more efficient means of management. The essence of this innovation lay in its emphasis on order, rationality, and self-control; and much of its appeal, both for the lunacy reformers and their audience, derived from the high value it placed on work as a means to these ends. The new approach could only be fully developed and applied in an institutional setting. So that, just as the separation of the insane into madhouses and asylums helped to create the conditions for the emergence of an occupational group ('mad-doctors') laying claim to expertise in their care and cure, so too the nature and content of the restorative ideal these doctors espoused reinforced the commitment to the institutional approach. Thereafter, the existence of both asylums and psychiatry testified to the 'necessity' and 'naturalness' of distinguishing the insane from other deviants.

A vital feature of this radically new social control apparatus was how much its operations became subject to central control and direction. As both the Weberian and the Marxist analyses have stressed, precapitalist societies were overwhelmingly localized in their social organization. The mechanisms for coping with deviance in pre-nineteenth century England placed a corresponding reliance on an essentially communal and family-based system of control. The assumption of direct state responsibility for these functions thus marked a sharp departure from these traditional emphases.

While administrative rationalization and political centralization are not only or wholly the consequence of economic rationalization, it seems inescapable that the advance of the capitalist economic order and the growth of the central authority of the state are twin processes intimately connected with each other.

> On the one hand, were it not for the expansion of commerce and the rise of capitalist agriculture, there would scarcely have been the economic base to finance the expanded bureaucratic state structures. But on the other hand, the state structures were themselves a major economic underpinning of the new capitalist system (not to speak of being its political guarantee) (Wallerstein 1974: 133).

In a very literal sense, institutional control mechanisms were imprac-

ticable earlier, because of the absence both of the necessary administrative techniques and also of the surplus required to establish and
maintain them.

The creation of more efficient administrative structures, both the
precondition and the consequence of the growth of the state and of
large-scale capitalist enterprise, possessed a dual importance. On the
one hand, it allowed for the first time the development of a tolerably
adequate administrative apparatus to mediate between the central
and local authorities, and thus to extend central control down to the
local level. On the other, it provided the basis for the development
of techniques for the efficient management of large numbers of
people confined for months or years on end. Without these structures, institutional methods of social control would scarcely have
achieved the importance they did. State construction and operation
of institutions for the deviant and the dependent was very costly.
Hence the importance, as a transitional arrangement, of the state
contracting with private entrepreneurs to provide jails, madhouses,
and the like. Under this method, the state allows the 'deviant farmer'
to extort his fees however he can, and turns a blind eye to his
methods; in return, the latter relieves the state of the capital expenditure (and often even many of the operating costs) required by a
system of segregative control. Movement to a system directly run by
the state required the development of large stable tax revenues and/
or the state's ability to borrow on a substantial scale. These in turn
were intimately tied to the expansion of the monetary sector of the
economy and the growth of the sophisticated credit and accounting
mechanisms characteristic of capitalist economic organization
(Ardant 1975).

Likewise, the development of national and international markets
produced a diminution, if not a destruction, of the influence
traditionally exerted by local groups (especially kinship groups) in
the patterning of social life. More directly, the growth of a single
national market and the rise of allegiance to the central political
authority to a position of over-riding importance undermined the
rationale of locally-based responses to deviance, based as they were
on the idea of settlement and the exclusion of strangers. As local
communities came to be defined and to define themselves as part of
a single overarching political and economic system, it made less and
less sense for one town to dispose of its problems by passing them
on to the next. There was a need for some substitute mode of

exclusion. In combination, these developments contributed to 'the monopolization of all "legitimate" coercive power by one universalist coercive institution . . .' (Weber 1968 Vol. I: 337), and to the development of a state sponsored system of segregative control.

The struggle to legislate and to implement lunacy reform in England involved just such a transfer of the locus of power and responsibility to the central authority and necessarily took place in the face of fierce local resistance (Scull 1974: Ch. 4). This opposition reflected both a parochial defensiveness against the encroachments of the state, and the uneven spread of a new outlook on the insane. Local authorities generally accepted the traditional paradigm of insanity, along with its emphasis on the demonological, almost bestial character of madness. In consequence, they were frequently unable to comprehend why the reformers saw the treatment of lunatics within their jurisdiction as brutal and inhumane; why conditions they saw as unexceptionable produced shock and outrage in others. The reformers had fixed on the fundamentals of a new system for dealing with the insane – asylums constructed at public expense, and regular inspection of these institutions by the central authorities – as early as 1815. But before the plan was given legislative approval in two 1845 Acts of Parliament (8 and 9 Vict. c. 100, 126) there were three decades of Parliamentary manoeuvering and compromise designed to placate local opposition; a series of official inquiries producing a stream of revelations of the abuses of the old system (1815–1816, 1827, 1839, 1842–1844); and a mass of propaganda in popular periodicals and reviews extolling the merits of their proposed solution.

III

Most historical writing on lunacy reform perpetuates the illusion that the whole process represented progress toward enlightenment, the triumph of a rational, altruistic, humanitarian response over ancient superstitions, the dawn of a scientific approach to insanity. Yet this is a perspective made possible only by concentrating on the rhetoric of intentions to the neglect of the facts about the establishment and operation of the asylum system. Even a superficial acquaintance with the functioning of nineteenth century mental hospitals reveals how limited was the asylum's concern with the human problems of its inmates.

The consistent structural limitations of the total institution (Goffman 1961) operated from the asylum's earliest years to reduce its ostensible clients to the level of cogs to be machined and oiled till they contributed to the smooth running of the vast apparatus of which they were each an insignificant part. In such a place, said John Arlidge (1859: 102)

> a patient may be said to lose his individuality and to become a member
> of a machine so put together as to move with precise regularity and
> invariable routine; a triumph of skill adapted to show how such
> unpromising materials as crazy men and women may be drilled to
> order, but not an apparatus calculated to restore their pristine condition
> and their independent self-governing existence.

Certainly, the equanimity with which the English upper classes regarded this development cannot have been unrelated to the fact that the inmate population was overwhelmingly drawn from the lower segments of society. Nor can there be much doubt that the influential classes' emphasis on the centrality of efficiency and economy in the daily operations of the asylum (an insistence likewise reflecting the low social status of the bulk of the insane) functioned only to worsen the drab awfulness, the monotonous custodial quality of institutional existence

Asylums quickly assumed gigantic proportions. Within twenty-five years of the establishment of the first state-supported institution of this sort; the larger asylums already contained between five hundred and a thousand inmates. By mid-century, some had facades which stretched for nearly a third of a mile, and contained wards and passages of more than six miles (Quarterly Review 1857: 364). Thereafter, wing was tacked on wing, story upon story, building next to building, as the demand grew to accommodate more and more 'lunatics.' In the words of one critic, they began to 'partake more of the nature of industrial than of medical establishments' (Arlidge 1859: 123), where 'all transactions, moral as well as economic, must be done wholesale' (Browne 1864: 18). In such places, the mad-doctors of the period 'herd lunatics together in special institutions where they can be more easily visited and accounted for by the authorities' (Bucknill 1880: 122).

In addition to the broader sources of the commitment to the asylum model, the activities of a committed group of lay reformers and of that segment of the medical profession with an interest in the mad business obviously played an important role in legitimizing the institutional approach. In the second quarter of the nineteenth century, such men developed an increasingly elaborate pro-institutional ideology. Moreover, the fact that the asylum was presented as an arena for professional practice had much to do with the stress on rehabilitation and the marked utopian strain so characteristic of its early years. In the process, the defects inherent in the asylum's structure were largely, though not entirely, overlooked (Cf., e.g., Browne 1837).

The drawbacks of choosing an institutional response *were* elaborated, with striking prescience, by a few early critics of the asylum (Hill 1814; Reid 1816; Conolly 1830), and were repeated some years later by a handful of disillusioned reformers (e.g., Bucknill 1880; Arlidge 1859). By then, the operations of the system had revealed the basic accuracy of the criticisms; yet the authors of them continued to be ignored. A major source of the resistance to these objections is undoubtedly to be found in the unattractiveness to the English bourgeoisie of the alternative policies that might have been pursued. In particular, given that many of the conditions which so aroused the lunacy reformers were little or no worse than the conditions large numbers of the *sane* lower classes were forced to endure (cf., e.g., Chadwick 1842; Engels 1969), to have attempted to improve the condition of the insane while leaving them in the community would necessarily have entailed questioning the fundamental structure of nineteenth century English society.[5] In view of the social background of the lunacy reformers, and their concern with incremental change, it is scarcely surprising that they failed to do this. But in the absence of a coherent alternative plan, their carpings about the defects of the asylum could be (and were) simply ignored (cf. Scull 1977: Chs. 6 and 7).

Once the asylum was established, the psychiatric profession sought, without success, to secure a clientele not restricted to lower-class marginal elements of the population. The upper classes displayed an understandable reluctance to confine their nearest and dearest in a total institution. With a few exceptions (which in any event bore little resemblance to the conventional asylum of the period, save in the number of cures they could claim), the expansion of the English asylum system during the nineteenth century was substantially an expansion of the pauper sector.

Undoubtedly, this circumstance is a major explanation for the low prestige of the psychiatric profession throughout this period. The class focus of institutions at this time had a critical impact on the nature of the asylum itself, reinforcing the pressures to develop low cost custodial warehouses characterized by huge size, routine, and monotony. Under these conditions, moral treatment, never grounded in a well-developed theory of insanity, simply became a system of discipline and a convenient verbal camouflage for the psychiatric profession's questionable expertise.

The formal commitment to rehabilitation remained, but the practical concerns of those running the system were by now far different: the isolation of those marginal elements of the population who could not or would not conform or could not subsist in an industrial, largely laissez-faire society. But even as the optimism of the first years evaporated, the usefulness of custody for widely differing segments of society operated to sustain a system that had apparently failed, and helped to prevent the emergence of a constituency objecting to the asylum.

Working class opposition to the elimination of parish relief and their hatred of the new workhouse 'Bastilles' brought only a limited modification of the rigors of the New Poor Law and not its abandonment (Hobsbawm 1968: 229). The poor thus had little alternative but to make use of the asylum as a way of ridding themselves of what, in the circumstances of nineteenth century working class existence, was undoubtedly an intolerable burden, the caring for their sick, aged, or otherwise incapacitated relatives. From the bourgeoisie's perspective, the existence of asylums to 'treat' the mentally ill at public expense could be invoked as a practical demonstration of their own humanitarian concern with the less fortunate. But far from asylums having been 'altruistic institutions . . . detached from the social structures that perpetuate poverty,' (Gans 1971) one must realize that they were important elements in sustaining those structures; important because of their symbolic value and as a reminder of the awful consequences of non-conformity.

Ultimately, I contend that we must see the move toward an institutionalized and centralized social control apparatus as primarily the product of closely inter-related *structural* changes; the main driving force behind these changes being the commercialization of social existence and the advent of a full-blown capitalist market economy. What is crucial about the late eighteenth and the first half of the nineteenth centuries is that both the need and the ability to organize the necessary administrative structures and to raise the substantial sums required to establish such a control system were present in this period. Returning to the rival account of the rise of segregative control offered by Rothman: one may view the pervasive anxiety about the stability of the social order (which Rothman so persuasively describes but fails to explain) as the anxiety of a specific class. It was the way the bourgeois and professional classes made sense of the corrosive effects of capitalism on such traditional pre-capitalist social restraints as religion and the family. As such, the fears of the professional and entrepreneurial bourgeoisie were mediators through which structural pressures were translated into 'reform'; but they cannot plausibly be regarded as the primary or decisive cause of this change. A break with Rothman's cultural form of explanation has this further and crucial advantage: it moves us decisively beyond the implicit solipsism of his account, and allows us to see developments in England and the United States as part of a single phenomenon.

Notes

1 Of course, I am not suggesting here that prior to this process of differentiation the population at large were naively unaware of any and all differences between the various elements making up the disreputable classes – between, say, the raving madman and the petty criminal, or the blind and the crippled. (Obviously on a very straightforward level such distinctions were apparent and could linguistically be made.) The critical question is rather when and for what reasons such perceived differences became rigid and were seen as *socially significant* – i.e., began to provoke differential responses and to have consequential impact on the lives of the deviant.

2 For primitive mid-eighteenth century examples of this process of differentiation, cf. Marshall 1926: 49ff. On the necessity of such a classification, cf. MacFarlan 1782: 2–3. The increasing numbers of the poor:

> are thought to arise chiefly from the want of proper general views of the subject, and of a just discrimination of the characters of those who are the objects of punishment or compassion. Thus, while at one time the attention of the public is employed in detecting and punishing vagrants, real objects of charity are exposed to famine, or condemned to suffer a chastisement they have not deserved; at another time, while an ample provision is made for the poor in general, a liberal supply is often granted to the most slothful and profligate.

Hence arise two opposite complaints, yet both of them well-grounded. The
one of inhumanity and cruelty in our distressed fellow creatures; the other, of
a profusion of public charity, and an ill-judged lenity, tending to encourage
idleness and vice.

For an elaborate late eighteenth century classification and differentiation of the
various elements composing the poor, cf. Bentham 1797.

3 The negotiation of cognitive exclusiveness on the part of mad-doctors – whereby
   insanity came to be defined as a disease, and hence as a condition within the
   sole purview of the medical profession – was necessarily a prolonged and
   complicated process. As is usual in such cases, 'the process determining the
   outcome was essentially political and social rather than technical in character'
   (Freidson 197: 79). Persuasive rhetoric, the symbols (rather than the substance)
   of expertise, the prestige and ready access to elite circles of the more respectable
   part of the medical profession – all these resources were employed to secure
   and maintain a legally enforceable medical monopoly of the treatment of madness.
   For details, see Scull 1975 and Scull 1976.

4 One cannot readily summarize in a phrase or two what moral treatment consisted
   of, nor reduce it to a few standard formulae, for it was emphatically not a
   specific technique. Rather, it was a general, pragmatic approach which aimed at
   minimizing external, physical coercion; and it has, therefore, usually been
   interpreted as 'kind' and 'humane.' Instead of merely resting content with
   controlling those who were no longer quite human, the dominant concern of
   traditional responses to the mad, moral treatment actively sought a transformed
   lunatic, remodeled into something approximating the bourgeois ideal of the rational
   individual. Those advocating moral treatment recognized that external coercion
   could force outward conformity but never the necessary internalization of moral
   standards. Instead, lunatics must be induced, by playing on their 'desire for
   esteem,' to collaborate in their own recapture by the forces of reason and
   conformity; and their living environment must be reconstructed so as to encourage
   them to reassert their own powers of self-control. As moral treatment evolved in
   the large public asylums, it was increasingly simplified and reduced to a set of
   internal management devices: the crucial elements here were the development
   of the ward system, and the creation of an intimate tie between the patients'
   position in this classificatory system and their behavior – still among the major
   weapons mental hospitals use to control the uncontrollable.

5 Thus, improving the conditions of existence for lunatics living in the community
   would have entailed the provision of relatively generous pension or welfare
   payments to provide for their support; implying that the living standards of
   families with an insane member would have been raised above those of the
   working class generally. Moreover, under this system, the insane alone would
   have been beneficiaries of something approximating a modern social welfare
   system, while their sane brethren were subjected to the rigors of a Poor Law
   based on the principle of less eligibility. Such an approach would clearly have
   been administratively unworkable, not least because of the labile nature of lunacy
   itself, and the consequent ever-present possibility that given sufficient incentive
   (or rather desperation) the poorer classes would resort to feigning insanity. (This

possibility probably provided an additional incentive for keeping the conditions in the lunatic asylums as unattractive as possible, as 'ineligible' as workhouses.) These obstacles presented an absolute barrier to the development of a plausible alternative, community-based response to the problem of insanity – in fact none of the critics of the asylum was ever able to suggest even the basis of such a program: a *sine qua non* if their objections were to receive serious consideration.

References

Ardant, G. 1975.
  Financial policy and economic infrastructure of modern states and nations. In C. Tilly (ed.) *The Formation of National States in Western Europe*. Princeton: Princeton University Press, 164–242.
Arlidge, J. T. 1858.
  On the State of Lunacy and the Legal Provision for the Insane. London: Churchill.
Bailey, W. 1758.
  A Treatise on the Better Employment and More Comfortable Support of the Poor in Workhouses. London.
Becker, H. S. 1963.
  Outsiders. Glencoe, Illinois: Free Press.
Bellers, J. 1696.
  Proposals for Raising a College of Industry of All Useful Trades and Husbandry. London.
Bentham, J. 1791.
  Panopticon; or the Inspection House. London: Payne.
  1797. *Pauper Management*. London.
  1843. *Works*. Ed. J. Bowring. Edinburgh.
Browne, W. A. F. 1837.
  What Asylums Were, Are, and Ought to Be. Edinburgh: Black.
  1864. *The Moral Treatment of the Insane*. London: Adlard.
Bucknill, J. C. 1880.
  The Care of the Insane and their Legal Control. London: Macmillan.
Chadwick, E. 1842.
  Report on the Sanitary Conditions of the Labouring Population of Great Britain. London.
Chambliss, W. 1964.
  A sociological analysis of the law of vagrancy. *Social Problems*, 12, 67–77.
Conolly, J. 1830.
  An Inquiry into the Indications of Insanity. London: Taylor.
Dobb, M. 1963.
  Studies in the Development of Capitalism. New York: International Publishers.
Engels, F. 1969.
  The Condition of the Working Class in England. London: Panther Books.
Fessler, A. 1956.
  The management of lunacy in seventeenth century England. In Proceedings of the Royal Society of Medicine, Historical Section, 49.

Foucault, M. 1965.
Madness and Civilization. New York: Mentor Books.
Freidson, E. 1970.
  Profession of Medicine. New York: Dodd, Mead.
Furniss, E. 1965.
  The Position of the Laborer in a System of Nationalism. New York: Kelly.
Gans, H. 1971.
  Preface to Colin Greer, *The Great School Legend*. New York: Basic Books.
Goffman, E. 1961.
  Asylums. Garden City, New York: Doubleday.
Hill, G. N. 1814.
  An Essay on the Prevention and Cure of Insanity. London: Longman.
Hobsbawm, E. 1968.
  Industry and Empire. London: Penguin Edition.
Hobsbawm, E. and Rudé, G. 1969.
  Captain Swing. London: Penguin Edition.
MacFarlan, J. 1782.
  Inquiries Concerning the Poor. Edinburgh: Longmans and Dickson.
Malthus, T. R. 1798.
  An Essay on the Principle of Population. London: Murray. First and Sixth
  Editions.
  1826. *Essay on Population*. Sixth Edition, Book II.
Mantoux, P. 1928.
  The Industrial Revolution in the Eighteenth Century. London: Cape.
Marshall, D. 1926.
  The English Poor in the Eighteenth Century. London: Routledge.
Marx, K. 1967.
  Capital. (3 vols.) New York: International Publishers.
Marx, K. and Engels, F. 1968.
  The Communist Manifesto. In *Selected Works*. New York: International
  Publishers.
Mechanic, D. 1969.
  Mental Health and Social Policy. Englewood Cliffs, New Jersey: Prentice-Hall
  Inc.
Moffett, J. T. 1971.
  Bureaucracy and social control: A study of the progressive regimentation of the
  western social order. Unpublished Ph.D. dissertation, Columbia University.
Parry-Jones, W. Ll. 1972.
  The Trade in Lunacy. London: Routledge and Kegan Paul.
Perkin, H. 1969.
  The Origins of Modern English Society, 1780–1880. London: Routledge and Kegan
  Paul.
Polanyi, K. 1944.
  The Great Transformation. Boston: Beacon Edition.
Poor Law Report, 1834.
  Report of the Royal Commission on the Poor Laws. London.
Quarterly Review, 1857. Lunatic asylums. 101, 353–393.

Reid, J. 1816.
Essays on Insanity. London: Longmans.
Rimlinger, G. 1966.
Welfare policy and economic development: A comparative historical perspective. *Journal of Economic History*, 556–571.
Rock, P. 1974.
The sociology of deviancy and conceptions of the moral order. *British Journal of Criminology*, 139–149.
Rothman, D. 1971.
The Discovery of the Asylum. Boston: Little, Brown.
Scull, A. T. 1974.
Museums of madness: The social organization of insanity in nineteenth century England. Unpublished Ph.D. dissertation, Princeton University.
1975. From madness to mental illness: Medical men as moral entrepreneurs. *European Journal of Sociology*, 16, 219–261.
1976. Mad-doctors and magistrates: English psychiatry's struggle for professional autonomy in the nineteenth century, *European Journal of Sociology*, 17, 279–305.
1977. *Decarceration: Community Treatment and the Deviant – A Radical View*. Englewood Cliffs, New Jersey: Prentice-Hall Inc.
Smith, Adam 1776.
The Wealth of Nations, New York: Modern Library Edition.
St. Luke's Hospital, 1750.
Considerations upon the Usefulness and Necessity of Establishing an Hospital as a Further Provision for Poor Lunaticks. Manuscript at St. Luke's Hospital, Woodside, London.
Stark, W. 1810.
Remarks on the Construction of Public Hospitals for the Cure of Mental Derangement. Glasgow: Hedderwick.
Stephen, L. 1900.
The English Utilitarians. (2 vols.) London.
Temple, W. 1770.
An Essay on Trade and Commerce. London.
Thompson, E. P. 1963.
The Making of the English Working Class. New York: Vintage.
Townsend, J. 1786.
A Dissertation on the Poor Laws, by a Well-Wisher of Mankind. London.
Wakefield, E. 1812.
Plan of an asylum for lunatics, etc. *The Philanthropist*, 2, 226–229.
Wallerstein, I. 1974.
The Modern World System. New York: Academic Press.
Webb, S. and Webb, B. 1927.
English Poor Law History: Part One – The Old Poor Law. London.
Weber, A. F. 1899.
The Growth of Cities in the Nineteenth Century. New York: Columbia University Press.
Weber, M. 1930.
The Protestant Ethic and the Spirit of Capitalism. London: Allen and Unwin.

1946. From *Max Weber: Essays in Sociology*. (Eds. H. Gerth and C. W. Mills.) London: Oxford University Press.

1961. *General Economic History*. New York: Collier.

1968. *Economy and Society*. (3 vols.) Totowa, New Jersey: Bedminster Press.

CHAPTER 2

The enduring asylum*

David Rothman

In the opening decades of the twentieth century, new ideas and new programs transformed public attitudes and social policies toward the criminal, the delinquent, and the mentally ill. The innovations are well known for they have dominated every aspect of criminal justice, juvenile justice, and mental health right through the middle 1960s. They include probation, parole, and the indeterminate sentence; the juvenile court and the outpatient clinic; and novel designs for the penitentiary, the reformatory, and the insane asylum. Yet we know surprisingly little about the origins and initial consequences of these procedures: how they were conceived, how they were translated into practice, and how they actually worked.

This gap in our knowledge is all the more glaring because we are today in revolt against inherited wisdom and established programs. For the first time, vigorous debate is challenging the legitimacy of each of these measures. Should criminal sentences be open-ended or fixed? Should the authority of the juvenile court be narrowed? Should prisons and mental hospitals be dismantled and juvenile institutions be abolished? My goal is to inform both history and social policy, to analyze a revolution in practice that has an immediate relevance to present concerns.

To a remarkable degree, American historians have ignored these programs for the criminal, the delinquent, and the insane. There is

* From *Conscience and Convenience: The Asylum and Its Alternatives in Progressive America*, pp. 3–11, 325–331, 335–337, 360–366, 370–375. Copyright © 1971 by David Rothman. By permission of Little, Brown and Company and the author.

not a single history of probation or parole or indeterminate sentences, not more than two or three accounts of prisons, mental hospitals or training schools in the twentieth century, and only a handful of studies of juvenile courts or outpatient clinics. Perhaps the fault rests with the substance of the story. One French student of the Parisian underworld in the mid-nineteenth century counseled a friend to avoid the subject, to leave to others the 'warts and pustules' of his society. But the problem goes deeper, in many ways reflecting the obfuscating character of the term 'reform.' All of the measures that this book will be analyzing carried that label and were prominent on the Progressive agenda. Their enactment appeared so appropriate, so logical a step forward in humanitarian and scientific progress, that their principles did not have to be analyzed in depth. But in the longer history of the response of the public to the deviant, reform is an altogether misleading designation. To the Jacksonians, who in the decades following 1820 first created the prisons, insane asylums, and reformatories (a phenomenon I explored in *The Discovery of the Asylum*), those institutions were reforms. Then, to the Progressives, inherited procedures seemed so inadequate that they had to undertake reform; and now, in turn, Progressive solutions appear to stand in need of reform. In brief, reform is the designation that each generation gives to its favorite programs.

To recognize the repetitive quality of this process makes the subject more fascinating and clarifies the essential questions to be addressed. How does each generation arrive at its reform program What elements come together to earn a proposed innovation the title of reform? Who makes up the cadre of reformers? Perhaps even more important, where do they find their constituents? How do their programs win enactment? And then a second order of questions emerges: what difference do the programs make? How consistently are they translated into practice? Put more forcefully, why is it that reforms so often turn out to be in need of reform? With these types of inquiries in mind, this work is ultimately about the enterprise of reform.

Two words, 'conscience' and 'convenience,' point to the dynamic and tension that are at the core of the analysis. We begin first with conscience, for the Progressive programs were the invention of benevolent and philanthropic-minded men and women and their ideological formulations were essential to promoting change. Coming from the world of the college, the settlement house, and the medical school, the Progressive reformers shared optimistic theories that at once clarified the origins of deviant behavior and shaped their efforts to control it. They marched under a very appealing banner, asking citizens not to do less for fear of harm, but to do more, confident of favorable results.

Their principles can be summarized succinctly. Progressives aimed to understand and to cure crime, delinquency, and insanity through a case-by-case approach. From their perspective, the Jacksonian commitment to institutions had been wrong, both for assuming that all deviants were of a single type, the victims of social disorder, and for believing that they could all be rehabilitated with a single program, the well-ordered routine of the asylum. To Progressives, knowledge about and policies toward the deviant had to follow a far more particular bent. The task was to understand the life history of each offender or patient and then to devise a remedy that was specific to the individual.

In that effort, two seemingly different approaches competed for favor among Progressives. Some reformers were environmentalists, locating the roots of the individual's problem in one or another of the wretched conditions of the immigrant ghetto. Others adopted a psychological explanation, looking to the mind-set of the deviant for the causes of maladaption. But whatever the orientation, the two schools agreed that each case had to be analyzed and responded to on its own terms. One offender was best treated in the community – and hence the need for probation. Another offender would have to be incarcerated until he proved himself able to reenter society – and hence the propriety of an indeterminate sentence to a prison or training school that would resemble a 'normal' community. Yet another patient might best be treated at home – and hence the need for outpatient clinic care; or require short-term intensive treatment – hence, the psychopathic hospital; or need long-term care – which the mental hospital would provide. In effect, all Progressive programs assumed one outstanding feature: *they required discretionary responses to each case.* Rules could not be made in advance. Every person had to be treated differently. Fixed codes or set procedures were both unfair and ineffective.

That these measures would expand the power of the state, enlarging the freedom of action of public officials, did not disturb reformers. To the contrary, another distinguishing mark of the Progressive mentality was its willingness to increase the scope of

state action and widen its exercise of power. Julia Lathrop, Hull
House resident and later Chief of the Children's Bureau, summarized
the credo well: 'The success of our future civilization lies in government adding to their responsibility and taking on work which people
have not hitherto been willing to entrust to them.' Thus, Progressives
were eager to relax the formal rules under which juvenile court
judges, probation officers, parole boards, wardens, superintendents,
and psychiatrists operated. In this way, the needs of justice and the
aims of therapy, the welfare of the individual and the security of
society would be satisfied.

But conscience is only one part of the record. To understand the
speed with which the new measures took hold, one must reckon
with convenience as well. Progressive proposals found a favorable
response among the administrators of criminal justice and mental
health – indeed, a much more favorable response than among the
public at large. Wardens, district attorneys, judges, mental hospital
superintendents, and directors of child care agencies welcomed the
enlargement of their discretionary authority. The innovations
brought them numerous practical advantages, enabling them to carry
out their daily assignments more easily and efficiently. For operational reasons, they supported the Progressive innovations with
enthusiasm. Accordingly, the process of reform is far more complicated to trace in the twentieth century than in the early nineteenth.
In the Jacksonian era, one can rightly describe *a* reform position
without especial attention to the special interests of its advocates. In
the Progressive decades, the cast of characters is longer and their
particular agendas much more varied.

These distinctions are all the more important because convenience
assumed a critical role in determining the outcome of the new measures. For reform proposals to find a constituency among administrators may well be a precondition for the success of any movement.
What is most important, however, is that this Progressive alliance
undercut the aims of the original design. What remained was a
hybrid, really a bastard version – one that fully satisfied the needs
of those within the system but not the ambitions of reformers.

Although it is simple and almost fashionable now to talk about
the inevitable 'failure of reform,' to insist that nothing works, the
story here raises more complicated considerations. Clearly, the label
of 'failure' is often attached to a program too quickly and uniformly;
the question should be, 'failure, or success, to whom?' As we shall

see, the administrators of criminal and juvenile justice and mental health in the decades 1900–1940 did not define the Progressive measures to be failures at all. To the contrary, the innovations satisfied them in countless ways, from helping them to clear crowded court calendars, to maximizing their control over inmates and patients, to buttressing the legitimacy of their institutions.

From the perspective of the designers of the system, the programs did appear to be failures; that is, they did not meet expectations. The architects recognized all the flaws and cracks that appeared when blueprint became structure. But what conclusions follow for us from this finding? Should we use the occasion for whipping the reformers, for denigrating the effort to do good, for bolstering the judgment that doing nothing may be the only sensible public policy? Or does the result become the text for preaching on the evils of modern society, for lamenting that good intentions do not produce good results, for making the reformers into tragic heroes? Or ought we to step back and view the whole enterprise with a detachment that borders on wonderment, to analyze the weaknesses of reform theory as though its proponents were attempting to fly by flapping their arms? Or finally, ought we to recall the horrors of the nineteenth-century prison and asylum and then go on, more or less complaisantly, to conclude that the legacy in corrections and mental health was so grim that anything reformers did to try to improve conditions must be applauded? Nevertheless, this list of choices is incomplete and must be expanded.

There is little arguing that the reform effort should be evaluated in light of the social context and the state of knowledge available at the time. The horrors of the jails, prisons, and asylums were real enough to encourage a belief that any change would be for the better; to fault reformers for not having stronger weapons at hand with which to combat deviant behavior would not only be unfair but presumptuous, considering that we are now not well equipped either. Yet, these points made, we must also recognize that Progressives never paused to reckon with their own limitations. They never considered whether, given their knowledge, they should move more cautiously and circumspectly in implementing their policies; whether it was right for them to leave the deviant so helpless before their desire to treat and cure. Reformers, to a fault, were enthusiasts, so certain of their ability to achieve success that they were unwilling to qualify or to moderate their programs, to protect the objects of their wisdom from the coercion of their wisdom.

Moreover, for all their awareness of how great the gap was between the rhetoric and the reality of programs, Progressives were unable to perceive any of the underlying causes for failure. They never understood, for example, the nature of the alliance that linked them to the administrators of the system. In this respect, the Progressives active in criminal justice were at one with their co-reformers who were attempting to regulate the corporations: neither group could appreciate how the very parties that were to be regulated might capture the regulating agency or turn ostensibly corrective legislation to their own advantage. As a result, throughout the 1920s and 1930s, criminal justice and mental health reformers never reconsidered the premises of their programs. Failure, they believed, reflected faulty implementation, not underlying problems with theory or with politics; incompetent administrators and stingy legislators, not basic flaws within the design, undercut the strengths of the innovations. Hence, reformers responded to disappointment in one-note fashion: they urged better training for probation and parole officers; better programs for prisons and training schools; more staff for juvenile courts and more attendants for mental hospitals. Do more of the same so that the promise of these innovations would be realized. So however sympathetically one may respond to reformers' initial determination to improve the system, it is more difficult to condone their die-hard unwillingness to review their own record, to ring the bell on their own policies.

Finally, is it true that whatever else, Progressive innovations were better than the procedures that they replaced? Whatever their weaknesses, were the new practices improvements on the old? The data are too complex for rapid summary. One needs to know first a good deal about the implementation of probation, parole, the juvenile court, and outpatient programs; and about their effects upon prisons, reformatories, and mental hospitals – all of which makes up the substance of the chapters that follow. Yet let it be clear from the start that the answer to the question may well be, no, that Progressive reforms did not significantly improve inherited practices. To raise but one theme to which we will frequently return, innovations that appeared to be substitutes for incarceration became supplements to incarceration. Progressive innovations may well have done less to upgrade dismal conditions than they did to create nightmares of their own.

For all this, the most interesting and important enterprise remains that of appreciating the dynamics of reform, not in order to denigrate or applaud the would-be reformer but to analyze the strengths and weaknesses of the movement. This commitment may well reflect a sense that those who would attempt to do good today have much to learn from the history of reform, in terms of why ambitious programs were not realized and how men and women of good conscience responded to the course of events. In this spirit, it becomes relevant to understand that a peculiar reading of history made Progressives fearful that alternatives to their own program inevitably would be harsh and cruel. For another, they were not about to give any appearance of being allied with hard-line critics of these new measures who considered them ways of coddling the criminal. Even more important, reformers were never deeply disturbed by the fact that administrative convenience had become so well served in their programs; for they were convinced that their innovations could satisfy *all* goals, that the same person and the same institution could at once guard and help, protect and rehabilitate, maintain custody and deliver treatment. They perceived no conflict between these goals, no clash of interest between the deviant and the wider society, between the warden and his convicts, between the hospital superintendent and his patients, between the keeper and the kept. The 'friend' or social workers who did probation work could simultaneously be an 'officer'; the juvenile court judge who was charged to protect society could also be a parent to the delinquent. This belief was among the most fundamental in the reformers' canon, and in retrospect, perhaps the most dubious. The study of the past does not give license to predict the future, but it is more than a little tempting to argue that such goals can never be satisfied together, that they are too diametrically opposed, at least in this society, to be joined. More modestly it can be said that the Progressive effort to link them failed. In the end, when conscience and convenience met, convenience won. When treatment and coercion met, coercion won.

Nowhere was the gap between Progressive ambitions and day-to-day realities greater than in the field of mental health. When one looks to accomplishments, the record is meager even by standards of criminal and juvenile justice. In probation, parole, and juvenile courts, the critical question is why the letter of the law survived without the spirit. In mental health the question moves back one step: why were proposals for change so rarely put into effect? The issue is not so much the distortion of aims as the failure even to establish the new programs. In the years 1900–1940, neither the insane nor their doctors returned to the community.

This blunt statement carries not only a descriptive but an analytic import. To understand the minimal success of outpatient clinics or psychopathic hospitals or after-care measures, one must confront the asylum and its residents, the chronic insane. Mental hygiene proponents were eager not to abolish asylums but to restrict them to a back-up and secondary role. The major concern of the mental health system was to be the treatment of acute cases within the new community facilities. Reality, however, did not fulfill their expectations. The asylum never lost its centrality and its needs shaped the outcome of all reform ventures.

The fate of the psychopathic hospital at once reveals the priorities that rules in public policy. More than any single innovation in mental health, the psychopathic hosital carried the burden of reform; and yet only a handful of these hospitals came into existence. The first one opened at Ann Arbor (affiliated with the University of Michigan) in 1909; soon, psychopathic hospitals appeared in Boston, Chicago, New York, Denver, and Baltimore. But at no time before World War II were there over a dozen such places. Even more critical, the psychopathic hospitals became the handmaidens of the asylums. Rather than fulfill the ambitious programs of mental hygiene, they satisfied the narrow aims of the state institutions.

The course of events at Boston Psychopathic is an apt and not atypical case in point. In 1911, the Massachusetts State Board of Insanity, persuaded by Adolf Meyer's arguments, successfully urged on the legislature the creation of such a facility.The first function of the psychopathic hospital, the Board explained, was to 'receive all classes of mental patients for first care, examination and observation.' Its inpatient service would then 'provide short, intensive treatment of incipient, acute and curable insanity. Its capacity would be small, not exceeding such requirement.' In contrast to the asylum, it would be a hospital ranking with 'the best general and special hospitals . . . in any field of medical science.' Moreover, the new institution would provide clinical instruction to medical students ('who would thus be taught to recognize and treat mental disease in its earliest stages, where curative measures avail most'). It would also conduct an outpatient clinic (giving 'free consultation to the poor and such advice and medical treatment as would . . . promote the home care of mental patients'). Finally, it would promote research through 'the clinical study of patients on the wards and scientific investigation in well-equipped laboratories.' Boston Psychopathic, in other words, would have nothing to do with custodial care – it was to be advancing 'cure and prevention.'[1]

Nevertheless, from its moment of creation as a ward within the Boston State Hospital (1912), through its subsequent development as a separate institution (after 1921), the facility could not carry out this mandate. The inpatient department, to begin with this aspect, did not provide systematic, let alone effective treatment of the acute insane. It was not that Boston Psychopathic became one more storehouse for the chronic insane, indistinguishable from the state institutions. Rather it turned into a 'diagnostic center,' or more accurately put, a first stop on the road to the state hospital. Boston Psychopathic examined patients and offered a recommendation – it did not make a sustained effort to treat or to cure. In this sense, it was much less like a hospital than like a prison reception center.

In part, this development reflected the prevailing strengths and weaknesses of psychiatric knowledge – or lack of knowledge. As we shall see later in more detail, the available treatments for insanity were crude, at best capable of calming a patient, but unable to attack the disease itself. Under such circumstances, even the best-trained psychiatrists like those at Boston Psychopathic, were, predictably, more willing to attach labels than to try to conduct therapy. They were more eager to make referrals than to deliver treatment.

But in part, too, the issue transcended the skills of psychiatry and involved broader social considerations: specifically, the ways in which families, judges, and legislators preferred to handle cases of insanity. The fate of Boston Psychopathic was tied to the operation of commitment laws, the mechanisms by which someone suspected of being insane was confined, against his will if need be, to a state institution. Ever since the 1870s, commitment laws had posed difficult and complicated policy problems. In the pre-Civil War period, the widespread belief in the ability of the asylum to cure the insane made the issue of commitment procedures appear simple; the promise of effective treatment seemed to obviate the need for procedural protections. Then, as superintendents in the post-Civil War decades reduced their claims of cures and as horror stories about institutional conditions grew more prevalent, many jurisdictions began to impose more stringent requirements. Massachusetts, for example, demanded that a certificate of insanity be signed by two doctors and that a court hearing take place, with a judicial finding that the individual was insane. Some states, like Illinois, even insisted upon a jury trial before allowing involuntary commitment.[2]

The Progressive reformers, sharing the optimism of their Jacksonian predecessors, also shared their impatience with procedural barriers to quick and simple commitment. From their perspective, there was no reason why a doctor who wished to treat a mentally ill patient should have to satisfy numerous legal stipulations that his colleague who wished to treat a physically ill patient did not. To equate commitment with deprivation of liberty for the insane seemed to make as little sense as equating hospitalization with deprivation of liberty for the tubercular. The entire thrust of the mental hygiene movement, after all, was to make insanity into a disease like all others, to make asylums into hospitals and psychiatrists into doctors – and hence it seemed unfair, punitive, and retrogressive to single out mental illness for special restrictions.[3]

Under the press of these arguments, the Massachusetts legislature, like many others, enacted a series of laws designed to simplify the commitment process. The legislature could not abandon all procedural requirements; the stigma that the insane asylum continued to bear was too powerful to permit that. But it could and did establish alternate modes of commitment that substantially eased the placement of a patient in a mental hospital. In 1909 the legislature enacted a 'temporary commitment' statute, so that someone believed to be mentally ill could be confined for observation and treatment for seven days (in 1911, it became ten days) without a court finding of actual insanity; a guardian or a police officer or a member of the Board of Health could obtain this temporary commitment order from a judge by submitting a certificate signed by one physician. At the expiration of the period, the hospital would either release the patient or go through regular court channels to obtain a formal and permanent commitment. The Massachusetts State Board of Insanity was proud of its role in winning this new legislation. 'A total of 1,705 persons,' it boasted in 1915, 'secured the benefits of treatment in our public or private hospitals for the insane without the formality of a procedure before a judge, which would have been attended with delays, legal exactions, semi-publicity and the stigma of having been pronounced insane, all of which was thus obviated, to the comfort and satisfaction of the patients and friends.'[4]

Temporary commitment quickly became the preferred route into the mental hospital, so much preferred that it soon affected the entire operation of Boston Psychopathic. The founders of that institution were enthusiastic about the temporary commitment statute, believing it fitted perfectly with their desire to carry out 'short, intensive treatment.' What they did not anticipate, however, was that the temporary commitment order would become the most attractive and convenient method of committing all insane, chronic as well as acute, to the state's mental hospitals. The State Board of Insanity had expressly defined the first purpose of Boston Psychopathic as the examination and observation of 'all classes' of patients; but the Board, according to the institution's first director, had not really meant 'all' but rather, all 'except to that class of patients which can and should be committed under the regular law.' In other words, the psychopathic hospital was not to admit the chronic and obvious cases of mental illness; those could go directly to the state hospital. It was to examine and treat the borderline case or the acute case, where the diagnosis was difficult or the disease was not so crippling as to require long-term confinement in a mental hospital. Boston Psychopathic, in short, was designed for the curable insane, not the incurable.[5]

The widespread use of the temporary commitment statute for all types of mental illness undercut that original mission of the Boston Psychopathic. Families and physicians found it especially convenient to bring their patients to the institution under this order, regardless of the state or prognosis of the illness. The facility was located in the city, not the countryside; its image as a hospital reduced, at least somewhat, the stigma of confinement; patients may well have objected less to a temporary initial commitment to such a place. In all, the first step to permanent hospitalization could be accomplished with a minimum of fuss and trouble. As the director of the Boston institution well appreciated: 'The special role of a psychopathic hospital, its close affiliation with the general hospital, the absence of the large accumulation of chronic patients, make it easier for a patient to accept the suggestion of admission to a psychopathic hospital than . . . to a large hospital for mental disorders.' Moreover, 'to send the patient to a large state hospital at an early stage of a mental disorder often seems to the family a rather drastic step. The family accepts more readily admission to a psychopathic hospital; should the patient have to go later to a state hospital for continued treatment, the relatives feel that the step has been taken after due consideration and a thorough diagnosis.'[6]

The sympathetic tone of these remarks makes it evident that the administrators would do little to interfere with this process. Although they had the statutory authority to refuse admission to any patient whom they considered inappropriate, they rarely exercised it. They did complain periodically about 'the employment of our hospital as a mere vestibule to the custodial institutions, a tendency somewhat easy for physicians to slide into under the operation of Chapter 395' (the new temporary commitment law); and they did occasionally send circulars to physicians requesting them to commit the chronic patients directly to state hospitals. But these efforts were without effect. The director conceded that 'it has not been easy to put a stop to the practice of sending obviously commitable cases into the State institutions by this [temporary commitment to Boston Psychopathic] route.' In fact, the members of 'the medical profession and of the community in general, accept this as the main role of the hospital.'[7]

Confronted with this distortion of their purpose, the administrators of Boston Psychopathic would not take a tough stand on admissions policy. They would not restrict themselves to accepting only the non-chronic cases so as to make the facility into something other than the most convenient route into custodial care. There were ample explanations for their reluctance, and by no means were the explanations without merit. One official noted: 'If any insane patient is brought to the admitting office, it is not easy to deny him admission on the ground of his not needing "temporary" care, simply because he needs permanent or prolonged care.'[8] Or, 'Theoretically, cases of alcoholic intoxication and of delirium tremens are not admitted to the hospital,' since they were obviously chronic conditions. Nevertheless, 'practically, the danger of overlooking some serious physical or mental condition that is masked by the intoxication or delirium is so great that any such case brought to the hospital is admitted in order that a satisfactory diagnosis be made.' In other words, the admissions officer would not say no – for humanitarian as well as for medical reasons.[9]

The price that Boston Psychopathic paid for this decision was heavy, at least if its performance is judged by its original purposes.

Designed to bring a new dedication and effectiveness to treatment, it became instead a processing mill for some two thousand patients a year. They came, spent their ten days, and then left, going back to their families or on to the state hospital. The institution could make few claims for recovery; in one year, for example, it reported that six of its discharged patients had recovered; 640 had improved; and 1,086 were unimproved. Clearly, treatment had little relevance in the daily routine. As one superintendent declared, treatment 'is a complicated activity'; and 'with the limited number of beds at the hospital [under one hundred] and its large admission rate [over two thousand], it is obvious that only in a small proportion of the cases admitted can psychotherapeutic treatment be carried to a termination in the hospital itself.'[10]

Occasionally the directors took refuge in the argument that the institutional milieu, quite apart from therapeutic programs, had a remedial value. 'Students are apt to think,' one of them noted, 'that there is little treatment being carried on in the wards because the familiar apparatus for treatment of medical and surgical cases is comparatively little in evidence.' But they should not be misled. They may not at first realize . . . how important for the treatment of the individual case are not only removal from the ordinary social and economic responsibility of the everyday environment and adaptation to the hospital routine, but also the repeated interviews with the physician, the contacts with the nurses, the atmosphere of the department of occupational therapy. But the bankruptcy of that position was altogether evident. By focusing on the patient's removal from the community as valuable in and of itself, on 'interviews' whose purpose was to gather data not provide therapy, on 'contacts' not intimate encounters, and on the 'atmosphere' of a program not its substance, Boston Psychopathic was offering rationales that were not very different from what superintendents of frankly custodial state institutions had been saying for a very long time.[11]

Other psychopathic hospitals did no better in fulfilling the mental hygiene design. The majority followed the Boston model, whose procedures were, as one director accurately noted, 'more or less applicable to psychopathic hospitals in general.' Thus, the Syracuse State Psychopathic Hospital, a sixty-bed institution affiliated with Syracuse University, admitted the great majority of its six hundred patients under a thirty-day observation order; it then devoted practically all of its energies to diagnosis. Its routine appeared so imbal-

anced – spending thirty days in making a diagnosis and then releasing
the patient immediately thereafter – that a very defensive tone
entered the director's reports. 'It has been our policy,' he explained,
'to carefully examine . . . and to make a thorough social study of
every case possible regardless of the length of time we may expect
to have the patient under treatment. Although many cases remain
with us for only a brief period and then go on to another hospital,
we feel . . . that the patients' interests are best served by this pains-
taking and thorough method although at times it would seem a great
deal of work is being done without adequate return.' The result was
that somewhere between 40 and 50 percent of Syracuse Psychopathic's patients moved on to a state hospital. The institution
intended to revitalize the system had itself become an adjunct to the
system.[12]

By one route or another, then, the psychopathic hospitals failed
to realize the goals of their founders. Most of them became diagnostic
centers, processing patients rapidly; a handful, like Psychiatric Institute, went the route of administering psychotherapy. But none of
them became the central institutions for the care of the mentally ill,
even the acute and treatable mentally ill. The ultimate function of
the psychopathic hospital, in fact, may well have been to legitimate
the state hospital, to endow it with a propriety that was as necessary
as it was important. The message put out by a Boston Psychopathic
or a New York Psychiatric Institute was that those committed to a
state hospital belonged in a state hospital. In the one instance the
judgment was explicit (based upon a diagnosis); in the other it was
implicit (reflecting the patient's unsuitability for psychotherapy).
How the state hospitals fulfilled this mandate we shall now see.

Beginning in the 1890s and continuing right through the pre-World
War II decades, some state institutions for the insane did attempt to
associate themselves in one way or another with the model of a
treatment hospital. To this end, the 'asylum' of the nineteenth
century became the 'hospital' of the twentieth, with the change
in name intended to signal a change in operation. In 1900, the
superintendent of the New Hampshire Asylum for the Insane
successfully requested an alteration in 'corporate title.' 'The name
"asylum",' he argued, 'is identified with the care of the chronic and
incurably insane.' Since the institution's 'chief primary present and
future mission has been and always will be the care and treatment
of the curable insane,' since it was 'a hospital in the true sense of

the word,' and since 'in nearly all other states the word asylum has ceased to be applied to institutions that are remedial in character,' it was appropriate that 'the title should be changed from asylum to hospital.' By the same token, institutional attendants became nurses, State Boards of Lunacy (as in Massachusetts before 1899) became State Boards of Insanity (1899), then Commissions on Mental Diseases (1916). So too, the Rhode Island Asylum for the Pauper Incurable Insane (1869) became the State Hospital for the Insane (1897) and then the State Hospital for Mental Diseases (by 1922). Indeed, many states, sensitive to the stigma of insanity, preferred not to designate at all the type of disease that these hospitals were treating. So whenever one noted the signpost 'state hospital,' and in ignorance asked, 'hospital for what?' the correct answer, of course, was 'mental illness.'[13]

The contrast between 'asylum' and 'hospital' became the point of departure for a host of speeches and newspaper articles anticipating improvement in the care and treatment of the mentally ill. 'What every asylum requires in order to become a curative institution,' declared one doctor, 'is a hospital for the treatment of recent and acute cases. . . . Although in certain particulars this might require special arrangements, it need not differ very materially from the general arrangements of a fever hospital.' Or, as a journalist noted, 'We are making a beginning when we throw over the "retreat" idea and call our institutions for the insane "hospitals" – which is what they should be, in fact as well as in name.'[14]

But, to encapsulate in one phrase the history of the mental hospital in the period 1900–1940, 'fact' and 'name' bore practically no relationship. With a candor that was rare, one superintendent asked: 'Is it not a confession of weakness to commit an act of grand larceny by assuming a name which we have not earned and thus take a short cut to popular favor? There is nothing to gain by masquerading in borrowed plumage. . . . Unless a name has behind it the merit of good works . . . it will be but a term of reproach.'[15]

Grand larceny was not too strong a charge. To be sure, mitigating facts must be mentioned. Progressive penal institutions did the same thing; the Norwich, Connecticut, asylum superintendent who in 1908 wanted his 'Hospital for the Insane' to be known as 'The Norwich State Hospital' properly noted that 'Prisons are becoming known as reformatories and correctional institutions as schools.'[16] The insane was entitled as much courtesy as the criminal. Moreover, name

changes to reduce stigma were certainly not confined to the
Progressive years. In 1978, a special act of the New York legislature
altered the designation of the Willowbrook Development Center
(itself an updated term for an institution for the retarded that even
earlier had been known as an institution for the feeble-minded), to
make it the Staten Island Development Center. 'Willowbrook' simply
conjured up too many horror stories. But the grand larceny indict-
ment stands. Label asylums hospitals, claim to be as concerned with
and capable of cures as doctors are, refer to attendants as nurses;
and yet, in the end, the state hospital was not very different from
the post-Civil War asylum. Both were custodial institutions.

The state hospital, like the asylum, was caught in a cycle from
which it could not escape. The routine, almost without exception,
amounted to custodial care for the chronic patient, which meant that
for the most part, the institution received chronic patients, which in
turn meant that the routine had to be designed for the chronic
patient, and the cycle commenced all over again. Under these
circumstances, to sort out cause from effect, to weigh the impact of
overcrowding as against the state of psychiatric knowledge as against
the quality of the staff, is not only difficult but relatively unimportant.
The critical consideration is that every influence that bore on the
functioning of the state hospital promoted and reinforced a holding
operation.

The custodial quality of the state institutions not only undercut
the mental hygiene design for the hospitals but also thwarted the
effort to extend the reach of treatment and the principles of prevention into the community. Reformers had looked to promote alternative procedures, from outpatient clinics to after-care, which would
cure and prevent mental illness. Their goals, however, were not to
be realized. The traditional needs of the state hospital shaped, and
finally distorted, the implementation of the mental hygiene agenda.

The fate of family care, or boarding-out as it was also known, is
a useful first case in point. Although mental hygiene proponents did
not so much promote the idea (that some among the chronic could
be better cared for in community homes) as use it as a starting point
for a much more novel approach (that acute and curable cases should
be treated in clinics), still the disappointing history of the program
begins to clarify the barriers to change. One might have anticipated
a broad popularity for family care. After all, the institutions were
perpetually overcrowded and offered little to the back-ward chronic

patient. And in the 1920s and 1930s, some psychiatrists and social workers did contend that family care had therapeutic effects. 'The boarding home,' one of them declared, 'becomes, not a permanent residence, but a stepping stone to mental health, independence, and self-support.' Nevertheless, only three states, Massachusetts, New York, and Ohio, even experimented with the procedure; and none of them went very far with it. Massachusetts, the pioneer in the field, had a total of 124 patients in family care in 1900, 255 in 1919, 164 in 1925, and 311 in 1935. In 1939, only a mere 1,300 patients were in family care throughout the nation, about 3 percent of the total institutional population.[17]

Why did family care make so little progress? One reason, as Massachusetts' officials explained, was that patients were often reluctant to leave the institution. 'They dislike leaving the comforts of the hospital for unknown conditions. . . . They think they will be less comfortable or will have to work hard or will miss the companionships formed at the hospital.' Moreover, relatives frequently objected to family placement for fear that 'they themselves will be subjected to criticism for not taking the patients home instead of allowing strangers to care for them.' Then too, community protest interfered. 'Our assistant,' reported the director of the Northampton State Hospital, 'has noticed at times an opposition by the citizens of some of the smaller towns to the placing out of State dependents.' Although the legislature authorized placing out only for non-dangerous and non-troublesome patients, some towns did not want any type of ex-inmates in their midst. Superintendents also complained of the difficulty of finding responsible families to take in the inmates, families that could meet the needs of chronic patients and at the same time not exploit them for whatever labor they could perform.[18]

But however pertinent all these considerations, the major stumbling block to family care remained the hospitals' own needs. It was not in their best interest to board out patients. First, the inmate who was most suitable for family care – who was most likely to find a family ready to take him in – was the steady working inmate whose labor was critical to the institution's functioning. Why should some family benefit from his work when the hospital desperately required it? TheMassachusetts State Board noted frankly that 'the lack of proper development of this [family care] department' reflected 'the want of interest on the part of hospital authorities, their objection to losing the workers (which means increasing the maintenance cost).' And superintendents conceded the validity of the point. 'It seemed,' one of them admitted, 'as if every good worker among the insane in that whole institution was, if he or she was quiet (and most good workers are quiet and manageable), turned over . . . to be boarded out, so that the institution was absolutely stripped of all the good workers it had developed.' With production figures and institutional maintenance to mind, superintendents were not eager to discharge their best laborers.[19]

Second, direct financial considerations worked against hospitals boarding out patients. Legislatures had no intention of supporting family care in ways that would increase the total amount of state expenditures; the program would have to operate within the same annual allotment of funds. (Legislators were probably short-sighted here; boarding-out might well have saved them later capital construction costs as institutions swelled beyond a point which even they could ignore. But such a saving would not turn up on an annual budget sheet, and their focus tended to be limited to the two-year periods from election to election.) What this constraint meant to the institutions was that any increased staff time for administering outpatient care would have to come out of existing positions; a hospital staff already overburdened would have to assume new obligations, to arrange for placements and visit the patients at least on an annual basis; and superintendents, again understandably, were unwilling to do this. 'The principal reason why my interest has not taken more practical effect,' explained one of them, 'is the fact that there was no one person in the hospital, no one officer, whom we could take off for that work because their duties were already so arduous.'[20]

Moreover, since the legislature would not add new funds for family care, expenditures had to come, directly or indirectly, from the institutions' budgets. For the hospital to subtract from its funds the $3.50 to $4.50 weekly per capita stipend to give to community caretakers was almost unthinkable. Not only was the patient's labor being lost, but since the costs of supervising him were lower than the costs of supervising the troublesome cases, an important margin of income disappeared. Further, superintendents were eager to keep their own enrollments high, either because state reimbursement came on a per capita basis or because a large number of patients was the most powerful argument for appropriations, or both. Again, an occasional superintendent candidly made these points: 'The cost of boarding out patients,' the Northampton Hospital director explained, 'will keep the number small so long as the expense must be met from our maintenance appropriation. Patients who are suitable to be boarded out are of the quiet class, who need but little supervision. Removal from the hospital of ten or twenty of their class will not noticeably reduce our expenses . . . but to board out ten patients will reduce by about $1,500 our maintenance appropriation.' In sum, economic incentives ran counter to family care and promoted keeping chronic but steady working patients within the institution.[21]

In much the same way, the state hospitals frustrated reformers' hopes for an extensive network of outpatient facilities. Mental hygiene proponents had anticipated that patients near to recovery would be paroled from institutions and would receive subsequent support in after-care clinics; these clinics would also serve the wider community, thereby reducing the number of hospitalizations. But again, the state facilities paid minimal attention to the program. Neither the legislatures, nor the hospital boards, nor the trustees, nor the superintendents ever devoted major energies to concerns or activities that went beyond institutional boundaries. To be sure, the mental hygiene movement did enjoy some success in the private sector; philanthropic agencies in the 1920s began to establish clinics and, especially, to administer child guidance programs. In the public realm, however, state dollars and state policy continued to buttress the state hospitals.

If ever a procedure seemed tailored to fit the needs of the mental hospital, it was the parole of patients. Given the overcrowded condition of the facilities, the hospitals ought to have been eager to arrange for parole. In fact, the first use of parole antedated the mental hygiene movement. It was initially designed to solve a special problem: sometimes patients left the institution to visit with relatives; they would initially adjust well and remain for a few weeks, when suddenly things would take a turn for the worse and the relatives would bring them back to the institution. The difficulty was that by law the several weeks' absence constituted an automatic discharge, and so the entire commitment procedure had to be repeated. To avoid this legal requirement, the institutions in the 1880s and 1890s secured legislation allowing patients to remain on visit – on furlough or parole – for thirty days, with the right to return at will. This initial

period was soon increased to sixty days – and then, with the support
of mental hygiene proponents, to one or two years.[22]

Nevertheless, parole did not become standard practice. Patients
on parole did increase, from a few thousand in 1910 to 23,000 (8
percent of all patients) in 1923, to 49,250 (11 percent of patients) in
1939. In Massachusetts the number rose from 539 in 1910, to 1,675
in 1925, to 2,555 in 1939; and in New York, from 196 in 1906, to
3,362 in 1925, to 6,809 in 1939. But the percentages, particularly in
the states with the greatest institutional populations, rarely exceeded
one in ten; as of 1939, Massachusetts and Pennsylvania had only 10
percent of their hospital inmates on parole, New York had 9 percent
and Illinois, 4 percent. And even these figures were somewhat
inflated because institutions often included escaped patients in the
parole category, which (as we will see) is very revealing about the
quality of outpatient care.[23]

The constraints that hindered the implementation of parole
resemble the considerations that restricted family care. Once again,
relatives' reluctance, together with community opposition, discour-
aged release: 'We often cannot obtain the cooperation of relatives
in the parole,' declared a New York superintendent. He also went
on to note that because of a recent upstate murder of a physician
'by an insane man (so far as I know, never a State hospital patient)
. . . there was an active opposition to the parole of patients from
the hospital, and had any patients been paroled . . . they would
have encountered an absolutely antagonistic environment.' Yet, with
parole as with family care, the institution itself erected major barriers
to release. Not only did it fail to prepare the inmates (thereby making
them fearful about release), but more important, it placed the maintenance needs of the institution above the discharge of the patients.
As two close students of New York staff practices discovered: 'Active
opposition to the point even of threats of resigning is apt to be
met with when patients are about to be removed who have been
familiarized with some important part of the routine work and
trained to perform it automatically and without supervision. Such
patients are to be found in almost every ward and working department of every hospital.' The superintendents criticized the ward
attendants for this opposition. Still, in light of personnel shortages,
administrators were quite prepared to give the staff its way. After
all, it was the superintendent who was ultimately responsible for
operating within the hospital budget.[24]

One unusual investigation of parole practices at the Chicago State Hospital in the early 1930s confirmed this generalization. Under the auspices of Edith Abbott, dean of the social work school at the University of Chicago, physicians and social workers examined 290 patients on the 'improved' wards to analyze why they had not been released. In some cases, there were no relatives to provide care; in others, no jobs were available. For almost three-quarters of the male patients, however, the failure to release reflected 'the policy of not encouraging the parole of patients who were useful workers. . . . When threatened with the loss of this 'staff,' the institution interposed to block their parole.' Just how powerful this interposition was should be clear from the fact that even after this policy was exposed, only twenty-one patients from the group went onto parole. Publicity did not affect practice.[25]

The hospitals were also unwilling or unable to support the staff or the facilities essential to a parole system. The demands of such a program were even greater than those for family care. By design at least, psychiatric and social work staff were to screen the appropriate cases for release, investigate the family circumstances, make the various arrangements, and then be responsible for providing after-care in community outpatient clinics. All of this took personnel and funds – and the hospitals begrudged them both. Reformers may have agreed that 'back of this whole system of trial visit is social service,' but the numbers of social workers employed in the state hospitals remained very low. As late as 1938–39, there were no social workers at all in one-third of the state hospitals, and even where they were in greatest supply, they were far too few in number to deliver much assistance. In New England, the ratio was one social worker for every 833 patients; in the mid-Atlantic states it was 1:775; elsewhere the figure was 1:1,600. In only seven of the nation's institutions was the ratio better than 1:400. Under these circumstances, few of the prescriptions for pre-release or post-release practices could be satisfied. What could five social workers do for the 2,285 inmates of the Boston State Hospital? What could four of them do for the 2,403 at Worcester?[26]

Given the central significance of outpatient clinics in the theories of the mental hygiene proponents, the failure to implement this part of the program was perhaps the most disappointing result of all. Through the 1920s and 1930s, the clinics remained few in number and severely limited in operation. As late as 1937, almost one-third of state hospitals had not organized any outpatient facility; and those institutions that did administer clinics operated on a small and indifferent basis. A 1935 national survey of mental hygiene facilities revealed that 62 of 127 state hospitals were administering outpatient clinics; and while it is true that most of the clinics were located off the institution's grounds, in a local hospital or school building, still they met only intermittently. Almost 60 percent were open only once a month or less, and a mere 6 percent met twice a week or more. So too, three-quarters of the sponsoring state hospitals were unwilling to allocate significant staff time to the clinics; they assigned less than half the time of one psychiatrist to outpatient work. The survey concluded that only five institutions took the mandate seriously.[27]

The clinics themselves established only very superficial contact with clients. A few exceptions aside, intensive treatment was not to be found. In New York, which actually invested more heavily in outpatient care than most states, a Committee on Mental Hygiene reported that 'the state hospital clinics gave insufficient time to individual examinations and had inadequate provision for following up their recommendations.'

Boston Psychopathic, for its part, ran a clinic that was as diagnostically oriented as its hospital, and no more capable of delivering treatment. In 1921 the clinic calculated that it was serving 1,439 patients in 1,500 clinic hours. It disposed of 660 of the cases with one meeting each: 'To a very large extent this group is made up of the frankly psychotic cases which are referred to the Boston Psychopathic Hospital or a State hospital.' These patients took up a total of 450 hours. Accordingly, 'we find that we are left with 1,050 hours with which to examine and treat 779 patients, which allows us about one hour and twenty minutes to each patient per year. That such a limited amount of time for each individual patient makes adequate treatment difficult is obvious.'[28]

As in the case of family care and parole, a lack of community cooperation hindered the outpatient program. But in this instance, it was not so much the general public as the local physicians and county medical societies who blocked reform goals. Some of them were fearful of state intrusions into health care. To them, outreach meant encroachment, and so just as they did battle with the clinics established with federal funds to deliver maternal and child health care (eventually succeeding in cutting off appropriations), so they opposed public clinics to deliver psychiatric care. In Illinois, one researcher noted 'the opposition of county medical societies to extra-mural work by the hospitals . . . [because] the state was infringing on the field of the private practitioners.' As he explained, 'This was ground sacred to the feet of the private physician. If he wished, he might call in the hospital physician in consultation; that was his professional privilege. But should the hospital attempt to reach out into the community in furthering the cause of mental health, the whole foundations of medical practice were immediately endangered! Hence there was strong and continuous opposition to the parole clinics.' Other doctors simply showed a fatal indifference. As one national survey discovered: 'The attitude of local physicians to state hospital clinics was . . . neutral, uninterested or uninformed rather than either antagonistic or definitely favorable. The effect of such an attitude on the work of the clinics seemed to be reflected chiefly in the scarcity of referrals from private medical sources.'[29]

Yet these considerations were not nearly as critical as the apathy or hostility of the medical superintendents. The notion that an insti-tutional staff would be willing to conduct an outpatient program was altogether fanciful. To superintendents, the clinics did not even offer the modest conveniences of boarding-out or parole. From their consistently narrow perspective, aftercare or community clinics were not part of what they were budgeted to do; outpatient care was a distraction and one that would siphon off their already slim resources. A superintendent explained to Helen Witmer of the National Committee for Mental Hygiene that 'in his judgment, a hospital's first duty was to its inpatients and that an extensive community program was not warranted unless a staff specially equipped for such work was provided [read: on someone else's budget line]. He deplored the tendency to "oversell" mental hygiene and said he believed that clinic work carried on by a staff of ward psychiatrists not only handicapped the hospital's normal work but was of little value to the outpatients as well.' In other words, superin-tendents' vision was so completely bounded by institutional walls that they were not about to give attention to the outside community. They would not release their inmates, their staff, or their funds to alternative programs.[30]

The consequences of this perspective to the mental hygiene move-ment were fatal. The superintendents' attitudes meant that with a handful of exceptions, public expenditures in mental health would be devoted primarily, almost exclusively, to institutional care. In the

1920s and still more clearly in the 1930s, the needs of the state hospitals dominated the agenda of the state departments of mental hygiene, and by extension, controlled the budgets of governors and legislators. Between 1930 and 1937, only twelve state departments of mental hygiene made any attempt to organize and to fund outpatient work apart from the control of the state hospitals, and these occasional efforts were typically short-lived and sporadic. Only three state departments, New York, Massachusetts, and Pennsylvania, were able to establish something of a network of outpatient clinics – and even there, the facilities were devoted not to adults or to patients on parole (where alternatives to institutionalization were most at stake), but to children.[31]

Moreover, the outcomes in two of these same states demonstrated just how powerful institutional interests were. Pennsylvania's Bureau of Mental Hygiene actually hoped to work with the state hospitals, to coordinate their clinic effort, and to give independent funding only to clinics in rural areas that were distant from the institutions. But cooperation proved impossible. The dominant figure in each clinic was supposed to be a psychiatrist on loan from the nearest mental hospital. But as the Pennsylvania Bureau learned: 'Having for the most part, responsible positions on the staffs of hospitals, the consultant's time is very limited.' Moreover, 'difficulties centering around state supervision developed in two hospitals'; superintendents were not eager to come under direct state agency control and certainly not to come under control by an agency looking to outpatient care. Finally, the Depression killed off what personnel shortages and discord did not. By 1939, the Pennsylvania Bureau abandoned outpatient work altogether: 'The provision of clinics has been left largely to the state hospitals,' which was, in effect, their death sentence.[32]

In much the same way, the Massachusetts Division of Mental Hygiene did manage for a time to administer a network of clinics within Boston. But it was not able to move out into the rest of the state and even half of the Boston clinics soon disappeared. Officials believed that part of the problem might have been the reluctance of first- and second-generation immigrants to use the clinics. But more, 'for years the Division consistently viewed its clinic program as temporary, its aim being to stimulate the state hospitals to offer comprehensive mental health services to the districts in which they were located.' The plan, however, could not succeed. As the

Commissioner of Mental Diseases explained in 1936: 'It has been demonstrated beyond all doubt that we cannot expect the state hospitals to operate these clinics with the byproducts of their hospital staff.' If clinic services were to be offered, 'it is absolutely necessary that each institution be provided with funds with which to secure adequately trained psychiatrists, psychologists, and social workers and that the clinic personnel should not have duties connected with the institution.'[33] But such advice merely demonstrated the extraordinary difficulties that the Massachusetts Division, indeed the entire mental hygiene movement, confronted. Reformers thought in terms of cooperation and a division of labor, but such a hope was doomed to disappointment. Perhaps it was because the funding was too limited so that the institutions, wanting to guard their every penny, blocked attempts to support alternate programs. Perhaps it was because superintendents were determined to preserve their monopoly over the care of the insane. No matter, the outcome was the same: the institutions undercut the effort to promote outpatient care.

What few successes the mental hygiene movement enjoyed came in the private sector. Some of the leading urban social welfare agencies did organize outpatient clinics, particularly for children, and by the close of the 1930s, about a hundred of them were in operation. Individual psychiatrists and social workers, too, began to affiliate with these agencies, preferring to work with clients in the community than with inmates in the asylums. But the private sector did not have adequate resources to transform the system of care for the mentally ill. Public funding was necessary for that – but the institutions, at least through the World War II period, controlled the sources of funding, the state budgets. Eventually, federal interventions would alter the balance – but even then, the contest between the institution and community care would not be easily or quickly resolved.[34]

It may well be, with all the advantages that hindsight allows, that reformers made a fateful mistake in helping to justify a custodial role for the state hospitals. The institutions consistently and successfully used this rationale to their best advantage. Superintendents were often prepared to describe their function as taking care of the 'social waste,' the senile, the alcoholic, the syphilitic, and the schizophrenic. It may be difficult to imagine a less inviting task, a more troublesome or unrewarding mandate, but its very grimness gave the state hospitals a powerful warrant for survival.

And survive they did. In 1950 the Council of State Governments examined 'The Mental Health Programs of the Forty-Eight States' and reported that while the general population had increased 2.6 times between 1880 and 1940, the mental hospital population had increased 12.6 times. In 1903, the resident population of the state hospitals was 159 per 100,000 of general population; in 1948 the figure was 322 per 100,000. And every indicator confirmed the chronicity of the patients. The number of insane in county and city almshouses decreased over these years as custodial care became the more exclusive province of the state hospitals; during the same period private mental hospitals witnessed very little growth in number, precisely because the chronic were not filling their wards. And the diagnostic classifications of entering state hospital patients in 1946 repeated the familiar pattern: 6 percent syphilitic, 4 percent alcoholic, 28 percent senile, 19 percent schizophrenic. (The private hospitals, by contrast, admitted only 1 percent syphilitic, 9 percent senile, 2.5 percent alcoholic, and 14 percent schizophrenic.) The resident institutional population was even more pronounced in its chronicity: schizophrenics, for example, made up one-fifth of admissions but more than half of hospital inmates. Duration of hospitalization pointed in the same custodial direction. In a state like New York only 16 percent of patients resident on April 1, 1947, had been confined for less than one year; one-third had been confined five to fourteen years, and a staggering 27 percent, fifteen years or more.[35]

These figures gave superintendents their final retorts to would-be critics. First, they could point to the long list of custodial problems (overcrowding, staff shortages, chronic patients, and the like) and argue that *if only* they had more doctors or more beds or a better trained nursing staff or a better class of patients, *then* recoveries would increase, treatment would go on, research would take place, and the institution would become a hospital. If that was not sufficient, they had a last-ditch defense, as useful in the twentieth century as it had been in the nineteenth: if not us, who? Surely it was better to care for the mentally ill in state hospitals than in county almshouses or in poor farms or in household attics or in unsupervised boarding homes or in families looking to exploit patients for their labor. But in retrospect, such arguments had more to do with convenience than with conscience. As the performance of the state hospitals over these decades makes amply clear, institutional survival, and not patient welfare, was the ultimate consideration.

Notes

1 Massachusetts State Board of Insanity, *Annual Report, 1910*, 30–31.

2 A substantial history of changing commitment laws remains to be written. Deutsch, *The Mentally Ill*, ch. 19, is an introduction to the material. See also the several articles in the American Social Science Association *Journal* 19 (1884), 66ff.

3 Meyers, *Papers*, vol. 4, 168, 186–187, 205, 230–231. See also Winfred Overholser, The Voluntary Admission Law, *American Journal of Psychiatry* 2 (1924), 476–481; Report of the Committee on Institutions, *First International Congress on Mental Hygiene* (1930), 58ff.

4 Massachusetts State Board of Insanity, *Annual Report, 1915*, 92; *Annual Report, 1917*, 93–94.

5 *Idem*, Annual Report, 1914, 93–94.

6 C. M. Campbell, The Work of the Psychopathic Hospital, *First International Congress on Mental Hygiene* (1930), 358. See also Trustees of the Boston Psychopathic Hospital, *Annual Report . . . 1921*, 20; L. Vernon Briggs, *History of the Psychopathic Hospital of Boston* (1922).

7 Massachusetts State Board of Insanity, *Annual Report, 1914*, 94; Trustees of the Boston Psychopathic Hospital, *Annual Report . . . 1921*, 3.

8 Massachusetts State Board of Insanity, *Annual Report, 1914*, 14.

9 Campbell, Psychopathic Hospital, 357–358.

10 Trustees of the Boston Psychopathic Hospital, *Annual Report . . . 1938*, 7, 37.

11 Trustees of the Boston Psychopathic Hospital, *Annual Report . . . 1931*, 9.

12 Syracuse State Psychopathic Hospital, *First Annual Report* (1931), 10; *Fifth Annual Report* (1935), 5.

13 New Hampshire Asylum for the Insane, *Report . . . 1900*, 17; James Russell, 'Asylum Versus Hospital,' *Proceedings of the American Medico-Psychological Association* 5 (1898), 242–244.

14 Burton Chance, 'Needed Reforms in the Care of the Insane, *Outlook* 78 (1904), 1037; Asylum or Hospital, *Literary Digest* 51 (1915), 153.

15 Russell, *Asylum Versus Hospital*, 245.

16 Norwich (Connecticut) Hospital for the Insane, *Second Biennial Report* (1908), 14. See also William F. Lorenz, Educational Value to the Community of Mental Hygiene Agencies, *National Conference of Social Work, 1921*, 380.

17 Helen Crockett, Boarding Homes as a Tool in Social Case Work with Mental Patients, *Mental Hygiene* 18 (1934), 194; Massachusetts Commissioner of Mental Health, *Annual Report . . . 1939*, 146; US Bureau of the Census, *Patients in Institutions, 1939*, 8.

18 Northampton State Hospital, *Fifty-Seventh Annual Report* (1912), 14; *Fifty-Eighth Annual Report* (1913), 13–14.

19 Massachusetts State Board of Insanity, *Annual Report, 1912*, 190, 200.

20 *Ibid.*, 206.

21 *Ibid.*, 195, 203; Northampton State Hospital, *Fifty-First Annual Report* (1906), 12.

22 Horatio M. Pollack, The Development and Extension of the Parole System in New York State, *Psychiatric Quarterly* 1 (1927), 53–56; M. B. Heyman, A Plea for the Extension of the Parole Period, *New York State Hospital Quarterly* 2 (1916), 13–17.

23 US Bureau of the Census, *Patients in Hospitals, 1923*, 17–18, 88–89; *Patients in Institutions, 1939*, 99; Hamilton, *Public Mental Hospitals*, 34–35.

24 Discussion of Russell Blaisdell, What Patients May be Safely Paroled?, *New York State Hospital Quarterly* 7 (1922), 438; Aaron J. Rosaroff and Thomas Cusack, The Parole System and its Relation to Therapy, *AJI* 7 (1920), 151. See also E. H. Howard, The Parole System and After Care Treatment, *New York State Hospital Bulletin* 6 (1913), 150–157.

25 The study is reported in Stuart K. Jaffary, *The Mentally Ill and Public Provision for their Care in Illinois* (Chicago, 1942), 129–130; the full analysis is in Florence Worthington, *Suggested Community Resources for an Extensive Parole System for Mental Patients in Illinois* (Smith College Studies in Social Work, 1933).

26 Massachusetts Commissioner of Mental Health, *Annual Report . . . 1939*, 132; June F. Lyday and Maida H. Solomon, 'The Problem of the Supply of Psychiatric Workers for State Hospitals,' *American Journal of Psychiatry* 7 (1928), 629–631; Hamilton, *Public Mental Hospitals*, 44–45; Illinois Department of Public Welfare, *Fourteenth Annual Report*, 161. See also, *First International Congress on Mental Hygiene*, 76.

27 National Committee for Mental Hygiene, *Research in Mental Hospitals* (New York, 1938), 99–101; Helen L. Witmer, *Psychiatric Clinics for Children* (New York, 1940), 108–111, 128; 'Directory of Psychiatric Clinics in the United States, 1936,' *Mental Hygiene* 20 (1936), 72–129. Only a handful of hospitals, no more than seven, set up clinics to serve only adults. In fact, there were many more clinics that accepted only children as clients.

28 New York State Psychiatric Institute and Hospital, *First Annual Report*, 8–9; *Eighth Annual Report*, 8; Trustees of the Boston Psychopathic Hospital, *Annual Report . . . 1921*, 33.

29 Sheila M. Rothman, *Woman's Proper Place* (New York, 1978), ch. 4; Jaffary, *The Mentally Ill*, 148–149; Witmer, *Psychiatric Clinics*, 87.

30 Witmer, *Psychiatric Clinics*, 87.

31 *Ibid.*, 182ff.

32 *Ibid.*, 198–205; Secretary of Welfare of the State of Pennsylvania, *Second*

Biennial Report (1924), 38–39; Paul Homer, 'A State-Wide Mental-Hygiene Program for Pennsylvania,' *Mental Hygiene* 18 (1934), 205–211.

33 Witmer, *Psychiatric Clinics*, 211–212; see also, *Report of the Boston Mental Hygiene Survey* (Boston, 1930), 90–94.

34 In addition to Witmer's *Psychiatric Clinics*, see the articles by Ethel Dummer and William Healy in *Orthopsychiatry, 1923–1948: Retrospect and Prospect*, and George S. Stevenson and Geddes Smith, *Child Guidance Clinics* (New York, 1934), which traces the pertinent work of the Commonwealth Fund. The child guidance movement, like so much else in this field, still lacks a competent history.

35 Council of State Governments, *The Mental Health Programs of the Forty-Eight States* (Chicago, 1950), 30–37.

CHAPTER 3

Cycles of institutional reform*

Joseph P. Morrissey, Howard H. Goldman and Lorraine V. Klerman

From its founding in 1830, Worcester State Hospital (WSH) in Massachusetts has mirrored the cyclical pattern of reform and retrenchment, of hope and despair, which has characterized institutional care of the mentally ill in America. This pioneering hospital has served as a model for the rest of the nation (Bockoven, 1972; Grob, 1966; Shakow, 1972). Its well-documented social history provides a telling record of the best and worst features of the institutional care of the mentally ill in America and illustrates the cyclical patterns of institutional reform during the past 150 years.

In the early 1970s, WSH embarked on a concerted program intended to supplant its predominantly custodial and social control functions with an active therapeutic role in the mental health service network of central Massachusetts. Although initially successful, the transformation of WSH into a network of institutional and community-based services was ultimately halted in the late 1970s. The administrative, political, and economic forces that led to the demise of this organizational arrangement parallel the conditions that undermined its role as a therapeutic asylum over a century ago.

Today, WSH serves more as the 'floor' rather than the 'hub' of the mental health service system in Worcester. It continues to perform its historical treatment, custody, and social control functions for a sizeable residue of the most disadvantaged and most disturbed patients.

* Reprinted with minor editorial changes by permission of the authors and publisher, from *The Enduring Asylum: Cycles of Institutional Reform at Worcester State Hospital*, New York: Grune and Stratton, Inc., pp. 7–8, 281–91, 294–305. © 1980 by Grune and Stratton, Inc. All rights reserved.

Other local service agencies, created in part with staff and resources formerly assigned to WSH, are thereby able to deal selectively with more-advantaged and less-disturbed clients. In effect, WSH endures as an institution of last resort and it continue to anchor a two-class system of mental health care.

Just as its institutional history provides unique insights into the environmental and organizational forces that have led to the endurance of public asylums for the past 150 years, its recent deinstitutionalization experiences reveal, in microcosm, the social forces that will insure their continued existence in some form. In this chapter, the meaning and significance of the Worcester story for the larger mental health field will be reviewed and evaluated.

Current evidence indicates that like earlier attempts at institutional reform, deinstitutionalization as practiced in the 1970s failed to develop a system of humane care for the chronically mentally ill. This assessment will be supported by a review of the parallels in the cycles of institutional reform, in the context of the fundamental social forces that have conditioned American social policy toward the care of the mentally ill. This review, in turn, will highlight the enduring functions of state mental hospitals and the fundamental changes required for the dissolution of the two-class system of care in this country. Short of a major technological breakthrough in understanding the causes and cures of mental disorders, progress toward the development of a truly humane system of mental health care requires a commitment of societal resources commensurate with the personal and social costs of these intractable problems. Moreover, such a system will remain elusive until mechanisms are developed to overcome the fragmentation of the current service network and the penchant to polarize the organizational and ideological approaches to the problem of mental illness.

Cycles of reform: persistence and change

Since the reform movements of Horace Mann and Dorothea Dix at WSH that led, in turn, to the rise and proliferation of state mental hospitals in the early and middle decades of the nineteenth century, American social policy toward the care of the mentally ill has been a reflection of social values and ideologies. The belief that man could be perfected by manipulating his social and physical environment,

the reformist zeal of Evangelical Protestantism, and the spirit of
noblesse oblige were prominent features of the social climate at the
time of the founding of WSH. As a seed bed of moral treatment
during its first decades of operation, it provided the model that was
followed by the rest of the nation and established the precedent for
the state to assume exclusive responsibility for the indigent mentally
ill. As the intellectual, social, and technological base of society
changed, however, so too did the structure and functions of the
institutions devoted to the care and treatment of the mentally ill.

The lack of an effective technology for treating large numbers of
chronically ill patients drawn from lower class and immigrant groups,
and the consequent decline in the rates of therapeutic success associated with hospitalization, gradually transformed WSH and other
public mental hospitals from small, therapeutic asylums into large,
human warehouses that provided cheap custodial care and segregation for the mentally ill, the medically infirm, the aged, and a miscel-
lany of other social rejects. The cause of the 'therapeutic asylum'
became an ambiguous legacy of the past and a rhetoric for periodic
institutional reform. Institutional change, however, was administrative and contextual, emphasizing the locus more than the modes
of care and treatment. Some reformers favored large, centralized
institutions; others advocated small, decentralized facilities such as
general hospitals and other community-based settings. Over the past
150 years, while the pendulum of social and institutional reform
oscillated between these extremes, a sharply divided two-class system
for mental health care emerged and became firmly entrenched.

A careful analysis of these institutional reforms indicates that the
social forces that shaped American social policies toward the
mentally ill have remained largely unaltered. Social policies are principles or courses of action designed to influence the overall quality
of life in a society; the circumstances of living of individuals and
groups in that society; and the nature of intrasocietal relationships
among individual groups, and society as a whole (Gil, 1973). Such
policies operate through three interrelated, universal processes or
societal mechanisms:

1 *Resource development*: the generation of life-sustaining and life-
   enhancing material and symbolic resources, goods, and
   services;
2 *Division of labor*: the allocation of individuals and groups to

specific statuses (social positions) within the total array of
societal tasks and functions, involving corresponding roles, and
prerogatives intrinsic to these roles; and
3   *Distribution of rights*: the assignment to individuals and groups
of specific rights to resources, goods, and services through
general and specific entitlements, rewards, and constraints.

The mental health referents of these key processes are readily
identifiable in relation to the characteristics of the organizations and
clientele which constitute the mental health service system in its
historical and contemporary context. In the late eighteenth and early
nineteenth centuries, the general hospital became the first medical
institution to care for the mentally ill in America, supplementing
other social institutions, such as the family and the almshouse. The
early general hospitals developed 'insane departments' and later built
separate asylums, many of which have become today's private mental
hospitals. The general hospital did not become the dominant model
because it was unable to provide care for the indigent insane who
had become a great burden to their community. The public mental
hospital was created to meet this need.

Accordingly, since the mid-nineteenth century, mental health care
has been divided into a public and a private sector (*resource development*). Public resources were allocated for the establishment of
separate asylums for the indigent mentally ill; private resources were
used almost exclusively to build facilities for paying patients.
Following this initial schism, organizations within each sector
developed specialized functions (*division of labor*) to serve different
populations. Some facilities primarily treated acutely ill patients,
while others provided predominantly long-term custodial care to the
chronically disturbed. Some hospitals accepted only voluntary
patients, while others were licensed to detain patients involuntarily.
The differentiation of voluntary and involuntary care reflected not
only a *division of labor*, but also a difference in the *distribution of
rights*, in this case, the right to liberty and to refuse treatment.
Further, because of the unequal distribution of rights to resources,
the separation into public and private sectors also meant that each
sector served a different population. State hospitals cared for the
disadvantaged patients, while private hospitals treated the advantaged patients. This distribution of rights to resources, in turn,
weighed the right to treatment in favor of the advantaged. As the

care system evolved, private sector facilities tended to specialize in providing treatment to wealthier, acute, quiet, primarily voluntary patients. The state hospitals were left to provide long-term custodial care to poor, chronic, disturbed, involuntary patients. The differentiation of the mental health care delivery system during the past century has resulted in a pluralism of institutions, patient populations, methods of treatment, and professional ideologies.

The failure of institutional reforms throughout this period at WSH and elsewhere resides in their ad hoc or 'cosmetic' nature (Talbott, 1978): changes *in* rather than changes *of* this dual system of care. An early effort to alter the institutionalization of the mentally ill occurred in the 1860s and early 1870s in the form of the cottage hospital movement. Merrick Bemis, the medical superintendent at Worcester, was one of the principal spokesmen and innovators in the effort to decentralize state hospitals in a way that would sustain their role in caring for all social classes and ethnic groups while providing humane custody of the chronically ill in family-like residences (Grob, 1966). Professional and economic considerations led to the defeat of Bemis's proposals (and of similar proposals in other locales) and the institutionalization of the mentally ill continued unabated. As a consequence, well-to-do families resorted to private facilities for the care of their mentally ill members and state hospitals became filled with lower class and ethnic minorities.

Subsequent reforms followed a similar course. The mental hygiene movement of the early twentieth century was originally dedicated to improving the care and treatment of mental hospital patients (Deutsch, 1944). Much of its impetus came from Adolf Meyer, who formulated many of his ideas while working at WSH. As it matured, however, the movement began to concentrate on prevention in the form of early detection and treatment of mental disorders. The movement spawned the development of psychopathic hospitals within the state system for the reception and evaluation of acute cases, but most admissions were still funneled into large custodial institutions. The lasting contribution of the movement, however, were the child guidance clinics and parental education programs which were championed as interventions that would reduce the need for mental hospitalization. As Gruenberg and Archer (1979: 488) note, however,

(I)n hindsight . . . it is clear that the child guidance clinics were treating, as best they could, a new set of problems that had not before received psychiatric attention – disorders of childhood. They enlarged the spectrum of cases receiving attention; but they were not arresting later psychoses through early effective treatment on a significant scale.

The middle-class biases of the mental hygiene movement and the rejection of the poor by private social welfare and psychiatric agencies has been apparent for decades (Davis, 1938; Hollingshead and Redlich, 1958; Hunt *et al.*, 1958; Cloward and Epstein, 1965; Fisher, 1969). Likewise, the Community Mental Health Center movement initiated in the early 1960s quickly became oriented to meeting the needs of a new or 'underserved' clientele in local communities that rarely consisted of people with severe mental disorders who often needed inpatient care (Chu and Trotter, 1974; Cameron, 1978; Bassuk and Gerson, 1978; Scherl and Macht, 1979). And the more recent state hospital 'deinstitutionalization' movement of the early 1970s, justified as a broad-based plan to provide humane care for the chronically mentally ill, has led to their abandonment in the eyes of many critics (Reich and Segal, 1973; Kirk and Therrien, 1975; Rose, 1979; Gruenberg and Archer, 1979). These reform movements shifted attention from one administrative solution to another, from institution to community and from centralized to decentralized services. Each expanded and diversified the mental health system but none fundamentally changed the two-class system of care.

The evidence of cyclical patterns in the social and institutional reforms at WSH as well as in the mental hospital arena as a whole, however, goes much deeper. There are a number of striking parallels in the processes as well as the outcomes associated with the two principal 'reforms' of the past 150 years: the *rise* of state mental hospitals, or 'institutionalization,' and their apparent *demise*, or 'deinstitutionalization.' These parallels can be found in the exaggerated success claims of the early advocates of both reform movements and in the two distinct phases within which the reforms were carried out.[1]

With regard to exaggerated success claims, each movement was launched with little or no appreciation of the practical limits to which the core ideas could be pushed. In the case of the mental hospital movement of the nineteenth century, institutionalization proved beneficial only for milder and acute cases of mental illness; moral treatment had little success with chronic, long-term cases. The early successes of moral treatment at WSH, however, spawned the diffusion of asylums throughout America even as the original hospitals were floundering under the pressure of an ever-expanding chronic caseload. Proponents of institutionalization, such as Dorothea Dix and Samuel Woodward, were so wedded to the idea that environmental change and removal to state hospitals was intrinsically beneficial (Rothman, 1971), that institutions continued to be built regardless of their deteriorating quality of care and inadequate resources.

In the case of the community mental health movement of the mid-twentieth century, the development of new psychosocial techniques (e.g., milieu therapy, therapeutic communities, 'open hospitals') and later the discovery and widespread use of psychoactive drugs made deinstitutionalization or community-based treatment possible for relatively acute cases of mental disorder. Research documented the value of short-term hospitalization and alternatives to hospitalization for acute episodes, but there was little research evidence that the new technologies could reverse the course of chronic deterioration in long-stay patients (Klerman, 1977; Gruenberg and Archer, 1979). Community mental health ideologues, nonetheless, saw the state hospital census decline following 1955 as evidence that the majority of patients could benefit by transfer to the community, with little appreciation for the absence of life-support systems needed to maintain chronic patients outside of these hospitals. Social science research on conditions in many state hospitals (e.g., Goffman, 1961), also contributed to '. . . the romantic notion that all chronic deterioration was the product of institutional life' (Klerman, 1977: 624). Shifting the locus of care by removing chronic patients to community settings rested on naive environmentalist assumptions similar to those advanced in favor of mental hospitalization in the nineteenth century (Caplan, 1969).

With regard to phases of reform, both the mental hospitalization and the community mental health movements were initially stimulated by therapeutic innovations but were ultimately accelerated by political-economic considerations. In the nineteenth century, the mental hospital movement got underway during the era of moral treatment (roughly between 1830 and 1855) when humane psychosocial treatment in small, intimate asylums led to high rates of recovery for persons who were ill less than a year. In the twentieth century, the community care movement (roughly between 1950 and 1965) was occasioned by the resurgence of psychosocial treatment approaches and early release policies (Gruenberg and Archer, 1979), and then by the use of psychotropic medications (Klerman, 1977). Active treatment programs and renewed optimism about the treatability of mental disorders led to dramatic census declines in state hospitals throughout the country.

Although political-economic factors played a crucial role in the subsequent development of each movement, it was the growing belief in the incurability of mental disorders and the pervasive therapeutic nihilism of the late nineteenth century that led to expansion of large custodial mental hospitals, while it was the near-opposite belief – that the technological advances of chemotherapy provided an effective basis for treating all state hospital patients in the community – that transformed the community care movement into a program of 'deinstitutionalization' in the past decade. History has shown that both beliefs were misleading. With the apparent failure of moral treatment, concern shifted to providing custodial care for the largest number of patients at the lowest possible cost in large centralized institutions removed from the mainstream of community life. Contrary evidence, such as the Park-Eastman studies at Worcester State Hospital which clearly showed that with proper care a significant number of patients recovered without relapse (Bockoven, 1972), was ignored and the burden for caring for the mentally ill and other social problem cases was shifted from local communities to the state.

In the late 1960s, under the banner of 'deinstitutionalization.' state hospital phase-down became 'a slogan and a de facto policy decision' (Klerman 1977: 624). The coalescing of interests among community mental health advocates, civil libertarians, and fiscal conservatives led to a sharp break with the state hospital reform movement of the 1950s and early 1960s. As Gruenberg and Archer (1979: 500) note, the

. . . recognition that [state hospitals] can sometimes do more harm than good . . . developed into a belief that they can never do any good . . . (T)he court decision that mental patients must be treated in the 'least restrictive care' setting has been interpreted to mean that any care is less restrictive than state mental hospital care, even though these hospitals can often provide care with less restriction on the patient's life than can nursing homes, adult residence hotels, and general-hospital, locked psychiatric wards.[2]

Moreover, as Klerman (1977: 624) relates:

. . . right-wing fiscal conservatives were interested in reducing the budgets of state governments. If they could shift the fiscal burden of responsibility to the Federal level, they did so. Transferring a patient into a nursing home meant that the cost was borne by Medicare, and discharging patients into the community, even if they were sent to state-subsidized boarding homes, was still less expensive per diem. If the patients could be certified as disabled, they were eligible for Social Security, with costs being borne in large part by Federal rather than state or local funds.

The result was a rapid depopulation of state mental hospitals despite little documentation of the relative cost-benefit ratio of dein-stitutionalization. Thus, in a number of respects, recent reforms in mental health care have committed the counterpoint error of the late nineteenth century: assuming that all patients would benefit by release to the community, while ignoring evidence that many chronic patients require some kind of institutional care for the rest of their natural lives (Klerman, 1977; Gruenberg and Archer, 1979). More-over, the claims that community care would be more cost-efficient than state hospitals – so appealing to the fiscal conservatives who endorsed rapid deinstitutionalization policies – have proved to be exaggerated (Arnhoff, 1975). 'Although the release of patients to the community,' as Mechanic (1978: 6) points out, 'is always less expensive in direct care costs than other alternatives if this is all that is done, required welfare expenditures and indirect social costs to the patients, their families and the community measured by patient deterioration, disruption of family life, and social control problems may be large. Effective community care requires not only adequate medical services and the provision of supportive services but also efforts in teaching patients coping skills that enhance their social capacities and life satisfactions.'

The Group for the Advancement of Psychiatry (GAP, 1978: 339–340) has also noted the marked parallels in the ideological, social, and economic climate of society a hundred years ago and the current post-deinstitutionalization era:

(The) ideological emphasis *then* on the interpersonal and humanistic understanding of the mentally ill was replaced by an emphasis on cellular and brain pathology and on classification of mental illness. *Now*, the humanistic concern for mental patients, which reappeared in the middle years of this century, is endangered by preoccupation with advances in psychobiology and psychopharmacology.

Educationally, the inspired leaders of moral treatment failed *then* to train successors to counteract the pessimistic view of mental illness that evolved with the development of scientific medicine. *Now*, the pioneers in community care have failed to train new leaders and new clinician-administrators prepared to accept the responsibility for the formulation of new policies and the development and operation of community programs for psychiatric rehabilitation.

Culturally, the advocates of moral treatment, dependent on familiar interpersonal relationships, were not prepared *then* to adapt their treatment approach to the mentally ill members of a mass of immigrants who differed in language, socioeconomic status, and education. *Now*, the advocates of community care, also dependent on familiar types of interpersonal relationships, have not sufficiently adapted their treatment approach to the growing demands of new consumer groups, recent migrants from a broad range of ethnic and cultural backgrounds, and people such as drug abusers who have been diverted from the correctional system.

Then, the locus of segregation of the mentally ill was shifting from jails and almshouses to state hospitals away from our communities. *Now*, the locus of segregation is again shifting, this time from state hospitals to ghettoes and residential care facilities still isolated from our communities.

Then, rising costs and financial distress caused cutbacks in hospital services and virtually made moral treatment impossible to carry out. *Now*, recession and inflation have led to cutbacks in community care that have made its ambitious goals virtually impossible to attain.

These parallels are disturbing and suggest that history may be repeating itself, that the hope that the chronic mentally ill in this country will be rehabilitated or at least given humane and dignified care is being abandoned, and that they are doomed either to return to custodial institutional care or to drift, rejected and unattended, in the back-waters of our cities.

In a number of respects, therefore, the ambiguous legacy of institutional care is now being supplanted by the ambiguous legacy of community care. In the past decade, the gap between the ideal of a community-based mental health system and its reality has widened considerably. Similar to the early private asylums, CHMCs and general hospitals have not provided the comprehensive care required for chronic as well as acute patients; social and rehabilitative services have not been put into place; and the state hospital system has been dismantled prematurely. Rather than 'deinstitutionalization' a process of 'transinstitutionalization' has occurred in many instances, with 'back wards' moved to nursing homes (Schmidt *et al.*, 1977) and other residential care facilities (Reich and Segal, 1973) and 'front wards' moved to general hospitals and CMHCS (Windle and Scully, 1976). Thus segregation of the mentally ill persists in a new ecological arrangement.

These observations are not meant to imply that nothing has changed in the American mental health system, nor that the changes have not been beneficial to many patients. Indeed, the past two decades have witnessed dramatic increases in outpatient services, private-sector care, and community-based services (cf., Kramer, 1977; Redlich and Kellert, 1978; Regier *et al.*, 1978; Klerman, 1979). Nevertheless, as long as social forces shape policies toward the mentally ill, the basic functions of the state mental hospital will continue to be needed even if the institutions are phased down, consolidated, or closed. The following section will examine briefly the enduring functions of the state mental hospital in the present and future mental health care system.

The multiple functions of state mental hospitals

It is overly simplistic to view the history of the public mental hospital as a fall from the 'grace' of moral treatment into the 'snakepit' of custodialism. It is certainly true that Worcester State Hospital and the institutions modeled after it never lived up to the exaggerated expectations of their founders. However, neither is it accurate to regard the public asylum as 'dead' (Talbott, 1978) or even as an institutional failure – its 'premature obituary' has been noted elsewhere (Lamb and Goertzel, 1972). The endurance of public asylums beyond the era of moral treatment attests to the multiple 'usages' (Perrow, 1978) or functions they came to serve for the larger society, for their staff, and for other community organizations. Although officially a medical institution in which treatment was presumed to be the legitimate, announced purpose, in practice, the actual functions served by state mental hospitals were (1) to provide inexpensive custody, control, and segregation of persons who were disruptive of social order or burdensome to their families; (2) to provide stable employment and health-welfare benefits for their staff (and, historically, they did serve as the arena for the professionalization of psychiatry); (3) to provide a cottage industry in towns with few or no other economic resources; and (4) to operate as a backup or 'dumping ground' for cases deemed inappropriate or unacceptable by other health and welfare organizations and community practitioners (Belknap, 1956; Fowlkes, 1975; Bachrach, 1976; Goldman, 1978). In each of these respects, state mental hospitals for the past century or more have been remarkably successful as 'tools' (Perrow, 1972) or resources for realizing the purposes of a variety of internal and external interest groups.[3]

Within the last two decades, however, many of the political-economic supports for the social functions of state hospitals have been altered by the opportunities to transfer patients to community settings and the financial burden of their care from state to Federal and local government budgets, by the growth of the nursing home and other rehabilitation service industries, and by the proliferation of general hospital psychiatric units and community mental health centers as alternative practice settings for the professional staff of these institutions. However, despite the rapid depopulation of state hospitals, most continue to exist (albeit 'creamed,' 'dumped upon,' and 'exposéd'). Their residual social functions are still needed and they have not been supplanted by other institutions.

Enduring functions of state mental hospitals

Today, state mental hospitals continue to serve their historic patient care and social control functions, albeit at a reduced level. Data available from the National Institute of Mental Health (Goldman and Rosenstein, 1979) indicate that:

1   These hospitals still serve a substantial acute care function. In 1975 approximately 400,000 admissions (duplicated count), consisting largely of persons from socially and economically disadvantaged backgrounds, were recorded by the 313 state and county mental hospitals in the United States;

2   These hospitals still serve a major social control function

through civil, criminal, and emergency commitment. In 1972, some 200,000 persons were admitted to these hospitals on involuntary status; and

3 These hospitals still serve a sizeable custodial care function. In 1975 there were some 100,000 to 125,000 resident patients in state hospitals who could not be moved permanently into community facilities, either because they were 'inappropriate' (too disturbed or too disturbing) for current types of residential alternatives or because the alternatives are not available.

Thus, despite the rhetoric of deinstitutionalization, public resources are still required to maintain state mental hospitals. Many disadvantaged patients are still barred from admission to nonpublic facilities because of a lack of resources to pay for care and treatment. Courts, police, private physicians and other agencies continue to commit mental patients involuntarily to public hospitals because most nonpublic facilities do not have (or seek) licenses to treat involuntary cases. In addition, a substantial residue of the most difficult and undesirable patients remain to be cared for in the state mental hospitals because nonpublic facilities refuse to accept (or keep) them even if they are able to pay and are admitted voluntarily. From their inception, state hospitals have served as a buffer or (less euphemistically) 'dumping ground' for the mental health and social welfare system, and this role continues to be performed today. As Shore (1979: 770) notes, the relationship between state hospitals – the 'institutions of last resort' – and the rest of the mental health system involves a 'tacit social contract':

> Maintenance of the system of private entitlement depends upon the co-existence of a public system in which the quality of care is infinitely dilutable by the addition of new patients to a fixed resource pool. Thus the private sector of psychiatry needs the public institutions as they are currently set up and is subtly but strongly motivated not to look too deeply into their functioning.

The state mental hospital is not unique in this regard. Similar organizations or parts of organizations can be found in the medical care system (cf., Roth and Eddy, 1967 on chronic disease hospitals), the public school system (cf., Carlson, 1965 on 'special' classrooms for the educationally handicapped), higher education (cf., Clark, 1960 on community colleges), and in many other direct services arenas. By managing the 'failures' and tough problem cases in each institutional sphere, these organizations allow other more powerful or prestigious agencies to provide high-quality services to carefully selected client groups.

The expansion of a pluralistic (public-private, acute-chronic, inpatient-outpatient) mental health services system has occurred at the expense of the state mental hospitals. While the phase-out of many of these institutions – especially those established during the era of institutionalization as overflow chronic care facilities in remote rural areas – can be justified on clinical, administrative, and fiscal grounds, it is clear that the closure of *all* state hospitals is premature. To date, the private sector has accepted the more acute, less disturbed, voluntary patients with financial resources, leaving the public sector with the residue of the patient population. The growth of the nursing home industry and the development of alternative community residences has reduced the number of long-term chronic patients who once languished on back wards in state mental hospitals. However, many authorities question the categorical claims that their relocation has led to demonstratable benefits. Indeed, rather than 'deinstitutionalization,' the process has often resulted in their 'transinstitutionalization' or movement from one debilitating environment to another (Talbott, 1979b).

The existence of a 'pluralism' of services – so enticing in the context of the American political creed – has had unanticipated or counter-intuitive consequences for the state mental hospital. The Joint Commission on Mental Illness and Health (1961) had encouraged the expansion of the mental health system, including the proliferation of community mental health centers and psychiatric units in general hospitals. The Community Mental Health Centers Act of 1963 largely ignored the state mental hospital but it created the expectation that the new centers would prevent hospitalization and would provide aftercare for patients released from these hospitals. Likewise, there was a hope that psychiatric units in nonpublic general hospitals would assume the acute inpatient function of state mental hospitals. Neither expectation has been realized fully. Further, the expansion of mental health services siphoned away professional staff and the most treatable patients from the public hospitals. This 'creaming' left them to perform an increasingly more difficult set of tasks with diminished resources. Rather than replacing the state mental hospital, however, the proliferation of community-based facilities reinforced the role of the public asylum as a 24-hour backup and institution of last resort and ultimate responsibility. The continued existence of the state hospitals permits other facilities and practitioners to maintain the privilege of treating a selected target population, referring the most difficult problems and abdicating responsibility for the least desirable and most costly patient care (Shore, 199; Shore and Shapiro, 1979). The endurance of the two-class system of care throughout these administrative change processes can be attributed to the persistence of the fundamental social forces that have shaped policies toward the care of the mentally ill for the past century.

Prerequisites for fundamental reform

'Images of the future,' as Paul Starr (1978: 175) reminds us, 'are usually caricatures of the present. They inflate some recognizable features of contemporary life to extravagant proportions, and out of fear or hope respond to every vagary of historical experience, as if it were a sign of destiny.' So it is with images of the mental health service system. After a brief period of quiescence in the late 1970s, calls for the closure of state mental hospitals are again being heard.[4] To avoid the shortcomings of the past, however, it is imperative for policy makers and planners to consider the prerequisites for fundamental reform in the American mental health care system. Until effective cures are developed for the major mental disorders – thereby allowing state hospitals to take their place alongside TB sanitoriums in museums for archaic social institutions – the residual functions of state hospitals, and the two-class system which they anchor, can only be supplanted by fundamental changes in the resource base, division of labor, and distribution of rights (Gil, 1973) underlying current policy toward mental health care.

Consistent with this view, Goldman *et al.* (1979) have pointed out that a viable plan for the elimination of state mental hospitals will require three broad-based reforms:

1 A comprehensive *national health insurance* program for inpatient as well as ambulatory care, and the expansion of services in general and private mental hospitals to accommodate 400,000 additional admissions of severely disturbed patients;

2   A shift in the locus of *involuntary care* into the private sector
    or into specialized correctional facilities, or more radically, its
    outright abolition at all mental health facilities; and
3   A comprehensive *national social insurance* program for essential
    psycho-social rehabilitation services, and the expansion of
    intermediate care facilities or psychiatric nursing homes for
    more than 100,000 very disturbed chronic patients.

The first and third proposals would go a long way toward eroding
the economic underpinnings of the present two-class system of care.
Comprehensive health and social insurance programs would enrich
the resource base of the mental health system and alter the distribution of rights to resources. Insurance benefits would enfranchise
the disadvantaged and thereby universalize the purchase of services
in the private sector. This would presumably shift the burden of
acute care farther away from the public sector and the state mental
hospitals toward general hospitals and Community Mental Health
Centers. In addition, broad insurance benefits for long-term as well
as short-term care would be required to encourage community residential and aftercare facilities to increasingly become involved in
chronic care functions once left by default almost exclusively to
state institutions. Moreover, these health benefits would have to be
complemented by a comprehensive social insurance program or some
other mechanism for insuring that the chronically mentally ill have
access to the psychosocial, recreational, and vocational supports
needed for optimal functioning (cf., Group for the Advancement
of Psychiatry, 1978; Sharfstein, 1978; Turner and TenHoor, 1978;
President's Commission, 1979; Schulberg, 1979; Talbot, 1979a).

Alterations in the resource base and distribution of resources
alone, however, would not be sufficient to shift the division of labor
completely away from state mental hospitals. Before public asylums
could be closed, their role in civil and criminal commitment would
have to be supplanted. The elimination of all forms of involuntary
care would obviate the problem by fundamentally altering the
division of labor as well as the distribution of rights, both to seek as
well as to refuse treatment. Although the abolition of involuntary
care is strongly advocated by some critics of current psychiatric
practice (e.g., Szasz, 1968) its near-term occurrence would seem
unlikely. Short of this dramatic change, the closure of state mental
hospitals could be facilitated by the transfer of responsibility for

civil and criminal commitment to private facilities or specialized correctional units. However, such transfers would have to avoid the simple 'dumping' of difficult cases from one institutional sphere to another and the associated risks of 'criminalizing' the mentally disordered (cf., Abrahamson, 1972; Rachlin *et al.*, 1975; Stelovich, 1979). Otherwise, policymakers may inadvertently recreate the very conditions in local jails and prisons that led Dorothea Dix and other nineteenth-century reformers to crusade for the decarceration of the insane and their relocation in separate asylums.

The implementation of these reforms, by opening equitable access to the private sector and by sharing the burdens of involuntary treatment among a pluralism of providers, would allow for the closing of state mental hospitals. Unlike the case of the TB sanitoriums, however, the patient care functions now served by state mental hospitals would not cease to exist. Short of a major therapeutic breakthrough, provisions in some type of organized inpatient setting will still have to be made for the violent, the seriously disordered, and the chronically disabled. *Thus, under present circumstances, even if state hospitals were closed, the residual functions of public asylums – relabeled and relocated within the boundaries of different organizations – would endure in the resultant system of care.*

Clearly, it is one thing to recognize the scope of the fundamental changes that are required for the closure of state mental hospitals and the dissolution of the two-class system of care; it is quite another to design and implement the organizing and financing mechanisms that will lead to their accomplishment. Without a firm grasp of the ultimate goals toward which public policy should be directed, however, technical planning often deteriorates into the search for administrative 'fixes' for pressing problems. Moreover, as is made abundantly clear from the history of Worcester State Hospital, the failures of institutional reform in American mental health care have often resided in their unidimensional or segmental approach to a multidimensional and recalcitrant set of problems. In the absence of a critical assessment of the 'goodness of fit' between proffered solutions and the magnitude of the problems of mental health care, each generation endorsed proximate solutions that soon became the basis for another cycle of institutional reform. To avoid the failures and partial successes of the past, policymakers and planners must be sensitive to the potential for unanticipated consequences in the implementation of fundamental reforms. These reforms transcend the capacities of any individual community or state, acting alone – they necessitate a comprehensive national policy based on public–private sector collaboration. Even then, a number of organizational, professional, and civic problems will have to be addressed and resolved, especially if a truly humane system of care for the chronically mentally ill is to emerge in the aftermath of deinstitutionalization.

Chronic mental patients: the next cycle of reform?

It is fashionable to offer proposals for reform on the assumption that current modes of service delivery constitute a 'nonsystem' that requires 'rational' realignment (e.g., Talbott, 1979b). While it is true that pluralism in the mental health service arena has promoted the growth of a fragmented or loosely connected network of agencies, it is naive to assume that interorganizational relationships in this network are either nonrational or easily realigned. There is a deeply rooted 'natural system' underlying this network. It is organized according to the special interests of individual agencies and professional groups if not the recognizable needs of the populations in need of mental health care.[5] Moreover, many of the specific proposals under active consideration for transforming this network into a more comprehensive and continuous delivery system to meet the needs of the chronically mentally ill may well have opposite effects. The impact of national health insurance is one case in point.

Many mental health administrators and policymakers look forward to a national health insurance program to solve the financing problems for all forms of mental health care. While an insurance program with liberal psychiatric benefits (most proposals now are exceedingly conservative with regard to psychiatric care) would help to subsidize short-term acute psychiatric care in general hospitals, it would have little impact on the care of the chronically mentally ill (Astrachan *et al.*, 1976; Sharfstein, 1978). Moreover, it would promote the 'medicalization' of mental health care and its transfer to the general hospital. While many observers see these trends as the ultimate solution to present problems in the delivery of acute care, they may exacerbate rather than mitigate the problems of chronic care. The medical profession has a long-standing bias toward acute ('curing') versus chronic ('caring') services and a narrow concern for the medical rather than the health status of its clients. Accordingly, fueled by insurance reimbursements, a general hospital model of psychiatric practice might solidify the retreat form chronic mental patients whose problems involve a myriad of social as well as medical deficits. 'Housing, opportunity for some significant activity, and protected arrangements for interpersonal relationships,' as Morris (1978: 17) notes, 'constitute essential, tangible [social] support elements that, for this population, must be provided . . . if the mentally disabled are to cope with the uncertainties and hostilities of "making it" among their largely able-bodied fellow human beings.'

Consistent with the earlier recommendations of the Joint Commission on Mental Illness and Health (1961), some observers advocate the change-over of state mental hospitals into chronic care institutions to serve the chronically mentally ill and other long-term care populations with physical and social disabilities. Such a policy might help to destigmatize the mentally ill. It would also provide a broader base for developing the nonmedical, social support programs needed in common by all chronically disabled populations. And it would provide a socially constructive use for the capital plant of many state hospitals. However, the costs as well as the benefits of this policy must be carefully assessed. Chronic-care institutions, for example, may blur the distinctive needs of the mentally ill and blunt the formation of the political constituencies that other observers see as essential for effective relief in a pluralist political system (Talbott, 1978; Scherl and Macht, 1979). In addition, the growing recognition that chronic patients are susceptible to episodic relapses suggests that a rigid separation of the acute and chronic care systems may exacerbate problems in continuity of care for the chronically mentally ill. Should this occur, it may well substitute a 'two-caste' system (acute versus chronic) for the present two-class system of care.

In the view of some professionals, just as effective treatment today requires a combination of psychopharmacological and psychosocial interventions (Klerman, 1977), an effective organization of the mental health system requires the integration of hospital and community care (e.g., Morris, 1978). According to Gruenberg and Archer (1979: 500):

> Even the best community mental health service cannot provide the type of long-term psychiatric attention that is most beneficial to chronic seriously mentally ill patients, even if it has a close cooperative relation

with an inpatient service . . . What is needed is a unified clinical team, to take responsibility for conducting aftercare and follow-up after its own decision to release. If, when these team members readmit, they themselves continue the treatment of the same patient within the inpatient service, they will not have any grounds for feeling that someone else had failed the patient, and will learn to respond realistically to what they can do for that particular patient.

The integrated team was a core feature of the state hospital-based community mental health services developed in New York by Hunt and Gruenberg (cf., Gruenberg, 1974) and of the services developed at Worcester State Hospital by Flower and Myerson in the 1960s and early 1970s. These programs were casualties of the deinstitution-alization movement, but they represent prototypic models that will have to be reevaluated in the emergent mental health system.

The recent diversification of the mental health system has frag-mented rather than integrated the care of chronic patients. There are many proposals that seek to overcome these problems, ranging from centrally funded but decentralized services to administratively unitized, comprehensive service agencies (cf., Talbott, 1978). However, the relative merits and benefits of these administrative structures remain to be carefully evaluated:

. . . a multiple provider, pluralist system with many relatively small units may meet the innumerable wants and needs of a large and diverse population much more satisfactorily than a large hegemony of integrated or tightly controlled subunits. Good data is simply lacking to decide when small units may be more flexible, effective, and responsive, and for what conditions of distress, and when large units can overcome the cumbersomeness of size through mobilization of resources. Efforts have been made to isolate and define conditions suitable for large-scale human service organization and conditions favorable for small-scale organization, but convincing evidence for or against any one paradigm is lacking (Morris and Hirsch-Lescohier, 1978: 28).

Nor are financing mechanisms the only barrier to developing a responsive delivery system for the chronically mentally ill. It has been noted, for example, that the fragmentation of acute, hospital-based care and chronic, community-based care has occurred in the mental health services of the National Health Service in Britain where economic barriers have been removed (Jones, 1979). 'We have learned,' as Mechanic (1975: 314) also reports, 'that health delivery systems, even when they involve no financial barriers to care erect a variety of other social and psychological barriers that keep certain patients out of their systems or induce a lack of continued participation and cooperation. There is a wide variety of ways in which services come to be rationed: by the resources provided to deal with a given patient load, and the limitation of these resources; by the location of sites of care, and the difficulties involved for patients and their families in reaching such locations; by creating social distance between providers and patients; by over-professionalization and other barriers to communication; by wasting time to obtain services and other noneconomic costs that divert those who particularly have ambivalence about using services to begin with; and by the stigmatization of patients and their families.'

Traditionally, little prestige or professional fulfillment has been associated with the care of the chronically ill. Organizations as well as their professional staff have tended to disassociate themselves from such clients.[6] The prospects for a more responsive delivery system in the future will turn on the extent to which humane custodial and supportive care is legitimized as socially and professionally important and, equally challenging, the extent to which functions and caring services are subsidized rather than particular organizations or professional groups. That is, the elusive goal of a client-centered versus an organizational-professional centered delivery model may be the *sine qua non* of humane care for the chronically mentally disabled. The task in this case resides in the design of treatment organizations that can respond to the needs of chronic mental patients while avoiding pressures toward the extremes of 'elitism' (i.e., creaming, and the selective acquisition of 'nice' clients) or 'dumping ground' (i.e., serving as repositories for patients unwanted by other agencies).

As part of the growing trend for government at both the federal and state levels to disengage from the provision of direct patient services, it appears that many programs will be financed by 'purchase-of-service-contracts' between state mental health authorities and human service vendors (both public and private) at the local community level. The underlying rationale is that a system of incentives can thereby be created that will induce local agencies to take responsibility for the needs of chronically disabled patients in a manner that is presumed to be more cost-effective than institutionally based programs. In the longer run, it is hoped that these programs will evolve into a totally community-based mental health service delivery system.

Whether the reliance on marketplace mechanisms in the mental health arena will actually lead to a more responsive and comprehensive service delivery system remains to be carefully evaluated. An opposite effect is equally plausible. Namely, confronted with year-to-year performance contracts, vendor agencies may resort to 'creaming' practices whereby the tough problem cases are rejected in favor of those clients who will show up as 'successes' in end-of-year performance reviews. In other words, without explicit provisions to the contrary, purchase-of-service arrangements may operate as *disincentives* for taking on chronic cases that require disproportionate amounts of staff time and effort relative to the probability of ever demonstrating effective outcomes. Moreover, these initiatives are being launched at a time when the resource base for mental health service programs is shrinking. Given the press of other social problems that have received even fewer societal resources to date and the ominous citizens tax revolt now sweeping the country (Talbott, 1979c), the goal of community-based mental health services seems even more remote than it did in the recent past. Ironically, the transfer of responsibility to the community without secure, long-term funding may make the mentally disabled more vulnerable to the capriciousness of public opinion on the question of who and what deserves to be funded from the public treasury. Will community groups today accept responsibilities that their counterparts rejected 150 years ago? The chronically mentally ill are even more resource-poor, more heterogeneous, and more anomic now than they were then. And, in no small measure, the current climate of public opinion mirrors the socioeconomic forces and social prejudices that eroded the support base of the early public asylums.

Will history repeat itself again? The administrative changes of recent years have improved the care of many patients and current proposals offer hope to many more. However, unless this generation of policymakers addresses the problems of mental health care as reflected in the institutional history of Worcester State Hospital, the public asylum will endure as a repository for the unwanted. Short of fundamental change, today's 'solutions' will surely become the target of another cycle in institutional reform.

Notes

1 Many radical critics of the efforts at institutional reform in the mental health field
(e.g., Scull, 1977) fail to recognize the discontinuities between origins (starting
mechanisms) and outcomes (maintenance mechanisms). By noting the repressive
features that often characterize the outcomes or end states of reform, they
erroneously infer that these consequences were part of the original motives and
intentions of early reformers. To argue from outcomes to motives is not only a
logical fallacy but it also distorts the historical record of mental hospitals in
America (cf., Grob, 1977; Grob, 1978). For a similar assessment of Piven and
Cloward's (1971) critique of the functions of public welfare, see Higgins (1978).

2 As Mechanic (1978b: 6) points out, the institutionalism syndrome can be found
in varying degrees in a variety of settings: '(M)ost discussions of
deinstitutionalization are misleading in their failure to differentiate the impact of
varying community settings on the quality of life of patients and the course of
their illnesses and handicaps.' Moreover, social science research in the past decade
suggests that Goffman's (1961) depiction of state hospitals as 'total institutions'
may be accurate only for large hospitals – that are extremely bureaucratic,
understaffed, and underfinanced – rather than an inevitable feature of institutional
care (see Goldstein, 1979: 399–401).

3 Perrow (1978) suggests that the conventional view of human service agencies in
mainstream organizational theory – that they are rational instruments in pursuit
of announced goals – is a 'mystification' of reality. Rather, he argues that all
organizations are resources for a variety of group interests within and without
the organization, and the announced purposes (e.g., therapy, treatment), while
they must be met to some limited degree, largely serve as legitimating devices
for these interests.

This view is compatible with Carlson's depiction of state mental hospitals, prisons,
and public schools as *domesticated organizations*. 'By this is simply meant,' Carlson
(1965: 266) notes, 'that they are not compelled to attend to all of the ordinary and
usual needs of an organization . . . they do not compete with other organizations
for clients; in fact a steady flow of clients is assured. There is no struggle for survival
for this type of organization. Like the domesticated animal, these organizations
are fed and cared for. Existence is guaranteed. Though this type of organization
does compete in a restricted area for funds, funds are not closely tied to quality
of performance. These organizations are domesticated in the sense that they are
protected by the society they serve. Society feels some apprehension about
domesticated organizations. It sees the support of these organizations as necessary
to the maintenance of the social system and creates laws over and above those
applying to organized action in general to care for domesticated organizations.'

And, in another context, Perrow (1972: 184) comments on the consequence of
their protected status: '(P)risons, mental hospitals, and many small welfare agencies
exist to show that *something* is being done about some problems, but few care just
what it is or how effective it is; those who control the organization's resources
(legislators, religious boards, etc.) care only that the "something" should not involve
scandals and should not cost too much.'

4 In November 1979, following growing criticisms of the Commonwealth's deinstitutionalization plans and the deaths of several patients in state hospitals, the Commissioner of the Massachusetts Department of Mental Health established a Blue Ribbon Commission to make recommendations on the future of the eight remaining state mental institutions (Dietz, 1979a). A few weeks later, he proposed the abolition of the state mental hospital system and the creation of inpatient units in existing general hospitals and private psychiatric hospitals (Dietz, 1979c), and announced plans for a pilot program at a general hospital in the Boston area (Dietz, 1979e). His proposals met with divided reactions (Dietz, 1979d) and the prospects for their full implementation were uncertain at the close of 1979. In a separate action, the Commissioner of the Department of Mental Hygiene in New York requested legislative authorization to close two of that state's twenty-four mental hospitals (Goldman, 1979).

5 The work of Warren *et al.* (1974) on the model cities program (including mental health agencies) provides a comprehensive understanding of the social order underlying community health and welfare networks. The authors indicate the ways in which an 'institutionalized thought structure' – shared interagency paradigms on the nature of clients, the ameliorative steps that should be taken, and the basic soundness of the existing system – serves to stabilize the status quo and protect agency domains and prerogatives.

6 The critique of professions has been a prominent theme in recent literature. The most trenchant critic of medicine has been Ivan Illich (cf., Illich, 1976; Illich *et al.*, 1977) but his assessment extends to professions in general, namely, modern professional activity has a debilitating rather than enhancing effect because it is designed to 'manufacture' needs in accord with professional satisfactions rather than client interests. Other insightful evaluations of professions can be found in Freidson (1970), Yarmolinsky (1979), and Starr (1979).

References

Abrahamson, M. 1972.
  The criminalization of mentally disordered behavior: A possible side effect of a new mental health law. Hospital and Community Psychiatry 23: 101–105.
Arnhoff, F. 1975.
  Social consequences of policy towards mental illness. *Science* 188: 1277–81.
Astrachan, B., D. Levinson, and D. Adler 1976.
  The impact of national health insurance on the tasks and practice of psychiatry. *Archives of General Psychiatry*, 33 (July): 785–93.
Bachrach, L. 1976.
  Deinstitutionalization: An analytical review and sociological perspective.
  Rockville, MD: National Institute of Mental Health.
Bassuk, E. L. and S. Gerson 1978.
  Deinstitutionalization and mental health services. *Scientific American*, 238: 46–53.
Belknap, I. 1956.
  Human Problems of a State Mental Hospital. New York: McGraw-Hill.

Bockoven, J. S. 1956.
   Moral treatment in American psychiatry. *Journal of Nervous and Mental Disease*,
   124 (August-September): 193–5.
   1972. *Moral Treatment in Community Mental Health*. New York: Springer.
Caplan, R. B. 1969.
   Psychiatry and the Community in Nineteenth Century America. New York: Basic
   Books.
Carlson, R. 1965.
   Environmental constraints and organizational consequences: The public school
   and its clients. Pp. 262–270 in D. E. Griffiths (ed.): *Behavioral Science and
   Educational Administration*, 63rd Yearbook of the National Society for the Study
   of Education. Chicago: University of Chicago Press.
Chu, F. and S. Trotter 1974.
   The Madness Establishment. New York: Grossman.
Clark, B. 1960.
   The Open Door College: A Case Study. New York: McGraw-Hill.
Cloward, R. A. and I. Epstein 1965.
   Private social welfare's disengagement from the poor. The case of family
   adjustment agencies. Pp 623–44 in M. Zald (ed.): *Social Welfare Institutions*.
   New York: Wiley.
Davis, K. 1938.
   Mental hygiene and the class structure. *Psychiatry*, 1: 55–65.
Deutsch, A. 1944.
   The history of mental hygiene. In American Psychiatric Association, *One Hundred
   Years of American Psychiatry*. New York: Columbia University Press.
Dietz, J. 1979a.
   Deinstitutionalization debate: Plan for mental patients faces stiff fight. *The Boston
   Globe* (November 22): 1.
   1979b. Mental health system blasted. *The Boston Globe* (December 4): 17, 23.
   1979c. State urged to shut its mental hospitals. *The Boston Globe* (December 12):
   1, 26.
   1979d. Call to abolish mental hospitals brings intensely divided reaction. *The
   Boston Globe* (December 16): 1.
   1979e. Hospital in Somerville to pioneer mental health plan. *The Boston Globe*
   (December 19).
Fisher, B. M. 1969.
   Claims and credibility: A discussion of occupational identity and the agent-client
   relationship. *Social Problems*, 16: 423–33.
Fowlkes, M. 1975.
   'Business as usual – at the state mental hospital.' *Psychiatry* 38: 55–64.
Freidson, E. 1970.
   The Profession of Medicine. New York: Dodd, Mead.
Gil, D. 1973.
   Unraveling Social Policy. Cambridge: Schenkman.
Goffman, E. 1961.
   Asylums. New York: Doubleday.
Goldman, H. H. 1978.
   Within and between: The role of the psychiatric resident in the psychiatric unit

in the general hospital. Unpublished doctoral dissertation. Heller School, Brandeis University.

Goldman, H. and M. Rosenstein 1979.
Pluralism and hospital psychiatry: The future of the state mental hospital revisited. I. The continuing role of the state mental hospital. Rockville, MD: Division of Biometry and Epidemiology, National Institute of Mental Health (unpublished).

Goldman, W. 1976.
Change in a state department of mental health: A view from within, *Administration in Mental Health* 4 (Fall): 2–9.

Goldstein, M. S. 1979.
The sociology of mental health and illness. *Annual Review of Sociology* 5: 381–409.

Grob, G. N. 1966.
The State and the Mentally Ill: A History of Worcester State Hospital in Massachusetts, 1830–1920. Chael Hill: University of North Carolina Press.
1973. *Mental Institutions in America: Social Policy to 1875*. New York: The Free Press.
1977. 'Rediscovering asylums: The unhistorical history of the mental hospital.' Hastings Center Report 7 (August): 33–41.
1978. Public policy making and social policy. Paper presented at the Conference on the History of Public Policy in the United States. Harvard University Business School, November 3–4.

Group for the Advancement of Psychiatry 1978.
The Chronic Mental Patient in the Community. New York: GAP.

Gruenberg, E. 1974.
The social breakdown syndrome and its prevention. Pp. 697–711 in S. Arieti (ed.), *American Handbook of Psychiatry*. New York: Basic Books.

Gruenberg, E. and J. Archer 1979.
Abandonment of responsibility for the seriously mentally ill. *Milbank Memorial Fund Quarterly/Health and Society* 57 (Fall): 485–506.

Higgins, J. 1978.
Regulating the poor revisited. *Journal of Social Policy* 7 (April): 189–98.

Hollingshead, A. and F. Redlich 1958.
Social Class and Mental Illness. New York: Wiley.

Hunt, R. G., O. Gurrslin, and J. Roach 1958.
Social status and psychiatric service in a child guidance clinic. *American Sociological Review* (February): 81–3.

Illich, I. 1976.
Medical Nemesis: The Expropriation of Health. New York: Pantheon.

Illich, I., I. Zola, J. McKnight, and H. Shaikin 1977.
Disabling Professions. London: Marion Boyars.

Joint Commission on Mental Illness and Health 1961.
Action for Mental Health. New York: Basic Books.

Jones, K. 1979.
Deinstitutionalization in Context. *Milbank Memorial Fund Quarterly/Health and Society* 57 (November): 552–69.

Kirk, S. A. and M. E. Therrien 1975.
'Community mental health myths and the fate of former hospitalized patients.'
Psychiatry 38: 209–17.
Klerman, G. L. 1977.
Better but not well: Social and ethical issues in the deinstitutionalization of the
mentally ill. *Schizophrenia Bulletin* 3: 617–31.
Kramer, M. 1977.
Psychiatric Services and the Changing Institutional Scene, 1950–1985. Rockville,
MD: National Institute of Mental Health, Series B., No. 12.
Lamb, H. R. and V. Goertzel 1972.
The demise of the state hospital – a premature obituary. *Archives of General
Psychiatry* 26: 489–95.
Mechanic, D. 1975.
Medical Sociology, 2nd Edition. New York: Free Press.
1978. The community integration of the mentally ill: Problems in
deinstitutionalization. Madison, Wisconsin: Center for Medical Sociology and
Health Services Research, University of Wisconsin (mimeo).
Morris, R. 1977.
Integration of therapeutic and community services: Cure plus care for the mentally
disabled. *International Journal of Mental Health* 6 (Winter): 9–26.
Morris, R. and I. Hirsch-Lescohier 1978.
Service integration: Real versus illusory solution to welfare dilemmas. Pp 21–50
in R. Sarri and Y. Hasenfeld (eds): *The Management of Human Services*. New
York: Columbia University Press.
Perrow, C. 1965.
Hospitals: Technology, structure and goals. Pp. 910–971 in J. March (ed.):
Handbook of Organizations. Chicago: Rand McNally.
1972. *Complex Organizations: A Critical Essay*. Glenview, Scott Foresman.
1978. Demystifying organizations. Pp. 105–22 in R. Sarri and Y. Hasenfeld
(eds.): *The Management of Human Services*, New York: Columbia University
Press.
Piven, F. and R. Cloward 1971.
Regulating the Poor: The Functions of Public Welfare. New York: Vintage Books.
President's Commission on Mental Health 1979.
Final Report, Washington DC: President's Commission on Mental Health.
Rachlin, S., A. Pam, and J. Milton 1975.
Civil liberties versus involuntary hospitalization. *American Journal of Psychiatry*
132: 189–91.
Redlich, F. and S. Kellert 1978.
Trends in American mental health. *American Journal of Psychiatry* 135 (January):
22–8.
Regier, D., I. Goldberg, and C. Taube 1978.
The de facto mental health services system. *Archives of General Psychiatry* 34
(June): 615–93.
Reich, R. and L. Siegel 1973.
Psychiatry under siege: The chronically mentally ill shuffle to oblivion. *Psychiatric
Annals* 3 (November): 35–55.

Rose, S. 1979.
Deciphering deinstitutionalization: Complexities in policy and program analysis. *Milbank Memorial Fund Quarterly/Health and Society* 57 (Fall): 429–60.

Roth, J. and E. Eddy 1967.
Rehabilitation for the Unwanted. New York: Atherton.

Rothman, D. J. 1971.
The Discovery of the Asylum. Boston: Little-Brown.

Scherl, D. J. and L. B. Macht 1979.
'Deinstitutionalization in the absence of consensus.' *Hospital and Community Psychiatry* 30 (September): 599–604.

Schmidt, L., A. Reinhardt, R. Kane, and D. Olsen 1977.
The mentally ill in nursing homes: New back wards in the community. *Archives of General Psychiatry* 34: 687–91.

Schulberg, H. 1979.
Community support programs: Program evaluation and public policy. *American Journal of Psychiatry* 136 (November): 1433–37.

Scull, A. 1977.
Decarceration: Community Treatment and the Deviant – A Radical View. Englewood Cliffs, NJ: Prentice Hall.

Sharfstein, S. 1978.
Will community mental health survive in the 1980s? *American Journal of Psychiatry* 135 (November): 768–71.

Shakow, D. 1972.
The Worcester State Hospital research on schizophrenia (1927–1946). *Journal of Abnormal Psychology Monograph* 80 (August): 67–110.

Shore, M. 1979.
Public psychiatry: The public's view. *Hospital and Community Psychiatry* 30 (November): 768–71.

Shore, M. and R. Shapiro 1979.
The effect of deinstitutionalization on the state hospital. *Hospital and Community Psychiatry* 30 (September): 605–8.

Starr, P. 1978.
Medicine and the waning of professional sovereignty. *Dedalus* 107 (Winter): 175–93.

Stelovich, S. 1979.
From the hospital to the prison: A step forward in deinstitutionalization? *Hospital and Community Psychiatry* 30 (September): 618–20.

Szasz, T. 1968.
Law, Liberty, and Psychiatry. New York: Collier Books.

Talbot, J. A. 1978.
The Death of the Asylum. New York: Grune and Stratton.
1979a. *The Chronic Mental Patient.* Washington, DC: American Psychiatric Association.
1979b. Deinstitutionalization: Avoiding the disasters of the past. *Hospital and Community Psychiatry* 30 (September): 621–4.
1979c. The impact of proposition 13 on mental health services in California. *Hospital and Community Psychiatry* 30 (October): 677–85.

Warren, R., S. Rose, and A. Bergunder 1974.
  The Structure of Urban Reform. Lexington, MA: D. C. Heath.
Windle, C. and D. Scully 1976.
  Community mental health centers and the decreasing use of state mental hospitals.
  Community Mental Health Journal 12: 239–43.
Yarmolinsky, A. 1978.
  What future for the professional in American society? *Dedalus* 107 (Winter):
  159–74.

Part II

*The changing
mental health system*

INTRODUCTION

The selections in Section I discussed similarities in problems over time, and pointed to fundamental structural factors which shape mental health care. In the last article of that section, 'Cycles of institutional reform,' analogies were made with current psychiatric services. In this section we will explore the variety of present-day institutions and programs. While there have always been new institutions and new modes of care, there has never been such a change in the psychiatric landscape as at present. As the Introduction to this book pointed out, the state hospital is no longer the preeminent psychiatric facility; community mental health centers, nursing and boarding homes, and general hospitals have achieved positions of strength in the caregiving system.

No longer is most mental health care provided in the public sector. Nor is the distinction between the public and private sectors as clear as it used to be. Presently, the private sector includes many less-privileged people as well as more well-off clients. This results from the expansion of third-party reimbursements, both governmental and private. These payments for service come from government social welfare programs or private insurance carriers, rather than out of individuals' resources. No longer is the classic two-class system of care so easily demarcated. Rather, there is something of a two-caste system based more on availability of third-party payment than on social class. This has led to a new bifurcation, whereby the private sector largely treats acute mental illness and the public sector emphasizes chronic care. To be sure, those with money can still purchase the best care, but those without large reserves are not always excluded from quality care.

The selections here offer an overview of the contemporary mental health institutional network and of the structural forces behind this system. Darrel Regier, Irving Goldberg and Carl Taube's well-documented article, 'The de facto US mental health services system,' opens the section. This work by biometricians from the National Institute of Mental Health is the first systematic attempt to enumerate the prevalence and incidence of mental illness by the various sectors where persons are treated. It is important in providing some base-point for the rest of the selections; it is also of particular interest in showing that very few mentally ill persons are treated, and of those who are, very few are seen in specific psychiatric facilities. Such basic epidemiological data, historically elusive and methodologically diverse, are a clear prerequisite for assessing mental health resources and their allocation.

Ellen Bassuk and Samuel Gerson's 'Deinstitutionalization and mental health services' provides an overview of the deinstitutionalization phenomenon. The authors detail the huge state hospital discharges, the rise of community mental health centers, and the new role of nursing and boarding homes in caring for chronic mental patients. Bassuk and Gerson document the preponderance of flaws in the mental health system, while remaining cognizant of the successes. But they locate those successes as deviations from the norm. Bassuk and Gerson show us the incompleteness of the psychiatric system, and the many holes into which a psychiatrically needy person may fall.

For Bassuk and Gerson, lack of financial resources is the principal, though not the only, barrier to adequate services. They provide a sketch of reimbursement obstacles – particularly at the federal level – which detract from appropriate service delivery. The authors close with a plea to fulfill the humanitarian goals of mental health care, rather than eschewing them because of economic, political, administrative, and clinical shortcomings.

The general hospital's growing role in mental health care has been one of the major institutional transformations due to deinstitutionalization. This is the one case where deinstitutionalization has strongly affected the medical care system as a whole. Leona Bachrach, in 'General hospital psychiatry: Overview from a sociological perspective,' presents us with the general outline of this development and offers a forecast for the future.

Bachrach observes that the increase in psychiatric services provided in general hospitals is one of the unintended consequences of recent mental health practices. Deinstitutionalization, she points out, is 'superimposed' on existing service delivery patterns. The effects of deinstitutionalization on general hospital psychiatry will therefore vary according to the interaction of three factors: state hospital depopulation, the range of alternative services available, and the policies for selecting patient populations within that range.

Of particular importance is the wide patient mix in general hospital psychiatric services, including some of the most and some of the least disturbed. As Bachrach remarks, many general hospitals have not yet been able to navigate their course in this situation. Importantly, some of the problem is that general hospitals have been picking up some of the chronic patient load which CMHCs were supposed to handle. Thus we see how policy diversion in one sector has major ramifications in other sectors. This includes not only general hospital inpatient and outpatient care, but also the treatment of mentally ill persons in emergency rooms. The problems facing general hospitals, including the acceptance of civilly committed persons, are further testimony to the difficulties created when mental health services are unplanned, uncoordinated and prone to the vagaries of the marketplace.

The community mental health center was designed to be the great new experiment in mental health care. This cornerstone of 1950s and 1960s planning has indeed taken over a large part of the psychiatric caseload, and has helped expand service availability. Yet the larger social goals of the CMHC have not been fulfilled, nor is it clear that they were ever plausible goals. This is the subject of Alberta Nassi's 'Community control or control of the community: The case of the community mental health center.' Like Morrissey *et al.* in the first section, Nassi discusses how recent mental health reforms echo the ideas of fifty and one hundred years ago. She focuses on a problematic reform issue – that of community control – which was one of the least defined yet most provocative aspects of the program's social impact.

Nassi shows that professional and governmental bodies had notions of community *involvement* which were far from the democratic process of community *control*. Professionalist approaches to service delivery possess little or no belief in client participation, especially when the clients are already labeled as mentally ill. Further, the local mental health power structure, which is integrated with the local political and financial powers, seeks to preserve the status quo of its agencies. Nassi's analysis extends itself to a critical level by comparing community control of CMHCs to popular control of health facilities in the Popular Unity period under Salvador Allende in Chile. There, conservative medical practitioners and their professional organization actively opposed popular participation, and became key partners in the reactionary coup against the Allende government. While the stakes are clearly not that high in the US, the comparison is rich in its assessment of the ways in which true community power threatens various elements of the power structure.

Concern for the rights of mental patients has been an important force in recent mental health policy and treatment. Perhaps more than any other recent development, this issue has remarkably different meanings for varied parts of the mental health system. Arising out of the civil rights orientation of the 1950s and 1960s, patients' rights were heralded by mental health professionals and administrators who could readily support a development which demanded positive care for persons committed to mental institutions. In fact, such legal pressures could even be used to increase mental health budgets from state and federal legislatures. But as patients' rights activists pressed on to urge the right to refuse treatment, providers and officials could hardly support such a challenge to psychiatric authority. Phil Brown's 'The Mental Patients' Rights Movement and mental health institutional change' details the history of the development of mental patients' rights, and explores the diverse points of view concerning this matter. Brown's discussion of cooptation and reform can be applied to a wider range of change efforts in the mental health sphere.

CHAPTER 4

The de facto US mental health services system: A public health perspective*

Darrel A. Regier, Irving D. Goldberg and Carl A. Taube

In establishing the President's Commission on Mental Health, the White House Executive Order of February 17, 1977 requested as a first priority that the Commission seek to identify how the mentally ill are being served, to what extent they are being underserved, and who is affected by such underservice.[1] The need for such information is compelling indeed, since establishing the parameters of mental illness is prerequisite to any reformulation of a national mental health services-manpower-research policy.

However compelling the need for such information, there are several important requirements for fulfilling the Executive Order request. Such a mandate requires, first, that there exist valid epidemiological research data on the *true* prevalence, or total number, of persons who have a mental disorder. Second, it requires that there exist comprehensive mental health services research data on the *treated* prevalence, or number of such persons receiving mental health services from known service settings. Third, it requires a known relationship between the presence of a mental disorder and the type and amount of treatment needed. Knowledge in these three areas enables one to address the questions posed to the President's Commission.

A public health approach to accomplishing the Commission's goals

* Reprinted from *Archives of General Psychiatry*, vol. 35, pp. 685–93, 1978, with permission of the authors.

concerns itself not only with those 'showing up at the door' of specialty mental health facilities, but rather with the mental health service needs of the entire population. An ideal public health approach to obtain such basic information would commence with an epidemiological sample survey to determine the prevalence and incidence of mental disorder in a total population. Individuals so identified would subsequently be followed up on a longitudinal basis to determine their utilization of mental health services in all general medical, specialty mental health, or other human service facilities. Both prevalence and utilization data would then allow analysis of the population groups most affected by mental disorder and by an under-utilization of services. However, such comprehensive mental health information does not yet exist, and there are several major deficiencies in the available data.

The major shortcomings of present data include both the paucity of recent epidemiological studies and the lack of attention in mental health services research to the number of persons served. The major epidemiological population surveys are now almost twenty-five years old and thus fail to reflect recent advances in diagnostic and case identification technology. Sharing a recently noted deficit with most health services research, mental health services data are generally concentrated on the number of service events (for example, visits, admissions, bed days, discharges, or episodes of care) rather than on the number of treated persons who account for these events.[2] Finally, the lack of any linkage between mental disorder epidemiological and health services research studies makes it difficult to obtain treated prevalence data, and to understand the complex interaction between multiple social and economic factors that determine whether persons with mental disorders actually seek or receive services.[3]

Despite these major deficiencies in our information base, it is, nonetheless, possible to utilize the existing data to answer provisionally some of the questions addressed to the Commission. The state-of-the-art presentation that follows is thus intended to provide a first step in forging a more functional linkage between available epidemiological and mental health services research findings.

Epidemiological research findings are initially reviewed to present our current best estimates of the true prevalence of mental disorder in the population. Second, the results of a separate examination of the general medical practice and specialty mental health service sectors (as defined below) are presented to determine the number of individuals with mental disorder diagnosed and/or treated in these settings. Finally, some consideration is given to the affected persons not seen in the health or mental health sectors – some of whom may receive other human services. A detailed description of the estimation procedures is provided, both to clarify current deficiencies and to enable a better focus for filling information gaps through future research.

The major objectives of this analysis, then, are as follows: (1) to produce the best available estimates of the number of individuals in the population who have mental disorders, and (2) to determine from available data the number who are identified and/or treated within specified sectors of the mental health and health services system in a single year. Further analyses, beyond the scope of this article, are required to describe the adequacy of the services provided to patients in each sector, and the characteristics of those persons who are most affected by underservice.

Definitions

At a time when psychodynamic principles are being popularized on a mass scale for consciousness-expanding purposes,[4] and psychotropic drugs are among the most widely prescribed of all medications,[5] it is necessary to define the mental health services system, mental disorders, and mental health services as used in this article.

Mental health services system

When defining the US mental health services system, it is important to acknowledge that – in the absence of any national- or state-level approach for coordinating health/mental health service setting relationships – we are speaking about a largely unorganized and de facto 'system.' The 'system' definition utilized in the present discussion is thus an operational one, aimed at the best possible understanding of where persons with mental disorder receive services. To that end, we have identified four major sectors where mental health services may be provided.

The specialty mental health (SMH) sector encompasses a wide range of facilities, listed in Table 4.1, that provide both outpatient and inpatient care. Excluded from this analysis are special

alcoholism, drug dependence, or mental retardation facilities –
persons who exclusively use these facilities are consequently not
accounted for. Although individuals with alcoholism, drug dependence, and mental retardation disorders treated in the currently
listed SMH facilities are counted, future analyses will hopefully be
able to draw on comparable and unduplicated data from these
additional special purpose facilities.

In addition to the usual focus on the SMH sector, it is necessary to
take particular note of our inclusion of the general hospital inpatient/
nursing home (GHI/NH) and the primary care/outpatient medical
(PC/OPM) sectors – these two being collectively referred to as the
general medical practice (GMP) sectors. No health specialty sector,
whether surgical, medical, or mental health, can provide preventive,
diagnostic, and treatment services for all patients with disorders in
its area of special expertise. Hence, it is important to acknowledge
the necessary division of patient care responsibility currently existing
between the major sectors of our mental health services system.

The remaining sector is collectively referred to as the not in
treatment/other human services (NT/OHS) sector, to reflect our lack
of longitudinal follow-up information on those individuals identified
with mental disorders in total population surveys whose mental
disorders are not detected or who receive no treatment in the health
care system. It is clear that a large number of persons may well
receive some mental health service from the other human services
sector, although we are not aware of comparable surveys of utilization data in this sector.

Mental disorders

Insofar as the data permit, the mental disorders referred to here
include the organic and functional psychoses, neuroses, personality
disorders, alcoholism, drug dependence, behavioral disorders,
mental retardation, and other disorders encompassed in section V
of the *Eighth Revision International Classification of Diseases,
Adapted for Use in the United States (ICDA)*. (The section on mental
disorders, section 5, is compatible with the American Psychiatric
Association *Diagnostic and Statistical Manual of Mental Disorders
[DSM-II]*, although the latter contains several additional diagnostic
categories.) However, because of the multiple disorders in some
individuals, and the limited experience with more recently developed

differential diagnostic instruments and surveys, the percent distribution of these disorders in the population is difficult to determine. In addition, most population surveys do not account for individuals who are institutionalized, and thus may underestimate the true prevalence of some of the more severe disorders in the total population. Despite the difficulties in applying the above definition consistently, its use is intended to exclude the more ubiquitous 'problems of living' and emotional symptoms that may affect up to 85 percent of the population.[6] Such exclusion is essential for providing functionally useful estimates of the total true prevalence of mental disorder.

The application of these same diagnostic criteria to persons utilizing the various treatment settings is also somewhat difficult. In the SMH sector, for example, the *DSM II* is used in most US facilities for persons classified as having a mental disorder. However, there are certainly some persons with no mental disorder receiving evaluations, collateral interviews, or other direct mental health services in this sector. The actual number of individuals in this category is relatively small and, for reasons later discussed in the section on findings, these individuals were not deducted from the total number of persons receiving services in this sector.

With regard to the remaining sectors, somewhat different but related diagnostic criteria apply. Section V *ICDA* diagnoses are used in the admission and discharge diagnoses of the GHI/NH sector. The survey prevalence indexes used in the PC/OPM sector are less precise, with one major study finding formal *ICDA* diagnoses for approximately two thirds of the conditions identified, and with the remaining third identified as having 'psychiatric-associated' conditions.[7]

Mental health services

For purposes of this article, the mental health services of the SMH sector are limited to direct patient treatment services. Data on most of these services in the SMH sector are routinely collected by the National Institute of Mental Health (NIMH) and are relatively more comprehensive than in the remaining sectors. Data on the indirect services of prevention, consultation, and education for persons not identified as patients remain outside the purview of this analysis.

In contrast to the SMH sector, mental health services in the GMP sectors are limited to the detection and diagnosis of mental disorder, as indicated by diagnoses on admission to or discharge from care, or in surveys, without regard to the actual treatment provided. Because of the limited nature of current data, information on actual treatment in GMP settings is only briefly discussed.

It is essential to recall that one objective of this article is to determine where persons with mental disorder may receive some mental health services, including the essential first-level services of screening and diagnosis. No attempt is made to address the major issues of the adequacy or effectiveness of the mental services provided in any of the SMH or GMP sectors. Hence, discussions of data relating to the intensity, appropriateness, effectiveness, or cost of treatment in any sector are beyond the scope of this article.

Methodology

While a brief summary of the methodological approach is included in this section, those particularly interested in our estimation procedures are directed to the detailed footnotes to Table 4.1. The general approach consisted of arranging all pertinent epidemiological and health services data into a parallel, one-year time frame. This was necessitated by the fact that most epidemiological studies are cross-sectional (point prevalence) estimates of the number of individuals with a disorder at one point in time. On the other hand, most health services research studies are usually concerned with the volume of services provided over a time interval of up to one year.

Any attempt to link such dissimilar data requires that an estimate of the number of new cases of mental disorder in one year (annual incidence) be added to point prevalence estimates to obtain an annual interval (period) prevalence. In addition, it is necessary to 'unduplicate' the volume of service data (for example, visits, admissions) to obtain the total number of individuals with mental disorder treated in any facility during one year (annual treated prevalence).

Findings

The results of the data synthesis and estimation procedures are summarized in the extensively annotated Table 4.1 and the accompanying Figure 4.1. The major highlights are discussed briefly

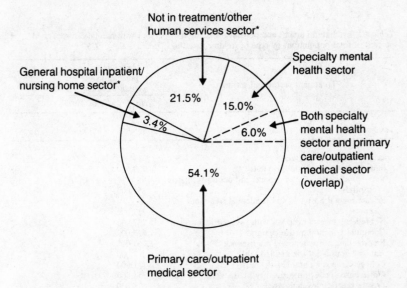

Fig. 4.1 Estimated percent distribution of persons with mental disorder, by treatment setting, in United States in 1975. Data relating to sectors other than specialty mental health sector reflect number of patients with mental disorder seen in those sectors without regard to amount or adequacy of treatment provided.
Asterisks indicate exclusion or overlap of unknown percent of persons also seen in other sectors.

in this section. In general, the estimates are conservative to assure a baseline minimal estimate both of the extent of the problem and of the available treatment provided.

Estimated national true prevalence of mental disorder

Clearly, policy planners have available no definitive epidemiological survey that is based on a national probability sample and thus capable of providing the desired data on the annual period prevalence of mental disorder in the total US population. The technical difficulties of mental health epidemiological studies have been amply detailed by the Dohrenwends,[8] and the need for improvements in case identification and standardized diagnoses has been emphasized by Kramer.[9] However, a considerable number of epidemiological investigations in smaller community populations have occurred over the

Table 4.1 Estimated number and percent distribution of persons with mental disorder, and percent of total population, by type of treatment setting: United States, 1975

Treatment sector and setting	Estimate of persons with mental disorder[1]		%of total US population
	No.	% of Total	
Total[2]	31,955,000	100	15
Specialty mental health sector			
State and county mental hospitals[3]	789,000		
VA – psychiatric units of general and neuropsychiatric hospitals[3]	351,000		
Private mental hospitals and residential treatment centers[3]	233,000		
Nonfederal general hospitals with psychiatric units[3]	927,000		
Community mental health centers[3]	1,627,000		
Freestanding outpatient and multiservice clinics[3]	1,763,000		
Halfway houses for the mentally ill[4]	7,000		
College campus mental health clinics[5]	131,000		
Office-based private practice psychiatrists[6]	854,000		
Private practice psychologists[7]	425,000		
Subtotal	7,107,000		
Unduplicated sector total[8]	6,698,000	21.0	3.1
General hospital inpatient nursing home sector			
General hospital inpatient facilities			
Nonfederal general hospitals without separate psychiatric units[9]	812,000		
Federal general hospitals (excludes psychiatric units of VA hospitals)[9]	59,000		
Nursing homes[10]	207,000		
Nonpsychiatric specialty hospitals[11]	22,000		
Unduplicated sector total	1,100,000	3.4	0.5
Primary care/outpatient medical sector			
Office-based primary care physicians[12]	10,710,000		
Other office-based nonprimary care physicians[12]	2,337,000		
Community (neighborhood health centers)[13]	314,000		
Industrial health facilities[14]	314,000		
Health department clinics[15]	941,000		
General hospital outpatient and emergency rooms[16]	6,391,000		
Subtotal	21,007,000		
Unduplicated sector total[17]	19,218,000	60.1	9.0
Unduplicated subtotal across specialty mental health and general medical sectors[18]	25,094,000	78.5	11.8
Not in treatment/other human services sector			
Unduplicated sector total[19]	6,861,000	21.5	3.2

Notes to Table 4.1

1 The numbers shown include adjustments within and across settings to avoid duplication of individuals seen in multiple settings and sectors to the extent possible. The nature of adjustments are explained in the respective footnotes.

2 Based on estimated total US resident population of 213,032,000 persons as of July 1, 1975. The estimate that 15% of the population is affected by mental disorder in a one-year period (annual period prevalence) is derived from epidemiologic surveys of community populations as discussed in the text. Source of population data: *Current Population Reports*, series P-25, No. 705. Bureau of the Census, July 1977.

3 Based on National Institute of Mental Health, Division of Biometry and Epidemiology, unpublished data from the 1975 surveys of US mental health facilities. Patient care episodes derived from these surveys were multiplied by a conversion factor of 0.83 (approximately 1.2 episodes per person per year) to obtain the total number of different individuals treated. In addition to unduplicating individuals within settings by a constant factor, this procedure, in effect, also unduplicates individuals across settings by distributing those seen in multiple facilities to the respective settings in proportion to the number of episodes they experience in each. The conversion factor was obtained from the only reported analysis of psychiatric register data in the United States, namely, the Maryland psychiatric case register, which tracked a total state population in its use of virtually all then existing specialty mental health facilities except halfway houses, college clinics, and mental health professionals in private office practice. Each type of facility was found in that study to require slightly different unduplicating factors depending on average length of stay and readmission rates. Hence, the application of a uniform unduplicating factor for all facilities should result in a reasonable estimated total number of persons served in all facilities, but may not be as reflective of the experience of the specific facilities listed. A cross-check on the appropriateness of this factor in 1975 for community mental health centers, where actual patient counts were made, showed a relative difference of less than 0.5 percent between the unduplicating factor estimate and the actual count. However, the conversion factor may not be as accurate for other settings. Source of conversion factor: Bahn A K, Gorwitz K, Klee G D, *et al.*: Services received by Maryland residents in facilities directed by a psychiatrist. *Public Health Rep* 90: 405–416, 1965.

4 National Institute of Mental Health, Division of Biometry and Epidemiology, Survey and Reports Branch: unpublished data from the 1975 inventory of psychiatric halfway houses and community residences. Number of admissions unduplicated across facilities was obtained by multiplying by the 0.83 factor cited in footnote 3.

5 Estimate derived by applying the 3.1 percent general population utilization rate of specialty mental health services to the 5.1 million full-time students in four-year colleges and universities who may use campus mental health facilities, and multiplying that result by the 0.83 conversion factor cited in footnote 3. Source of student population: National Center for Educational Statistics, Statistical Information Branch.

6 National Center for Health Statistics, Division of Health Resources Utilization Statistics, Ambulatory Care Statistics Branch: unpublished data from the 1975 National Ambulatory Medical Care Survey of the 11,275 office-based psychiatrists who practice 15 hours per week or more – the total visits accumulated was estimated from the sample survey as 14,806,000 in 1975. The number of patients seen was obtained by unduplicating these visits by the average 26 visits per patient per year found for nonanalyst psychiatrists in an American Psychiatric Association survey. The nature of that survey was such that it tended to oversample high utilizers as reported by G. W. Albee in his book review (Into the valley of therapy rode the six thousand. *Contem Psychol* 21: 525–527, 1976). To adjust for this bias, the average of 26 visits per patient per year was employed, rather than the survey-weighted average of 42 visits per patient per year for both analyst and nonanalyst psychiatrists combined, thus yielding a somewhat higher but more realistic estimate of individuals seen. The 569,000 patients derived from this procedure were then increased by 50 percent to account for patients seen by the approximately 15,000 psychiatrists who may be engaged in less than 15 hours per week of private practice. (The 50 percent adjustment seems reasonable and would represent an average of about 10 hours per week over 47 weeks and 26 visits per patient per year.) The resulting total for private practice psychiatrists in the Table includes persons also seen in other specialty mental health settings (see footnote 8 for unduplicating adjustment). Source: Marmor J: *Psychiatrists and Their Patients: A National Study of Private Office Practice*. Washington, DC, Joint Information Service of the American Psychiatric Association and the National Association for Mental Health, 1975.

7 Council for the National Register of Health Service Providers in Psychology: unpublished data from the 1976 (October to December) surveys of the 18,882 licensed/certified psychologists who are health service providers. Of the 15,422 such psychologists engaged in private practice, 4,683 are full-time and 10,739 are in part-time practices. On the basis of specific questionnaire items, it was estimated that 204,336 different individuals were seen in a one-week period and that these persons averaged 25 sessions per year. Hence, the total number of individuals seen by private practice psychologists is estimated to be approximately 425,000 per year (204,336 × 52 + 25 = 425,000). This total for private practice psychologists includes persons also seen in other specialty mental health settings (see footnote 8 for unduplicating adjustment).

8 This unduplicated sector total was obtained by subtracting the number of patients seen by private practice psychiatrists and psychologists who are also seen in other mental health facilities. Reported data from the Monroe County (New York) psychiatric case register indicate that 32 percent of patients seen in 1971 by psychiatrists in private office practice were also seen in other psychiatric settings during that year. This same factor was used to unduplicate patients of psychologists who were also seen in other psychiatric settings. The duplication of persons seen by both psychologists and psychiatrists in their private office practices, not already accounted for by the 32 percent adjustment factor across other specialty settings, is probably relatively small and can be ignored. Source: Sharfstein S S, Taube C A, Goldberg I D: Private psychiatry and accountability: A response to the APA task force report on private practice. *Am J Psychiatry* 132: 43–47, 1975.

9 Based on the number of discharges from nonfederal and federal general hospitals with a primary diagnosis of mental disorder, less those discharges from hospitals with separate psychiatric units that are surveyed by NIMH. This conservative estimate (4.4 percent of all general hospital discharges) was unduplicated by multiplying by the 0.83 factor cited in footnote 3, the only reasonable such factor available in the absence of special studies of these settings. Source: Ranofsky A L: *Utilization of Short-Stay Hospitals: Annual Summary for the United States, 1975.* National Health Survey, Series 13, No. 31, US Dept of Health, Education, and Welfare, Public Health Service, 1977.

10 Based on primary diagnosis at admission as a criterion. Data from the National Center for Health Statistics indicate that 11.3 percent of primary diagnoses on admission to nursing homes in 1973 were mental disorders (which excludes diagnosis of senility). In the absence of any later inormation, this proportion was applied to the 2.2 million persons served in nursing homes in 1973 (assumed to be the same for 1975), which includes those already resident at the start of the year The resulting estimate is undoubtedly conservative, particularly in light of Levine and Levine's (Levine D S, Levine D R: *Cost of Mental Illness: 1971,* series B, No. 7. Rockville, Md, NIMH, 1975) estimate that 42 percent of nursing home resident patients were considered to be incapacitated by mental disorder. Because of the extremely conservative nature of the estimate used here, which is based on primary diagnosis utilization data, no attempt has been made to adjust for duplication of nursing home patients also seen in other settings. Thus, the resulting total shown for the general hospital inpatient/nursing home sector may be considered as an unduplicated total. Source: *The Nation's Use of Health Resources,* publicaion (HRA) 77-1240. Department of Health, Education, and Welfare, 1976.

11 Based on the number of discharges from nonpsychiatric specialty hospitals in 1975. In the absence of other available data it was assumed that 4.4 percent of such discharges (the same proportion as for general hospitals without separate psychiatric units, see footnote 9) were of patients with a diagnosis of mental disorder. This estimate was multiplied by the 0.83 unduplicating factor cited in footnote 3, assumed applicable here in absence of any other data, to yield an unduplicated estimate of persons seen in these hospitals. Sources: (1) *The Nation's Use of Health Resources,* publication HRA 77-1240. Department of Health, Education, and Welfare, 1976. (2) National Center for Health Statistics: unpublished data.

12 Data from the National Center for Health Statistics 1974 Health Interview Survey showed that 57 percent of the civilian noninstitutionalized US population was seen in a physician's office during one year – this would amount to 119 million persons in 1975. Since 60 percent of all visits in the 1975 National Ambulatory Medical Care Survey (NAMCS) were accounted for by the primary care specialties of family-general practice, internal medicine, and pediatrics, the same percent of the total patients seen were attributed to these specialties. Thus, 71,400,000 patients are attributed to primary care physicians and all but a small proportion of the remaining 40 percent (less 854,000 to psychiatrists) or 46,747,000

(Notes to Table 4.1 contd.)

are attributed to other nonpsychiatrist office-based physicians. Based on multiple special surveys of general practice populations, 15 percent of primary care physician patients are estimated to have a mental disorder. Other nonpsychiatrist physicians, however, recorded a diagnosis of mental disorder at about one third the primary care physician rate in the 1975 NAMCS. Hence, 5 percent of their patients are estimated to have emotional disorders. The above approach is an estimate based on a primary assignment of patients to one physician type in proportion to the volume of visits made to these providers, and does not adequately account for the duplication across types of physicians or settings in this sector, which is dealt with in footnote 17.

13 The National Center for Health Statistics 1974 Health Interview Survey found that an estimated 1 percent of the US civilian noninstitutionalized population received care in neighborhood health care centers in 1974; the same proportion was assumed to apply in 1975. A 15% rate of mental disorder (see footnote 12) was applied to the approximately 2,090,000 total patients, to obtain the estimated number of persons with mental disorder in neighborhood health care centers. Source: *The Nation's Use of Health Resources*, publication HRA 77-1240. Department of Health, Education, and Welfare, 1976.

14 This estimate is based on the National Center for Health Statistics 1974 Health Interview Survey data indicating that 3 percent of the US civilian noninstitutionalized population used commercial or industrial health facilities in one year. A 5 percent rate of mental disorder diagnoses was used based on the findings of a special survey of industrial clinics. Sources: (1) *The Nation's Use of Health Resources*, publication HRA 77-1240. Department of Health, Education, and Welfare, 1976. (2) Rosen B M, Locke B Z, Goldberg I D, *et al.*: Identifying emotional disturbance in persons seen in industrial dispensaries. *Ment Hyg* 54:271-279, 1970.

15 This estimate was based on the National Center for Health Statistics 1974 Health Interview Survey data indicating that 3 percent of the US civilian noninstitutionalized population received services from health department clinics. The primary care nature of these clinics resulted in the use of a 15 percent mental disorder diagnosis rate (see footnote 12) for health department clinics. Source: *The Nation's Use of Health Resources*, publication HRA 77-1240. Department of Health, Education, and Welfare, 1976.

16 The National Center for Health Statistics 1974 Health Interview Survey showed that 20 percent of the US civilian noninstitutionalized population used general hospital emergency rooms and/or outpatient facilities as a source of health care in one year. This utilization rate was applied for 1975 to the larger total resident population to account for military and other use of these facilities. The use of hospital emergency rooms and general medical clinics for primary health purposes is now a well-established pattern not only for military personnel, but for a large sector of the general population as well. Although one study of patients seen in general medical clinics indicated an identification rate of mental disorder in 22 percent of patients seen, it was decided to continue use of the conservative estimate of 15 percent (see footnote 12) for patients seen in these settings. Sources: (1) *The Nation's Use of Health Resources*, publication HRA 77-1240. Department of Health, Education, and Welfare, 1976. (2) Rosen B M, Locke B Z, Goldberg I D, *et al.*: Identification of emotional disturbance in patients seen in general medical clinics. *Hosp Community Psychiatry* 23: 364-370, 1972.

17 Duplication across all primary care settings is accounted for by reducing the total number of individuals seen in general hospital outpatient and emergency room settings by 28 percent. This reduction is based on a National Center for Health Statistics finding that 28 percent of all hospital outpatient visits are made on referral of a physician. Source: *The Nation's Use of Health Resources*, publication HRA 77-1240. Department of Health, Education, and Welfare, 1976.

18 The total number of patients treated in all three health care sectors is reduced by 10% of those treated in the primary care sector. This reduction is made on the basis of studies in Monroe County, New York, of office-based primary care physicians' patients with mental disorders, 10 percent of whom were identified as having also been seen within the previous year by specialty mental health settings. Source: Goldberg I D, Babigian H M, Locke B Z, *et al.*: Role of nonpsychiatrist physicians in the delivery of mental health services: Implications from three studies. *Public Health Rep*, to be published.

19 This is the balance of the estimated 31,955,000 persons (15 percent of the 213,032,000 US resident population) with mental disorder. Thus, this unduplicated figure excludes an unknown overlap of persons seen in any of the three health care sectors in addition to the other human services sector.

past twenty-five years, as indicated by the following selected examples. The state-of-the-art limitations that necessitate combining prevalence and incidence data from independent community studies and then projecting to the national level are clearly recognized. However, the large-scale nature of these respected studies should result in estimates that are grossly reflective of the US as a whole.

Even the most conservative true prevalence survey estimates in community populations indicate that at least 10 percent of the total population is affected by a mental disorder at any one point in time. The most conservative of these studies was the 1954 survey of the entire noninstitutionalized Baltimore population, in which it was determined that at any given point in the year, 10 percent of the total population (all ages) had a mental disorder classifiable by the *ICDA*.[10] Using different case identification criteria, the 1954 Midtown Manhattan Study found that 23 percent of the adult population (age, twenty to fifty-nine years) were affected by serious psychiatric impairments at any point in time.[6] In addition, a 1967 study in New Haven, Conn, which has recently been updated, found a point prevalence mental disorder rate of about 16 percent in the adult population (age, twenty +).[11] (Both the Midtown and the New Haven studies would have yielded somewhat lower rates by the addition of children to the respective study populations, and the Midtown Manhattan rate would be additionally altered by including persons over fifty-nine years of age. These surveys are limited to the noninstitutionalized population and hence may underestimate the total population rates of some disorders, such as severe mental retardation or psychoses, that receive substantial institutional care.) Finally, the most recent update of the New Haven study showed a definite current mental disorder in 15.1 percent of the population (age, twenty-six +), and a probable mental disorder in an additional 2.7 percent of the population (a total of 17.8 percent).[12]

Given the point prevalence (that is, number with a disorder at the time of the survey date) nature of these surveys, it should be noted that the addition of persons who develop a mental disorder over a one-year interval (annual incidence) would generally result in a higher annual period prevalence rate than the respective rates produced in each of the above-mentioned studies. Although actual population studies of the true incidence of mental disorder are extremely rare, it is possible to extrapolate a 5 percent annual US mental disorder incidence rate from the treated incidence rate provided by a community-wide psychiatric case register.[13]

The Monroe County (New York) register is maintained by the Department of Psychiatry at the University of Rochester School of Medicine and Dentistry, and receives reports on persons receiving services from virtually all SMH facilities in the county, including psychiatrists in office-based practice. This register showed that almost 1 percent of the population were persons who had no previous Monroe County or other SMH treatment services, but who received SMH services for the first time in 1973 (annual SMH treated incidence). An additional 2 percent of this population, who were under active treatment or had a mental disorder, as indicated by prior SMH treatment at the start of the year (SMH treated point prevalence), received SMH services during 1973. Thus, there was a total of 3 percent of the population receiving SMH services in one calendar year (annual SMH treated prevalence).

If it is assumed that SMH treated incidence and prevalence rates are proportional to true incidence and prevalence rates, it is possible to extrapolate a true incidence rate from the psychiatric case register. Using our previously discussed conservative 10 percent true point prevalence rate and the corresponding 2 percent treated point prevalence rate, a 5:1 true prevalence/treated prevalence ratio may be derived. If the same 5:1 ratio holds for both true/treated annual incidence and prevalence rates, the 1 percent treated annual incidence would correspond to a 5 percent true annual incidence rate. Likewise, the 3 percent treated annual prevalence rate would correspond to a 15 percent true annual prevalence rate. The point prevalence could remain at 10 percent if the 5 percent annual incidence rate were offset by, in addition to other factors, effective treatment or spontaneous remissions of mental disorders for 5 percent of the affected population during the year.

Hence, by taking into considerations the counterbalancing biases and ranges of the available studies, and even using the lowest point prevalence estimate of 10 percent, it is possible to estimate that the annual period prevalence of all mental disorders in the United States is conservatively at least *15 percent of the population per year* (31,955,000 persons in 1975). Indeed, it is likely that application of the newer case identification methods[14] in large-scale population studies will provide added evidence for *point* prevalence rates of at

least 15 percent, with *annual* prevalence rates of over 20 percent of
the population per year.

Specialty mental health (SMH) sector

Given the substantial number of persons identified in the previous
section as having mental disorders, it is reasonable to ask how many
are under the care of mental health specialists during a year. This
study's review of SMH service settings, including private practice
psychiatrists and psychologists, showed that approximately 3.1
percent of the 1975 US population, or 6,698,000 persons, received
SMH services (see Table 4.1). Of these, approximately 1.5 million
persons (0.70 percent of the population) were actually hospitalized
in SMH facilities (NIMH, Division of Biometry and Epidemiology,
unpublished data from 1975 surveys of US mental health facilities).

Although the 3.1 percent rate represents all persons receiving
SMH services rather than the number with mental disorder receiving
such services, no attempt was made to adjust for persons seen in
SMH settings who were determined to be without mental disorder.
Such data as are available indicate that they form a relatively small
proportion of total persons seen in the SMH sector and this number
is more than offset by the conservative estimates used in this article.
(Unpublished data from the NIMH surveys of mental health facilities
for 1975 indicate that less than 0.5 percent of inpatient admissions
and less than 2 percent of outpatient admissions were assigned a
diagnosis of 'no mental disorder.' With regard to persons receiving
no diagnosis at all, a reported analysis of data from the Maryland
psychiatric case register found that among persons undiagnosed at
admission to psychiatric facilities, three fourths received a specific
diagnosis of mental disorder at separation or discharge, and only 2
percent received a separation or discharge diagnosis of 'no mental
disorder.'[15])

There are two relatively comprehensive, independent studies that
lend added confirmation to the general range of annual SMH service
utilization rates detailed in this article. The only major active
community-based psychiatric case registry in the United States,
located in Monroe County, New York, found that 2.7 percent of the
total 1973 county population used SMH services, not including
private practice psychologists or student mental health clinics, during
the year (annual treated prevalence). Of these, about 1.9 percent

had previously been identified and received SMH services (treated point prevalence), with an additional 0.8 percent new patients starting treatment at some time during the year (annual treated incidence), and 0.75 percent receiving a psychiatric hospitalization during the year.[13] (It is clear that these treated prevalence and incidence rates reflect the number of persons under treatment and thus include persons with totally new disorders, recurrent disorders, disorders continuing from previous years, and even some with no disorders. Although the usage of such prevalence and incidence terms does not correspond precisely with the more usual epidemiologic definitions, they are parallel and provide a useful public health focus in mental health services research.[16, 17]) Additional unpublished data from the 1977 National Center for Health Statistics (NCHS) Health and Nutrition Examination Survey (HANES) also found that approximately 2.6 percent of the 1974 noninstitutionalized population acknowledged use of either outpatient mental health facilities or of a psychiatrist, psychologist, or psychoanalyst during the preceding year.

Hence, only about one fifth of the 32 million persons (15 percent of the 1975 US population) estimated to have mental disorder during one year, and thus potentially requiring services, received care during the year by trained specialists in SMH settings. While it is clear that persons treated in this sector receive the most intensive and costly services, these data serve to disabuse us of the notion that all mental health needs can be cared for by mental health specialists. It is thus to the remaining persons (12 percent or more of the US population) who rely on treatment resources other than the SMH sector that we now turn our attention.

The general hospital inpatient/nursing home (GHI/NH) sector

Because of the absence of reliable survey data on the treated prevalence of mental disorders in this sector, we are left entirely with utilization data in which a primary diagnosis of mental disorder is indicated on discharge or admission. Estimates derived in this manner undoubtedly miss a number of patients who have a significant mental disorder in addition to another primary medical condition. The estimated number of patients served in this sector (about 1,100,000 in 1975), represent only 3.4 percent of the estimated total number of individuals with mental disorders. However, although not evident from Table 4.1, which combines inpatient and outpatient services for SMH facilities, the importance of general hospitals without psychiatric units is evidenced by the fact that they account for approximately twice the number of inpatient discharges for mental disorder as those reported by general hospitals with separate psychiatric units.[18]

The transfer of chronic psychiatric patients from long-term state and county hospitals to nursing homes as a result of economic and other factors has produced a major change in the locus of care for these patients.[19] Additional studies are required to document both the prevalence of psychiatric disorders in nursing home settings and the relative benefits or liabilities of this insufficiently examined change in mental health services policy.

The primary care/outpatient medical (PC/OPM) sector

This analysis of existing research studies has shown that a large number of individuals with mental disorder are identified in the PC/OPM sector. Since approximately 75 percent of the US noninstitutionalized population see a physician in one or more settings during a year, the finding that a high number of persons are identified with mental disorder in this sector is not surprising.[20] Special surveys of general practitioners and internists, supported by the NIMH and others, have shown the relatively consistent findings that about 15 percent of their patients are affected by a mental disorder over periods of one month to one year.[21, 22] Lower rates were found in industrial clinic settings, with somewhat higher rates found in hospital outpatient departments.[23, 24]

By applying prevalence estimates from the above studies to the NCHS data on the number of individuals in the population using the PC/OPM settings, an estimate of the number of individuals with mental disorder served in this sector was derived. Over 60 percent of the total persons affected by mental disorders in 1975, or 19,218,000 persons, are estimated to have had contact with general medical professionals in these settings. With regard to overlapping care, only about one tenth of these 60 percent are estimated to have also been seen in the SMH sector during the year, as indicated in footnote 18 to Table 4.1.

Screening for, or diagnosing, mental disorder is an important first level of mental health service, and the number of individuals receiving this service is appropriately reflected in the PC/OPM sector total. However, it is clear that physicians and other health providers in the sector may not offer any direct mental health treatment to some identified patients for a variety of reasons. In a remarkably comprehensive study of general medical physicians, Shepherd *et al.* found that 67 percent of those with identified mental disorder received some form of treatment from the physician himself. Another 5 percent were referred for specialty mental health care, with 28 percent receiving no treatment in the year.[7] There is wide variation in what is defined as treatment, and some of the cited GMP studies found psychotropic drugs prescribed for 60 percent to 80 percent and 'supportive therapy' provided in up to 96 percent of those identified with mental disorder.[23-25] Although further studies of the number actually treated are clearly indicated, if Shepherd's finding holds that no specific treatment is provided in up to one third of those identified, then the actual number treated in this sector would be reduced from 9 percent to some 6 percent of the total population.

Available data on this sector's volume of both general medical and mental health services for persons with diagnosed mental disorder are only briefly examined. A recent NIMH collaborative study of multiple organized medical care settings has found, in concert with other studies, that patients with an identified mental disorder appear to utilize general medical services at a rate that is at least double that of other patients.[26, 27] Routinely reported data on diagnosed mental disorders in this sector are generally understated because organic illnesses are more often the major presenting problem. This reflects the nonpsychiatrist physicians' organic illness orientation, and their preference to avoid a mental disorder diagnosis whenever an alternative is available. Our analyses of 1973 and 1975 National Ambulatory Medical Care Survey (NAMCS) data showed that only 5 percent of visits to general practitioners, internists, and pediatricians combined result in any *ICDA* section (5) diagnosis of a mental disorder. Although a 5 percent mental disorder diagnosis rate was also found in a 1973 National Drug and Therapeutic Index (NDTI) survey of office-based physician visits, an antianxiety or sedative agent was prescribed in 12 percent of these visits.[5] While it requires further exploration, supplemental methods of case identification might include consideration of other recorded problems related to mental disorder, symptoms and/or the intended use of a prescribed drug in general medical practice utilization data.

However, even with the above described underreporting biases of GMP physicians, it is clear from available data that the large number of nonpsychiatrist medical services, at a rate that is at least double that of other patients physicians, provide a substantial share of the total volume of mental health services in the US. Our analyses of the NAMCS data show that of all office-based physician visits resulting in a primary diagnosis of mental disorder, 47 percent are accounted for by nonpsychiatrist physicians, and 53 percent are accounted for by psychiatrists. Likewise, although nonpsychiatrists acknowledge use of a 'psychotherapy-therapeutic listening' service in only 2 percent of their visits, compared with 73 percent of psychiatrists' visits, by sheer weight of numbers nonpsychiatrists account for as many as 46 percent of visits and 27 percent of the total time devoted to such therapeutic listening treatment by office-based physicians.[28, 29]

Given the substantial mental health service responsibilities of the PC/OPM sector, there remains a pressing need for additional research that would enable primary health care providers to fulfill their vital primary care, public mental health function.[29, 30] Improved information is needed concerning the prevalence of specific psychiatric disorders, the type and efficacy of treatments provided, and the appropriate training required for these health professionals.

Not in treatment/other human services (NT/OHS) sector

Following an accounting of the unduplicated total number of persons identified and/or treated in the defined SMH and GMP sectors for one year, this number is subtracted from the 15 percent of the population estimated as having a mental disorder to obtain the number in the NT/OHS sector. Unfortunately, data are not available to differentiate between the number of persons with mental disorders who receive no treatment and those who are served by family service agencies, religious counselors, and other social welfare agencies outside the usually defined 'health' arena. This is a critical area for future research in that the other human services sector undoubtedly provides some mental health services to a substantial number of individuals in the US population.

Although there is obviously duplication between this and the other designated health and mental health sectors, the balance of 6,861,000 persons attributed to the NT/OHS sector in 1975 is indicative of those who would be treated here exclusively, or receive no treatment at all, if the 15 percent annual prevalence figure and the estimates of treated prevalence are correct. If a 15 percent annual prevalence estimate is as much as 5 percent too low (and the rate was 20 percent), then the balance of persons in this sector would actually be as many as 17,513,000, or 41 percent of the total 42.6 million with such disorders in 1975.

Conclusions

Available epidemiological survey and mental health services utilization data are used to show that a substantial proportion of the population (at least 15 percent) is affected by mental disorder in a given year. In addition to presenting the most recent data from the specialty mental health sector where 3 percent of the population is served, particular note is made of the primary care/outpatient medical sector where over 9 percent of the population, or 60 percent of those estimated to have mental disorders, are identified and/or receive treatment.

A principal implication of these findings is that mental disorder represents a major US health problem, which, although requiring active specialist attention, is beyond that which can be managed by the specialty mental health sector alone. Hence, there is a need both for further integration of the general health and mental health care sectors and for a greater attention to an appropriate division of responsibility that will maximize the availability and appropriateness of services for persons with mental disorder. Given the limitations of specialty resources, improvements in the mental health training of primary health care providers are needed to maximize the quality of mental health services for those fully or partially dependent on the general medical practice sectors. In addition, greater attention must be focused on the human services sector and on the social and economic costs incurred by those with mental disorder who receive no mental health services from the 'health' arena – concerns that relate at a minimum estimate to more than 3 percent of the population.

In conclusion, greater specificity is needed in epidemiological and mental health services research data to facilitate more effective and targeted public health service intervention programs. Recent improvements in mental health epidemiological survey technology

will need to be applied on a broader scale to obtain overall population prevalence estimates for specific disorders. There is also
additional need for more direct and reliable methods of estimating
the number of persons with mental disorder receiving specific mental
health services in the facilities of all four defined sectors.

While the data presented in this article provide a provisional and
broad perspective on the dimensions of mental disorder and mental
health services, more definitive responses to the President's
Commission must depend on future research findings. Support for
research in the epidemiology of and services for persons with mental
disorders is vitally needed to assure that an improved data base will
buttress future public policy decisions.

References

1 The White House: Executive Order No. 11973 – President's Commission on
Mental Health. Office of the White House Press Secretary, Feb 17, 1977.
2 *Health Statistics Plan, Fiscal Years 1978–1982*. US Department of Health,
Education, and Welfare, Public Health Service, 1977.
3 Jeffers J R., Bognanno M. F., Bartlett J. C.: On the demand versus need for
medical services and the concept of shortage. *Am J Public Health* 61: 45–63,
1971.
4 Parloff M.: Shopping for the right therapy. *Saturday Review*, Feb 21, 1976, pp.
14–20.
5 Balter M. B.: Coping with illness: Choices, alternatives and consequences, in
Helms R. B. (ed.): *Drug Development and Marketing*. Washington, DC,
American Enterprise Institute Center for Health Research, 1974.
6 Srole L., Langner T. S., Michael S. T., *et al.*: *Mental Health in the Metropolis:
The Midtown Manhattan Study*. New York, McGraw-Hill Book Co Inc, 1962.
7 Shepherd M., Cooper B., Brown A. C., *et al.*: *Psychiatric Illness in General
Practice*. London, Oxford University Press, 1966.
8 Dohrenwend B. P., Dohrenwend B. S.: Social and cultural influences on
psychopathology. *Ann Rev Psychol* 25: 417–452, 1974.
9 Kramer M.: Issues in the development of statistical and epidemiological data
for mental health services research. *Psychol Med* 6: 185–215, 1976.
10 Pasamanick B., Roberts D. W., Lemkau P. V., *et al.*: A survey of mental disease
in an urban population. *Am J Public Health* 47: 923–929, 1956.
11 Tischler G. L., Heinsz J. E., Myers J. K., *et al.*: Utilization of mental health
services: I. Patienthood and the prevalence of symptomatology in the
community. *Arch Gen Psychiatry* 32: 411–418, 1975.
12 Weissman M. M., Myers J. K., Harding P. S.: Psychiatric disorders in a United
States urban community: 1975–1976. Read before the annual meeting of the
American Psychiatric Association, Toronto, May 4, 1977.

13 Babigian H. M.: The impact of community mental health centers on the utilization of services. *Arch Gen Psychiatry* 34: 385–394, 1977.

14 Spitzer R. L., Endicott J.: *Schedule for Affective Disorders and Schizophrenia: Life-Time Version (SADS-L)*, ed 3. New York, New York State Psychiatric Institute, 1977.

15 *Comparison of Psychiatric Diagnosis on Admission to and Separation from Psychiatric Facilities*, statistical note 62, publication HSM-72-9012. National Institute of Mental Health, 1972.

16 Kramer M.: A discussion of the concepts of incidence and prevalence as related to epidemiologic studies of mental disorders. *Am J Public Health* 47: 826–840, 1957.

17 Kramer M., Pollack E. S., Redick R. W.: Studies of the incidence and prevalence of hospitalized mental disorders in the United States: Current status and future goals, in *Comparative Epidemiology of Mental Disorders*. New York, Grune & Stratton Inc, 1961, pp. 56–100.

18 Ranofsky A. L.: *Utilization of Short-Stay Hospitals: Annual Summary for the United States, 1975*. National Health Survey, Series 13, No. 31. US Dept of Health, Education, and Welfare, Public Health Service, 1977.

19 Redick R. W.: *Patterns in Use of Nursing Homes by the Aged Mentally Ill*, statistical note 107. Rockville, Md, Survey and Reports Branch, Division of Biometry and Epidemiology, NIMH, 1974.

20 *Current Estimates from the Health Interview Survey, 1973: Vital and Health Statistics*, series 10, No. 95, DHEW publication No. HRA 75–1522. National Center for Health Statistics, Health Resources Administration, 1974.

21 Locke B. Z., Gardner E.: Psychiatric disorders among the patients of general practitioners and internists. *Public Health Rep* 84: 167–173, 1969.

22 Locke B. Z., Krantz G., Kramer M.: Psychiatric need and demand in a prepaid group practice program. *Am J Public Health* 56: 895–904, 1966.

23 Rosen B. M., Locke B. Z., Goldberg I. D., et al.: Identifying emotional disturbance in persons seen in industrial dispensaries. *Ment Hyg* 54: 271–279, 1970.

24 Rosen B. M., Locke B. Z., Goldberg I. D., et al.: Identification of emotional disturbance in patients seen in general medical clinics. *Hosp Community Psychiatry* 23: 364–370, 1972.

25 Locke B. Z.: Patients' psychiatric problems and nonpsychiatrist physicians in a prepaid group practice medical program. *Am J Psychiatry* 123: 207–210, 1966.

26 Regier D. A., Goldberg I. D., Burns B. J., et al.: Epidemiological and health services research findings in four organized health/mental health service settings. Read before the annual meeting of the Alcohol, Drug Abuse, and Mental Health Administration Conference on Health Maintenance Organizations, Chicago, Nov 30, 1977.

27 Eastwood M. R., Trevelyan M. H.: Relationship between physical and psychiatric disorder. *Psychol Med* 2: 363–372, 1972.

28 Regier D. A., Goldberg I. D.: National health insurance and the mental health services equilibrium. Read before the annual meeting of the American Psychiatric Association, Miami, May 13, 1976.

29 Brown B. S., Regier D. A.: How NIMH now views the primary care practitioner.
   Practical Psychol Physicians 5: 12–14, 1977.
30 Reynolds R. E.: Primary care, ambulatory care, and family medicine:
   Overlapping but not synonymous. *J Med Educ* 40: 893–895, 1975.

CHAPTER 5

Deinstitutionalization and mental health services*

Ellen L. Bassuk and Samuel Gerson

Fifteen years ago the US undertook a massive reform in the delivery of mental health services under the banner of 'community mental health.' A major objective, urged by a spirit of reform and presumed to be brought within reach by the availability of new psychoactive drugs, was the release from institutions and the rehabilitation within their own community of people with severe mental illness. Today the population of mental hospitals has indeed been reduced by two-thirds. That achievement is offset, however, by huge increases in the rate of admissions to those hospitals (signifying a high turnover of patients through short periods of hospitalization) and in the number of discharged but severely and chronically disturbed former patients consigned to bleak lives in nursing homes, single-room-occupancy hotels and skid-row rooming houses.

Does 'deinstitutionalization' represent an enlightened revolution or an abdication of responsibility? It is probably too early for a definitive judgment, but it is not too soon to review the issues raised by this aspect of the community mental health movement and to consider how such a well-intentioned reform as deinstitutionalization could have created so many problems.

The mandate of those who attend to the mentally ill has always been shaped by the social, economic, religious and philosophical temper of the times, and in no case is that effect more clearly illustrated than in the history of the institutional segregation of

* Reprinted from *Scientific American*, vol. 238, no. 2, pp. 46–53, February 1978, by permission of the authors and the publisher.

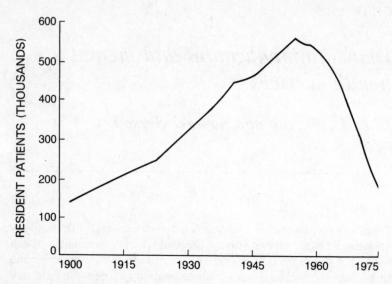

Fig. 5.1 Inpatient population of state and county mental hospitals rose steadily from the turn of the century until 1955, since when it has decreased sharply. These data do not include private or Federal hospitals, whose population has held fairly constant at between 50,000 and 75,000.

people who are labeled 'mad.' The movement toward institutionaliz-ation started with the growth of secularism in the seventeenth and eighteenth centuries. As the power of the churches waned, so did the view that disturbed behavior was a symptom of demonological possession, to be dealt with by exorcism or death. In its place came the belief that deviance was a reflection of sloth and moral turpitude, best managed by disciplinary measures and segregation from society. Institutionalization replaced witch-hunting, but the basic objective continued to be to protect society rather than to care for the indi-vidual. It was not until the ascendancy of 'moral treatment,' advo-cated primarily by Philippe Pinel at the Hôpital Salpêtrière in Paris, early in the nineteenth century that concern for the welfare of the institutionalized person competed with concern for the protection of society. As inhuman living conditions and harsh punishment began to give way to a more humane approach, there was growing interest in understanding the nature and causes of disturbed behavior from a medical perspective. Concepts of illness replaced concepts of social deviance; medical treatment became the new rationale for institutionalization.

In the US parallel efforts to treat disturbed behavior as a medical problem in special hospitals were limited at first to a few large Eastern cities; by the mid-1840s only some twenty-five such hospitals had been established with a total capacity of perhaps 2,500. The great majority of those who were segregated because they could not function appropriately within the community lived under squalid conditions, sequestered in county homes or almshouses or even in jails with people who were simply poor or old or physically sick – in any case without treatment. In the second half of the nineteenth century, however, there was a revolution in the care of the mentally ill, brought about by a convergence of social, medical and economic influences. Public attention was drawn to the plight of the severely disturbed by a reform movement led by Dorothea Dix, which coincided with the development of new medical models of disturbed behavior. As the mentally ill began to be transferred from local homes and jails to small county institutions, it became evident to state legislatures that larger state institutions would more economically assuage the reform movement. By 1900 more than a hundred new state institutions were built.

In time the large, cost-effective mental hospitals came to serve as receptacles for a wide range of socially troublesome individuals, including many of the indigent and disturbed – or seemingly disturbed – people among the waves of late-nineteenth-century immigrants. As the proportion of chronically ill patients increased, the hospitals became overcrowded, patient care deteriorated and both psychiatrists and the public lost faith in the possibility of cure and return to the community. The reform movement, having seen its original objectives apparently accomplished, had ceased to be a significant influence. By early in this century the network of state mental hospitals, once a proud tribute to an era of reform, had largely turned into a bureaucratic morass within which patients were interned, often neglected and sometimes abused.

That was the general situation after World War II, when social, economic and medical developments prompted a reassessment of the delivery of psychiatric services. The rejection of large numbers of young men from military service on the ground of diagnosed psychiatric disturbance had made the country aware of the prevalence of mental disorders and of the lack of adequate resources for prevention

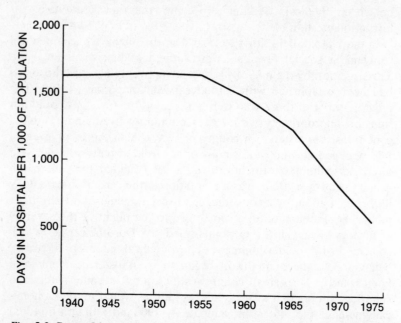

Fig. 5.2 Rate of hospitalization, or the number of days in the hospital per 1,000 of US population, has decreased by 65 percent in state, county and private mental hospitals since 1940.

or treatment. The new awareness led to more funding of research and training programs in the area of mental health. Then came a major medical development: the widespread and effective introduction of antipsychotic drugs in the early 1950s. The possibility arose that thousands of patients previously considered manageable only within the confines of an institution could now be treated as outpatients. That possibility increased the growing pressure for the development of comprehensive programs of community-based treatment. The pressure was further augmented by the desire of state legislatures to reduce the financial burden of state mental hospitals.

These various trends combined to lead Congress to establish in 1955 the Joint Commission on Mental Illness and Health to evaluate services for the mentally ill and to formulate a national mental health program. The commission's recommendations, reported in 1960, provided the groundwork for a landmark address to Congress by President Kennedy urging a 'bold new approach' to the management

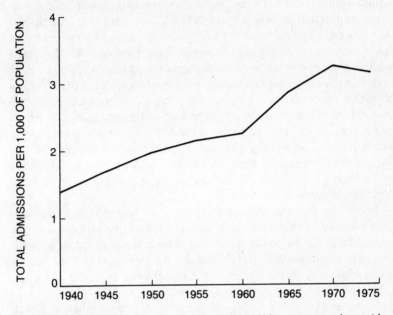

Fig. 5.3 Rate of admissions has increased by 129 percent as the resident population and hospitalization rate of mental hospitals have dropped. The drop is the result of shorter average stays.

of mental illness, which led in turn to the passage of the Mental Retardation Facilities and Community Mental Health Centers Construction Act of 1963. The legislation and related guidelines from the Department of Health, Education, and Welfare called for the establishment of a new kind of community-based center and promised Federal funding for such facilities if they provided five essential services: inpatient care, outpatient care, emergency treatment, partial hospitalization and 'consultation and education.' The legislation marked a momentous shift in the ideology of treatment for mental illness and led to radical changes in the delivery of psychiatric services.

The concept of 'community mental health' implied a dual promise: treatment and rehabilitation of the severely mentally ill within the community and the promotion of mental health generally. The first promise was to be fulfilled by the development of an extensive support system for the mentally ill, based on community mental health centers and offering comprehensive and coordinated treatment and rehabilitation services. These new and 'less restrictive' services were to take over the traditional function of large custodial institutions in caring for chronically disturbed individuals. The quantitative goal set for this deinstitutionalization process was a 50 percent reduction in the patient population of state hospitals for the mentally ill within two decades – a statistic that, as we mentioned above, has already been achieved. The second aim of the program, the broad improvement of the nation's mental health status, was to be accomplished largely by preventive programs originating in the mental health centers, each of which would be responsible for a population of 75,000 to 200,000 people in a geographically defined 'catchment' area.

Implicit in these objectives was an expectation that mental illness could indeed be prevented and that even chronic patterns of severely disturbed behavior could be altered. There was a mood of enthusiastic optimism, which in retrospect can be seen to have bordered on blind faith. The shortcomings of the initial legislation, the lack of an adequate system of follow-up care, the hard realities of insufficient funding, the probable impact of patients on communities and even the uncertainties as to effective therapy that continue to plague psychiatry – all of these were largely ignored in the rush to implement the new goals. In some programs established by the legislation ignoring the realities has only made for confusion and waste. For thousands of hospitalized patients released haphazardly to a nonsystem of community aftercare, however, it has meant real hardship and even tragedy.

As of mid-1975, 507 community mental health centers were in full operation; an additional ninety-six centers had received large grants from the National Institute of Mental Health for construction and staff. (According to NIMH estimates, however, the 603 centers would provide coverage for only some 40 percent of the US population; some 1,500 centers are needed.) Outpatient facilities, which include the community centers, other clinics and emergency rooms, now account for more than 65 percent of all mental health patient-care 'episodes,' an increase from 23 percent in 1955. (An episode is an entry into care; the total number of episodes in a year is the sum of the inpatient and outpatient rolls and the additions to those rolls in the course of the year.) At the same time that outpatient episodes were more than doubling between 1955 and 1975, there was a 65 percent decrease in the census of resident patients in the state mental hospitals, from 559,000 to 193,000.

The deinstitutionalization statistics are illusory, however. Although the annual census was decreasing, admissions to state hospitals increased from 178,000 in 1955 to a peak of 390,000 in 1972 and had declined only to 375,000 by 1974. That trend reflects a new philosophy of short-term hospitalization. Moreover, a growing proportion of the admissions were readmissions (in 1972, 64 percent of them); about half of the released inpatients are readmitted within a year of discharge. Those statistics must surely reflect the lack of a fully effective community-based support system. As a matter of fact, the Department of Mental Health in Massachusetts, where we work (at Beth Israel Hospital and Cambridge Hospital and the Harvard Medical School), has estimated that between half and three-fourths of the readmissions could have been avoided if comprehensive community facilities had existed.

And they generally do not exist. As contemplated in the 1963 legislation and made more explicit in an amendment in 1975, the deinstitutionalized patient was to be supported by a spectrum of aftercare services delivered by halfway houses, family and group homes, therapeutic residential centers, fostercare arrangements and so on, with the local community mental health center as the coordinator. In 1977 a report issued by the General Accounting Office concluded that the centers have not fulfilled their intended function in behalf of patients returned to the community. There are some obvious reasons. One is that the centers developed and have been administered without connection with the state hospitals; the two systems are most often completely unintegrated and frequently not even in communication with each other, so that the discharges are inadequately coordinated with the availability of community facilities. Moreover, in the rush to reduce their census the hospitals discharged patients long before most of the community centers had been established and before supporting programs had been developed.

There are, to be sure, a few centers that have devised innovative programs to enhance the quality of life for chronically ill patients; there are some experimental programs that offer total care for discharged patients in a community setting. Such centers and programs are few, however, and they are the results of efforts by particular individuals or institutions, special funding or other special

circumstances rather than of any consistent plan. In part this inconsistency results from a deliberate choice: the development of
community services was not based on data collected by systematic
research; rather, it was assumed that each center would be shaped
by the particular needs of its area as they were perceived by the
community itself.

A major problem in gauging the effectiveness of the community
support programs is the paucity of follow-up studies whose data
can be generalized and compared and that trace the movement of
discharged patients through the labyrinth of psychiatric facilities and
living conditions after their release. The existing evidence is clear,
however, particularly to those of us who are engaged in the emergency care of severely disturbed people in outpatient departments of
city hospitals. Time and time again we see patients who were released
from state hospitals after months or years of custodial care; who
then survived precariously on welfare payments for a few months on
the fringe of the community, perhaps attending a clinic to receive
medication or intermittent counseling; who voluntarily returned to
a hospital or were recommitted (which in Massachusetts is possible
only if the patient is acutely suicidal or homicidal or manifestly
unable to care for himself); who were maintained in the hospital on
antipsychotic medication and seemed to improve; who were released
again to an isolated 'community' life and who, having again become
unbearably despondent, disorganized or violent, either present themselves at the emergency room or are brought to it by a police officer.
Then the cycle begins anew.

The generally ineffective functioning of community mental health
centers in caring for discharged patients means that there is an
inadequate system of follow-up psychiatric treatment for them, or
even of basic guidance in coping with the mechanics of daily living.
The failure to establish sheltered housing shunts former patients into
nonpsychiatrically oriented facilities. Most patients are placed in
nursing homes (a category that includes skilled nursing facilities,
intermediate-care facilities, rest homes and homes for the aged), a
process of 'reinstitutionalization,' since most homes have more than
a hundred beds (and yet offer only custodial care). A national survey
in 1974 of skilled-nursing facilities revealed that 22 percent of their
284,000 patients less than sixty-five years old were diagnosed as being
mentally ill or retarded. Of the patients sixty-five years and over, a
third had chronic brain disease and a tenth were diagnosed as being

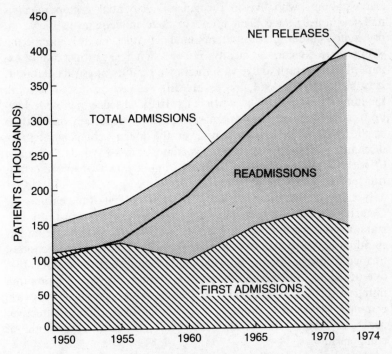

Fig. 5.4 Readmissions of patients previously discharged from institutions have exceeded first admissions since 1960; in 1972 they accounted for 64 percent of admissions. Rise in net releases (discharges minus returns from long-term leaves) reflects shorter periods of hospitalization.

neurotic or psychotic. The inappropriate occupying of nursing-home beds by these former patients means that the beds are not available for patients with chronic physical illnesses, whose stay in general hospitals is therefore unnecessarily prolonged.

Untherapeutic though many nursing homes are, living conditions in most of them are at least tolerable. Conditions may be worse for discharged patients living on their own, without enough money and usually without any possibility of employment. Many of them drift to substandard inner-city housing that is overcrowded, unsafe, dirty and isolated. Often they come together to form a new kind of ghetto subpopulation, a captive market for unscrupulous landlords. Their appearance and their sometimes bizarre behavior may disturb the neighborhood, and they are usually shunned and frequently feared.

Even patients who live in recognized residential centers such as halfway houses have been found to have inadequate medical and psychiatric care or none at all, minimal activities and little interaction with people outside the facility. For the significant proportion of ex-patients who return to live with their own families physical conditions may be relatively good, but severe stresses can be placed on both the family and the patient, particularly in the absence of close follow-up treatment; there may be long-term effects, especially on children in the household. Finally, whatever the living arrangement for a discharged patient may be, he is almost sure to find a shortage of vocational rehabilitation, sheltered employment or job referrals, transportation and recreation.

It is not enough to review and deplore the plight of the chronically disturbed ex-patient. It is important to see just where deinstitutional-ization has encountered difficulties, and that requires some under-standing of the dynamics of the program: the complex interaction of financial, professional, political and administrative factors that operate almost independently of the intentions or the legislation that initiated it. Perhaps the most important single element in this case is money – the lack of money in general, the issue of cost ineffective-ness and more specifically the effect of various methods of compensation.

Community mental health centers were constructed and originally staffed by grants of Federal 'seed' money, but they were expected eventually to become self-supporting. The idea was that enough income would be generated by individual fees, third-party (insurance) reimbursements and budget expenditures by state and local governments. The expectation of fees turned out to be unreal-istic. The great majority of the people who apply for community mental health services are poor; people with money go to private or voluntary hospital clinics or to individual practitioners. In recognition of these facts the Federal Government kept amending the original legislation and now helps to fund the centers for a twelve-year period. A major burden is nevertheless placed on third-party reimbursement. Insurance coverage of the mentally disabled has always been incom-plete, biased in favor of inpatient care and markedly inferior to coverage for physical illness. (In 1968 a fourth of all physical patient episodes were covered by insurance and only an eighth of all mental-care episodes; reimbursement for inpatient treatment is usually more time-limited for mental illness than it is for physical illness.)

The major Federal insurance plans are the Medical Assistance Program, or Medicaid (for the medically indigent), and Medicare (for the elderly), and their specifications have been important determinants of the community mental health centers' growth and activity. Medicaid pays the states between about 50 and 78 percent of the mental health costs of eligible individuals. Each state defines its own benefits, but Medicaid has established some restrictive general guidelines. Mentally ill people between twenty-one and sixty-five ordinarily are not eligible for Medicaid if they are hospitalized in facilities that care for mental disorders exclusively, including even residential treatment centers such as halfway houses. Medicaid benefits are available, on the other hand, for inpatient psychiatric care in general hospitals – and for maintenance in most nursing homes. That is why the nursing home, rather than more psychiatrically oriented facilities, has become the principal alternative to the state hospital. Medicaid coverage of outpatient care in mental health clinics is very limited (although there has been a trend toward increasing the benefits), and in most states the coverage for day-care programs is inadequate.

Medicare provides limited inpatient coverage in state hospitals and more extensive coverage in general hospitals. It allows no more than $250 a year for outpatient coverage, a figure that has been frozen since Medicare was initiated in 1965 in spite of marked increases in the cost of psychiatric services. A third source of Federal money that has an impact on mental health care is the Supplemental Security Income program, which provides income-support funds for some mentally ill individuals. It ordinarily provides monthly payments of $167.80 to ex-patients (with some states adding a supplement), but generally not if they live in a halfway house, a group home or a similar institution – actually giving the individual an incentive to choose a welfare hotel or nursing home rather than a psychiatrically oriented facility.

The combined effect of the Federal programs has been to limit development and use of community-based alternatives. Their eligibility requirements have channeled many patients into nursing homes and substandard housing with minimal opportunities for psychiatric services and have undermined the development of a full range of outpatient services and residential treatment programs.

Apart from insurance programs the financial support of community mental health centers and their services has had to come from

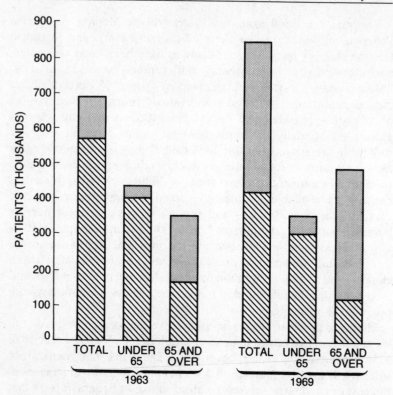

Fig. 5.5 Nursing homes have absorbed many patients released from hospitals. Bars show population of nursing homes (color) and of state and private mental hospitals (gray) in 1963 and 1969.

Federal grants and state and local budgets. At the state and local level funds for community services have had to compete with funds for the traditional mental-hospital system. Between 1968 and 1974 the cost of that system increased from $1.7 to $2.8 billion. There is little indication that the reduction in the population of large institutions has freed funds for less restrictive services. The hope was that the community approach would save money, but it is now clear that effective care requires very large expenditures. The political influence of discharged mental patients is small, to say the least, and appropriations by state and local legislatures are inevitably guided more by political priorities than by clinical concerns.

It is hard to see how the fiscal viability of the community mental health system can be improved except by the passage of some form of comprehensive national health insurance. As such legislation is debated it is important to bear in mind the great potential for shaping public policy that is inherent in the details of the insurance coverage. For example, the Kennedy-Corman Health Security Act, one of the most comprehensive proposals, encourages ambulatory care by providing coverage for unlimited visits to a community mental health center. Yet it would cover only twenty visits per benefit period (which in existing insurance programs is generally one year) to a private practitioner. Inpatient treatment would be covered for up to forty-five days in a benefit period. The effect of such coverage would be to make the centers the major source of outpatient care, which may well be desirable, but it would strictly curtail visits to private practitioners and clinics except by the affluent.

In addition to being short of funds the community mental health centers are short of personnel. The demand for services far exceeds the supply. There is a relative lack of well-trained professionals in psychiatry in general, and their concentration in large urban centers compounds the scarcity. In 1975 the National Institute of Mental Health estimated that psychiatrists constituted less than 6 percent of the staffs of the centers and that most of them were engaged in administration. Over the past decade there has been a decrease in the proportion of psychiatrists in the centers and only a small increase in the number of other relevant specialists such as psychologists and social workers.

To make up for the shortage of professionals, special programs for the training of paraprofessionals have been instituted, and an attempt has been made to enroll volunteer workers. These trends have resulted in a blurring of professional roles and in controversy over the qualifications and training required to treat severely mentally ill patients effectively. Moreover, the centers' deviation from traditional methods of psychotherapy and their frequent preoccupation with nonclinical issues involving public health, social problems and economics have made many academic professionals reluctant to become engaged in community mental health programs. It is important that specific roles and tasks be defined for the personnel staffing the centers and that adequate recruitment and training programs be developed.

Psychiatry still lacks criteria for selecting patients to be treated with most of the various therapeutic methods; the methods themselves are

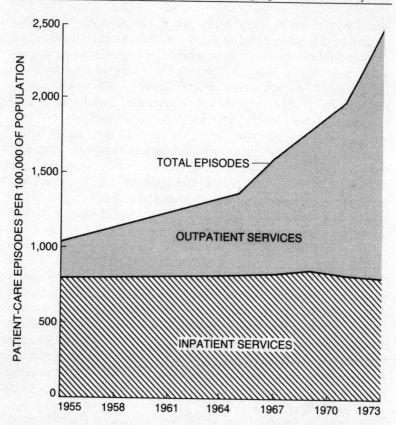

Fig. 5.6 Patient-care 'episodes' (the number of people on inpatient and outpatient rolls plus the number of additions during the year) have risen sharply in proportion to the population. The increase is due almost entirely to the growth in outpatient services. Inpatient episodes have remained constant in spite of the drop in the population of hospitalized patients. These data cover most public and private psychiatric services except for offices of private practitioners.

not well defined and there is only a small body of data on the efficacy of particular approaches. It is clear that some patients cannot be treated with any existing technique, so that new approaches need to be developed. The very nature of many conditions psychiatrists attempt to treat is still not well understood. In view of this lack of basic knowledge it is not surprising that there are no accepted guidelines for establishing comprehensive systems for the delivery of mental health care – notably systems for reaching disadvantaged people, who may be subjected to particular stresses and may respond to them in ways requiring specific interventions with which many psychiatrists are not familiar. Systematic basic research is needed if comprehensive and effective treatment is to be provided for varied groups of patients.

The complex and interrelated tasks of reducing the patient population in state hospitals, providing alternative community facilities and ensuring the best possible outpatient treatment would be difficult ones in any case, and the difficulty is compounded by organizational chaos. The bureaucratic fragmentation, diffusion of responsibility and lack of coordination begin at the Federal level and extend through the state and local mental health apparatus. Eleven major Federal departments and agencies share the task of administering 135 programs for the mentally disabled. Inevitably (as in the case of Medicaid and Medicare coverage) the provisions of one program may undercut the objectives of another. Some agencies have not considered deinstitutionalization a major goal; other agencies have given it a high priority but lack the power to distribute funds or monitor Federally funded programs. At the state and local levels there is a similar fragmentation of roles, and in particular there are lack of coordination, competition for funds and even enmity between the administrators of the old state hospital systems and the managers of community programs.

The problem of conflicting governmental jurisdictions in mental health has been exacerbated in recent years by increased judicial involvement. Significant decisions by courts in several states have asserted the civil liberties of patients and have established a constitutional right to treatment, have defined minimum standards of care and have delineated objective criteria for involuntary commitment. Many of these decisions have advanced the cause of human and civil rights, but in some cases the immediate effect has been damaging to patients. For example, a landmark right-to-treatment case in Alabama, *Wyatt* v. *Stickney*, defined minimum standards of care and stated that unless a hospital could provide specific treatment for a patient's condition it could not hold that patient against his will. Providing such treatment would have required the expenditure of large sums of money. The Alabama state legislature chose not to appropriate the additional funds, thus in effect mandating the release of thousands of patients – who ended up in substandard housing and with still less in the way of psychiatric services.

Officials at the National Institute of Mental Health have recognized that a comprehensive national strategy needs to be adopted, agreed to at all levels of government and carried out in a coordinated manner. The institute's new Community Support Program requires coordination of the relevant activities of all Federal agencies and careful delineation of the roles of each and defines responsibility for policy making. A 'fiscal partnership' would be established among the various levels of government to develop a genuinely integrated system of direct services to meet the needs of the severely and chronically ill patient. Although some details of the system are still to be worked out, $3.5 million has recently been allotted to sixteen states for program development. What is most important is that the NIMH plan asserts the willingness of the Federal Government to accept more responsibility for the mentally ill and that it acknowledges the specific needs of the chronic, severely disabled patient. For the first time in several decades the proposal explicitly affirms the existence of chronic disability, an implied denial of which has permeated the mental health movement, and asserts the importance of supportive and rehabilitative services as well as preventive measures.

The view that a massive shift in the locus and form of treatment can in itself combat mental illness is not new. It was, after all, the view of Dorothea Dix and her supporters a hundred years ago, when they urged the development of large state institutions as both sheltering asylums and centers of treatment. Their movement gained impetus from a cult of curability, and the community mental health movement may have been a victim of a similar faith. Although the institutionalization movement of the nineteenth century and the recent push for deinstitutionalization were nominally opposite in their objectives, they suffered from a similar confusion of goals. In both cases the aims of social reform and of more effective treatment became entangled; the improvement of living conditions or the assertion of civil rights was somehow expected to bring advances in treatment and rehabilitation. Social justice may be a necessary condition for successful treatment, but it is not a sufficient condition.

Even too narrow an emphasis on 'treatment' can be inappropriate if it shifts attention from the patient's daily life situation. This is true particularly in the case of the chronically mentally ill, for whom

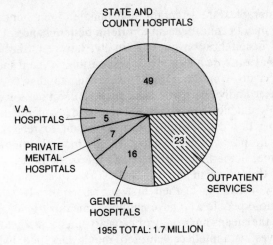

STATE AND
COUNTY HOSPITALS

49

V.A.
HOSPITALS — 5

7

PRIVATE
MENTAL
HOSPITALS

16

23

OUTPATIENT
SERVICES

GENERAL
HOSPITALS

1955 TOTAL: 1.7 MILLION

STATE AND
COUNTY HOSPITALS

COMMUNITY
MENTAL HEALTH
CENTERS

V.A.
HOSPITALS

PRIVATE
MENTAL
HOSPITALS

GENERAL
HOSPITALS

12   4

3   4

19

9

49

OTHER
OUTPATIENT
SERVICES

1973 TOTAL: 5.2 MILLION

Fig. 5.7 Shift to outpatient services is illustrated by the two pie charts. The numbers give the percent of total episodes accounted for in 1955 and 1973 by various facilities offering either inpatient (gray) or outpatient (grid) services. The community mental health centers that have been established since 1963 account for much of the outpatient increase, but other outpatient facilities have also expanded.

definitive therapies are generally unavailable. Treatment within a community may in concept seem to offer a better chance of rehabilitation than hospitalization does. Actually, however, the quest for treatment may obscure a more basic responsibility: the responsibility to provide living conditions that ensure human dignity and that offer refuge to individuals who seek such refuge themselves or are demonstrably unable to manage their lives independently.

In meeting this responsibility it is important to remember that neither the hospital nor the community approach is inherently the more humane. Some hundred years ago the trustees of the Willard Asylum for the Insane in western New York explained the purpose of their new institution in their first annual report. It would be a home 'for those people who have neither home nor friends, and who are without the means financially or capacity intellectually to provide for themselves, with intellect shattered, minds darkened, living amid delusions, a constant prey to unrest, haunted by unreal fancies and wild imagining. They now have in their sore misfortune a safe refuge, kindly care, constant watching, and are as comfortable as their circumstances will allow. This is a result over which every humane and Christian citizen of the state will rejoice.' The subsequent failure to maintain and improve institutions with that purpose seems to us to reflect economic, political, administrative and clinical realities rather than any inherent fallacy in the goals themselves.

Priorities must be established. The first task is to provide decent places of habitation – of asylum (which is a humane term in spite of its association with the old label 'insane asylum'). New approaches to treatment should be undertaken only after rigorous research, and those approaches must not ignore and thus jeopardize the individual life situation of patients whom the treatment presumes to serve. One must accept the fact that psychiatry is not now able to cure some forms of severe emotional disability, and that psychiatry alone cannot assume the broad responsibilities of a society to care for its helpless fellows.

CHAPTER 6

General hospital psychiatry: Overview from a sociological perspective*

Leona L. Bachrach

In *Death of the Asylum* John Talbott (1) discussed four sources of change that have influenced the history of state mental hospitals: 1) changes generated within the hospital itself and specific to a particular institution, 2) changes brought about by policy decisions on the part of the authorities or auspices controlling the hospital, 3) changes in patterns of service delivery in the greater mental health system, particularly deinstitutionalization efforts, that shift and redefine a particular hospital's role, and 4) changes in societal values, attitudes, and sensitivities that influence directions and priorities in psychiatric care. These same factors have been no less influential in determining the history and course of development of general hospital psychiatry.

This tells us something important: that general hospital psychiatry responds to the same kinds of pressures and social forces as do other psychiatric service modes. It tells us also that general hospital psychiatry is intertwined with the concerns of, and the service patterns within, the rest of the psychiatric service delivery system.

Acknowledgments of this complementarity abound. For example, the Hospital Association of Massachusetts has appointed a special task force to identify problems and formulate recommendations, 'in view of changing societal trends,' concerning the general hospital's role in 'matters relating to mental health and retardation' (2, p. 7).

* *American Journal of Psychiatry*, vol. 138: 7, pp. 879–87, 1981. Copyright 1981, the American Psychiatric Association. Reprinted by permission of the author and the publisher.

Similarly, the Massachusetts Psychiatric Society has seen fit to appoint a task force to investigate factors affecting changing patterns of psychiatric care in general hospitals (3).

Striking statistical evidence for the complementarity of various psychiatric service modes is provided in a federal report that compares selected occupancy trends in psychiatric inpatient facilities (4). For example, between 1971 and 1975 the number of beds in state hospitals decreased by 39 percent but the number in psychiatric inpatient units of general hospitals increased by 23 percent. Over the same period the average daily census in state hospitals decreased by 41 percent, but the census in general hospital psychiatric inpatient units increased by 22 percent. Once again, changes in average length of stay in these facilities showed, respectively, a decrease of 41 percent and an increase of 4 percent (4). On the basis of such statistics NIMH acknowledges that general hospitals are increasingly being used as alternatives to long-stay state mental hospitals (5).

As one part of a larger system of care, general hospital psychiatry is currently in the process of sorting out its specific role and functions in relationship to those of the rest of psychiatry. As it defines its limits, it is experiencing something of an identity crisis, not a novel situation for general hospital psychiatry. The effort to establish boundaries has been part of its history from the beginning (6). But there are elements in the current identity crisis that are somewhat new and different. Today there are extraordinary external social forces that are profoundly affecting all of psychiatry and altering traditional patterns of care and lines of command. General hospital psychiatry is caught up in the middle of that turmoil.

Even though this may seem paradoxical, general hospital's identity crisis is by no means paralyzing. In view of its many problems, general hospital psychiatry shows astonishingly great vitality. There is ample evidence that the field continues to initiate and evaluate varied and imaginative treatment strategies (7–12), to develop and improve programs of brief hospitalization for crisis intervention (13–20), to develop innovative training procedures (8, 9, 21) and unusual collaborative service arrangements (22, 23), and to engage in productive research (24–28).

Before I get into the major focus of this presentation, a conceptualization of some of the problems that general hospital psychiatry faces today, I want to clarify what I consider to be some important semantic and definitional problems.

Statistical materials concerning psychiatric services in general hospitals are in short supply, so that much of what passes for established fact is based on anecdotal evidence. This is not, I think, entirely without value. The problems of general hospital psychiatry are in many ways best understood by those who practice and receive care in these settings – people who do not necessarily think statistically or write reports. Still, it is necessary to rely on statistical evidence for documentation, and it is important to establish that the available statistics on psychiatric services in general hospitals are neither complete nor conclusive. The principal source of nationwide data is the Division of Biometry and Epidemiology of NIMH. Although these data are not current in a field where change is occurring rapidly, they are useful because of their breadth and variety. However, it should be noted that other available nationwide statistics on general hospital psychiatric services, supplied by the American Hospital Association (29) and the National Association of State Mental Health Program Directors (30), are sometimes at considerable variance with the NIMH data.

According to NIMH, in 1976 (the latest year for which such data are available) separately designated psychiatric services were provided in 870 general hospitals in the nation.(This number does not include those services which operate as parts of federally funded community mental health centers. Nor does it include psychiatric services in VA general hospitals.) Of these, 791 hospitals provided inpatient care, 303 provided outpatient care, and 176 provided day treatment. A total of 171 of these hospitals were operated under public auspices and 699 under private auspices (31, 32).

A federal report (31) reveals, however, that the overall role of general hospitals in providing psychiatric care is considerably more extensive than what these numbers might suggest. Much of the psychiatric treatment that is provided in general hospitals is given in units that are *not* specifically designated as psychiatric. In 1975 there were about 1.5 million inpatient admissions to general hospitals with primary psychiatric diagnoses, but only about 516,000 of these were admissions to designated psychiatric inpatient units. In other words, only about 35 percent of general hospital inpatient admissions diagnosed with primary psychiatric disorders actually occupied designated psychiatric beds (31). A similar statistic is provided by the State of Maryland, where in 1978 only 37 percent of general hospital admissions with primary psychiatric diagnoses occupied designated psychiatric beds (33).

Public versus private hospitals

It is also important to point out that general hospital psychiatry is not an undifferentiated phenomenon. Whether a particular hospital is operated under public or private auspices is of critical importance in determining who receives psychiatric services for what purposes and how those services are financed. Public and private general hospitals differ considerably in their admissions according to primary diagnoses: depressive disorders lead in private facilities and schizophrenic disorders in public ones. In 1975 depressive disorders accounted for 43 percent of admissions to private inpatient units, as contrasted with 24 percent to public units. On the other hand, schizophrenic disorders accounted for 36 percent of admissions to public units and 20 percent to private units (34).

NIMH data also reveal substantial differences in the financing of inpatient psychiatric care between public and private general hospitals. In 1975, approximately 40 percent of the admissions to public units listed Medicare or Medicaid as the principal expected source of payment as contrasted with 26 percent of private hospital admissions. By comparison, the leading principal expected sources of payment at private units were Blue Cross and commercial insurance funds, which accounted for 60 percent of the total (35).

The important point I wish to make is that public and private general hospital psychiatry are different entities. Although there is considerable overlap in some of their problems, and although they share many basic concerns, they should really be treated separately in discussions of psychiatric programs in general hospitals. Generally speaking, one of the major differences between them lies in the respective patient populations that they serve. Historically, public general hospitals have been more closely identified with the most severely disabled of mental patients, while private hospitals have tended to focus on patients who are somewhat less impaired (36). The failure of political activists and service planners, and even of practitioners, to make this distinction has resulted in some difficulties for general hospital psychiatry because it has confounded the problem of delimiting target populations. I shall return to this theme several times in the discussion that follows.

Having established that public and private hospitals are essentially different, I must also point out that, numerically, general hospital psychiatry is today increasingly dominated by the private sector. Between 1971 and 1975 there was a net increase of 5 percent in the number of additions (admissions plus returns from extended leave) to the psychiatric inpatient units of all general hospitals. This is a particularly deceptive summary statistic, however, because although additions to public hospital units *decreased* by 35 percent over this time period, those to private hospitals units *increased* by 32 percent (37). It appears that the private general hospital has become a focal point for the diminution of publicly provided psychiatric services (32). Nevertheless, except for the NIMH data, the literature contains only isolated acknowledgments of the distinctions in general hospital psychiatric service delivery in public versus private settings (38, 39).

Whatever the differences between public and private general hospital psychiatric services may be, they have one important problem in common: they are in trouble financially. In both cases there is competition for scarce funds both within the hospital and from outside third-party sources (40). Greenhill (6) wrote that 'there is probably no area of the economics of health care that is so poorly documented as cost–accounting for general-hospital psychiatric units.' In most states, third-party reimbursement rates are the same for psychiatric beds as for beds in other units, even though the latter, according to Greenhill, have 'become much more costly to maintain because of modern technology.' Psychiatric units must thus bear a portion of the extraordinary operating costs of medical/surgical and intensive care units.

In public general hospitals, the financial problems of psychiatric service delivery are not really separable from the greater survival problems of these facilities. Wolfe (41) sees these problems in the historical perspective of continuing undercapitalization of public health facilities. In many instances, public general hospitals must underwrite the costs of care for those 'who lack insurance and the means to pay their own bills' (42), and this is true for psychiatric (43) as well as other patients (44). In addition, public general hospital psychiatry is increasingly encumbered financially by the admission of patients who receive emergency psychiatric care in private hospitals and are subsequently transferred to public hospitals for more intensive treatment. For their part, the private hospitals very frequently have 'neither the financial resources nor the space to accommodate most of the medically indigent who frequent their emergency rooms' (43) and who represent fallout from the deinstitutionalization movement.

Issues in general hospital psychiatry

The decline of the public sector as the primary provider of psychiatric services resounds throughout the system and affects the delivery of services in all settings. Accordingly, general hospital psychiatry today shares a number of problems with the rest of psychiatry. Training issues and related funding problems, for example, affect psychiatry irrespective of service setting. However, there is a series of issues that general hospital psychiatry has to deal with and that have to do with the identity crisis that is uniquely its own. These issues fall into five rather broad categories.

First, there are problems of *boundaries*. What are, or should be, the limits of the responsibility of general hospital psychiatry? Here, not one but two sets of boundaries must be considered: 1) how general hospital psychiatry relates to the whole patchwork of services that make up the psychiatric service system and 2) its status within the more concrete sphere of a geographical entity known as the general hospital.

Second, there is a question of *target populations*. Who is, or should be, served by general hospital psychiatry? Another way of asking this question is by inquiring into the functions that general hospital psychiatry performs or is supposed to perform on behalf of patients.

Third, there is a problem of *appropriate service provision*. In what way or ways is the target population served? In what ways should it be served?

Fourth, what are, or should be, the physical boundaries or *structural characteristics* of psychiatric services within general hospitals? Are they, or should they be, segregated and specifically designated as psychiatric? Or are they, or should they be, integrated into other services without specific labeling?

Finally, how do, or should, all of these questions relate to the major social process affecting general hospital psychiatry today – *deinstitutionalization*?

It is immediately apparent that none of these issues is discrete and clean. Each of them is contaminated by the others, with the result that they can be separated only academically. Their discussion necessarily entails a great deal of overlap.

Boundaries

Within the psychiatric service system.   Goldman (36) conceptualized an ecological approach for understanding the array of facilities that make up the psychiatric service system. In this scheme, general hospitals, particularly with reference to their psychiatric inpatient capabilities, are cited

> for their special competence in acute care for voluntary (private sector) and involuntary (public sector) patients. . . . They are especially suited for this type of care because of their proximity to higher quality general medical and surgical services (for diagnosis, consultation, and treatment) and their affiliation with active emergency care departments.

As an integral and organic part of the community, the general hospital psychiatric service's boundaries in relation to the rest of the service system are defined both in terms of its functional relationship to other branches of medicine and its sociological complementarity to other community-based agencies. Thus the importance of general hospital psychiatry's proximity to other medical services is a recurrent theme in the literature (40, 45–50). Similarly, the qualities of comprehensiveness and continuity of care are also stressed in defining general hospital psychiatry's relationship to other service facilities (2, 6, 13, 46, 48, 51–54). Dressler and Fitzgibbons (47) pointed out that the general hospital is not only 'an established base for health care in the community,' but also, in many communities, 'the only available facility' in which psychiatric care can be provided.

Within the general hospital.   The territorial concerns of general hospital psychiatry, as pointed out in the earlier part of this paper, are two-pronged. In an excellent review article Greenhill (6) wrote that the general hospital's psychiatric unit,

> like Janus, must watch in both directions. On the one hand, it has its obligation to the large extramural community from which it receives

and to which it returns the mentally and emotionally ill, while on the other it has a responsibility to the inner community, the general hospital in which it resides.

Much of the literature concerning the relationship between psychiatry and the rest of the general hospital focuses on the care of chronic psychiatric patients, a situation that potentially increases psychiatry's visibility and emphasizes its differences from other medical specialties within the general hospital (6, 45, unpublished 1979 paper by Leeman). Flamm (52) cautioned that

> it becomes very important to . . . to be on guard against some growing efforts to convert general-hospital units into miniature state hospitals; such efforts are earmarked by recommendations to admit unmanageable, committed, and chronic patients for whose care we are neither structured nor equipped.

Although many share and endorse Flamm's point of view, the practitioners of general hospital psychiatry are by no means unanimous on this issue. The question of boundaries within the hospital, to the extent that it is dependent on whether chronic patients are to be admitted, remains very much unresolved.

Another area where the problem of boundaries within the hospital has surfaced concerns accreditation standards. As outlined in the Winter 1980 issue of the *Newsletter* of the American Association of General Hospital Psychiatrists, two basic approaches are currently being considered. Both have inherent problems, and both apparently require some compromises if they are to be made acceptable to a majority of psychiatrists practicing in general hospitals.

One approach, represented in the new 'consolidated standards' covering free-standing mental hospitals, substance abuse programs, and general hospital psychiatric inpatient units of more than a hundred beds, supports an effort to coordinate and integrate basic standards for psychiatric services and to reverse the trend of developing separate categorical program standards. The difficulty with this approach is that it emphasizes psychiatry's differences from the rest of medicine. It also plays down the uniqueness of the general hospital setting.

The second alternative favors application of regular general hospital standards, as contained in the manual of the Joint Commission on Accreditation of Hospitals, to psychiatric services.

The difficulty with this approach, of course, is its inattention to concerns that are basic to psychiatry.

Gould (55), a proponent of the consolidated approach, stated that the geographical location of a psychiatric program should not serve as a 'parameter' for deriving standards: 'It is my judgment that the consumer should not be the victim of chance and should be able to know that a single standard of care has been utilized whenever that care is from a JCAH accredited program.' Conversely, adoption of standards that would integrate psychiatric services into the mainstream of general hospital services is primarily supported by those who represent general hospitals at large. Flamm (56) wrote that this alternative might be made more attractive 'if the standards for general hospitals included some suggestions' mandating emergency room psychiatric care as well as consultation-liaison services.

Target population

There is considerable controversy over who 'rightfully' should be served by general hospital psychiatry, and much of the argument centers on patients who are involuntarily admitted to inpatient units and/or who are characterized by severe management problems (6, 52, 57, 58). The issue of target populations becomes critical in those instances where specific facilities – particularly private ones – are required by extrahospital forces to adapt their admission policies to include a previously unserved, and often unwanted, patient population. These facilities' spokespersons feel that they have had far too little say in determining policies that affect them profoundly.

Viewpoints concerning target populations tend to be extremely polarized and are characterized by persuasively worded arguments. Leeman, for example, asserted that 'therapeutic success' in a general hospital psychiatric inpatient program depends largely on 'the unit's ability to control who gets in,' and he concluded that the 'admission of a few involuntary patients can lead to the treatment of all as if they were involuntary patients' through destruction of the therapeutic milieu (unpublished 1979 paper).

By contrast, Becker (59) wrote that 'the involuntarily committed patient can be treated within the general hospital without disruption of its therapeutic milieu.' In fact, Becker went so far as to say that when the general hospital psychiatric inpatient unit is 'unwilling to accept the involuntarily hospitalized patient, is unwilling in many cases to accept the indigent patient, feels incapable of managing the disruptive, aggressive, or acutely suicidal patient . . . it is failing to serve the psychiatric needs of an appreciable segment of the community.'

This controversy frequently, but not necessarily, results from a failure to distinguish between public and private hospital general psychiatry. Psychiatrists in public hospital programs appear generally to accept the hospital's role in treating involuntary and unmanageable patients. Thus Robbins and associates (22) characterized the service population of a public general receiving hospital as consisting of those patients who are 'too disturbed to be treated safely, who may not be responsive to therapy, and for whom "no bed is available" ' at other hospitals in the community. Similarly, an article in the *New York Times* (60) describes a public general hospital that admits psychiatric patients whom 'other hospitals choose not to admit because, in an official's words, it is a "hospital of last resort," a psychiatric dumping ground for the mentally ill.'

In actual practice, both public and private general hospital psychiatric services are used by people with a wide range of disorders. Who is served where depends in large measure on historical patterns of service delivery in a given community, on what other facilities are available to patients, and on what requirements are imposed by external policy-making bodies that exercise control over hospital procedures (51).

Appropriate service provision

Although general hospitals provide a variety of psychiatric services ranging from education, training, and community consultation to direct patient care, the major services discussed in the current literature are 1) inpatient care, particularly of a short-term nature, to people with both acute-onset illness and chronic disabilities, 2) outpatient care, 3) emergency services, and 4) consultation and liaison services.

Inpatient care. Of the direct services to psychiatric patients provided in general hospital settings, inpatient care is by far the most widespread. As noted previously in this paper, inpatient psychiatric care is more often dispersed throughout the medical/surgical wards than it is provided in specially designated units. However, literature dealing with inpatient general hospital psychiatry typically refers to segregated units, as do nearly all available statistics. This bias should be understood because it affects the discussion that follows.

Of the 870 general hospitals that NIMH reports as having separate psychiatric services, 791 (90 percent) provide inpatient care (31). The total number of days of care in psychiatric inpatient units of general hospitals increased by 11 percent between 1971 and 1975, even though psychiatric inpatient care in the nation is generally declining (31).

Outpatient care. Often overlooked as a major modality among psychiatric services, the general-hospital-based psychiatric outpatient clinic nevertheless provides a considerable amount of care. More than one-third of all general hospitals that NIMH reports as having separate psychiatric services – a total of 303 hospitals – provide outpatient psychiatric care (31).

There is a distinct paucity of literature dealing with the provision of psychiatric outpatient services in general hospitals, although local statistical reports containing relevant information occasionally appear (2). This general absence of journal literature is interesting in view of the fact that continuity of care is emphasized so strongly by service planners and providers. This very important element in the continuum of community-based services does not, for some reason, emerge as a proper focus for investigation or analysis. Two possible explanations present themselves. Either the importance of outpatient care in the spectrum of psychiatric services is seriously overlooked, or else the service providers are too deeply involved in clinical and/ or administrative responsibilities to take the time to write about them.

Emergency services. If general hospital psychiatric outpatient services are largely overlooked in the literature, quite the opposite is true of emergency services. Indeed, the literature on emergency psychiatric services in general hospitals is so rich that it deserves to be reviewed thoroughly and independently and not simply as one element in an overview of general hospital psychiatry (61, 62).

The literature on emergency services abounds with penetrating discussions of the changing role and functions of psychiatric services in general hospitals, and of the relationship of the psychiatric emergency ward to other divisions of the hospital and to the community at large. Bassuk and Gerson (61) wrote that general hospital emergency psychiatry 'occupies a unique position. It faces the difficult task of reconciling community needs with traditional organizational structures.'

Nationally, about one-half – an estimated 435 – of the general hospitals with separate psychiatric services list emergency care as a modality (31). Specific hospital-based psychiatric emergency services include walk-in clinics, telephone crisis services, suicide prevention centers, and home visit programs. In general, the availability of psychiatric emergency services in general hospitals is correlated with the bed-size of the psychiatric inpatient unit. The larger the inpatient unit, the more likely the hospital is to provide emergency care (63).

A number of general hospital emergency psychiatry studies show considerable methodological and conceptual sophistication. What is most striking about this corpus of literature is the distinctly socio-logical slant that pervades it (61, 62). Those who analyze emergency psychiatric services in general hospitals are concerned with such continuity of care issues as 1) patient characteristics and other circumstances that lead individuals to seek help in emergency wards (64–67), 2) patient and therapist variables influencing the transfer of psychiatric emergency patients to other programs in and out of the hospital (61, 62, 68–71), and 3) factors affecting compliance with psychiatric emergency service treatment recommendations and refer-rals (61, 65, 71).

Consultation and liaison services.   General hospital consultation-liaison psychiatry, like emergency psychiatry, is the subject of numerous investigations and theoretical articles. Although some studies (72, 73) deal with patients' reactions to psychiatric consul-tations, this body of literature is primarily concerned with consul-tation-liaison's raison d'être: the collaboration between psychiatry and other medical disciplines within the hospital setting. In this broad context, the consultation-liaison literature appears to focus on several major categories of questions.

One portion of the literature is concerned with the overlap of psychiatric and nonpsychiatric medical disabilities among general hospital patients, the differential diagnosis of these disorders, and/ or appropriate treatment of patients with multiple disabilities (50, 74–77). Another portion concerns the functional relationships of this subspecialty to other departments within the hospital (53, 64, 74,

78–83). Still another segment of consultation-liaison literature is conceptual in nature and focuses on possible explanations for the resistances of nonpsychiatric physicians to psychiatry and psychiatric consultations (53, 80, 84–87).

Structural characteristics

There are strongly opposing views as to the desirability of specifically labeling psychiatric services in general hospitals instead of leaving them undesignated and integrating them into the rest of the hospital's activities. This issue, which is felt primarily in the areas of inpatient and emergency care, evokes considerable partisanship. Describing the situation in some rural communities, for example, Werner and associates (23) indicated that, in many small rural hospitals, 'there are insufficient numbers of patients to require a psychiatric unit, and there are not enough funds to establish and staff one.' Moreover, these authors asserted, 'in small communities, specific advantages to using the nonsegregated approach exist aside from the economic one. The general hospital floors are well known to patients and their families who often have been confined there for medical, surgical and obstetrical needs' and thus are perceived as being 'less stigmatizing' than separate units. Other writers have presented similar arguments favoring nonsegregation of psychiatric patients (46, 54).

In describing a serendipitous variant of unsegregated care, Breen (88) wrote of a general hospital where an outbreak of influenza forced the placement of medical/surgical patients in a designated psychiatric ward. This resulted in a number of apparent advantages to both patients and staff. For example, medical/surgical patients in this setting 'experienced the novelty not only of staff talking to them about their illnesses but of being able to discuss personal problems as well.' From the nonpsychiatric physicians' point of view, the high quality of the nursing staff emerged as an asset.

It appears that the 'right' answer to the controversy over designated versus undesignated units is largely a matter of cultural relevance: a hospital must do what is appropriate in and for its own community. What is appropriate for one community may, potentially, be entirely out of place in another. Whether or not psychiatry wishes to establish itself separately within the hospital depends to a considerable extent on practitioners' perceptions of what conditions are best suited for the delivery of effective services in a given community and of what that community's tolerance limits are.

Deinstitutionalization

Throughout the preceding discussion, the effects of deinstitutionalization on general hospital psychiatry have been apparent. Greenhill (6) summarized this issue when he asserted that the psychiatric unit in the general hospital is the 'core service to succeed the state hospital.' That deinstitutionalization is a critical element affecting the delivery of psychiatric services in general hospitals appears to be an incontrovertible fact, even though it is frequently overlooked. Although community mental health centers have defined for themselves a broad role in which services to chronic patients play only a part of total services – in some specific cases, a minor part (89, 90) – the role of general hospital psychiatry has been increasingly determined by state hospital population shifts. It is very probable that general hospitals are providing the bulk of community-based psychiatric inpatient care for state hospital dischargees and other chronically ill individuals who are effectively barred from state hospital admission by deinstitutionalization policies (37).

Moreover, it is possible that we have seen only the tip of the iceberg regarding the effects of deinstitutionalization on general hospital psychiatry. Bassuk (91) reported a substantial discrepancy between the time of initiation of a state hospital's depopulation practices and a visible increase in the use of a local private hospital psychiatric emergency service by people diagnosed with chronic psychotic disorders. In speculating on this time lag, Bassuk suggested that it may 'reflect the period required for dissolution of the patient's relationship with his support system, which may contribute to a recurrence of his psychotic illness.' To the extent that Bassuk's findings are generalizable, it is possible that we do not yet know the dimensions of deinstitutionalization's influence on general hospital psychiatric service delivery.

The inclusion of the most severely disturbed psychotic patients in general hospital psychiatric inpatient programs, as suggested earlier in this paper, is viewed positively by a number of psychiatrists, who perceive this trend as a challenge and a source of revitalization of their programs (8, 9, 59, 92, 93). Whatever one's view, it is evident that what Talbott (1) referred to as the problem of 'chronicizing' general hospital psychiatric inpatient services is occurring. A news story in the *Washington Post* (94) refers to 'mental patients [who are] inappropriately placed in the acute care hospital [and who] cause disturbances and are hard to manage.'

Emergency psychiatric services in the general hospital setting are also profoundly affected by deinstitutionalization. Because of deinstitutionalization, the general hospital emergency room has in some instances become a substitute for the state hospital. The elemental horror that this kind of situation has at times produced is epitomized in a simple statement in a 1979 newspaper account: 'Yesterday the hospital was attempting to relieve its overcrowding by discharging those judged to be least sick – a form of psychiatric triage that was being performed in the emergency room, where only patients who appear to be a danger to themselves or others are admitted' (60).

It seems clear that the inclusion of programs for chronic mental patients in general hospitals is most effective when those facilities have had a say in the matter and have been accorded resources and time sufficient for planning the effective integration of this new patient population. There are reports in the literature of slow but certain success in such planning efforts. Cotton and associates (8), for example, described a carefully planned program, with changes in treatment procedures and intensive staff training, to accommodate the flow of chronic patients into their hospital's inpatient unit.

Conversely, the literature suggests that there is confusion, resentment, and deterioration of services when admission of this patient population is forced. It is difficult to imagine successful general hospital treatment programs for chronic mental patients – or for any other patients – in the absence of consensus from the agency that delivers services.

Conclusions

I introduced this paper with a conceptualization of the sources of change that have been influencing the course of general hospital psychiatry in recent years. These may be summarized as changes generated by the hospital itself, by the authorities or auspices controlling the hospital, by trends in the greater service delivery system, and by shifts in societal values that redirect priorities in patient care.

It is clear that decisions concerning the major issues affecting general hospital psychiatry today – what services are provided to whom in what parts of the hospital – are frequently handed down. Psychiatry in general hospitals is thus often placed in a reactive, rather than a proactive, position in the determination of policy. General hospital psychiatry's current identity crisis is at least in part exacerbated by this necessity to conform to policies that originate at varying distances from day-to-day hospital operations (95–97).

In contradistinction to this reality, there is extensive document-ation – as indicated in the foregoing discussion – for the notion that programs in general hospital psychiatry are most likely to be effective when they are directly responsive to local needs. A report of the Massachusetts Hospital Association (2) cautions,

> To serve as an essential resource, the hospital must initiate the planning, development and administration of comprehensive services. In accepting its responsibility in the area of community mental health services, the hospital should carefully consider, and then define, its own role in the delivery of services. (p. 7)

This is surely a dilemma. General hospital psychiatry is supposed to be in tune with its own culture base, but its ability to do this is increasingly diluted by external directives. Planning that originates within the hospital structure – and, more specifically, with the psychi-atric staff – has the best potential for being culturally relevant, but planning that comes from extrahospital initiatives is also needed if the general hospital is to be functionally linked with other facilities within the psychiatric service network.

It is essential that general hospital psychiatry look toward developing skills that will enable it to maintain its integrity while it participates as a partner in the service system. A process of nego-tiated interfacility planning, with give and take, is prerequisite to delineating the role of the general hospital in the psychiatric service system (98). Because some general hospital planning will necessarily be generated outside the hospital, it is important that all changes be filtered through the hospital's internal decision-making process in order to reinforce a 'bottom-up' as opposed to a 'top-down' emphasis in planning.

References

1 Talbott J. A.: *The Death of the Asylum: A Critical Study of State Hospital Management, Services, and Care.* New York, Grune & Stratton, 1978.

2 Report of the Task Force on Psychiatric Services. Boston, Massachusetts Hospital Association, 1978.

3 Report of the Task Force on Standards and Criteria for Acute Inpatient Units. Boston, Massachusetts Psychiatric Society, 1979.

4 Occupancy Trends, Psychiatric Inpatient Services, 1971–1975: Memorandum 19. Rockville, Md, National Institute of Mental Health Division of Biometry and Epidemiology, Oct 7, 1977.

5 Trends in Length of Stay in General Hospital Psychiatric Inpatient Units, 1971 and 1975: Memorandum 15. Rockville Md, National Institute of Mental Health Division of Biometry and Epidemiology, Sept 9, 1977.

6 Greenhill M. H.: Psychiatric units in general hospitals: 1979. *Hosp. Community Psychiatry* 30: 169–182, 1979.

7 Collins G. B., Barth J.: Using the resources of AA in treating alcoholics in a general hospital. *Hosp. Community Psychiatry* 30: 480–482, 1979.

8 Cotton P. G., Bene-Kociemba A., Cole R.: The effect of deinstitutionalization on a general hospital's inpatient psychiatric service. *Hosp. Community Psychiatry* 30: 609–612, 1979.

9 Egri G.: A general hospital model, in *Chronic Mental Patients: Treatment, Programs, Systems.* Edited by Talbott J. A. New York, Human Sciences Press (in press).

10 Harbin H. T.: A family-oriented psychiatric inpatient unit. *Fam. Process* 18: 281–291, 1979.

11 Morgan C. D., Kremer E., Gaylor M.: The behavioral medicine unit: a new facility. *Compr. Psychiatry* 20: 79–89, 1979.

12 Schwab P. J., Lahmeyer C. B.: The uses of seclusion on a general hospital psychiatric unit. *J. Clin. Psychiatry* 40: 228–231, 1979.

13 Herz M. I.: Short-term hospitalization and the medical model. *Hosp. Community Psychiatry* 30: 117–121, 1979.

14 Rhine M. W., Mayerson P.: Crisis hospitalization within a psychiatric emergency service. *Am. J. Psychiatry* 127: 1386–1381, 1971.

15 Schwartz D.: A non-hospital in a hospital. *Am. J. Public Health* 61: 2376–2382, 1971.

16 Schwartz D. A., Weiss A. T., Miner J. M.: Community psychiatry and emergency service. *Am. J. Psychiatry* 129: 710–715, 1972.

17 Spaulding R. C., Edwards D., Fichman S.: The effect of psychiatric hospitalization in crisis. *Compr. Psychiatry* 17: 457–460, 1976.

18 Vonbrauchitsch H., Mueller K.: The impact of a walk-in clinic on a general hospital psychiatric service. *Hosp. Community Psychiatry* 24: 476–479, 1973.

19 Walker W. R., Parsons L. B., Skelton W. D.: Brief hospitalization on a crisis service: A study of patient and treatment variables. *Am. J. Psychiatry* 130: 896–900, 1973.

20 Dilts S. L., Berns B. R., Casper E.: The alcohol emergency room in a general

hospital: A model for crisis intervention. *Hosp. Community Psychiatry* 29: 795–796, 1978.

21 Karasu T. B., Rohrlich J. B., Stein S.: A model for individual supervision in a general hospital. *Compr. Psychiatry* 19: 323–329, 1978.

22 Robbins E. S., Hanin E., Moore A., *et al.*: Transfers to a psychiatric emergency room: A fresh look at the dumping syndrome. *Psychiatr. Q.* 49: 197–203, 1977.

23 Werner A., Knarr F. A., Stack J. M.: Psychiatric services in a rural general hospital. *Int. J. Psychiatry Med.* 8: 25–34, 1977–1978.

24 Lauer J. W.: Some demographic characteristics of a psychiatric inpatient unit in an urban general hospital. *IMJ* 152: 212–218, 1977.

25 Dimsdale J. E., Klerman G., Shershow J. C.: Conflict in treatment goals between patients and staff. *Social Psychiatry* 14: 1–4, 1979.

26 Greden J. F., Brandow M., Burpee C., *et al.*: Interdisciplinary differences on a general hospital psychiatry unit. *Gen. Hosp. Psychiatry* 1: 91–97, 1979.

27 Spencer J. H., Mattson M. R.: Utilization review and resident education. *Hosp. Community Psychiatry* 30: 269–272. 1979.

28 Taylor M. A., Abrams R.: The prevalence of schizophrenia: A reassessment using modern diagnostic criteria. *Am. J. Psychiatry* 135: 945–948, 1250, 1978.

29 American Hospital Association: Hospital Statistics, 1978. Chicago, AHA, 1978.

30 57,538 Inpatient Beds in Psychiatric Services in 1,087 General Hospitals. Washington, DC, National Association of State Mental Health Program Directors, Feb. 1979.

31 Taube C. A., Regier D. A., Rosenfeld A. H.: Mental disorders in Health, United States 1978. Hyattsville, Md, National Center for Health Statistics, 1978.

32 Bachrach L. L.: Utilization of Services in Organized Mental Health Settings in the United States: Staff Document. Washington, DC, President's Commission on Mental Health, Jan. 5, 1978.

33 Memorandum: Statistical Note 14. Baltimore, Md, State of Maryland Department of Health and Mental Hygiene, Maryland Center for Health Statistics, Sept. 26, 1979.

34 Faden V. B.: Primary Diagnosis of Discharges from Non-Federal General Hospital Psychiatric Inpatient Units, United States, 1975. *Ment. Health Stat. Note* 137, Aug 1977.

35 Expected Principal Source of Payment for Admissions to Selected Mental Health Facilities: Memorandum 17. Rockville, Md, National Institute of Mental Health Division of Biometry and Epidemiology, Sept. 23, 1977.

36 Goldman H. H.: Functional Analysis of Inpatient Psychiatric Units. Rockville, Md, National Institute of Mental Health, 1979.

37 Bachrach L. L.: General hospitals taking greater role in providing services for chronic patients (ltr to ed). *Hosp. Community Psychiatry* 30: 448, 1979.

38 Fowler D. R., Mayfield D. G.: Psychiatric hospitalization, I: Comparison of public and private delivery systems. *Dis. Nerv. Syst.* 38: 314–317, 1977.

39 Mayfield D. G., Fowler D. R.: Psychiatric hospitalization, II: Effect of social class and delivery systems. *Dis. Nerv. Syst.* 38: 320–323, 1977.

40 Sanders C. A.: Reflections on psychiatry in the general-hospital setting. *Hosp. Community Psychiatry* 30: 185–189, 1979.

41 Wolfe S.: Public hospitals caught up in discrimination. *Nation's Health*, April 1979, p. 7.

42 A new remedy for ailing hospitals. *New York Times*, Dec. 4, 1979, p. A26.

43 Katz S. E., Robbins E. S., Sabatini A.: Letter. *New York Times*, Jan. 6, 1979, p. 18.

44 Pomrinse S. D.: Letter. *New York Times*, Oct. 29, 1979.

45 Benson R.: The function of a psychiatric unit in a general hospital: a five year experience. *Dis. Nerv. Syst.* 37: 573–577, 1976.

46 Bey D. R., Chapman R. E., Kooker R., *et al*:. The normal treatment of chronic mental patients, in *Chronic Mental Patients: Treatment, Programs, Systems*. Edited by Talbott J. A. New York, Human Sciences Press (in press).

47 Dressler D. M., Fitzgibbons D. I.: The general hospital as a center for mental health services. *Conn. Med.* 40: 407–409, 1976.

48 Gaver K. D.: Considerations in providing psychiatric services in general hospitals. *Hosp. Community Psychiatry* 24: 252–253, 1973.

49 Slaby A. E.: Residents' Forum. *Psychiatric News*, Nov. 2, 1979, p. 14.

50 Weddige R. L.: Psychiatric consultation on medical-surgical wards. *Hosp. Community Psychiatry* 30: 377–378, 1979.

51 Bachrach L. L.: Psychiatric Bed Needs, an Analytical Review: Series D, Number 2. Rockville, Md, National Institute of Mental Health, 1975.

52 Flamm G. H.: The expanding roles of general-hospital psychiatry. *Hosp. Community Psychiatry* 30: 190–192, 1979.

53 Lipowski S. I.: Consultation-liaison psychiatry: past failures and new opportunities. *Gen. Hosp. Psychiatry* 1: 3–10, 1979.

54 Reding G. R., Maguire B.: Nonsegregated acute psychiatric admissions to general hospitals – continuity of care within the community hospital. *N. Engl. J. Med.* 289: 185–189, 1973.

55 Gould M.: Opinion 1: JCAH standards for general hospital psychiatry. *Newsletter of the American Association of General Hospital Psychiatrists*, Winter 1980, pp. 1–2.

56 Flamm G. H.: Summary of progress. *Newsletter of the American Association of General Hospital Psychiatrists*, Winter 1980, pp. 3–5.

57 Leeman C. P.: Involuntary admissions to general hospitals: Progress or threat? *Hosp. Community Psychiatry* 31: 315–318, 1980.

58 Leeman C. P., Brownsberger C., Carmichael W., *et al.*: Inadequacy of institutional psychiatric care (ltr to ed). *N. Engl. J. Med.* 294: 1067–1068, 1976.

59 Becker A.: Inadequacy of institutional psychiatric care (ltr to ed). *N. Engl. J. Med.* 294: 1068, 1976.

60 Sullivan R.: Hospital forced to oust patients with psychoses. *New York Times*, Nov 8, 1979, p. B3.

61 Bassuk E. L., Gerson S.: Into the breach: Emergency psychiatry in the general hospital. *Gen. Hosp. Psychiatry* 1: 31–45, 1979.

62 Gerson S., Bassuk E. L.: Psychiatric emergencies: An overview. *Am. J. Psychiatry* 137: 1–11, 1980.

63 Witkin M. J.: Emergency Services in Psychiatric Facilities, United States, January 1976. *Ment. Health Stat. Note* 136, July 1977.

64 Bartolucci G., Drayer C. S.: An overview of crisis intervention in the emergency rooms of general hospitals. *Am. J. Psychiatry* 130: 953–960, 1973.

65 Craig T. J., Huffine C. L.: Completion referral to psychiatric services by inner city residents. *Arch. Gen. Psychiatry* 31: 353–357, 1974.
66 Skodol A. E., Kass F., Charles E.: Crisis in psychotherapy: Principles of emergency consultation and intervention. *Am. J. Orthopsychiatry* 49: 585–597, 1979.
67 Summers W. K., Rund D. A., Levin M.: Psychiatric illness in a general urban emergency room: Daytime versus nighttime population. *J. Clin. Psychiatry* 40: 340–343, 1979.
68 Baxter S., Chodorkoff B., Underhill R.: Psychiatric emergencies: Dispositional determinants and the validity of the decision to admit. *Am. J. Psychiatry* 124: 1542–1546, 1968.
69 Feigelson E. B., Davis E. B., Mackinnon R., *et al.*: The decision to hospitalize. *Am. J. Psychiatry* 135: 354–357, 1978.
70 Hanson G. D., Babigian H. M.: Reasons for hospitalization from a psychiatric emergency service. *Psychiatr. Q.* 48: 336–351, 1974.
71 Jellinek M.: Referrals from a psychiatric emergency room: Relationship of compliance to demographic and interview variables. *Am. J. Psychiatry* 135: 209–213, 1978.
72 Koran I. M., Van Natta J., Stephens J. R., *et al.*: Patients' reactions to psychiatric consultation. *JAMA* 241: 1603–1605, 1979.
73 Schwab J. J.: Evaluating psychiatric consultation work. *Psychosomatics* 8: 309–317, 1967.
74 Hall R. C., Popkin M. K., Devaul R. A., *et al.*: Physical illness presenting as psychiatric disease. *Arch. Gen. Psychiatry* 35: 1315–1320, 1978.
75 Lipowski S. J.: Review of consultation psychiatry and psychosomatic medicine, III: Theoretical issues. *Psychosom. Med.* 30: 395–422, 1968.
76 Tuason V. B., Rhee Y. W.: Psychiatric disorders in patients of a general hospital. *South Med. J.* 65: 408–412, 1972.
77 Shevitz S. A., Silberfarb P. M., Lipowski Z. J.: Psychiatric consultations in a general hospital: A report on 1,000 referrals. *Dis. Nerv. Syst.* 27: 295–300, 1976.
78 Beresford T. P.: Alcoholism consultation and general hospital psychiatry. *Gen. Hosp. Psychiatry* 1: 293–300, 1979.
79 Guggenheim F. G.: A marketplace model of consultation psychiatry in the general hospital. *Am. J. Psychiatry* 135: 1380–1383, 1978.
80 Kramer B. A., Spikes J., Strain J. J.: The effects of a psychiatric liaison program on the utilization of psychiatric consultations: an evaluation by chart audit. *Gen. Hosp. Psychiatry* 1: 122–128, 1979.
81 Lipowski Z. J.: Consultation-liaison psychiatry: An overview. *Am. J. Psychiatry* 131: 623–630, 1974.
82 Romano J.: Chierurgions ought to be wyse, gentyll and sober: Part 2 (Andrew Boorde, 1547). *Contemporary Surgery* 15: 42–57, 1979.
83 Wellisch D. K., Pasnau R. O.: Psychology interns on a consultation-liaison service. *Gen. Hosp. Psychiatry* 1: 287–292, 1979.
84 Billowitz A., Friedson W.: Are psychiatric consultants' recommendations followed? *Int. J. Psychiatry Med.* 9: 179–189, 1978–1979.
85 Bloomberg S.: Problems associated with the introduction of a psychiatric unit into a rural general hospital. *Am. J. Psychiatry* 130: 28–31, 1973.

86 Gurian H.: A decade in rural psychiatry. *Hosp. Community Psychiatry* 22: 56–58, 1971.

87 Sasser M., Kinzie J. D.: Evaluation of medical-psychiatric consultation. *Int. J. Psychiatry Med.* 9: 123–134, 1978–1979.

88 Breen H.: The benefits of placing medical-surgical patients on a psychiatric ward. *Hosp. Community Psychiatry* 30: 634–635, 1979.

89 Borus J. F. Issues critical to the survival of community mental health. *Am. J. Psychiatry* 135: 1029–1035, 1978.

90 Zusman J., Lamb H. R.: In defense of community mental health. *Am. J. Psychiatry* 134: 887–890, 1977.

91 Bassuk E. L.: The impact of deinstitutionalization on the general hospital psychiatric emergency ward. *Hosp. Community Psychiatry* 31: 623–627, 1980.

92 Meyerson A. T.: What are the barriers or obstacles to treatment and care of the chronically disabled mentally ill? in *The Chronic Mental Patient*. Edited by Talbott J. A., Washington, DC, American Psychiatric Association, 1978.

93 Smith C. M., McKerracher D. G.: The comprehensive psychiatric unit in the general hospital. *Am. J. Psychiatry* 121: 52–57, 1964.

94 Colen B. D.: Castoffs: DC General upset it is shelter of last resort. *Washington Post*, Jan. 22, 1979, p. C1.

95 Greenblatt M.: Special problems facing the psychiatrist-administrator. *Hosp. Community Psychiatry* 30: 760–762, 1979.

96 MacStravic R. E.: Inpatient bed needs for psychiatric care. *Adm. Ment. Health* 5: 14–20, 1977.

97 Pierce C. F.: Hospitals' future depends upon long-range planning. *Hospitals* 53: 80–86, 1979.

98 Bachrach L. L.: Developing objectives in community mental health planning. *Am. J. Public Health* 64: 1162–1163, 1974.

CHAPTER 7

Community control or control of the community? The case of the community mental health center*†

Alberta J. Nassi

Medical and mental health care in the United States is in a state of crisis
and a process of change. The crisis is the accumulation of urgent needs,
cost escalation, shortage of personnel, and a rapidly growing
dissatisfaction among most consumers with the prices and practices of
care-giving institutions and individuals. At the same time, the winds of
change, stirred by the deep and underlying crisis, have swept through
the nation's urban centers and inner cities during a decade of federal
attempts to restructure and modify some of the institutional bases of
social services, medical, and mental health care. One of the focal points,
of both progress and protracted conflict, has been the issue of consumer
participation and control. (Roman and Schmais, 1972, p. 63)

If mental health care is in 'crisis' now, then it was in crisis twenty,
fifty, and over a hundred years ago as well. The annals of American
psychiatry and psychology reveal that the solutions considered most
progressive today have emerged and disappeared over and over in
the past. For example, the Association of Medical Superintendents
in 1864 and Adolph Meyer in 1909 formulated plans that closely
approximate the pattern of a catchment area served by a comprehen-

* The author assumes all responsibility for the viewpoints expressed in this paper,
but wishes to thank Stephen I. Abramowitz, Carlyle Folkins, and Larry D. Trujillo
for their thoughtful and detailed comments on an earlier draft. This paper was
presented at the meeting of the Western Psychological Association, Los Angeles,
April, 1976.
† Reprinted from *Journal of Community Psychology*, vol. 6, pp. 3–15, 1978, with
permission of the author and of the publisher, Clinical Psychology Publishing Co.

sive network of local facilities (Caplan, 1969). Indeed, even the notion of community involvement put forth by Adolph Meyer echoed the prescriptions of reformers earlier in the nineteenth century. Alford (1975) has argued that crises are usually creations of special interest groups seeking to make political capital out of a situation that has existed for many years and will continue to exist after the 'crisis' has disappeared from public view. In this light, the popular idea of community control in the community mental health movement may be employed by professionals and government bureaucrats to promote program funding and community acceptance of a large-scale federal project.

Citizen participation in the planning of health and welfare services has historical precedence. Until recently, control of voluntary hospitals or voluntary health agencies by boards of trustees, or control of official health departments by boards of health has not been questioned. Similarly, in the mental health field itself, there is almost a half century history of citizen participation built around volunteer programs of ward visits, financial support, and auxiliary aid. The major criteria have been civic leadership, wealth, and both the desire and the leisure to contribute time freely.

The noncontroversial nature of community participation by the wealthy is to be contrasted with the highly controversial nature of participation by the greater community to include the poor and ethnic minorities. A few crises have been precipitated moving outside the established framework of representation and influence to take disruptive, militant action. These actions have produced responses, usually in the form of 'new' programs or still more 'representation,' that maintain the traditional hierarchy (Alford, 1975).

This article is aimed at clarifying the concept of community control, raising the major issues surrounding it, and considering the varying degrees of control found in community mental health centers as reported in the literature. Toward those ends, the discussion is organized as follows: (a) Review of some community participation precedents in health and welfare services; (b) Distinction of the differences among community involvement, participation, and control and their corresponding ideologies; (c) Presentation of excerpts from case studies of community mental health boards; (d) Consideration of such major obstacles to community control as professionalism, prevailing mental health ideology, and the local mental health power structure; (e) Elaboration of the contradictory potentials within the community control proposition – demonstrated concretely in the case of consumer-worker control of health services in Chile during Salvador Allende's tenure.

Community participation as public policy
Neighborhood health centers

Community participation as a formal policy issue in health care had its origins in the neighborhood health centers of 1900–1930 (Stoeckle and Candib, 1969). The four concepts that dominated the health center movement at that time were district location, community participation, bureaucratic organization, and preventive care – strikingly similar to the major concerns of community mental health today.

The early health center period was characterized by substantial divergence of opinion with respect to the criteria for community participation. One definition was simply the utilization of services by residents. However, in 1915, Wilbur Phillips elaborated the 'social unit,' a complex plan of community participation for the actual governance of the health center and other community services (Stoeckle and Candib, 1969). Neighborhood residents, chosen on the basis of the block in which they lived, and advisors from the district, chosen on the basis of their occupation, composed part of the managing board of the unit and its health center. Since civic participation was considered to be minimal in lower-class communities, the health agency was conceptualized as a catalyst for its development. The outcome could be twofold: an enhanced sense of community and maximized use of health services. Participation itself was thought to be indicative of community health.

However, not every health center was designed for democratic participation. Most centers were bureaucratically run by municipal health departments and voluntary agencies. Innovative as Phillips's endeavors were, they were also shortlived, not from lack of neighborhood participation, but because they lacked political support within the municipal government and aroused public suspicions that the social unit might really be socialistic. Furthermore, simultaneous pressures for efficiency in bureaucratic organization often conflicted with the goal of community participation.

Although most of the ideas that underlie the recent development of community participation in health care have roots in the reform movement of the Progressive Era, many of them were not applied on a large scale until the 1960s. This may have been partly a reflection of the relatively quiescent political situation in the United States during the 1940s and 50s, when World War II and the post-war prosperity minimized domestic debate. During the past decade, however, a number of federal programs brought the issue of community participation in health and welfare services to national attention.

War on poverty

The Economic Opportunity Act of 1964 was the first piece of federal legislation specifically to mandate 'maximum feasible participation by the poor' (Notkin and Notkin, 1970). Although this mandate was not defined in a precise manner, a planning and programming environment was created in which the groups served could in principle, if not always in fact, play a decision-making role. The supporting documents and memoranda intended to implement this principle of consumer participation, however, were issued with a substantial volume of conflicting instructions, lack of precision as to purpose, and residual evidence of the traditional social service or 'welfare colonialism' (Alinsky, 1965). The commitment behind the legislation was sharply questioned by critics (Alinsky, 1965; Moynihan, 1969). Kosa (1969) noted that the Anti-Poverty Act allowed for the development of three alternative versions of participatory democracy: (a) containment, or confinement of the poor to essentially meaningless decision making; (b) co-optation, or luring the poor into voting as elitist members would have them vote; and rarely (c) co-determination, or the independent and self-interested action of the poor in public affairs.

Community participation and control in mental health

Community mental health boards were neither required by the Community Mental Health Centers Act of 1963 nor defined by federal regulations, although in the late 1960s the National Institute of Mental Health (NIMH) began to urge 'citizen participation' in the planning, decision making, and priority setting of community mental health programs (Chu and Trotter, 1974). The National Institute of Mental Health Policy and Standards Manual requires mental health agencies to 'involve the community in the planning, development, and operation of the program' (Feldman, 1973, p. 225). However, the guidelines further state that 'the exact form such involvement takes will vary from one center to another – may be formal or informal, and may include representation on policy and advisory boards' (Feldman, 1973, p. 225).

Professional organizations also have issued policy statements on community control. For example, the official position paper of the American Psychological Association read:

> For the comprehensive community mental health center to become an effective agency of the community, community control of center policy is essential. . . . The more closely the proposed centers become integrated with the life and institutions of their communities, the less the community can afford to turn over to mental health professionals its responsibility for guiding the center's policies. (Smith and Hobbs, 1966, pp. 500–501)

The meaning of community control
Definitions

The true meaning of community control has been diluted in the community mental health literature through interchangeable usage with the concepts of community involvement and participation. The distinction here is not merely semantic, but rather a real one between passive involvement, participation, and power. Geiger (1967) speaks to the same issue in referring to programs 'of the poor, by the poor, or for the poor.' Similarly, Holton, New, and Hessler (1973) have articulated three general models of citizen participation in community mental health: elitist, advisory, and consumer control. A brief review of these prototypes will be helpful in distinguishing the differences in meaning and their implications for the formation and functioning of community boards.

Community involvement.   Programs 'for the poor' reflect the classic public welfare formulation (cf. Wilensky and Lebeaux, 1965). This is an inherently elitist model, whereby community leaders and resident volunteers serve on boards largely for purposes of money raising, public relations, and image building. The board is not concerned with representing the interests of prospective clients, and professional delivery of services is seldom influenced. Involvement exists to the extent of professional tolerance. The composition of the board is usually reflective of the local power structure, and there is little tension between professionals and volunteers over preserving a public front. The professionals are most comfortable working with middle-class people and tend to fear local militancy, so that the board members are often handpicked by the program directors.

Community participation. Programs 'by the poor' characterize the advisory model – following the antipoverty legislation – which emphasized 'maximum feasible participation' by the target population in the implementation of services. These programs sometimes provide a 'share' of control, policy, and decision making, but questions of what is 'maximum,' what is 'feasible,' and what constitutes 'participation' are usually left in the hands of administrators (Geiger, 1967). The term 'advisory' is symbolic of the general powerlessness of this board. Indeed, the description of the local citizen's advisory board in the California Mental Health Services Act (1974) underscores this powerlessness: 'In general, each board functions to lend a helping hand in the overall planning and development of its community's mental health effort' (p. 7).

Community control. The third framework is 'programs of the poor, implying not merely participation but control and power – the real social power that comes from choice of programs and from control of money and jobs' (Geiger, 1967, p. 55). The consumer control model is the hardest of the generic concepts to define because of its far-reaching implications. Kunnes (1972) writes:

> Community control must be seen in its broadest sense, namely that in which a community itself controls and determines the political, social and economic realities of the community. . . . A community-controlled community will attempt to integrate all services into a human services network, including community-controlled schools, fire departments, and police (p. 43).

More specifically, one community included among its demands for community control of health care services (Kunnes, 1970): (a) total self-determination in health care planning for services and facilities through an incorporated community staff governing board: (b) removal of all outside-appointed administrators and staff working in the community; (c) immediate cessation of health care facility construction – pending review by a community-appointed review board; (d) publicly supported health care – eliminating all fee-for-service remuneration; (e) health education programs for all members of the community; (f) total control of budget allocations, overall policy, hiring, firing, salaries, construction, and health code enforcement by the community worker board; (g) total support from community and extracommunity organizations.

Ideological underpinnings

The above definitions correspond to three ideological positions that are discernable in the literature: the traditional or conservative, the liberal reformist, and the radical. Traditional theorists (cf. Hersch, 1972; Kolb, 1970, 1972; Zax and Specter, 1974) outline a delimited role of community involvement, thereby maintaining professional dominance. They are critical of radical positions which they believe to be quixotic, blatantly political, opportunistic, or even pathological. The liberal reformist position (Enelow and Weston, Jr., 1972; Feldman, 1973; Kellam and Schiff, 1968) supports greater community participation (e.g., advisory or shared responsibility), which is valued for its contribution to community solidarity as well as to mental health programming per se. What distinguishes this position from a more radical perspective is the fact that control is ultimately referred back to the existing power structure. Maximum control by the community and an end to professional power and autonomy are prescribed by the radical approach (cf. Chu and Trotter, 1974; Health Policy Advisory Center, 1972; Kunnes, 1970, 1972; Lowinger, 1970; Riessman and Gartner, 1970). Concomitant with the establishment of community control is a program for greater social and political change since, in the radical view, mental health cannot be considered apart from the broader political and economic system.

The Ambiguity of Community

Program implementation is further confounded by different interpretations of the word community, which has at least two distinct meanings, one sociological and the other geographical. Connery *et al.* (1968) point out that although the concept of community participation implies a sociological view of community, the provisions for a catchment area reflect geographic proximity stemming from administrative concerns. Every center funded by the National Institute of Mental Health serves a catchment area encompassing a population between 75,000 and 200,000 residing within a specific region.

The Community Mental Health Act of 1963 contained few traces of the rhetoric that had preceded its passage. Expansion of the notion of the 'therapeutic community' was to include a network of mental health services interwoven into the very fabric of local society. Instead, the federal interpretation of community is reminiscent of Tönnies's notion of Gesellschaft, an artificial construction of an aggregate of human beings as a practical way of achieving an objective. The Gesellschaft is to be distinguished from the Gemeinschaft, which derives from an a priori and necessarily existing unity (Zax and Specter, 1974).

Case examples of participation and control in community mental health centers

The inconsistency in governmental and professional references to 'community control' raises the question of whether similar 'slippage' has characterized the thrust toward community determination of mental health services. Holton, New, and Hessler (1973) used the elitist, advisory, and consumer control models in their study of six poverty area centers. Only the first two models were found to exist. The elitist model was found in three centers; potential consumers had a narrow advisory function in one center; community residents on the staff constituted participation in another center; and the remaining center was in the process of developing a consortium of consumer and agency representatives.

Similarly, in only two of six centers studied by the Health Policy Advisory Center (1972) could there be said to be direct community involvement. In both cases, the community was defined as the community mental health center's own professional peer group. While none of the centers relied exclusively on the peer group community for involvement, in several, efforts to involve the potential consumer community were perfunctory.

Roman and Schmais (1972) have characterized community boards under five general types according to their formal role in the policy-making process of the institutions to which they relate. This conceptualization encompasses more completely the various nuances of community participation. It provides a useful framework within which to consider certain instances of community participation in community mental health centers as they have been reported in the literature.

Incorporated body model

The incorporated body model is a legally viable structure, where the objective is maximum community participation and control. In this case, the board contracts for the services of an administrative and professional staff.

Hunts Point Multi-Service Center.   The Hunts Point Multi-Service Center (Ruiz and Behrens, 1973), a community corporation which operates its own psychiatric clinic in the South Bronx of New York, seems to embody the incorporated model. Funds are made directly available to the Center, which services 60,000 people in the central part of the Lincoln Community Mental Health Center catchment area. The Hunts Point Mental Health Unit began operation in February, 1970, with a complete staff of indigenous mental health workers, subject only to minimal guidelines of the Community Mental Health Center. Apparently, obtaining professional staff was a major difficulty, since professionals were offered almost no voice in the development of the program and were to be denied faculty positions in the Albert Einstein College of Medicine – unlike their counterparts at Lincoln Hospital. According to Ruiz and Behrens (1973), the unit was totally controlled by the local community, athough the form that this control took was not fully elaborated.

Delegated authority model

A board that embodies the delegated authority model typically receives complete operating authority from a prime contractor. The latter, however, retains administrative and professional personnel on its own staff.

Mott Haven Planning Committee.   The Mott Haven Planning Committee (Ruiz and Behrens, 1973) is a grassroots organization in the southern part of the Lincoln Community Mental Health Center catchment area whose institutional relationship approximates the delegated authority model. The Planning Committee agreed not to assume fiscal control of the program, but demanded and was granted veto power over the hiring of staff and the development of new programs. It appointed a Personnel Committee, which hired a psychiatrist-director and an indigenous administrator – both of whom were acceptable to the Community Mental Health Center Director. The Mott Haven Planning Committee was also instrumental in choosing a community location for the operation of a clinic.

Shared responsibility model

The third prototype (shared responsibility) is based on a commitment from administration and professionals to work with the community board. Legal responsibility is vested in the central affiliated institution.

Westside Mental Health Consortium. The planners of the Westside Consortium in San Francisco, California, recognised that the community would need to be involved as true partners — a decision that implied formal partnership (cf. consors, consortis) in the center and its decisional structure (Bolman, 1972). This meant that community members should be represented on the Board of Directors and on its committees in a manner reflecting the sociocultural composition of the community. Thus, the traditional Board of Directors with overall policy and fiscal responsibility for the Westside program is composed of equal numbers of institutional and community members. The Advisory Board is expected to reflect the conscience of the Westside community, to inform residents about the availability of services provided by the Center, and to aid in the coordination of mental health programs for their maximum utilization. In practice, the impact of the Advisory Board has been significant in influencing the direction of the Center.

Issue delegation model

In the issue delegation model, legal responsibility again reposes in the institutional staff, but decision-making authority on specifically delegated matters is reserved for the community board. The extent of community input is considerably attenuated in comparison to the models just discussed.

Hill-West Haven Division. Tischler (1971) described consumer participation and regulation in the Hill-West Division in the Connecticut Mental Health Center, which seemed to conform to the issue delegation model. Although counsel was sought from the community around issues of program goals and policy, the prerogatives of the community and the exact nature of its authority were never clearly articulated.

In the spring of 1969, consumer involvement in the regulation of the Division was formalized. Each community designated a Consumer Board to which the Division was accountable. These Boards had responsibility in the areas of program development, personnel practices, and the establishment of service and research priorities. Subsequent changes in the basic structure and direction of the Division were to be approved by the Boards, which could also initiate change. Despite this transition toward community involvement, Tischler (1971) acknowledged that structural impact was minimal; that is, the agency remained organized as it was previously and offered essentially the same services.

Purely advisory model

The most prevalent model is the community board that holds neither legal nor de facto power or control over agency policy. Several illustrative examples are provided by Chu and Trotter (1974). Additional examples of the purely advisory model have been described in studies by Holton, New, and Hessler (1971) and by the Health Policy Advisory Center (1972).

Area B and C Community Mental Health Centers.   The Area B and C Centers, located in Washington, DC, exemplify the purely advisory model of citizen participation. The Area B Center has had an Advisory Board with no policy-making powers, which was composed of a small core of actively concerned members. The Board was not adequately representative of the Spanish-speaking population within the catchment area, met sporadically, and tended to have a rapid turnover of membership. There was little outreach work, so that it was doubtful that residents were aware of the Center's existence, much less that of an advisory board to represent their interests (Chu and Trotter, 1974).

Similarly, the Area C Advisory Board fluctuated in popularity, its representativeness was doubtful, and it had no say in policy. There were no by-laws to outline the extent of the Board's responsibility or authority. The Board functioned apathetically and at the request of the center administration. Even the two outreach programs were regarded by professionals with hostility and were thought to threaten traditional professional wisdom.

Major obstacles to community control
The role of professionalism

The consumer movement and community control struggles over local health services are empirical manifestations of conflict that derive largely from dissatisfaction with professional dominance (Waitzkin and Waterman, 1974). The differential possession of technical knowledge is one source of professionals' power to influence the actions of their clients. Another manifestation of the power imbalance vis-à-vis the client is the manipulation of information. Withholding information about diagnosis and therapy contributes to the mystification of the client and prevents independent judgment about whether to accept, question, or reject professional advice (Freidson, 1970). Finally, the inherent claim of professionalism, that only highly trained 'craftsmen' are capable of evaluating the work of other 'craftsmen,' constitutes an additional formidable barrier to community control.

Graziano (1969) argued that such territorial claims are seldom challenged, but rather gain sustenance from professionals' experience, stability, and social status. The community's intimate knowledge of its own culture, its own priorities, and the local social structure is a valuable expertise that professionals seldom acknowledge (Ilfeld and Lindemann, 1971). A crucial policy issue in the provision of health care services underlies this debate: Who is to determine the goals of service and the models by which these goals are pursued? The thrust of the community control mandate is to insure effective and humane service delivery to the client through ultimate accountability to the identified needs of the local community.

The mental health ideology

Psychiatric labels imply personal failure, marginal status, and incompetence and are regarded as socially and economically stigmatizing (Scheff, 1966). As Ryan (1969) recognized, the mental health model embraces the brand of liberal ideology that blames the client rather than sociopolitical institutions for the client's predicament. To the extent that the individual is encouraged to focus on internal sources of stress, confrontation of the stresses generated by the social and political system is unlikely (Halleck, 1972). In addition to fortifying the status quo, such an ideology creates a caricature of an individual beset by dramatic internal conflicts that are somehow little affected by external realities (Davis, 1938).

By definition, the consumer class of mental health services is 'mentally ill' with the concomitant loss of legal status. Consequently, it is not surprising that citizen participation under federal law has been avoided. Fittingly, community leaders who become involved in struggles for community control are often given pathological labels. For example, Hersch (1972) notes: '. . . I think it can be said that in community control settings, with a certain regularity, there appear leaders who, by objective and clear-cut criteria, show evidence of thought disorder and psychiatric disability' (p. 753). Hence, both the consumer who colludes as the 'sub-adult' in relation to the 'wise expert' (Haug and Sussman, 1969) and the potential consumer who refuses to capitulate are thereby subject to stigmatization within this framework.

Local mental health power structure

Graziano (1969) described the mental health professions as a legitimized special interest segment of a community. The mental health power structure is composed of parallel bureaucratic agencies which, by virtue of their control over professional and financial resources, cooperate in their own mutual support and maintain the decision-making power within the field. There is a definable and relatively stable social structure through which agencies share leadership, make cooperative decisions, and wield legitimized social power, which tends to reinforce the viability of the structure itself. Primarily committed to self-preservation, the mental health power structure is alertly opposed to any events that might change it. When innovation intrudes, the structure responds with various strategies to deal with the threat. Some of these tactics include cooptation – the incorporation and alteration of change to fit the preexisting structure, or active rejection – utilizing all resources to 'starve out' change by insuring lack of support. The most subtle defense, however, is ostensibly to accept and encourage reform, to issue public proclamations in support of innovation [e.g., American Psychological Association's position statement (Smith & Hobbs, 1966) in support of community control], and simultaneously to build in various safeguards to ensure that all will be accomplished through channels of the power structure, thus virtually assuring no change.

Graziano (1969) coined the motto of 'Innovation without Change!' to underscore the tendency of the mental health establishment to maintain primary allegiance to the power structure and to perpetuate employment by creating innovations which never alter reality. The comprehensive mental health center is a case in point. The community is committed to the enormous expense of the center, but its control is referred back to the existing power structure. Most services are delivered by a professional staff compensated by government (i.e., bureaucratic) money. Without institutional changes in funding, the service aspects of community psychology will never be truly accountable to the community. Instead, the established structure will only be aggrandized, rendering it more entrenched and capable of absorbing the next 'innovation invasion.'

The dialectics of community control

According to a dialectical proposition, the whole determines the truth, not in the sense that it is greater than the sum of the parts, but in the sense that its structure and function determine every condition and relation (Marcuse, 1969). Thus, within a repressive system, even progressive movements threaten to become the very opposite to the extent that they are altered and incorporated to fit the preexisting structure. The exercise of political rights in such an atmosphere serves to validate the administration by testifying to the existence of democratic liberties which, in reality, have been eroded.

Conservative and radical implications

Within the context of community control, it would be irresponsible to ignore the cooptation of reforms in the past (cf. Alford, 1975). Community control is dialectical in the sense that it embraces both conservative and radical possibilities (Aronowitz, 1970). Reissman and Gartner (1970) have discussed the ways in which community control could favor and fortify the status quo: (a) Community control may become preoccupied with decentralization and neglect the issue of national power, which continues to determine the significant decisions on funds, resources, and basic policy; (b) The struggle for a redistribution of local resources may promote factionalism by pitting local groups against each other; (c) While community control is seen as a way of involving people in their own destiny – giving them greater power, resources, and competency – such involvement may become 'sociotherapy' or participation for its own sake, without power and without economic redistribution; (d) Community leadership could become co-opted with a consequent dilution of the objectives of community control; (e) The threat presented by the specter of consumer power could provoke a countermobilization of resources by professionals and governmental bureaucrats. As contended below, the latter process contributed to the overthrow of Allende's *Unidad Popular* government in Chile.

On the other hand, the vulnerabilities of the community control mandate do not negate its radical potential. The benefits of a shift in power to the local community would include: (a) a direct challenge to the prerogative of centralized bureaucracy to establish local policy: (b) a dramatic transformation and improvement in the health care service delivery system through accountability to the consumer and a transformation of traditional power relationships; (c) a mechanism for self-determination and the acquisition of greater competence, skills, and resources; and (d) an alternative model of government and social decision making, which rejects the efficacy of representative but distal institutions to reflect popular aspirations in a given locale.

Consumer-worker control of health care in Chile

The *Unidad Popular* government, headed by Salvador Allende, encouraged changes in the health system that portended essential shifts in financing and power. In particular, government policy supported increased consumer and worker control. These modifications produced strong resistance from health professionals. Modell and Waitzkin (1975) document the Chilean experience, which provides an excellent example of the difficulties of implementing community control in the health care system.

Consumer-worker control gradually emerged at the neighborhood and hospital levels. In the neighborhood health centers, which serviced populations between 50,000 and 75,000, local health councils were formed by representatives of health workers' unions and community organizations. The local health councils discussed community health problems, suggested solutions, cooperated in the promotion of health campaigns, and acted as an advisory link between the National Health Service and the community. A second council, which functioned as an executive body, was composed of representatives from the local health council and the director of the neighborhood health center. The executive body acted on the suggestions of the local health council, although ultimate authority rested with the medical director.

At the hospital level, parallel councils and executive groups were established with similar tasks and advisory functions. In addition, the area councils participated in comprehensive health planning and the coordination of services and facilities throughout the area.

The National Health Service also initiated a Program of Sociocultural Development, which provided for an integrated health team to work with community members in identifying local needs. The health team cooperated with local organizations, encouraged collective action to combat the diverse problems facing local residents, offered health information, and emphasized direct participation of the community as knowledgeable members of the local health council.

Although these innovations fostered community organization and promised a shift in existing power structures, traditional power relationships remained unchanged. Although a relatively low proportion of doctors were involved (10 to 20 percent), the local health councils and executive bodies remained advisory in nature. The major decision-making power was retained by the medical directors of the neighborhood health centers.

In late 1972 and early 1973, the local health councils consolidated their power by mobilization of popular support and by integration with other broadly based organizations. Among the popular goals were community control over the hiring and firing of health personnel and the training of community leaders to perform health-related functions, which later became critical during the periodic strikes and boycotts by the medical profession. At the hospital level, governing councils were formed from the spectrum of professional and nonprofessional ranks, and administrative and staffing decisions were made that previously were under the exclusive jurisdiction of high-ranking professionals.

It is of special importance for comparison with the United States that Chile, unlike other socialist governments, made no attempt to suppress private practice by either legal or economic means. Physicians, nonetheless, became increasingly anxious about the democratization and decline of professional dominance that the government encouraged. Several physicians were dismissed from the National Health Service when their private practices interfered with their public duties. Doctors feared that greater control would be exerted over the proportion of private patients that could be seen, especially within the National Health Service facilities. Furthermore, the training of paraprofessionals was viewed as another significant threat to professional hegemony.

In 1972, the Chilean Medical Association began a vigorous campaign against the *Unidad Popular*. Eventually, in the weeks immediately prior to the military coup of September, 1973, a doctors' strike organized by the Medical Association incapacitated the health care system. Finally, the medical profession, threatened by a redistribution of power and inconvenienced by economic instability, helped to lay the foundation for military dictatorship.

Modell and Waitzkin (1975) elucidate the *Unidad Popular* experience with health care to demonstrate the reluctance of those who hold professional dominance – as well as economic and political dominance – to accept a meaningful redistribution of wealth and power. The Chilean experiment suggests that the professional elite will uphold orderly, legal processes only as long as these processes do not threaten professional control. Thus, advisory boards were tolerated until they transcended their advisory function. Most importantly, the Chilean experience suggests the futility of incremental reforms in health care without a broader transformation of the social structure. Modell and Waitzkin (1975) conclude: 'More than ever before, health workers and consumers may learn that the struggle toward a humane health system cannot succeed without a concomitant struggle toward fundamental change in the social order' (p. 40).

Conclusion

The meaning of community control has been diluted by its application interchangeably with the concepts of community involvement and community participation. Whereas community involvement and participation were considered to be subordinate to existing government bureaucracies, community control rejects the prerogative of these centralized administrations to formulate local policy. Furthermore, community control in its broadest sense would extend to the control and determination of the social, political, and economic realities of the entire community.

Professional control is anticommunity control, since professionalism, by its very nature, rejects the input of the 'lay' public. The mental health power structure is also antagonistic to community control. Mental health agencies share leadership, make cooperative decisions, and monopolize social power. Strenuously committed to self-preservation, the mental health power structure subverts innovation by active rejection, cooptation, and destructive incorporation.

The community control mandate is indeed a double-edged sword, having conservative as well as radical potential. As a conservative force, community control could become preoccupied with local issues, encourage local factionalism, become an exercise in 'sociotherapy,' become co-opted and bankrupt of its original intentions or, as in the Chilean debacle, provoke a repressive backlash. With an eye toward radical social change, community control challenges federal intervention in the formulation of local policy, invites health care reform by demanding consumer accountability and upsetting professional equilibrium, provides a mechanism for self-determination, and suggests an alternative model of government and social decision making.

A significant redistribution of power and authority challenges professional hegemony and the mental health establishment. Such measures also demand a critical reformulation of current professional theory, practice, and research from the perspective of community autonomy. In the final analysis, anything less will relegate community control to the level of empty exhortation.

References

Alford, R. R.:
Health care politics. Chicago: University of Chicago Press, 1975.
Alinsky, S. D.
The war on poverty – Political pornography. *Journal of Social Issues.* 1965, *21,* 44–47.
Aronowitz, S.
The dialectics of community control. *Social Policy,* 1970, *1,* 47–51.
Bolman, W. M.
Community control of the mental health center: II. Case examples. *American Journal of Psychiatry,* 1972, *129,* 181–186.
California mental health services act. Sacramento, Calif.: California Office of State Printing, 1974.
Caplan, R. B.
Psychiatry and the community in nineteenth-century America. New York: Basic Books, 1969.
Chu, F. D., and Trotter, S.
The madness establishment. New York: Grossman Publishers, 1974.
Connery, R. H., Backstrom, C. H., Deener, D. R., Friedman, J. R., McCleskey, C., Meukison, P., and Morgan, J. A., Jr.
The politics of mental health: Organizing community mental health in metropolitan areas. New York: Columbia University Press, 1968.
Davis, K.
Mental hygiene and the class structure. *Psychiatry,* 1938, *1,* 55–66.
Duhl, L. J., and Leopold, R. L. (Eds.).
Mental health and urban social policy. San Francisco: Jossey-Bass, 1969.
Enelow, A. J., and Weston, W. D. Jr.
Cooperation or chaos: The mental health administrator's dilemma. *American Journal of Orthopsychiatry,* 1972, *42,* 603–609.
Feldman, S. (Ed.)
The administration of mental health services. Springfield, Ill.: Thomas, 1973.
Freidson, E.
Professional dominance. New York: Atherton Press, 1970.
Geiger, J. J.
Of the poor, by the poor, or for the poor: The mental health implications of social control of poverty programs. In M. Greenblatt, P. E. Emery, and B. C. Glueck, Jr., (Eds.), *Poverty and mental health.* Washington, DC.: American Psychiatric Association, 1967.
Graziano, A. M.
Clinical innovation and the mental health power structure: A social case history. *American Psychologist,* 1969, *24,* 10–18.
Halleck, S. L.
The politics of therapy. New York: Perennial Library, 1972.
Haug, M. R., and Sussman, M. B.
Professional autonomy and the revolt of the client. *Social Problems,* 1969, *17,* 153–161.

Health Policy Advisory Center. *Evaluation of community involvement in community mental health centers.* Health Policy Advisory Center, New York, 1972. (NTIS No. PB 211–267).

Hersch, C.
Social history, mental health, and community control. *American Psychologist*, 1972, 27, 749–754.

Holton, W. E., New, P. K., and Hessler, R. M.
Citizen participation and interagency relations: Issues and program implications. School of Medicine, Tufts University, Massachusetts, 1971. (NTIS No. PB 210–093).

Holton, W. E., New, P. K., and Hessler, R. M.
Citizen participation and conflict. *Administration in Mental Health*, Fall 1973, 96–103.

Ilfeld, R. W., Jr., and Lindemann, E.
Professional and community: Pathways toward trust. *American Journal of Psychiatry*, 1971, *128*, 583–589.

Kellman, S. G., and Schiff, S. K.
An urban community mental health center. In L. Duhl and R. L. Leopold (Eds.), *Mental health and urban social policy*. San Francisco: Jossey-Bass, 1968.

Kolb, L. C.
Community mental health centers. In J. Aronson (Ed.), *International Journal of Psychiatry*, 1970, *9*, 283–293.

Kolb, L. C.
Against the radical position in community mental health. In H. Gottesfeld (Ed.), *The critical issues of community mental health.* New York: Behavioral Publications, 1972.

Kosa, J., Antonovsky, A., and Zola, I. K. (Eds.).
Poverty and health – A sociological analysis. Cambridge: Harvard University Press, 1969.

Kunnes, R.
Will the real community psychiatry please stand up. In J. Aronson (Ed.), *International Journal of Psychiatry*, 1970, *9, 302–312.*

Kunnes, R.
Radicalism and community mental health. In H. Gottesfeld (Ed.), *The critical issues of community mental health.* New York: Behavioral Publications, 1972.

Lowinger, P.
Radical psychiatry. In J. Aronson (Ed.), *International Journal of Psychiatry*, 1970, *9*, 659–668.

Marcuse, H.
Repressive tolerance. In R. P. Wolff, B. Moore, Jr., and H. Marcuse, (Eds.), *A critique of pure tolerance.* Boston: Beacon Press, 1969.

Mental health for the masses. *Health-PAC*, May 1969, pp. 1–2.

Modell, H., and Waitzkin, H.
Health care and socialism in Chile. *Monthly Review*, 1975, *27*, 29–40.

Moynihan, D. P.
Maximum feasible misunderstanding. New York: Free Press, 1969.

Notkin, H., and Notkin, M. S.
Community participation in health services: A review article. *Medical Care Review*, 1970, *27*, 1178–1201.
Reissman, F., and Gartner, A.
Community control and radical social change. *Social Policy*, 1970, *1*, 52–55.
Roman, M., and Schmais, A.
Consumer participation and control: A conceptual overview. In H. H. Barten and L. Bellak (Eds.), *Progress in community mental health* (Vol. 2). New York: Grune & Stratton, 1972.
Ruiz, P., and Behrens, M.
Community control in mental health: How far can it go? *Psychiatric Quarterly*, 1973, *47*, 317–324.
Ryan, W. (Ed.).
Distress in the city: Essays on the design and administration of urban mental health services. Cleveland: Case Western Reserve University, 1969.
Scheff, T. J.
Being mentally ill: A sociological theory. Chicago: Aldine, 1966.
Smith, M. B., and Hobbs, N.
The community and the community mental health center. *American Psychologist*, 1966, *21*, 499–509.
Stoeckle, J. D., and Candib, L. M.
The neighborhood health center: Reform ideas of yesterday and today. *New England Journal of Medicine*, 1969, *280*, 1386–1391.
Tischler, G. L.
The effects of consumer control on the delivery of services. *American Journal of Orthopsychiatry*, 1971, *41*, 501–505.
Waitzkin, H., and Waterman, B.
The exploitation of illness in capitalist society. Indianapolis: Bobbs-Merrill, 1974.
Wilensky, H. L., and Lebeaux, C. N.
Industrial society and social welfare (3rd ed.). New York: Macmillan, 1965.
Zax, M., and Specter, G. A.
An introduction to community psychology. New York: Wiley, 1974.

CHAPTER 8

The mental patients' rights movement, and mental health institutional change*

Phil Brown

The social sciences have a long tradition that examines the social control functions of institutional psychiatry. Foucault (1) explored the way in which the early European asylums of the seventeenth and eighteenth centuries regulated the labor force in industrial areas. He also discussed the ideological aspects of replacing a religious and demonological world view with a rational, scientific psychiatry.

David Rothman (2, 3) found that the asylum in the United States, like the penitentiary, was a development of the early nineteenth century industrial revolution. The new mental hospitals housed a mainly working class and immigrant population who were the social victims of the new industrial capitalist order.

While not expressing themselves that explicitly in terms of social control functions, Hollingshead and Redlich's classic *Social Class and Mental Illness* (4) showed the higher rate of mental illness in working class people due to both social pressure and diagnostic bias. They noted that a middle or upper class person would be 'sentenced' to therapy for the same criminal action that would result in the commitment of a working class person to a state hospital. Related to this was the referral source: higher class people were referred to psychiatrists by physicians, while lower class people were referred by police and social work agencies. The higher one's class status, the

* Reprinted from *International Journal of Health Services*, vol. 11, no. 4, pp. 523–40, 1981, with permission of the author and the publisher, Baywood Publishing Co.

more likely one was to receive psychotherapy, while lower class status tended to yield 'organic' (e.g. electroshock) treatment. Of patients seen by private MDs, those of higher classes received considerably longer sessions. A majority of psychotic patients of the top two classes (based on the Hollingshead five class breakdown) were treated either by private psychiatrists or in private hospitals, while nearly all the psychotic people in the lower two classes were warehoused in state hospitals.

Over four decades ago, Kingsley Davis (5) wrote that the mental health movement of professionals had assumed a Protestant ethic long dominant in the US. Psychiatric textbooks took for granted a mobile class structure, and regarded competition as fundamental to human nature. Various types of psychological maladjustment were seen as resulting from an inability to compete. Individualism was also assumed in the following ways: (a) people were responsible for their own destiny; (b) individual happiness was the ultimate good; and (c) human behavior was observed and analyzed in isolation from society. This last point, what Davis termed a 'psychologistic conception of human nature,' was a 'means whereby an unconsciously held ethic may be advantageously propagated under the guise of "science".' Davis believed that mental health professionals ignored those elements of reality which didn't fit their social concerns. Thus, 'If human personality is understandable without reference to social reality, then naturally social reality need not be analyzed.' The criteria of mental health were always social criteria. Foreshadowing the popular antipsychiatry doctrines of the 1960s, Davis wrote, 'Sanity lies in the observance of the normative systems of the group.'

Beginning in the 1960s, many mental health professionals and social scientists provided extensive critiques of class, race, and sex biases in psychology and psychiatry. The works of R. D. Laing, David Cooper, Thomas Szasz, Thomas Scheff, Phyllis Chesler, and others showed that mental health ideology justified many existing inequalities by using a pseudo-scientific explanation. The essentially ahistorical and asocial view of mental health professionals toward individual mental illness allowed for a separation of emotional distress from its social causation.

The new revolt against psychiatry

In the 1960s and 1970s, the resurgence of political activism based on the civil rights, antiwar, and women's movements spurred new criticisms of psychiatry's role in preserving the status quo. Given their deep critical analysis of the social structure as a whole, those social movements were able to grasp the social control elements in what was supposedly a value-free, scientific approach.

But beyond this, some of the revolt against psychiatry was organized by its own clients. Mental patients' liberation groups pointed to the abuses they suffered at the hands of a system that couldn't understand their particular life crises, but could only warehouse them and give them the seclusion room, the chemical straitjacket, and other harsh treatments. Also important was the feminist critique of psychology and psychiatry, which demonstrated how professional ideology, private therapy, and institutional treatment mirrored the sexism of the whole society.

Broverman *et al.* (6) showed that psychiatrists' concepts of mental health for men and women were dramatically different. Psychiatrists' responses to a questionnaire held that mentally healthy men exhibited typical male sex role characteristics such as aggressiveness, competitiveness, and objectivity, and that mentally healthy women were characterized by passivity, nurturance, excitability, and subjectivity. The profile of a mentally healthy human being was found to correspond to that of mentally healthy men, thus effectively removing women from the human race in the eyes of the respondents.

Phyllis Chesler, in *Women and Madness* (7), cites innumerable sexist attitudes among a wide range of mental health professionals. Among them are the images of women common to the society as a whole: frigidity, seductiveness, promiscuity, the schizophrenogenic mother, and the like. Women were sometimes committed for being depressed housewives or 'sexually acting-out.' Further, the feminist critique of such practices was often seen as pathological in its own right.

The New Left also had a generalized antagonism to organized psychology and psychiatry. This often focused on the way that those fields psychologized social reality. Radicals were exceedingly critical of the practice of labeling political opponents as mentally ill rather than dealing with the actual opposition. 'Psychohistory,' as a recent example of this, focuses on psychopathology in political leaders such as Hitler and Nixon, rather than on the real political and economic forces represented by those leaders.

Perhaps one of the most dangerous extensions of this outlook can be seen in the psychologistic explanations of the black liberation, antiwar, and student movements of the 1960s. At the University of Chicago, for example, students occupied buildings to protest the firing of Marlene Dixon, a popular teacher long active in the antiwar movement. The students' program centered on the demand that the school end its research and development for war-related matters. Most opponents of this action simply argued against it on political grounds: the students were trying to overthrow legitimate authority, the Vietnam War was a justifiable defense against communist aggression, the university was value-free and above political matters. The noted psychologist Bruno Bettelheim had a different view. As he understood it, the students were acting out an unresolved Oedipal complex. They had no real political points to make, but were attacking the university as a surrogate for attacking their fathers. Therefore, Bettelheim explained, it was unnecessary to treat the protest as a political event. It was instead a manifestation of psychopathological behavior.

Psychologist Gustav Gilbert, formerly a US witness at the Nuremberg war crimes trials against Nazis, pursued a similar logic, but went further by equating the activists with the Nazis, based on their militant behavior and strong beliefs. Addressing the Detroit ghetto uprising of 1967, psychosurgeons Vernon Mark and Frank Ervin suggested that 'episodic dyscontrol syndrome' (their 'scientific' term for innate violence) caused the riots, and that preventive psychosurgery could prevent future outbreaks (8).

Such attitudes, quite common in the 1960s, prompted Kenneth Kenniston (9) to write an article, 'How Community Mental Health Stamped Out the Riots – 1968–1978,' in which he facetiously forecasted the creation of a psychiatric police force to take over urban counterinsurgency functions under a medical/scientific cover.[1]

On a more activist level, Psychologists for a Democratic Society (PDS) and other student-professional groups disrupted panels at psychology and psychiatry conferences where socio-political issues were being psychologized. The protesters staged guerrilla theater skits which posed questions such as: Why investigate why *some* people oppose the Vietnam war, racism, and genocide? Why not ask why *more* people don't join them?

The mental patients' liberation movement

The mental patients' liberation movement provided the first critique of psychiatry to come solely from the perspective of its clients. Small groups of ex-patients began to assert their anger at being committed for what they saw as minor deviant acts and then being resocialized into an institutional life style (11–13).

Mental patients' liberation fronts and similar organizations made their initial appearance with angry denunciations of mental hospital abuses, and sometimes with 'jailbreaks' in which they released friends who had been involuntarily committed. They also organized through publications, news conferences, demonstrations, and forums to oppose psychosurgery, electroshock, aversion therapy, and prison behavior modification programs. Further targets of the movement included legislative as well as litigatory challenges to involuntary commitment laws, denial of civil rights to patients and ex-patients, and treatment such as physical restraint and forced chemotherapy. Activists have leafleted at state hospitals, sometimes being arrested. They have also organized for increased Social Security Supplemental Security Income benefits for ex-patients.

A number of mental patients' organizations, especially the related antipsychiatry groups, see themselves as part of a larger radical social movement. Their journals publish articles on the women's, anti-nuke, and antiwar movements, making connections between them all. At the 1980 annual conference of mental patient activists, participants took time to leaflet at an anti-Nazi rally, an anti-nuke march, and a labor union rally (14).

This involvement is also clear in the international antipsychiatry movement, represented by the International Network: Alternatives Against Psychiatry, which includes member organizations and individuals in Mexico, Belgium, Italy, France, Holland, Canada, Austria, West Germany, Sweden, and the US. The international affiliates of this grouping are very involved in a wide range of general Left politics (14).

These groups also provided outlets for ex-patients to talk over their problems with others who would be sympathetic to them. From this consciousness raising and support group structure developed various forms of self-help organizations, providing drop-in centers and group residences.[2]

The patients' rights movement has been quite forceful, and has achieved some important successes. Yet its potential has been only partly fulfilled. This has been due to the cooptation of the movement by mental health professionals and planners, and to the conjuncture of the movement with the economic realities of deinstitutionalization.

The conjuncture with institutional reform

Patients' rights and institutional change posed a complex conjuncture of social forces. Favorable court rulings on patients' rights were definitely a product of the civil liberties upsurge of the period. But at the same time, these rulings provided judicial and political support for those professionals critical of custodialism. Efforts to deinstitutionalize patients from hospital to community were aided by the knowledge that state hospitals could not provide the treatment demanded by the courts. Budget cutting initiatives were thus reinforced, and hopefully less expensive community care was put on the agenda.

Further, the right to treatment issue raised the question of ordinary reform of the mental health system. Such reform and restructuring is often difficult to attain, given the plodding bureaucracy and traditionalism within many mental health administrations. The legal attacks, combined with a burst of popular exposés and civil libertarian protest, provided the necessary impetus and social justification for pursuing goals that might otherwise be challenged as too experimental.

Patients' rights litigation

A key element of the patients rights' legacy is in the area of litigation, especially in the matters of right to treatment, right to refuse treatment, safeguards on commitment proceedings, and patient labor. In the early 1960s, patients' rights litigation was not a direct result of the collective action of patients' rights groups, as they did not yet exist. Even many of the cases in the 1970s were initiated by individuals and/or professional advocates. The early cases were partly a result of the general upsurge of civil liberties activism in the 1960s, largely prompted by the civil rights movement. This provided a backdrop for the formation of patients' rights groups. Many later court cases were spurred by the patients' movement, even though most were not initiated by it. And, the movement's publicity, demonstrations, and other actions played an important role in the outcome of those suits and subsequent enforcement. That patients rights' groups don't initiate more law suits doesn't mitigate the importance they attach to such action. A leading movement magazine, *Madness Network News*, features a regular section on legislation and litigation, and other movement publications report on various cases.

In studying the significance of patients' rights litigation, it is first useful to examine the right to treatment issue. In 1966 Judge David Bazelon ruled in *Rouse* v. *Cameron* that Washington, DC, statutes provided for the right to treatment when confined to a mental hospital. Such rights could be derived from the US Constitution's Eighth Amendment guarantee against cruel and unusual punishment, and Fourteenth Amendment guarantees of due process and equal rights under the law. Bazelon ruled that inadequacy of resources was an unacceptable reason for failing to provide treatment. If a person was deprived of liberty on the grounds that he or she needed treatment, then such treatment had to be provided. The court made no specific ruling for remedies, but merely asked the hospital to make an honest effort. In 1968 a Massachusetts case supported the right to treatment for persons judged incompetent to stand trial by reason of insanity. Although these cases had little direct effect on mental health policy, since they involved persons originally charged with crimes, they were important in the history of right to treatment litigation (17, 18).

Wyatt v. *Stickney* was the real landmark case in the right to treatment. In a 1971 ruling, US District Court Judge Frank Johnson, Jr. held that 'involuntarily committed patients unquestionably have a constitutional right to receive such individual treatment as will give each of them a realistic opportunity to be cured or to improve his or her mental condition.' A 1972 decree followed, stating that the two mental hospitals and one retarded facility named in the case had failed to provide: '1) a human psychological and physical environment, 2) qualified staff at numbers sufficient to administer adequate treatment, and 3) individualized treatment plans.'

Unlike the 1966 *Rouse* v. *Cameron* case, *Wyatt* v. *Stickney* produced a definite set of specific standards. Patients were granted the right to privacy, mail, phone, and visitors. Concerning legal rights usually taken away from mental patients, the court ruled that 'no person shall be deemed incompetent to manage his affairs, to contract, to hold professional or occupational or vehicle operator's licenses, to register and vote, or to make a will, *solely* by reason of his admission or commitment to the hospital.' Patients were to be 'free from unrestricted or excessive medicine,' to receive weekly medication reviews from physicians, and medicine should not be used 'as a punishment, for the convenience of staff, or as a substitute for programs, or in quantities that interfere with the patient's treatment program.' Physical restraint and isolation were restricted, and human experimentation limited to express consent. Therapeutic labor was strictly defined, making hospital maintenance work voluntary and paid at minimum wages. Specific standards were promulgated on floor space, toilet doors, closets, and nutrition. Rigid staffing minimums were prescribed, and each patient was to receive a detailed individual treatment plan within 48 hours of admission (19).

Bruce Ennis, a leading mental patients' rights attorney, notes that the mental health professions actively supported the *Wyatt* v. *Stickney* suit. The American Psychiatric Association, American Psychological Association, American Orthopsychiatric Association, and American Association on Mental Deficiency all filed *amicus curiae* briefs and/or testified for litigants (20). This was likely motivated by an interest in obtaining further mental health funding, since the high standards ordered by the court couldn't possibly be attained within the limits of existing budgets. This motivation, whether implicit or explicit, is an excellent example of some overlapping interests of patients' rights groups and mental health professionals. Scheff (21) notes that no mental hospital in the US could afford to implement the individualized treatment plans, even if only for new admissions.

Patient labor has been an important area of litigation, with a high degree of success. Such labor was previously a major source of free, or extremely cheap, labor power for many state hospitals. As noted previously, it has now been outlawed, unless it is voluntary and is paid at minimum wages. In *Souders* v. *Brennan*, testimony disclosed that one patient worked twenty-nine days a month for thirty-three years at the rate of $10 a month. The court ruled that patients should receive competitive wages, and that the Secretary of Labor should find ways to apply the Fair Labor Standards Act to patient employees (22). High costs of paying regular workers are often cited as one reason for closing the expensive to maintain asylums. At times, mental health planners complained about the high cost of nonpatient labor, without comprehending the importance of ending asylum peonage. But once the mental health professionals got over their initial outrage at patient labor litigation, they found that such decisions added to their reasons for pursuing community care. Thus, as elsewhere, civil liberties issues promoted deinstitutionalization.

Another key issue is due process in commitment. In the 1972 case of *Lessard* v. *Schmidt*, the Federal district court ruled that an allegedly dangerous patient had a right to a speedy hearing, with advance notice of what expert testimony would be heard. Further, dangerousness had to be proved beyond a reasonable doubt, and indefinite involuntary commitment was to be a last resort after a less restrictive environment was tried (23, 24). In 1974 Federal judges overturned commitment statutes in Alabama (*Lynch* v. *Baxley*) and Michigan (*Bell* v. *Wayne County General Hospital*) for failing to provide constitutional guarantees of notice of hearing, right to be present at hearing, and right to counsel. The court also held that the commitment laws were unjust in failing to provide for such due process and for permitting such patients to be given shock treatment and chemotherapy unwillingly (18, 25).

But various states began to change their statutes without waiting for litigation. Massachusetts was one of several states that changed commitment laws in the early 1970s so that involuntary commitment was technically made more difficult and thereby less frequent. When the 1971 commitment law took effect, it increased the proportion of voluntary commitments from 27.9 percent in 1971 to 62.9 percent in 1972 (26). This drastic change was largely effected by pressuring involuntary patients to sign voluntary forms, and was therefore a technical, bureaucratic solution rather than a systemic change.

By 1973 a more significant change took place when the revised code contained a more restrictive definition of probability of harm to self or others. This replaced the previous code's wide range that included behavior 'which clearly violates the established laws, ordinances, conventions, or morals of the community.' Indefinite commitment has been abolished, with periodic reviews now required (24). Such commitment reform is quite typical of other states.

It is definitely a step forward to have abolished many of the arbitrary commitment procedures of the past. Yet humanitarian reasons may not necessarily be foremost. Psychiatric hospitals now cite legal reasons for refusing to admit persons in serious need. This is a type of 'defensive medicine,' which denies help for fear of legal consequences. Just as defensive medicine is a type of backlash against growing criticism of the medical establishment, defensive psychiatry may be a type of backlash against the patients' rights movement. It is also a rather callous method of cutting costs and shedding responsibilities.

A landmark case in 1975, *Donaldson* v. *O'Connor*, questioned the hospital's right to hold a patient to whom they failed to provide treatment. The US Supreme Court ruled that non-dangerous persons who were not receiving treatment should be released if they could survive outside of the hospital. Kenneth Donaldson was involuntarily committed to Florida's Chatahoochee State Hospital, where he spent 15 years. Well educated in legal matters, he began in 1960 to fight his unjustified confinement. Donaldson was so well versed in patients' rights law that he published an article in the *Georgetown Law Review* while in the hospital. The hospital superintendent constantly blocked Donaldson's legal efforts, saying that Donaldson was uncooperative for denying his illness, refusing electroshock, and for his legal battle for freedom (27, 28). However, the court failed to uphold a lower court's monetary award to Donaldson, thus partly taking pressure off mental health authorities (17), and probably defeating a significant precedent for malpractice suits.

The right to refuse treatment

Particularly important at present is the right to refuse treatment, which has been a major focus of patients' rights activists. Ultimately, the right to treatment is merely an affirmation that state hospitals are supposed to heal patients, not simply warehouse them. Staffing, sanitary, dietary, and residency standards are not a guarantee that humane and successful treatment will in fact occur. 'Proper' treatment in the eyes of a large number of mental health professionals may include psychosurgery, shock treatment, and abuse of psychiatric drugs and restraints. Expert testimony can often be marshalled by the administration and medical staff to prove 'dangerousness' and thus circumvent present safeguards against forced treatment. Patient organizers and civil liberties activists thus believe that it is insufficient to remain content with a statutory right to treatment.

Some suits had already touched on the right to refuse treatment. *Wyatt* v. *Stickney* resulted in a ruling that patients had the right to refuse electroshock, psychosurgery, or other major surgery. Other cases established similar rights in terms of electroshock and chemotherapy. In *Kaimowitz* v. *Department of Mental Health* a Michigan court held that an involuntarily committed patient's consent to psychosurgery was uninformed, and that no involuntary patient should be subjected to this procedure (29).

A major victory in a suit against the Massachusetts Commissioner of Mental Health and fourteen Boston State Hospital psychiatrists in 1979 established that patients be given the right to refuse psychotropic drugs and forced seclusion. The *Rogers* v. *Okin* case was particularly significant in that it was the result of several years of in-hospital organizing by the Boston Mental Patients' Liberation Front (MPLF). Several years before the suit was initiated, the organization started a discussion group in one of the hospital's wards. The group addressed general social and political topics, as well as patients' rights. Increasing attention to the latter topic generated staff opposition, which in turn led to barring the activists from the ward. Following this, a number of past and present patients sued the hospital, the Department of Mental Health, and various individual psychiatrists. Federal District Judge Joseph Tauro granted the plaintiffs a temporary restraining order in early 1975, and on October 29, 1979, the judge issued a permanent order. The order granted patients the right to refuse seclusion or forcible medication, except with express consent by themselves or their guardian, or in the event of substantial likelihood of extreme violence, personal injury, or attempted suicide (30).

Judge Tauro refused to order $1.2 million in damages from the psychiatrists named for assault and battery, infraction of civil rights, and malpractice. The court held that the doctors acted in 'good faith' and without attempt to deprive patients of their rights. Yet testimony from patients, lower-level staff, and even some professional staff revealed that seclusion was not used for emergency situation but rather as punishment for minor rule violations. The six-by-twelve-foot seclusion room had nothing in it but a plastic covered mattress, and patients had been incarcerated in such rooms for months (30).

Mental Health Department and hospital staff defended themselves by claiming that a committed patient was de facto incompetent to decide on treatment issues. The defendants also testified that there had been no forcible medication at all, except in cases of psychiatric emergency. Further, they stated that neither a voluntary nor involuntary patient had the right to refuse treatment, whether in emergency or nonemergency situations. Existing state law stated the opposite. The staff psychiatrists claimed that the temporary restraining order would encourage widespread refusal of medication, but in fact, in a twenty-five-month period from the time of the temporary order, only twelve of 1,000 patients refused medication over a prolonged period of time, and most changed their minds in a few days (30). Despite the overwhelming evidence in favor of the litigants, the state filed an appeal on the grounds that the state has a responsibility to treat committed patients, and that Tauro's ruling prohibits necessary exceptions to the right to refuse treatment (31).

An appeal by the state led to a partial reversal in November 1980 of Tauro's ruling. Federal Appeals Court Judge Frank M. Coffin sent the case back to Judge Tauro, asking for 'deference to the professional judgment of the state doctors in determining dangerousness.' The Appeals Court held that Tauro too narrowly limited forced medication to cases where patients were either mentally incompetent or were prone to harm themselves or others, and that Tauro's orders on these matters should be rewritten. Coffin also struck down the lower court's strict guidelines for appointing guardians for incompetent persons, as well as the court's stringent definitions of emergency situations in which regular safeguards could be abrogated. Despite these reversals, Judge Tauro and the patients' attorney, Richard C. Cole, see the appellate decision as upholding the essential rights of patients to refuse treatment in a wide range of situations (32).

The patients rights' suits of the 1960s were drastically needed to attain minimal democratic rights for mental patients. But it is likely that courts ruled as they did not only because of the resurgence of civil rights organizing, but also due to a serious fiscal crisis which pressured Federal and state officials to engage in rapid deinstitutionalization. This economic motivation increasingly appears in mental health planning documents and articles (33). State hospitals could not provide the standards of care demanded by right to treatment rulings, nor could they provide enough staff to avoid the abuses named in the right to refuse treatment cases. Nor could they replace the free patient labor of the past. Some progressive professionals and planners were happy to have a combination of humanitarian and economic reasons to reform the old snakepit asylums. Yet the overwhelmingly predominant conservatism of recent years has sought to attack social service spending despite the costs in human suffering. Thus, insensitive cost-benefit methods have led to hospital phase-downs without adequate funds for community facilities (34).

Cooptation and reform

Numerous state and Federal plans and documents cite the legal issues as part of the rationale for deinstitutionalization (25, 35–38), yet largely ignore the patients' rights movement which played such a major role in that legal presence and consequently evade the stated intent of the court decisions.

Cooptation here refers to professionals usurping control of situations in order to achieve an outcome favorable to them. It may be a purposeful subversion or minimalization, or may be an unintended consequence. Many hospitals began to post a Mental Patients' Bill of Rights, modeled after the original demands of the movement groups. Although enforcement of those rights was hardly guaranteed, the hospital could claim to be concerned with such issues. Most patients, however, are unaware of and/or unable to exercise their legal rights, even if there is a lawyer or law student in the hospital. In a sense, such recourse is available only *after* the fact of commitment, forced treatment, and denial of rights. Encouraging hospitals to nominally grant patients rights in this fashion may therefore be an abdication of responsibility by the state hospital and Department of Mental Health, which should have prevented rights violations in the first place.

Mental health officials are often motivated to promulgate new policies on patients' rights in the face of court challenges. For instance, during the Boston State Hospital suit discussed above, the Massachusetts Department of Mental Health ordered facilities to sharply limit seclusion, restraint, and excess medication. The same officials fought bitterly against the litigants, yet formulated policy involving many of the same issues (39). It appears that pressure from the Mental Patients' Liberation Front and public support for the complainants were catalysts for certain actions that the Department might have desired but couldn't grant as an explicit response to patient activists. Further, officials were probably trying to limit the magnitude of the outcome.

Mental health authorities themselves utilize the courts when it is to their advantage. Consent decrees, for example, are being used to overcome legislative and gubernatorial financial obstacles to deinstitutionalization. For example, nine plaintiffs filed a class action suit in December 1976 for the patients of Massachusetts' Northhampton State Hospital. They demanded that the hospital and the state mental health system as a whole provide the least restrictive environment for mental patients. Two years later, a consent decree was signed by the litigants and the Department of Mental Health whereby the Department would 'create and maintain a system of appropriate community residential alternatives and non-residential programs.' The decree included a phase-down from Northhampton's current 475 patients to 50 by mid-1980, ordered individual treatment plans, and required highly defined standards and evaluations for community programs. As manifested by legislative anger at the Mental Health Department, this decree was a method whereby the Department could circumvent the lawmakers' unwillingness to increase funding for deinstitutionalization (40, 41). Legislatures have been antagonistic toward mental health departments not only for fiscal reasons, but also due to their perception that professionals have had little success in treating mental illness.

Another form of governmental cooptation is the trend toward establishing state-run mental health advocacy offices (42). Also, patients rights' activists increasingly appear on panels at professional meetings, and have been placed on advisory boards for mental health planning, including the President's Commission on Mental Health, although there is no evidence that their input is significant in terms of policy decisions. This token representation allows professionals to assert their concern, and serves to legitimate the professionalist approach to patients' rights.

An interesting example of cooptation is provided by a 1972 situation in which administrators at a state hospital in the Northeast organized a weekend of workshops and visits on patients' rights. Organizers came from New York City's Mental Patients' Liberation Front, the Radical Therapist Collective, and Number Nine, a New Haven alternative free clinic. They worked with patients in the hospital who were seeking more rights and some control over treatment, such as patient-run halfway houses for predischarge patients. Some hospital staff who proposed the weekend activities were genuinely committed to these issues, but the administration was basically trying to coopt the cutting edge of the patients' demands. They vetoed a number of sensible plans (e.g. the halfway house) put forth by the patients and visiting advocates. They feared that the patients would sacrifice therapeutic treatment in favor of the patients' own notions of beneficial care.

Further, testimony at one large meeting showed that the hospital was particularly critical of some patient activists in community residences who were involved in demonstrations at the local trial of antiwar activists (43). One could argue that such involvement in supporting antiwar activists could be a beneficial and therapeutic activity, but to the administration it was a sign of the patients' inability to be serious. They may have also seen it as a threat to the hospital, since the state government would not feel comfortable with one of its state hospitals serving as an antiwar center.

It may be asked why reformers do not actually expect and desire cooptation, or at least institutional acceptance of reform goals. Certainly the activists shouldn't be surprised at institutional attempts to control the reform process. This question can be approached by looking at examples of state hospital reform. For some activists, the goal is patient-controlled facilities (16). Therefore, any institutional acceptance of activist-initiated programs may be seen as cooptative, since it would enable the hospital to operate more effectively as a traditional, professionally-dominated facility. But patient-run facilities are rare and typically are new facilities established by patients, rather than institutions which patients gained control of. The Mental Patients' Association in Vancouver, British Columbia, is the classic model of a treatment center originated by patients and ex-patients (16). In other countries, attempts have been made to extend a large degree of patient control, though often propelled by professionals. Franco Basaglia's efforts in Italy (44) and the Chinese psychiatric reforms (45) are cases of this type. Such efforts, however, are criticized by those ex-patient activists who demand total patient control. Chamberlin (46) holds that the radical antipsychiatry movement, as represented by the International Network: Alternatives to Psychiatry, is dominated by professionals, doesn't give ample power to patients, and engages in institutional practices such as continued use of psychiatric drugs.

For professionals and others who support a wide application of patients rights, total patient control is not usually the goal. Such people would seek reforms which diminish custodialism and hierarchy, increase patient involvement, and strive for community placements which might be modeled on the resident-run halfway houses of the Mental Patients' Association. In this sense, then, they would seek radical reforms which were not cooptative. These sympathetic professionals would share with the patient activists a pervasive critique of existing mental health facilities. Even if they did not adhere to a totally patient-run model of mental health treatment, these professionals would largely accept the ex-patients' self-concept as a social movement.

Anspach (47) terms as 'identity politics' the new movements of ex-patients and handicapped people who strive for not only social policy and institutional reform, but who also 'consciously endeavor to alter both the self-concepts and societal conceptions of their participants.' For these activists, both the goals and the participation in political action are important, for, as Anspach comments, purposive political action is a sign of health. Spitzer (48), contrary to Anspach, believes that identity politics keep people within the boundaries of the deviant-processing institution. Although ex-patients or ex-prisoners may achieve benefits by organizing against institutional coercion, such organizing 'also implies that the techniques of social control retain a binding validity.' Spitzer is correct to note the tendency to define oneself by the criteria of what is seen as the oppressor institution. Yet the similarity of experiences shared by ex-patients requires them to at least partly identify themselves as ex-patients, if they wish to change the mental health system.

Forceful cooptation will attempt to break down the strong self-image of political activists, for such identity politics presents a major challenge to mainstream institutional practices and ideologies and the power of the professional establishment. Support then may be distinguished from cooptation on the basis of whether or not the institution, agency, or professional accepts a significant level of ex-patients' identity politics. Such acceptance would be accompanied by reform work in the patients' and ex-patients' interest, and in particular would include the activists in that work. For instance, the Mental Patients' Civil Liberties Project in Philadelphia is a legal advocacy group headed by an attorney, but it works closely with the local rights group, the Alliance for the Liberation of Mental Patients.

The criteria discussed here indicate that it is not the location of a service or facility that determines whether it is cooptative, but rather its orientation to dominant professional power. The determination must be made in each case for halfway houses, ex-patient clubs, advocacy services, and other mental health reform features.

Professional self-interest

Many well-intentioned mental health providers are unable and/or unwilling to understand the activists' criticism and alternatives. Patients' rights organizers lack the tact and courtesies of professional debate, and have launched what they consider a full-scale assault on institutional psychiatry. Standard psychiatric terminology is often laden with meanings more conducive to promoting social control than improving the patient's health. Patient activists' language and style are partly a response to this phenomenon. Patients also accuse the psychiatric establishment of being unable to accurately diagnose mental illness, a failure documented by widely respected social science research (6, 49).

Unwilling to accept much of these criticisms, professionals have largely dismissed the whole critique. Many mental patients' liberation activists spurn the notion of 'mentalism,' which they define as the incorrect belief in the existence of any mental illness (16). In the face of such a purist and simplistic attitude, many professionals are in fact perplexed. Activist opposition to mentalism stems from the fact that much of what has been called mental illness is in fact a normal reaction to oppressive social conditions, a psychologistic explanation of nonpathological behavior, or detached, medicalized ways of not adequately dealing with emotional distress. The movement's purist attitude derives from rage at being victimized by an oppressive system which by its own admission has erred seriously. Hopefully professionals will translate at least some of that attitude into terms and concepts which are applicable, and which accept the basic justness of much of the patients' rights critique.

At the same time, the purist critique of mental illness is incorrect as well as detrimental to current patients, ex-patients, mental health providers, and the general population. Notwithstanding the poor history of psychiatric treatment, the inexactness of diagnosis, and the failure to grasp the social causes of emotional disorder, many people still have a good deal of severe suffering which requires intensive care. Some of that care may be provided by patient-run centers. But some will still necessarily take place in traditional mental health institutions. This does not mean that a flawed psychiatric system should be accepted without attempting to thoroughly restructure it, however. The total opposition to mentalism makes it harder to construct alliances with providers for such change. And by its disbelief in any form of mental illness, the purist approach remains idealist and unable to deal with serious disorder.

Another reason that mental health professionals have a hard time with the social movement of patients and ex-patients is that the field often adheres to a widely held ideology that sees mental health professionals and institutions as themselves a social movement. The long history of this belief has thus led many professionals to view the patients' rights movement as a threat to professionally defined social progress (34). Mental health professionals also have much self-interest in proclaiming a concern for patients' rights. If patients' rights continue to play a significant role in hospital restructuring and deinstitutionalization, then professionals expect to be in control of that process. Their self-interest necessitates expanding their net, broadening their professional dominance, and extending their monopoly of practice (50, 51).

Professionals and patients do share some interests, but the method of sharing may be perceived differently. One approach might be to view the two groups as having overlapping interests, i.e. there is a small area where both groups' interests are common ones. Alternatively, the interests may be seen as congruent, i.e. both have essentially the same interests.[3] Fiscal pressures, civil liberties awareness, and the need for institutional reform have led professionals to accept a small degree of patients' rights, but this only involves an overlap, not a congruence. Therefore it is likely to yield a cooptative approach, whereas a true congruence would be more likely to produce an alliance.

The Boston State Hospital suit discussed earlier demonstrates the overlapping model. Although the Department of Mental Health later granted a number of rights sought in the patients' litigation, it did so on its own terms because it did not believe that patient initiative was appropriate. Both groups had overlapping interests, and the officials acted in a cooptative manner, eschewing the alliance that would be possible were the interests truly congruent.

Not only do mental health professionals press for their own

concerns, but so do lawyers. While a small number of deeply committed patients' rights advocates have worked hard in radical reform effort, the typical commitment or rights case is not necessarily handled by a reform-minded lawyer. Fleming (52) claims that the legal profession has long been the main opponent of medical control of the mentally ill. She argues that Pennsylvania's 1976 mental health act legislated practices which were already judicial practice. The act included the right to treatment in the least restrictive environment, the right to due process, and the right to dignity, privacy, and human care. As Fleming put it, 'The legislation brought about an overall reduction of the discretionary power of the medical profession, together with an increase in the role and power of the legal profession in the involuntary commitment process.' The Philadelphia Psychiatric Society and the Pennsylvania Association of State Mental Hospital Physicians criticized the new law as hostile to the psychiatric profession. Fleming found that both public interest lawyers and commitment attorneys acted primarily to preserve the need for their services. They accepted a high level of psychiatric control, especially in the area of aftercare for discharged patients. Thus, Fleming concludes, the public interest bar paradoxically placed itself in support of the mental health establishment which it had fought earlier.

The role of mental health workers and unions

A major complicating factor in the patients' rights area is frequent opposition from state workers' unions. Mental health workers, like most people, hold many stereotypes of mental illness. For instance, they may feel that mental illness incapacitates people to the point that they can not make decisions about matters such as whether or not to accept a particular treatment. State hospital workers also fear violence from patients, and believe that reduction of restraint, seclusion, and forced medication will increase that violence. Patient violence is a real fear, but dangerous behavior could best be reduced by overall structural reforms in the mental health system, not by maintaining the status quo. Yet one major labor organization, The California State Employees Association, greatly exaggerates the level of patient and ex-patient violence (53). That union's publications reinforce many conservative notions of patient care which would lead to renewed stress on custodial institutional care.

Such opposition derives at least in part from mental hospital workers' understandable fear of job loss. Hospital closing and patient population reductions have resulted in large layoffs, without significant retraining programs to prepare aides for community mental health care (54–56). The American Federation of State, County, and Municipal Employees (AFSCME) estimates that 4,000–5,000 mental health and mental retardation workers have already lost their jobs due to closures and phase-downs (57). Workers and their unions may feel that future implementation of patients' rights measures would lead to further deinstitutionalization, and therefore to even more layoffs.

In the long run, patients and workers have a good deal in common. Both see the mental health administrators as antagonistic to their interests, and both are victims of fiscal cutbacks in mental health. Yet they organize at cross-purposes. They do not exhibit the unity sometimes observed in patient-community worker alliances in the medical care system, due to the dependent status of most psychiatric patients and the legacy of stereotyping, poor care, and even brutality by attendants. Mental hospital workers tend to want less external constraints over their work, and patients' rights demands result in more such constraints. In this sense, the two groups have conflicting interests. This is unfortunate, since more progressive mental health policies have the potential to make workers' tasks more interesting, creative, and even safer.

Conclusion

The patients' rights movement has had some important effects on recent change in mental health policy, particularly in the area of democratic rights. The movement has been extremely important to the general critique of psychiatric abuses, to the overall trend of anti-institutional attitudes, and to the practical activities of a small minority of sympathetic professionals and lower-level staff. Mental patients' liberation groups were central in the unsuccessful 1977 struggle against HEW approval of psychosurgery. They are providing important leadership in attempting to prevent the spread of psychosurgery. Since psychosurgery represents a dangerous social control method, often aimed at rebellious prisoners (8), the patients' rights activists are furthering the public good.

Patients' rights demonstrations against producers of major psychiatric drugs also serve a more general interest, in that they bring to light the increasing use of psychiatric drugs for non-institutionalized people. The activist critique of psychiatric ideology also helps others to better evaluate individual therapy, and puts pressure on therapists to rethink their approaches and orientation. Tied to this is a general change in public attitudes toward mental illness, in that the ex-patients offer a new picture of the commonality of problems which many non-hospitalized people share to some degree. This structural understanding of 'symptom-as-protest' puts an appropriate level of blame on social forces, rather than seeing emotional distress as merely individual pathology.

Still, state psychiatric systems plod along on their severely flawed deinstitutionalization path, a direction mainly determined by fiscal needs (28). Scull (58) is correct to note that psychiatric planners' professed concern for patients' rights is not at all a real determinant of recent policy, but rather an ideological justification for that policy. We should not, however, focus only on the cooptation of the patients' rights movement. That movement offers some important lessons in social change strategy. The patients' rights movement shows that the direct action of a relatively powerless group can have significant effects on overall social policy, even if its success in part depends upon support of more powerful groups intent on cooptation. After all, if the movement didn't pose certain demands, there would be nothing to coopt, and the existence of some degree of patients' rights guarantees makes it easier to pursue more rights. While sympathetic professionals might prefer a more polite form of strategy, it is probably necessary to have the sharp level of criticism and action provided by the patients' movement as a complement to 'mainstream' reform.

The fact that patients' rights issues are often pressed by a powerless group takes the direction of reform somewhat out of the hands of policy makers and higher-level professionals. This may provide lower-level professionals and paraprofessionals with more impetus to institute change from below. And, with the proper amount of respect for each other's needs, patients and ex-patients may find common goals with the mental health work force, though this will be a very difficult and somewhat unlikely outcome given the current situation.

Patients' rights organizing might be more successful if it took a more realistic approach to mental illness rather than adhering to the critique of mentalism. Activists will need to strengthen their sometimes existing links to other progressive social movements so that demands for patients' rights will be increasingly part of a broader social change effort.

Other changes are also necessary to improve the effectiveness of patients' rights activists. Mental health officials, planners, and providers will have to be more accepting of activists' criticisms, since these criticisms are very tied to the general crisis of the psychiatric care system. Unions, too, will need to be less hostile to patients' rights issues.

For many of the general public, the patients and ex-patients in the movement will have provided a salient critique of institutionalization. Much like the prisoners' movement, the mental patients' liberation movement has brought to public awareness the problems of the large physical institutions for the 'deviant' populations. It has also made it impossible for reform to be simply the province of the administrators, since the victims of the institutional process now have at least some control over the social definition of their condition, and therefore the possibility of control over changes in that condition.

Acknowledgments I would like to thank Ronnie Littenberg for her valuable assistance in a number of conceptual areas of this paper, particularly the relationship of reform and cooptation. Naomi Aronson, Stephen Pfohl, Michael Yedidia, and Sabrina Cherry also contributed useful suggestions on the issues of cooptation. An anonymous referee provided important comments on the political beliefs and actions of the patients' rights movement.

Notes

1 Interestingly, Kenniston later turned against the student movement, applying his own form of psychologizing. In an article with Michael Lerner (10), he accused the student left of being in an 'unholy alliance' with the right, their motive being the destruction of the university by the severe pathology of campus activism.

2 Judi Chamberlin's *On Our Own* (16) provides the best overview of the mental patients movement through the eyes of one of its most eloquent spokespersons. Current information can be obtained from magazines such as *Madness Network News*, *Phoenix Rising*, *Off the Shelf*, and *On the Edge*.

3 Michael Yedidia provided this formulation.

References

1 Foucault, M.
   Madness and Civilization: A History of Insanity in the Age of Reason. New
   America Library, New York, 1971.
2 Rothman, D.
   The Discovery of the Asylum: Social Order and Disorder in the New Republic.
   Little, Brown Publishers, Boston, 1971.
3 Rothman, D.
   *Conscience and Convenience: The Asylum and its Alternatives in Progressive
   America.* Little, Brown Publishers, Boston, 1980.
4 Hollingshead, A., and Redlich, F.
   Social Class and Mental Illness. Wiley, New York, 1958.
5 Davis, K.
   Mental hygiene and the class structure. *Psychiatry* 1(1): 55–65, 1938.
6 Broverman, K., Broverman, D., Clarkson, F., Rosenkranz, P., and Vogel, S.
   Sex role stereotypes and clinical judgments of mental health. *J. Consult. Clin.
   Psychol.* 34(1): 1–7, 1970.
7 Chesler, P.
   Women and Madness. Avon Books, New York, 1973.
8 Chavkin, S.
   The Mind Stealers: Psychosurgery and Mind Control. Houghton-Mifflin
   Publishers, Boston, 1978.
9 Kenniston, K.
   How community mental health stamped out the riots, 1968–1978. *Transaction,*
   July–August 1968, pp. 21–29.
10 Kenniston, K., and Lerner, M.
   The unholy alliance against the campus. *New York Times Magazine,*
   November 8, 1970.
11 Mental Patients Liberation Front (New York). Statement.
   The Radical Therapist 2(4): 1, 1971.
12 Glenn, M., ed.
   Voices From the Asylum. Harper & Row, New York, 1974.
13 Hirsch, S., Adams, J., Frank, L., Hudson, W., Keene, R., Krawitz-Keene, G.,
   Richman, D., and Roth, R., eds.
   Madness Network News Reader. Glide Publications, San Francisco,
   1974.
14 San Francisco Conference. *On the Edge* 1(6): 1–2, 1980.
15 Oaks, D.
   Eighth Annual Conference on Human Rights and Psychiatric Oppression.
   State and Mind 7(3): 38–40, 1980.
16 Chamberlin, J.
   On Our Own: Patient-Controlled Alternatives to the Mental Health System.
   Hawthorn Books, New York, 1978.
17 Stone, A.
   Overview: The right to treatment – comments on the law and its impact. *Am.
   J. Psychiatry* 132(11): 1125–1134, 1975.

18 Bernard, J. L.
   The significance for psychology of O'Connor v. Donaldson. *Am. Psychol.*
   32(12): 1085–1088, 1977.
19 Brown, P.
   Alabama federal court rules for patients rights. *Rough Times* 2(7): 7, 1972.
20 Ennis, B.
   The impact of litigation on the future of state hospitals. In *The Future Role
   of the State Hospital*, edited by J. Zusman and E. Bertsch, pp. 83–90.
   Lexington Books, Lexington, Mass., 1975.
21 Scheff, T.
   Medical dominance: Psychoactive drugs and mental health policy. *Am.
   Behavioral Scientist* 19(3): 299–317, 1976.
22 United States Senate Subcommittee on Long-Term Care. *The Role of Nursing
   Homes in Caring for Discharged Mental Patients (and the Birth of a For-Profit
   Boarding Homes Industry)*. US Government Printing Office, Washington, DC,
   1976.
23 Wisconsin federal district court rules on patients rights. *Rough Times* 3(3): 12,
   1973.
24 Flaschner, F. N.
   Constitutional requirements in commitment of the mentally ill: Rights to
   liberty and therapy. In *The Future Role of the State Hospital*, edited by J.
   Zusman and E. Bertsch, pp. 65–81. Lexington Books, Lexington, Mass., 1975.
25 Kopolow, L. E., Brands, A., Burtin, J. L., and Ochberg, F. M.
   Litigation and mental health services. Memorandum, National Institute of
   Mental Health, Rockville, Md., 1975.
26 Massachusetts Department of Mental Health. *Annual Reports.*
27 Greider, W.
   After 20 years, an ex-mental patient is vindicated. *Washington Post*, June 27,
   1975.
28 MacKenzie, J. P.
   'Right to liberty' proclaimed for thousands of mentally ill. *Washington Post*,
   June 27, 1975.
29 Ferleger, D.
   A patients' rights organization: Advocacy and collective action by and
   for inmates of mental institutions. *The Clearinghouse Review* 8: 597–604,
   1975.
30 The Boston State suit. *Mass. Psych. Wards* 1(8): 1, 10, 1979.
31 Dietz, J.
   State appeals treatment ruling. *Boston Globe*, November 21, 1979.
32 Dietz, J.
   Court expands mental patients rights. *Boston Globe*, November 30, 1980.
33 Rubin, J.
   Economics, Mental Health, and the Law. D. C. Heath, Lexington, MA, 1978.
34 Brown, P.
   The transfer of care: US mental health policy since World War II. *Int. J.
   Health Serv.* 9(4): 645–662, 1979.
35 Feldman, S.
   CMHCs: A decade later. *Int. J. Mental Health* 3(2): 19–34, 1974.

36 Bachrach, L. L.
Deinstitutionalization: An Analytical Review and Sociological Perspective.
National Institute of Mental Health Report Series on Mental Health Statistics
Series D., No. 4, Rockville, Md., 1976.

37 Becker, A., and Schulberg, H. C.
Phasing out state hospitals – A psychiatric dilemma. *New Engl. J. Med.* 294:
255–261, January 29, 1976.

38 General Accounting Office. *Returning the Mentally Disabled to the Community:
Government Needs to Do More.* US Government Printing Office, Washington,
DC, 1977.

39 Bruzelius, N. J.
New policy restricts restraints, seclusion. *Boston Globe*, January 8, 1978.

40 Booth, C. Brewster v. Dukakis.
Mass. Psych. Wards 1(3): 6, 11, 1979.

41 Booth, C. Brewster v Dukakis: Part Two.
Mass. Psych. Wards 1(4): 1, 4, 1979.

42 Brooks, A. D.
Hospitalization of the mentally ill: The legislative role, *State Government*,
Autumn 1977, pp. 198–202.

43 Brown, P.
Social change at Harrowdale State Hospital. *Rough Times* 2(6): 6–8, 1972.

44 Basaglia, F., and Basaglia, F.
Violence and marginality. *State and Mind* 7(3): 19–23, 1980.

45 Sidel, R.
Mental diseases in China and their treatment. In *Labeling Madness*, edited by
T. Scheff, pp. 119–134. Prentice-Hall Publishers, Englewood Cliffs, N.J.,
1975.

46 Chamberlin, J.
'Radical shrinks' meet militant ex-inmates. *Madness Network News* 6(2): 3–4,
1981.

47 Anspach, R.
From stigma to identity politics: Political activism among the physically
disabled and former mental patients. *Soc. Sci. Med.* 13(6A) 765–773,
1979.

48 Spitzer, S.
The political economy of therapeutic control: The commodification and
decommodification of mental health. In *The Community Imperative:
Proceedings of a National Conference on Overcoming Public Opposition to
Community Care of the Mentally Ill*, edited by Richard Baron, Irvin Rutman,
and Barbara Klaczynska, pp. 227–236. Horizon House Institute, Philadelphia,
1980.

49 Rosenhan, D.
On being sane in insane places. *Science* 179: 250–258, 1973.

50 Freidson, E.
Profession of Medicine. Harper & Row, New York, 1970.

51 Larson, M. S.
The Rise of Professionalism. University of California Press, Berkeley, 1977.

52 Fleming, S. Shrinks vs. shysters:
The latest battle for control of the mentally ill. *Law and Human Behavior*, in
press.
53 Chase, J.
Where have all the patients gone? *Human Behavior*, October 1973, pp. 14–21.
54 Meyer, N.
*Provisional Patient Movement and Administrative Data: State and County
Mental Hospital In-patient Services, July 1, 1973–June 30, 1974.* National
Institute of Mental Health, Statistical Note No. 114, Rockville, Md., 1976.
55 Weiner, S., Bird, B. J., and Arthur Bolton Associates.
Process and Impacts of the Closing of DeWitt State Hospital. Stanford Research
Institute, Menlo Park, Ca., 1973.
56 Greenblatt, M., and Glazier, E.
The phasing out of mental hospitals in the United States. *Am. J. Psychiatry*
132(11): 1135–1140, 1975.
57 American Federation of State, County, and Municipal Employees.
Patients for Sale. Washington, DC, 1980.
58 Scull, A.
Decarceration: Community Treatment and the Deviant – A Radical View.
Prentice-Hall Publishers, Englewood Cliffs, N.J., 1977.

Part III

*Providers
and treatments*

INTRODUCTION

In the provision of mental health care and in the formulation of policies and programs, practitioners clearly play important roles. The phenomenal growth of the mental health field in the post-World War II era included a dramatic rise in the number and variety of professionals. Mental health providers excelled in obtaining training and research funds, which allowed for an increase in the number of providers who could survive. Likewise, they engineered the creation of new facilities which required their labor. Psychiatry, and to a lesser degree clinical psychology and psychiatric social work, have attained much expanded status and power as professional groups. This section of readings provides material on several aspects of the psychiatric profession. All the selections deal with psychiatrists, not with other providers. This is due to the predominance of psychiatrists in mainstream mental health services. In the next section – on alternative care – attention will be paid to forms of treatment which do not include psychiatrists in either a predominant position or any position at all.

Donald Light's *Becoming Psychiatrists: The Professional Transformation of Self* is the best current description and analysis of the training of psychiatrists. A chapter from this book, drawing on Light's study of professional socialization at one of the nation's foremost psychiatric residency programs, shows how the clash of perspectives in the field has made psychiatry tangential to many mental health needs of the population. Of particular interest is Light's treatment of the contradictory elements of psychiatric expansion. On the one hand, community mental health represented a huge leap into a social level of psychiatry. On the other hand, forms of treatment were hardly changed from traditional hospital-based or individual practice-based forms. Further, psychiatry eschewed certain sociomedical problems that it might have properly addressed – alcoholism and sex therapy. Thus, contrary to many others who emphasise the *medicalization* aspects of psychiatric expansion, Light believes that there has been *demedicalization* of community mental health in the form of increased responsibility for nonpsychiatrists. Most recently, hostility from their medical colleagues has led psychiatrists to move towards a more strictly organic medical model, though as Light emphasizes, this change has occurred without a coherent overall framework or sense of professional development. Such myopia is possible, Light comments, since psychiatry generally has been very concerned with defending itself against justified criticism, and with preserving its own status and power despite the effects on patient care.

To study a specific example of psychiatrists' inability to deliver omnipotent expert opinion, we turn to Joseph Cocozza and Henry Steadman's 'Prediction in psychiatry: An example of misplaced confidence in experts.' The authors examine psychiatric testimony in court concerning the potential dangerousness of felony defendants considered incompetent to stand trial. Cocozza and Steadman show that the best prediction of dangerousness is the defendant's current charge, yet this data is not given priority. Psychiatrists may take this factor into account, but they nevertheless provide psychiatric rationales to justify public and legal belief in psychiatrists' expertise.

When patients were followed up to find out if they had engaged in assaultive behavior, been rehospitalized, or rearrested, there was no significant difference between those diagnosed as dangerous or non-dangerous. These data indicate that the prediction of dangerousness is inaccurate. This is important on several grounds. On a purely constitutional basis it is unjust, since psychiatric predictions are being used to incarcerate persons who have not been tried and found guilty. In terms of the sociology of professions, this data is useful to show that professional power to dramatically affect people's lives may be based on unfounded confidence. This is particularly salient in recent years, with the increase in the use of the insanity defense as a way to escape regular criminal trial for various heinous crimes. Perhaps people wish to believe that experts exist to deal with most or all difficult decisions, and therefore the public does not examine the basis of the experts' knowledge. This further interacts with the profession's often successful efforts to achieve public and governmental recognition and authority.

Thomas Scheff's contribution to the discussion of psychiatrists' medical dominance emphasizes a different aspect of practice – excess use of psychoactive drugs. In 'Medical dominance: Psychoactive drugs and mental health policy,' Scheff argues that by virtue of their training in the medical model, their high caseloads, and their legal and administrative responsibilities, psychiatrists rely on drugs without sufficient regard for their dangers. One major side-effect, tardive dyskinesia, has recently been found to have extensive prevalence, and the involuntary muscle movements it causes are irreversible. Like Cocozza and Steadman, Scheff utilizes Freidson's notion of professional dominance. Psychiatrists, like all physicians, seek to dominate the institutions and the relationships which they work in and deal with. This dominance includes a monopolization of knowledge and skills, reliance on medical technology, a public and legal basis for their special authority, and self-preservation without adequate regard for the client's welfare. Scheff believes that the legal power of psychiatrists to prescribe drugs and to control mental health facilities must be changed in order to improve mental health care. He urges the application of a true team method, another unfulfilled goal of the early community mental health theorists.

Continuing with the matter of psychiatric drugs, George Crane's 'Psychopharmacology in its twentieth year' offers a more technical base for the expansion of psychoactive drugs. Crane's emphasis is on side-effects, particularly tardive dyskinesia. In fact, Crane is one of the leading psychiatrists in the nation who have called this serious problem to both professional and public attention. As Crane notes, patients' families accept medical dominance in the form of psychiatric drugs, creating a ritual of mystification in which patient, family and staff participate. This ignores the need to examine larger background issues to the patient's illness. Crane does not seek the discontinuation of psychoactive drugs, but only a more judicious application. He calls for an end to indiscriminate usage, and more efforts at longitudinal studies on tardive dyskinesia and other side-effects. As Crane writes, psychiatric drugs are an 'example of large-scale and inefficient application of a potentially useful technical discovery without consideration for its long-term effects on the individual and his environment.'

CHAPTER 9

Professional training and the future of psychiatry*

Donald Light

Stepping back to view the relation of psychiatric education to the profession as a whole puts it in a different light. For ironically, this famous training program at University Psychiatric Center was setting its graduates on a trajectory that would be increasingly tangential to the profession and, more important, to the needs of society. These pages describe the end of an era, the final years of a great psychodynamically based program before it changed under pressure from the state and the profession. But it was not atypical in its values and techniques from the programs that trained the vast majority of psychiatrists in the profession today. Even at that time, one could see the signs of insularity from major shifts in mental health care: the disgust expressed at having to work with ordinary 'cases' from the community – black, uneducated, old, or some combination thereof; the poor attendance at required drug seminars and the view of drugs as tools of management rather than therapy; the disengagement from medicine; and the almost exclusive preoccupation with the inner dynamics of a patient, leaving work with the family, employer, and social agencies to the social workers. How did this insularity come about?

Professions are not unitary but are made up of factions or segments with their own view of what work is essential, of what techniques are best, and of how care should be organized.[1] Psychoanalysis, and

* Reprinted from *Becoming Psychiatrists: The Professional Transformation of Self*, by Donald Light, by permission of the author and of W. W. Norton & Co., Inc. Copyright © 1980 by W. W. Norton & Co., Inc.

its broad, diluted form known as dynamic psychiatry, had been the dominant segment for so long that it regarded the development of new therapies as epiphenomena or as irrelevant. Moreover, dynamic psychiatry has the fatal qualities of low paradigm development already discussed: strong on theory or ideology but weak on evidence and research. One consequence is a hierarchy built on authoritative figures, a deference to senior figures and the lore that surrounds them rather than a deference to research and new knowledge. These qualities have often been noted. The enlightened analyst, Robert Wallerstein, for example, has deplored the ideological factions that build up around authority figures and has called for rigorous research that involves other disciplines in the university.[2] But the argument here is sociological, namely that a weak technological base leads to these structural and cultural characteristics that promote a certain arrogant insularity in major scientific advances.

One consequence of these qualities was that dynamic psychiatry never integrated well with the rest of medicine. Theoretical incompatibility was not the central problem. Nor was psychiatry shut out of the curriculum. In fact, under the grandiose name of behavioral science it has gained more and more time in medical education, from 112 hours on the average in 1940 to 458 hours in 1966.[3] And leading psychiatrists would insist that they use the medical model of diagnosis and treatment. Nevertheless, courses in psychiatry have been consistently looked down on with disdain, and physicians in medicine have consistently regarded psychiatry with suspicion if not hostility. Besides the obstacles of clashing personalities and a certain queasiness around disturbed minds, the problem seems to lie in dynamic psychiatry's reliance on sages and insight rather than researchers and lab tests.

On the other side, dynamic psychiatry has done little until recently to bring about this integration. Residents at University Psychiatric Center and across the nation learned to dislike or belittle the most medical aspects of psychiatry. They learned that organic brain syndromes were not interesting because they were 'cut-and-dried' and did not involve psychodynamics. Electroshock therapy repelled most of them. Despite its quick, dramatic results for certain disorders, it was the treatment of last resort. We have already mentioned the belittling of psychopharmacology. Residents even learned to abandon the physical exam. A recent study of young psychiatrists trained at the University of California Medical Center found that none of the respondents performed a physical on outpatients and 85 percent did not do it on new inpatients.[4] Yet psychiatrists are quick to emphasize their medical affiliation as distinguishing them from other psychotherapists.

Besides keeping medicine in an ambivalent, arms-length position, the inbred qualities of the psychodynamic segment have made psychiatry slow to respond to the changing needs of the population. Although psychodynamic theory emphasizes the importance of the family, it was clinicians in social work and segments of psychology that expanded family therapy. The major cultural trends which have torn at the family led to a great need for this work, but psychiatry entered the field late. Group dynamics and group therapy were also picked up late, though Freud had written brilliantly about them. As recently as 1977, a survey by the American Psychiatric Association found that family and group therapy were still little used by psychiatrists.[5] Sociologically, group therapy was an important response to the widening demand for therapy from people who could not afford it individually. Group techniques were both developed and proliferated outside of psychiatry. As one observer put it, 'psychiatry is losing its grip on the non-psychotic world.'[6] The reasons, again, do not seem to lie in the limits of psychodynamic theory but in professional habits, a fixation on individual therapy.

Certain other kinds of therapy which would naturally seem to fall within the purview of psychiatry have grown tremendously but have not seemed quite proper or tasteful to most members of the profession. Public concern over alcoholism and the large government programs devoted to it reflect a major trend away from regarding it as a crime or the result of bad character toward a therapeutic and medical approach to the problem.[7] Naturally, psychiatrists work with alcoholics, but as little as possible. Although alcoholism inherently combines medical and psychological dimensions and therefore is an area in which psychiatry could have established a monopoly, it did not. A more recent field of growing demand has been sex therapy of the Masters and Johnson kind. Again, it combines physiological and psychological dimensions. Although psychiatrists deal with sex problems all the time, they do it in their own way and for the most part did not participate in developing the new techniques based on careful medical research. To summarize, the psychiatric profession and its association have passed up twenty years of extraordinary opportunities and creative developments. It is one of the few professions which, despite its prerogatives, lost ground in a period of expansion.

A preoccupation with the individual has contributed to psychiatry's unresponsiveness to the victims of discrimination. Therapists outside the profession were much quicker to understand the nature and pathologies of racism and sexism. Of course there were exceptions, both good and bad. In all of these areas, a certain number of psychiatrists pandered to social fads and another small number did pioneering work of enduring significance. But these exceptions are less important than the norms in training and practice.

An indication of psychiatry's insensitivity to social forces and cultural needs can be seen in how little it has done for blacks and women in its own training programs. A report commissioned by the American Psychiatric Association concluded: 'The meaning of being a woman to the woman resident and her teachers, to the woman therapist and her patients . . . has received scant attention.'[8] A recent survey reported in the study of residency training by the American Psychiatric Association that 'approximately 71 percent of the programs acknowledged that they had no affirmative action programs specifying active efforts to recruit women residents . . . 48 percent of the programs did not consider the supervisor's sex important . . . 87 percent of the programs did not offer courses on the psychology or sociology of women.'[9] The same study found only one recent article on the training of Afro-Americans and less than one hundred blacks in psychiatric residencies. Yet the APA study correctly anticipates a tremendous demand for therapeutic services among blacks. The survey found most of the residents critical of their program's understanding of racial issues. They felt that psychiatric theory had little to do with social problems and the needs of the patient population.[10] While psychiatry is certainly capable of addressing these needs, the residents are correct in their assessment of actual training and practice.

Similar qualities of the profession underlie the broken marriage between psychiatry and community mental health. The origins of this movement are complex.[11] They entail humanitarian, liberal politics both in psychiatry and in government, the hard politics of academic psychiatrists (who occupy key federal positions) wresting control of public psychiatry from the states and their mental hospitals by establishing a new institutional network to replace those hospitals, the advent of new drugs that could maintain hospitalized patients in the community, and the desire to cut hospital costs by transferring patients to programs of the welfare state.[12] The grandiosity of the project was staggering. 'The CMHC program would be one of the federal government's first attempts to raise national mental health by improving the quality of general community life through expert knowledge, not merely by more effective treatment for the already ill.'[13]

There was 'the fantasy of an omnipotent and omniscient mental health technology that could thoroughly reform society. . . .'[14] Given the difficulty psychiatry had in treating disturbed individuals, the assertion that it could also treat whole communities, carry out primary prevention, and eradicate mental illness was extraordinary.

No one inside the profession or out has yet explained such arrogance except to dismiss it as 'naive.'[15] But since highly sophisticated leaders of psychiatry, including the director of the University Psychiatric Center, promoted the idea, naiveté is too simple an answer. The profession needs to take itself on as a patient; for never has a profession carried out so grandiose a scheme on so large a scale with such widespread consequences.

We cannot digress to describe and explain the community mental health movement. For interested readers, the two most balanced accounts are by Musto and by Bassuk and Gerson.[16] Our interest is to understand the lack of genuine support for this movement once it was started and the consequences of the movement for the profession. For community mental health was a Trojan horse. Once psychiatry let it enter the city walls, thousands of its rivals poured forth from it. Over the years, psychologists and psychiatric social workers have gained increasing control over community mental health centers (CMHCs) and an increasing proportion of the professional positions, while the proportion and power of psychiatrists has steadily diminished. Specifically, in the six years from 1970 to 1976, the number of positions per center on the average decreased by 35 percent for psychiatrists, increased by 77 percent for psychologists, and increased by 35 percent for social workers.[17] The reasons are not hard to identify. First, community mental health further demedicalized 'mental illness' so that psychiatry's efforts to claim exclusive rights over it became nearly indefensible. Admonitions that psychiatrists should 'diplomatically point out that their rigorous medical and psychiatric training, extensive leadership experience in patient management, and ultimate legal responsibility for patient care differentiate them from other clinicians'[18] miss the point. These arguments have been made and other clinicians are not impressed. They feel that their training is just as rigorous, that medical expertise is usually not important, that they can manage patients as well or better than psychiatrists, and that 'ultimate legal responsibility' is usually not involved. Thus they need psychiatrists as a part-time resource because of their legal-medical monopoly over prescriptions and hospitalization. And this is exactly what has happened in many centers. Being a costly drain on an inadequate budget, psychiatrists' time is cut back to the minimum needed to carry out these functions. Aside from their legal-medical monopoly, psychiatrists do not have a clearly defined role and offer no distinctive model of how to do community mental health.[19]

Thus the fundamental problem with community mental health is that it created a new system of service without a new paradigm of care underlying it. Thomas Kuhn has pointed out that the organization of activities in a science is paradigm-specific.[20] One cannot successfully change the organization of research without a change in the underlying paradigm. It is illuminating to extend this argument to the delivery of services based on scientific work. Without a technology and clear examples of how community mental health differed from previous clinical work, community mental health has devolved into an outpatient variant of custodial practices previously found in state mental hospitals. This is what underlies the thoughtful assessment by Bassuk and Gerson:

> The very nature of many conditions psychiatrists attempt to treat is still not well understood. In view of this lack of basic knowledge it is not surprising that there are no accepted guidelines for establishing comprehensive systems for the delivery of mental health care – notably systems for reaching disadvantaged people.[21]

Besides the demedicalizing of mental illness and the lack of a new paradigm for mental health care, community mental health work did not attract the commitment of psychiatrists. As a study in 1974 showed, only 4 percent of psychiatrists listed community or social psychiatry as their area of specialization, though over 25 percent of them worked in the centers.[22] Unlike psychologists and social workers, they also tended to work part-time. Put simply, it is difficult to maintain a preeminent position when one is working part-time at an institution where one's competitors are working full-time and run it. He cannot lead who dabbles. The ensuing hostilities, when combined with inadequate and unstable funding, poor work conditions, and 'uninteresting' clientele, have left psychiatrists with alternatives to go elsewhere. Thus, a quarter of the profession worked in CMHCs in 1974 because the jobs were there for the young and/or less qualified. A downward drift has developed 'in which only those psychiatrists least qualified to work in other modes of practice perform [the CMHC's] long-term service and leadership roles. . . .'[23]

The lack of commitment and techniques is reflected in the poor training which most psychiatrists practicing today have had for community work. Like all training, appropriate preparation begins with appropriate recruitment. In the major study of psychiatrists, social workers and psychologists, Henry, Sims, and Spray found once more that therapists choose patients like themselves, and the modal psychiatrist is middle-class, educated, verbal, Jewish, and white.[24] The authors imply that one will have to recruit from a wider range than this if we expect therapists to work with the spectrum of patients found in any community.

Psychodynamic training does nothing to overcome the social and cultural biases of psychiatrists' background. A recent national survey concluded that 'To the extent that community mental health is rooted – in part, at least – in a sociogenic etiology and social remediation of mental disorders, then psychiatrists' unwillingness to assume any but the most modest of community activist stances may hinder the continued development and elaboration of the movement. . . .'[25] Psychiatrists were more likely than other staff to regard their community mental health center as a medical facility rather than as a social service facility, and they had been considerably less involved in community situations requiring them to be a change agent.

These findings stem from the psychoanalytically based training which so many psychiatrists receive and pursue. As usually taught, it is distinctly inappropriate for work in community mental health.[26] A number of books have appeared trying to show how they are compatible; but the diagnostic focus on unresolved tensions in early childhood; the slow, expensive, careful unravelling of these in treatment; and the trained inattention to physical surrounding, political manipulation, or economics is hardly what most CMHC clients want or what the centers can afford to give. No wonder residents disdained patients from the community when the challenges they presented differed so from those the staff at University Psychiatric Center emphasized.

A psychodynamic training is not only inappropriate; it can be dangerous. A recent, detailed study of staff relations at CMHC illustrated this when investigators found that such psychiatrists infused the rest of the staff with their professional biases.[27] The staff became stratified according to how trained they were to give dynamic psychotherapy, and the patients were stratified according to how eligible they were for such treatment. Thus the psychiatrists saved all the 'interesting' (articulate, neurotic, middle-class) patients for themselves and saw a few patients often. At the other end of the scale, any patient speaking Spanish or considered undesirable for individual therapy was given to the essentially untrained community mental health workers, many of whom could not speak Spanish either. Worse, these workers saw themselves as 'getting the dregs.' In this grotesque distortion of a community service, psychiatrists work the system to fulfill their own professional self-image which they acquired in residency.

To summarize, even when the omnipotent fantasies of psychiatry's leaders became manifest in the community mental health movement, the profession's elitist insularity prevented members from meeting the challenge. Meanwhile, what had been envisioned as an expanded power base for psychiatry turned out to be a power base for psychology and social work, albeit underfunded and pedestrian. Psychiatry developed an identity crisis of immense proportions, became disillusioned with community mental health, proclaimed over and over that it was 'dead' even as new centers were being rapidly built, and rediscovered its medical roots.

The return to medicine

In a prophetic article, Eugene Pumpian-Mindlin warned that if community psychiatry diverted the profession from the doctor-patient relationship by defining the community as the client, the identity of the profession would become dissipated. He warned the profession 'not to be corrupted by the wealth which is pouring our way. . . .'[28] The problem, it turned out, was not only losing sight of the doctor-patient relationship, but having patients who did not respond to psychotherapeutic techniques. Identity confusion results from working with an interprofessional team, yet seeing oneself as a 'doctor' and therefore leader. An early report on a residency in Cincinnati described many of the problems that appeared at other residencies and at University Psychiatric Center.[29] Residents considered their assignment in community psychiatry a drudge and disparagingly called the clinic in Cincinnati a 'drug clinic,' showing in the process the psychodynamic bias against drugs as significant therapeutic tools. By 1974, such reports were more common, one on Tufts describing the 'anxiety, loneliness, anger and disappointment' residents expressed toward their community psychiatry training.[30] By 1975, Roy Grinker declared, '. . . our discipline has lost its boundaries.'[31] He deplored the dichotomy of the medical vs. the social-model as 'one of the worst possible examples of dualistic thinking,'[32] but he called community and preventive psychiatry illusions, saying psychiatrists cannot be social engineers and change socioeconomic predispositions. Looking back in 1977, Francis Braceland concluded, 'We wandered too far afield in the 1960s, and some colleagues took on a sociologic cast of character that almost split our speciality in two.'[33]

The return to medicine became a broad movement in 1974. While just the year before, sessions at the annual meetings of the American Psychiatric Association on training were filled with educators openly expressing their confusion about what psychiatrists should learn, in 1974 the same sessions were filled with assertions about the importance of medicine in psychiatry, the tremendous gains in biopsychiatric research and the value of going through internship. Community psychiatry had confronted the profession with the inability of its own psychodynamic paradigm to consider extrapsychic forces, and it had admitted nonmedical competitors in a flush of egalitarianism.

The timing of this professional shift could not have been better. Both the public and leaders of the medical profession were pursuing primary care medicine. Family practice had finally become a specialty with its own residency and board exams. Federal funds were prompting medical schools everywhere to establish primary care programs, and the major specialties of internal medicine, pediatrics, and surgery were all designing primary care tracks. Given how common emotional problems are in any primary care practice, and considering the psychiatric dimensions of most serious medical procedures, psychiatry reaffirmed its medical roots at a time when the previous prejudices which specialists had had were breaking down. There was in this an historical symmetry. After World War II, medicine carried its obsession with specialty research and training to its practical conclusion – 80 percent became specialists when only 10 percent of all medical problems needed specialty care. During the same period, psychiatry was carried away from medicine by its psychoanalytic preoccupation. Now both sides were correcting and finding their common ground; therefore psychiatry could become full partner with the other major specialities in a new era of primary care and family medicine. It has not happened. In most schools, faculties in the other major specialities have not found their department of psychiatry very helpful or very willing to help. They feel perfectly capable of teaching psychiatry to their students themselves. An exception is 'liaison psychiatry,' a most interesting term, because it indicates that the profession had to have specialists to make itself useful and comprehensible to other physicians. A liaison psychiatrist recently wrote:

> The problem, then, is two-fold. We must persuade those in charge of psychiatric residency training of the need to inculcate candidates with the knowledge of the normal and abnormal psychological reactions to medical illness, including knowledge of recent findings derived from psychobiological research, and of the need to transmit this knowledge to the medical caretaker. At the same time we must persuade medical caretakers of the need for the liaison psychiatrist's clinical and educational services.[34]

But why has this not been a central part of training for *all* psychiatrists long before liaison psychiatry became fashionable? In short, through its pride and inflexibility, psychiatry succeeded in most medical schools during the seventies to make itself irrelevant even to its own parent profession. Not surprisingly, recruitment declined as those medical students more interested in people than organ systems found more versatile and expanding opportunities in family medicine or one of the primary care specialities.

Paradigm shift: The rise of biopsychiatry

During the past thirty years, research in biochemistry and psycho-pharmacology has steadily grown and produced important drugs that are universally used. What the predominantly psychodynamic profession did not seem to realize as it used these drugs along with psychotherapy was that they contained a fundamentally different paradigm of psychiatry. The etiology of disorders, the process of diagnosis, the kind of training, the nature of research, and the course of treatment implied by biopsychiatry are all different. Ultimately they are reconcilable – Freud recognized that – but they are strikingly different as presently practiced. Everyone in town knew about this work in the late sixties, when this study was done. Some of the most important work was going on down the street. But so long as this work did not constitute a major power base in the profession, most psychiatrists could ignore its journal articles full of strange hiero-glyphics and they could innocently reap the fruits of its research.

However, academic centers shape the future direction of a profession, and large grants for biochemical research gave biopsychi-atrists power. This same pattern was dramatically illustrated in medical schools, where Flexner's choice of the Johns Hopkins model for training put researchers in charge of education. As Rosemary Stevens has traced so well, the Johns Hopkins academic model steadily altered the entire character and politics of the medical profession.[35] In many ways, the Association of American Medical Colleges is today more influential than the AMA in policies affecting the profession. Starting in the late 1960s, the same process began in psychiatry. Behavioral scientists and community psychiatrists were replaced by biochemical researchers. Department after major depart-ment replaced a chairman trained in psychoanalysis with a biopsychi-atrist. One such chairman, who replaced a famous social psychiatrist, ordered that everyone start wearing white coats. At first, the staff joked about it: 'Oh, I see you're wearing your white coat today!' But soon the joking stopped.

Biopsychiatry now has control of major power centers in academic psychiatry. Its proponents are rewriting the Diagnostic Statistical Manual to emphasize the biomedical etiology of mental disorders. Students who cut up in class, alcoholics, 'antisocial' individuals, criminals, homosexuals, political dissidents, chain smokers, obese people, to mention a few, are increasingly seen to have biochemical imbalances, if not genetic defects. Like any social movement, it is rewriting history to show that before 1955 there was nothing but darkness and misery.

Pessimism about psychiatric disorders was widespread, admissions increased, and discharges remained low.

Living areas in public mental hospitals were poorly furnished and crowded. Hallucinating patients paced the floor, or rocked in chairs, and talked to their 'voices'; paranoid patients scanned the rooms, ever vigilant and ever fearful. . . .

The physicians responsible for the treatment of patients in public mental hospitals were poorly equipped for the task . . . [because] neither neurological diagnosis nor psychoanalysis had much to offer patients in public mental institutions.[36]

This account, in its exclusive focus on public mental hospitals as if their reality were the whole, glosses over so many issues irrelevant to physicians' techniques, and so ignores successful treatments without drugs, that only ideological distortion remains. Biopsychiatry now takes full credit for the community mental health movement; for it would not have been possible without the miraculous drugs it provided.[37] As Andrew Scull has shown, deinstitutionalization had less to do with new drugs than with saving money under the guise of humanitarianism.[38] And community mental health was hardly a movement which advocated proliferating the drugs of biopsychiatry to the underprivileged. To the extent that this has nevertheless happened, it has raised grave doubts about community psychiatry. While it began as a powerful humanitarian movement to break down class barriers in psychotherapy, to bring well-trained clinicians into close contact with the suffering of underprivileged people, to work jointly with ordinary citizens in campaigns against oppressive and dehumanizing forces from which they suffered, in fact community psychiatry has become a large set of underfunded centers that dispense drugs to large volumes of disturbed patients. It is estimated that the use of neuroleptics on patients in the community is 85 percent, at least as high as it was among hospitalized patients.[39] It is probably higher, because communities are less tolerant of deviant behavior than hospital staff, and life in a community requires more control.[40] Among discharged schizophrenics it reaches 95 percent.[41] The effects of these drugs extend beyond the individual to alter relations with his or her social network, reducing and distorting interaction in a variety of ways.[42] In California at least, most of the discharged patients have not returned to their families or communities of origin; so that patients do not have well-established social bonds with which to carry out the original ideals of community health work. On the contrary, many towns succeed in keeping state mental hospitals from discharging patients into their communities, so that large numbers of them are channelled into specific center-city areas.[43] These conditions further increase the dependence on drugs. The overall effect on health care is to medicalize it and play down educational, therapeutic, or rehabilitative alternatives.

As has been the case with previous new 'cures,' interesting doubts are being raised about how effective various drugs really are. Even lithium, 'the first specific treatment for major affective disorders,'[44] may turn out to be effective only on the subsample of people it is purported to 'cure.' In his review of psychotropic drugs, Thomas Scheff puts 'the phenothiazines (in the treatment of acute psychosis) and lithium carbonate closer to the positive value end of the continuum, the anti-depressants of lesser value, and the phenothiazines in the treatment of chronic psychosis and the anti-anxiety drugs, worse than useless.'[45] Since even small doses of Thorazine decrease social communication, the sociological side-effects may be significant.[46] The antianxiety drugs have a short but ominous history. Miltown, after being used by millions, was found ineffective and removed from the market, to be replaced by Valium and Librium, which now appear ineffective and also addictive.[47] But these problems are unlikely to slow down biopsychiatrists in their increasing influence over psychiatric practice. The technology of neuroleptics is increasingly imbedded in the social organization of care, subsuming more and more problems under its medical paradigm. Soon a complex division of labor may arise. In the model outlined by Fieve, one would have specialized clinics staffed largely by paramedics using routinized diagnostic tools, with a psychiatrist or two acting as supervisor and manager.[48]

Yesterday's training – tomorrow's practice

This portrait of the profession makes clear how most psychiatrists practicing today were trained with skills and professional values that have made them marginal to the paradigm shift in the profession and to the widening needs of society. Psychiatry today seems as confused about how to train its members and about their roles relative to physicians, paraprofessionals, and nonmedical therapists as ever. The confusion is less obvious, because spokesmen keep uttering to each other reassuring phrases about 'medical psychiatry.' As always, there are individuals who have thought through the issues and know what they are doing, but viewing the profession as a whole reveals confusion and unresolved questions around the classic fault lines in the profession. One of those concerns the relation between body and mind, between psychiatry and internal medicine, and a number of residencies seem to handle the internship year over which they now have control by asking themselves if residents should spend half or three-quarters of the first year 'on the wards.' It is, of course, the wrong question; for it barely addresses the integration of medicine with psychiatry for the future.

The garbled thinking which continues to plague the profession is found in the recent, major study of psychiatric education by the American Psychiatric Association. One section asks, 'What is a psychiatrist?' On the one hand, it admits that any physician can limit his/her practice to psychiatry without any training. On the other hand, psychologists, social workers and nurses 'contributed to the advancement of psychiatry.'[49] The board of trustees held an official discussion about the resulting problem of defining a psychiatrist. The report concludes that

> the psychiatrist is characterized by the medical assets he brings to the treatment of his patients. His distinct training includes patient responsibility, knowledge of psychodynamics, a cultivated sense of human growth and development, a heightened awareness of interpersonal process, professional objectivity, expert interviewing techniques and experience in negotiating counter-transference phenomena.

Hence it may be said that a psychiatrist can be defined as someone who has the knowledge and skills indicated as minimally necessary to function in order to cure and prevent mental illness. The complete psychiatrist exhibits these qualities to such an extent that as a result of his training (and lifelong education) he brings to his performance the highest degrees of patient responsibility, knowledge of psychodynamics, sensitivity about growth and development, compassionate objectivity, interviewing expertise and awareness of countertransference.[50] Besides the embarrassment of redundancy, vague terms and ideological bias, these medical assets are not medical at all. In a similar vein, the commission concludes with criteria for being declared a psychiatrist. They are amazing for their lack of substance and for tautological dependence on the professional monopoly they already hold. The first five criteria, for example, are: 1. has completed medical training; 2. could be employed as psychiatrist; 3. could be given a title which indicated psychiatric training; 4. defines himself/herself as a psychiatrist; 5. can meet requirements to join recognized professional societies.[51]

The basic problem with psychiatric training today is that it finds itself encumbered with years of medical school and decades of ideological bias, so that the profession is full of self-preservation, defensive thinking, and inhouse fighting. Psychodynamic psychiatry, as portrayed in this study, served a great purpose. It brought a level of human treatment and innovative study that the field had never seen before. But in the last fifteen years vested interests have entrenched themselves, and the profession has shown a remarkable inability to incorporate new developments, because the psychodynamic segment became too ingrown.

The situation today in some respects resembles the state of medicine around 1910, when Flexner issued his famous report. A large number of general psychiatrists, trained in programs of widely differing quality which admitted nearly anyone willing to apply, is treating patients with few specific remedies and little technology. But science has provided the basis for a new breed of psychiatrist, highly skilled and conversant with the expanding armature of drugs and medical technology. How practitioners assimilate this new technology will depend on the politics of legislation and the use of continuing education. But as in 1910, the new mandarins are narrowly focused on what their technology can do, not what it leaves out. The chance for the integration of biopsychosocial knowledge, which is so badly needed in medicine and psychiatry, is at present not great. People may have bodies, psyches, and live in a social world, but psychiatric paradigms do not.

To conclude, the economic, cultural and scientific opportunities for psychiatry are so great that it is bound to grow in the future. There will be an increasing demand for therapeutic services as better insurance gives all social classes the power to purchase services, as the population gets older and more educated, and as the expectations for a happy life rise.[52] At a deeper level, this is the age of therapy, of narcissistic self-nurturance in the face of a transient, fast-paced world that fragments time and community. The underlying forces of technology and industrial economy have led to each individual occupying several 'roles,' each outside the true self and yet leaving that self vaguely defined. Modern psychiatry arose to bridge this gap, to nurture the private self.[53] Yet its growth will be troubled by such confusion and ambivalence that neither psychodynamic therapy nor community mental health nor psychiatry in primary care nor biopsychiatry will develop in a constructive, cohesive way. Some of the obstacles have their origins in the kind of training described in this study. Some of them stem from the limited, self-preoccupied way in which psychiatry has medicalized itself. Others result from competition rather than enlightened cooperation with other mental health professions. Only a united effort between social scientists, psychiatrists, and other physicians could develop the integrated biopsychosocial model that all of medicine needs, but at present such an effort seems unlikely.

Notes

1 This perspective on professions was suggestively described by Rue Bucher and Anselm Strauss in Professions in process, *American Journal of Sociology* (1961) 66: 325–34.

2 Personal communication.

3 Donald G. Langsley, Alfred M. Freedman, Melvyn Haas, and James H. Grubbs, Medical student education in psychiatry, *American Journal of Psychiatry* 134 (1977), 15–20.

4 Charles W. Patterson, Psychiatrists and physical examinations: A survey, *Am. J. Psychiatry* 135: 8 (L978), 967–68.

5 Specifically, 7 percent of the national sample did family therapy with 50 percent or more of their patients, while 22 percent never used it at all. Ten percent did group therapy on half or more of their patients, and 48 percent never used it at all. Donald G. Langsley, Psychiatry and mental health manpower. 1978, typed, from the American Psychiatric Association, p. 14.

6 Eliot Marshall, It's all in the mind, *The New Republic*, August 5–12, 1978, 18.

7 Joseph W. Schneider, Deviant drinking as disease: Alcoholism as a social accomplishment, *Social Problems* 25: 4 (1978), 361–72.

8 Nancy Roeske, MD, Women in psychiatry, the American Psychiatric Association's *Conference on the Education of Psychiatrists, Commission I*, James N. Susses, MD, chairman, 1975, typed, pp. 17–42, esp. p. 26.

9 The A.P.A.'s *Conference on the Education of Psychiatrists, Commission III*, David R. Hawkins, MD, chairman, 1975, typed, p. 34.

10 The A.P.A.'s *Conference*, David R. Hawkings, MD, chairman, pp. 39–40. See
    also Chester M. Pierce, MD, Teaching cross-racial therapy, pp. 56–62 in the
    A.P.A.'s *Conference, Commission IV*, Milton Greenblatt, MD, chairman.

11 David F. Musto, Whatever happened to community mental health? *Psychiatric
    Annals* 7: 10 (1977), 30–55.

12 On the last point, see Andrew Scull, *Decarceration* (Englewood Cliffs, N.J.:
    Spectrum, 1976).

13 Musto, Whatever happened, p. 43.

14 Ibid., p. 50.

15 See, for example, Jonathan F. Borus, Issues critical to the survival of community
    mental health, *Am. J. Psychiatry* 135: 9 (1978), 1029–35.

16 Musto, Whatever happened; Ellen L. Bassuk and Samuel Gerson,
    Deinstitutionalization and mental health services, *Scientific American* 238: 2
    (1978), 46–53.

17 Langsley *et al.*, Medical student education, 23.

18 Borus, Survival of community mental health, 1031.

19 Table 13 of Langsley's reports shows that, aside from prescribing medications
    and managing inpatients, psychiatrists do not spend their time differently at
    community mental health centers than psychologists and social workers.

20 Thomas Kuhn, *The Structure of Scientific Revolutions*, revised edition (Chicago;
    University of Chicago Press, 1970). See Allen W. Imershein's explication of
    Kuhn in his suggestive article, Organizational change as a paradigm shift, *The
    Sociological Quarterly* 18 (Winter 1977), 33–43.

21 Bassuk and Gerson, Deinstitutionalization, p. 52.

22 Park Elliott Dietz and Jonas R. Rappaport, Professional activities of Maryland
    and US psychiatrists, typed, 1976.

23 Borus, Survival of community mental health, 1032.

24 William E. Henry, John H. Sims, and S. Lee Spray, *Public and Private Lives
    of Psychotherapists* (San Francisco: Jossey-Bass, 1973).

25 Morton O. Wagenfeld and Stanley S. Robin, Social activism and psychiatrists
    in community mental health centers, *American Journal of Community
    Psychology* 6(3) 1978; 253–64, esp. 263. See also the authors' article, Structural
    and professional correlates of ideologies on community mental health workers,
    Journal of Health and Social Behavior 15 (1974), 199–210.

26 For a precise analysis of the different models underlying psychoanalysis and
    community mental health, see Miriam Seigler and Humphrey Osmond. Models
    of madness, *The British Journal of Psychiatry*, 112: 493 (1966), 1193–1203.

27 Judith Lorber and Roberta Satow, Creating a company of unequals: Sources of
    occupational stratification in a ghetto community mental health center,

Sociology of Work and Occupations 4 (1977), 281–302. For a professional analysis of these problems, see *Racism, Elitism, Professionalism: Barriers to Community Mental Health*, Israel Zwerling *et al.*, eds., (New York: Jason Aronson, 1976).

28 Eugene Pumpian-Mindlin, Problems of professional identity in training psychiatrists, *The Journal of Nervous and Mental Disease* 144: 6 (1967), 535–138.

29 Marvin L. Kaplan, Richard M. Kurtz, and William H. Clements, Psychiatric residents and lower class patients: Conflict in training, *Community Mental Health* 4: 1 (1968), 91–97.

30 Paul G. Cotton and Kyle D. Pruett, The affective experience of residency training in community psychiatry, *Am. J. Psychiatry* 132: 3 (March 1975), 267–69.

31 Roy G. Grinker, The future educational needs of psychiatrists, *American Journal of Psychiatry* 132: 3 (1975), 259–62.

32 Ibid., p. 260.

33 Francis J. Braceland, Psychiatry and the Third Revolution, *Psychiatric Annals* 7:10 (1977), 4–5.

34 James J. Strain, The medical setting: Is it beyond the psychiatrist? *Am. J. Psychiatry* 134: 3 (1977), 253–56.

35 Rosemary Stevens, *American Medicine and the Public Interest* (New Haven: Yale University Press, 1971).

36 Philip A. Berger, Medical treatment of mental illness, *Science* 200: 4344 (26 May 1978), 974–81, esp. 974–75.

37 Ronald R. Fieve, The revolution defined: It is pharmacologic, *Psychiatric Annals* 7: 10 (1977), 10–28.

38 Andrew Scull, *Decarceration*, chap. 5.

39 G. E. Crane, 'Clinical psychopharmacology in its twentieth year, *Science* 181 (1973), 124–28; R. F. Prien and C. J. Kleu. An appraisal of the long-term use of tranquilizing medication with hospitalized chronic schizophrenics: A review of the drug discontinuation literature, *Schizophrenia Bulletin* 5 (1972), 64–73.

40 P. Allen, A consumer's view of the California mental health care system, *Psychiatric Quarterly* 48 (1974), 1–13.

41 E. Laska *et al.*, Patterns of psychotropic drug use for schizophrenia, *Diseases of the Nervous System* 34 (1973), 294–305.

42 H. L. Lennard *et al.*, *Mystification and Drug Misuse: Hazards in Using Psychoactive Drugs.* (San Francisco: Jossey-Bass, 1971).

43 H. R. Lamb and V. Goertzel, Discharged mental patients: Are they really in the community? *Archives of General Psychiatry* 24 (1971), 29–34; U. Aviram and S. P. Segal, Exclusion of the mentally ill: Reflections on an old problem in a new context, *Archives of General Psychiatry* 29 (1973), 126–31.

44 Fieve, Revolution defined, 13.

45 T. J. Scheff, Medical dominance: Psychoactive drugs and mental health policy. *American Behavioral Scientist* 19: 3 (1976), 299–317, esp. 301.

46 Ibid., pp. 305–06.

47 Ibid., p. 307.

48 Fieve, Revolution defined. A new book which purports to teach nonmedical therapists what they need to know about medicine to diagnose emotional problems with physiological aspects is *Primer for the Nonmedical Psychotherapist*, by Joyce A. Backar (New York: Wiley Spectrum, 1976).

49 The APA's *Conference on the Education of Psychiatrists, Commission VII*, Eric Pfeiffer, MD, chairman (1975, typed), p. 20.

50 Ibid., p. 20.

51 Ibid., p. 24. In all there were nine criteria, eight of them without substance and tautological.

52 Samuel Martin, Factors influencing the future of financing psychiatric residency education, in the A.P.A.'s *Conference on the Education of Psychiatrists Commission VI*, Herzl R. Spiro, MD, chairman (1975, typed), pp. 10–13.

53 See Peter L. Berger, Towards a sociological understanding of psychoanalysis, *Social Research* 32 (Spring 1965), 26–41; and Christopher Lasch, The narcissistic society, *The New York Review of Books* XXIII (15), (September 30, 1976), 5–13.

CHAPTER 10

Prediction in psychiatry: an example of misplaced confidence in experts*†

Joseph J. Cocozza and Henry J. Steadman

In discussing the relationship between attitudes and behavior, Deutscher describes prediction as a primitive scientific notion which 'is, in fact, as closely related to magic as it is to science' (1973: 91–92). While its precise role in science is disputed, prediction is more usually seen as an integral part of science, differing from explanation only in its time reference (Hempel and Oppenheim, 1948; Angel, 1967) or as an important validator of explanations (Sjoberg and Nett, 1968). Nonetheless, there may be specific instances when the predictors may function more as seers than as scientists.

The data we present in this paper suggest that the prediction of a patient's dangerousness may represent such a situation. These are concrete predictions of future behavior usually employed with regard to issues of involuntary confinement, differential treatment, and release of the mentally ill and criminally insane. These predictions are also increasingly used in the criminal justice system to deal with questions such as bail and parole. The final decision about the dangerousness of an individual in both civil and criminal matters generally rests with the court or special boards. However, these

* This is a revised version of a paper presented at the Annual Meeting of the American Sociological Association, Chicago, Illinois, September, 1977. The research was supported in part by PHS Grant No. MH 20367 funded by the N.I.M.H., Center for the Studies of Crime and Delinquency. The authors wish to thank Gwynn Nettler, Richard L. Henshel, William R. Avison and the anonymous reviewers for their helpful comments on an earlier draft.
† Reprinted from *Social Problems*, vol. 25, pp. 265–276, 1978, with permission of the Society for the Study of Social Problems and the authors.

decisions always require psychiatric testimony. The profession of psychiatry is seen by society as possessing the special technical knowledge necessary to make these complex assessments. It is the psychiatrist who is constantly identified in mental health laws as the appropriate professional to render these evaluations and who has emerged as *the* expert in the prediction of dangerousness.

The process by which psychiatrists have assumed this position has been alluded to by Deutsch (1949) and discussed more fully by us elsewhere (Steadman, 1972). Briefly, what seems to have happened is that psychiatrists have been granted this responsibility of predicting dangerousness because of their attained status as experts in the treatment of mental illness and the historically strong association perceived between mental illness and violent behavior. In the mid-nineteenth century, the American public began to demand protection from involuntary mental hospitalization in the form of commitment laws, in which the primary justifications for involuntary institutionalization became dangerousness and the need for care and treatment. Psychiatrists, as they became the legitimated deliverers of mental health treatment, were assumed to be competent to judge the bases for medical intervention and hospitalization. One of these judgements related to the perceived potential of the individual for dangerous behavior. Thus, historical processes resulted in an acceptance of psychiatrists as society's experts in predicting dangerousness.

This situation has become all the more important because the prediction of dangerousness through psychiatric evaluation is rapidly becoming the single most important factor in the commitment of the mentally ill in the United States. Tens of thousands of individuals are involuntarily confined each year on the basis of their perceived dangerousness (Rubin, 1972). This criterion is commonly used in commitment and placement decisions for 'mentally ill offenders,' 'sexual psychopaths,' 'defective delinquents,' those found not guilty by reason of insanity, and those incompetent to stand trial. Furthermore, dangerousness is rapidly becoming the most important criterion for involuntary civil commitment (Levinson and York, 1974; Stone, 1975). Recent legal decisions (e.g., *Lessard v. Schmidt* 349 F. Suppl. 1078) have, in fact, suggested that dangerousness may be the sole criterion for involuntary confinement of the mentally ill. Since the landmark 1969 Lanterman-Petris-Short Act in California, every state that has revised its mental health statutes has declared the primary, if not the exclusive, bases for emergency involuntary commitment to be dangerousness. Yet, despite this importance, little concern has been expressed over the need to examine the nature and limits of the supposed psychiatric expertise in predicting dangerousness.

Such a situation appears to approximate the one which concerns Freidson in his discussion of the application of professional knowledge. He writes:

> As opposed to the medical knowledge which is medicine as such, there are the practices which grow up in the course of applying that knowledge to concrete patients in concrete social settings. The 'pure' medical knowledge is transmuted, even debased in the course of application. . . . Perhaps most important, because of the practitioner's moral commitment to intervention, action takes place even in the absence of reliable knowledge (1970: 346).

The purpose of this paper is to report research examining one application of professional expertise, where the reliability of knowledge has yet to be systematically reviewed. In order to address this issue objectively, we collected data on predictions of dangerousness by psychiatrists on a group of incompetent felony defendants. Information was obtained on the psychiatrists' decisions and their reasons for them, on the impact of non-psychiatric factors on their findings, on the extent to which the psychiatric findings were accepted by the court, and, most important, on the accuracy of the psychiatric predictions. These data provide unusually direct evidence to evaluate whether the confidence society has in the application of a special body of psychiatric knowledge in assessing dangerousness is justified.

Research setting and sample

On September 1, 1971, New York State's Criminal Procedure Law (CPL) became effective. One section[1] of the revised statutes mandated a determination of dangerousness for all indicted felony defendants found incompetent to stand trial. The determination as to the defendant's dangerousness was a judicial one based upon oral and written testimony by two psychiatrists.[2] A court finding of dangerousness permitted placement of the incompetent, indicted felony defendant in a facility run by the Department of Correctional

Services (DCS). A finding of not dangerous required commitment in a Department of Mental Hygiene (DMH) civil mental hospital. The major intent of the new statute was to reduce the number of incompetent defendants placed in maximum security correctional facilities and to send all but the dangerous accused felony defendant to more therapeutically-oriented mental health facilities. The implementation of this statute provided a unique opportunity to examine a situation in which psychiatrists were mandated to provide specific estimations of dangerousness.

All male, indicted felony defendants for whom a court psychiatric report on dangerousness was made between September 1, 1971 and August 31, 1972 were included in this study. This selection resulted in a group of 257 defendants. Several data sources were used to gather information on these 257 defendants. The first source was the judicial hearings themselves. For each defendant, data were collected on the current criminal charge which had led to their hearing, on the psychiatric finding regarding the dangerousness of each defendant, and on the final determination of dangerousness made by the court. In addition, copies of the formal reports prepared by the 118 psychiatrists who were involved in these proceedings were obtained. These court reports contained their recommendation for a finding of dangerous or not dangerous. In those cases where a finding of dangerousness was offered, the psychiatrists were also required to detail the reasons for their finding. Each reason given by a psychiatrist was coded up to a maximum of six.

The second source of data on these defendants were psychiatric and court records. From these files, social and demographic information on each individual was abstracted. The final set of data was gathered on all defendants over a three year follow-up period. These data centered around outcome measures of the defendant's actual behavior subsequent to the determination of dangerousness. This included examining hospital ward notes and incident reports for indicators of institutional behavior, and New York State's Department of Mental Hygiene and Division of Criminal Justice Services computerized files for indicators of community behavior.

Psychiatric findings of dangerousness

The developing trend toward the use of a diagnosis of dangerousness for institutionalization and differential treatment has not been accompanied by a clarification and specification of the meaning of the concept. While there have been some attempts to define dangerousness more clearly (Goldstein and Katz, 1960; Cocozza and Steadman, 1974), it remains amorphous. The New York CPL, unfortunately, provided an excellent example of this problem. In the revised law, a dangerously incapacitated person was defined as '. . . an incapacitated person who is so mentally ill or mentally defective that his presence in an institution operated by the Department of Mental Hygiene is dangerous to the safety of other patients therein, the staff of the institution, or the community.' Thus, the statutory definition tautologically defined a dangerous person as one who is dangerous . . . to the safety of other people. Accordingly, not only were the criteria for predicting dangerousness left to psychiatric judgement, but also the definition of dangerousness was relegated to the psychiatric and judicial participants at each hearing.

We suspected that this vagueness in the law would increase the possibility that non-psychiatric variables would influence the official decisions made by the psychiatrists. The importance of such contingencies in mental health decisions has been shown by others (Haney and Miller, 1970; Rushing, 1971). Thus, our first interest was in examining the impact of non-psychiatric variables on psychiatric decision making.

Of the 257 indicted, male, felony defendants found incompetent to stand trial, 154 (60 percent) were evaluated as dangerous by the reporting psychiatrists. In fact, there was very little difference between the 154 defendants evaluated as dangerous and the 103 defendants evaluated as not dangerous. Three sets of background variables were examined: social characteristics (age, race, marital status, and education); past criminal behavior (a record of juvenile delinquency, prior arrests, prior convictions, and prior convictions for violent crimes); and past mental hospitalizations (prior mental hospitalization and number of months hospitalized for mental illness). As seen in Table 10.1, none of these variables appeared to play a significant role in the psychiatric evaluations. There was, however, one factor which significantly differentiated the predicted groups. This factor was the offense with which the defendant was

Table 10.1 Background characteristics of incompetent defendants psychiatrically evaluated as not dangerous and dangerous

Background characteristics	Psychiatric evaluation	
	Not dangerous (N = 103)	Dangerous (N = 154)
Social		
Mean age of admission	30.8	30.7
Race		
% white	35.9	29.9
% black	47.6	44.2
% Puerto Rican	15.5	22.7
% other	1.0	3.2
Marital status		
% never married	56.9	47.3
% div., sep., widowed	28.3	33.3
% currently married	14.8	19.4
Mean education	9th	9th
Criminal behavior		
Juvenile delinquency		
% none	84.3	79.2
% some	15.7	20.8
Mean prior arrests	4.0	3.6
Mean prior convictions	2.3	2.1
Violent crime convictions		
% none	45.6	42.9
% some	54.4	57.1
Mental hospitalizations		
Prior mental hospitalizations		
% none	22.3	19.9
% some	77.7	80.1
Mean no. of months previously in mental hospital	24	21

currently charged. This piece of information was available to the psychiatrists and appeared on the front sheet of the court reports they submitted with their finding.

The data revealed that the more serious the crime the defendant was charged with, the more likely was the psychiatrists to reach a finding of dangerousness. Using the legal classification of arrest charges, it was found that those defendants who had been arrested for a Class A felony were almost always found dangerous. 83 percent of this group were evaluated as dangerous by the psychiatrist as compared to 50 percent of all other defendants. A more meaningful classification was developed which grouped all crimes into categories based on the type of crime. We hypothesized that more important than the legal categories was the actual or perceived level of violence associated with the crime. Thus, we classified each crime into one of four groups, those involving violence against persons (murder, manslaughter, assault and rape), those potentially violent in nature (for example, robbery and arson), property crimes (for example, burglary, grand larceny), and all other crimes (for example, forgery, gambling, sodomy). The resulting data are shown in Table 10.2. As can be seen, there is a statistically significant linear relationship between the type of alleged offense and psychiatric findings of dangerousness. While almost three-fourths of those charged with violent crimes were found dangerous, only 30 percent of those who fell into the residual category of other crimes were seen as dangerous. Thus, knowing just this single piece of information, one could have successfully predicted the findings of the psychiatrists in over 73 percent of the 108 cases in which the defendant was charged with a violent crime.

Table 10.2 Relationship between type of alleged offense and psychiatric evaluation of dangerousness

Psychiatric evaluation	Type of alleged offense							
	Violent		Potentially violent		Property		Other	
	%	N	%	N	%	N	%	N
Not dangerous	26.8	29	46.0	40	47.6	20	70.0	14
Dangerous	73.2	79	54.0	47	52.4	22	30.0	6
TOTAL	100.0	108	100.0	87	100.0	42	100.0	20

$X^2 = 17.56$
$P < .001$
$C = .25$

Psychiatric justifications for findings

The second issue we were interested in exploring concerned the reasons given by the psychiatrists to justify their findings. Of particular interest was how far their stated reasons coincided with non-psychiatric factors found to impinge upon their decision. As we have just seen, the one factor which seemed to most influence their evaluation was the defendant's alleged offense.

Information on the psychiatrists' reasons for a finding of dangerousness were obtained from the official examination report submitted to the court. On these forms, following the section related to the capacity of the defendant, was this additional paragraph:

> It is the further opinion of each of us that the above named defendant (is) (is not) a dangerous incapacitated person, that is, an incapacitated person who is so mentally ill or mentally defective that his presence in an institution operated by the Department of Mental Hygiene is dangerous to the safety of other patients therein, the staff of the institution or the community. The following is a detailed statement of the reasons for finding the defendant to be a dangerous incapacitated person.

In those cases where the psychiatrist evaluated the individual as dangerous the phrase 'is not' would be crossed out and reasons for the finding would be offered.

Despite the request in this form for a 'detailed statement,' most were very brief, frequently not more than a sentence. For example, one report gave the following reason: 'He is a dangerous incapacitated person because of his delusions of grandeur and of feeling influenced by cyclops.' Another read 'Because of his admitted numerous fights with people.' Rarely were these statements longer than two sentences.

Complete information on these stated reasons was available for 149 of the 154 defendants evaluated as dangerous. These reasons were examined and general categories were established. Each of these statements were then coded and verified with multiple reasons allowed up to a maximum of six. The reasons were, first of all, divided according to their time reference, whether they referred to events occurring before arrest or to events occurring during the observation period subsequent to arrest. The before arrest reasons were further broken down into four main categories. These were reasons related to the defendant's current charge, to prior anti-social behavior (for example, assaults, criminal history, history of gun possession), to prior mental illness or mental hospitalization, or to other behavior. Those reasons focusing on behavior subsequent to arrest were grouped into the following categories: anti-social behavior (for example, assaults, threats of assaults, management problem); mental illness (delusional thinking, unpredictability, impulsiveness); and other.

The total 390 reasons thus classified are given in Table 10.3. In addition to showing that post arrest behavior was more frequently cited than behavior prior to arrest, Table 10.3 also indicates that the two major types of reasons given by psychiatrists for a finding of dangerousness are mental illness and anti-social behavior. The mental illness category accounts for 42 percent and the anti-social behavior category for 41 percent of all reasons cited. The reporting of psychiatric symptoms and indicators is less surprising than the large number of cited reasons related to anti-social behavior, particularly those referring to behavior occurring prior to the current arrest. As will be recalled from the data presented in Table 10.1, there was no difference between those found dangerous and not dangerous in the level of prior criminal behavior, including prior violent criminal behavior.

Table 10.3 Psychiatric reasons for a finding of dangerousness cited in court reports (N = 149)*

Type of reason cited	% of reports citing reasons
Behavior prior to or leading to arrest:	
Nature of current charges (e.g., type of crime)	11.5
Anti-social behavior (e.g., criminal history, assaults)	15.9
Mental illness (e.g., prior mental hospitalization, impaired thinking)	10.3
Other	3.1
(Sub-total)	(40.8)
Behavior subsequent to arrest:	
Anti-social behavior (e.g., assaults or threatened assaults)	24.6
Mental illness (e.g., delusions, impulsiveness)	31.3
Other	3.3
(Sub-total)	(59.2)
TOTAL	100.0

* Multiple reasons up to a maximum of six were coded. The percentages are based on the total 360 reasons given in the 149 court reports submitted by the psychiatrists.

Of most interest in Table 10.3 is the fact that only 11.5 percent of the reasons cited by the psychiatrist for a finding of dangerousness refer to the defendant's current charge. Despite the empirically demonstrated importance of this factor in their decisions, the psychiatrists rarely justified their predictions on the basis of the defendant's current arrest charge.

Judicial concurrence with psychiatric findings

The accuracy of psychiatric predictions would not be so serious were it not for the confidence placed in the expertise of these professionals. Others have found psychiatrists to be influential in courtroom decisions dealing with involuntary commitment (Scheff, 1966; Miller and Schwartz, 1966). Our data showed the same with regard to dangerousness. Although the psychiatrists were mandated to submit their findings to the court, the final decision as to the dangerousness of the defendant rested legally with the judge. While by law the decision was a judicial one, in reality it was made by the psychiatrists. In 86.7 percent of the cases, the psychiatrists' recommendation as to the defendant's dangerousness was accepted by the court.

Most of the disagreements, twenty-eight of the thirty-four, that did occur between the court and psychiatrists, resulted in the court finding the defendant not dangerous after the psychiatrists had recommended dangerousness. In the other six cases, the court concluded dangerousness despite the psychiatric recommendation of not dangerous.

Two factors appeared to contribute to these judicial/psychiatric disagreements. The first was the cross examination skills of the Legal Aid attorneys. For example, at one of the locations we attended seven of the hearings in which the court ruled against a psychiatric finding of dangerousness. In all of these cases, the Legal Aid attorney attacked the psychiatric report through detailed questioning of whether the alleged offense actually occurred and focused on differences between his client's reports of the alleged events and those offered by the psychiatrists. Wenger and Fletcher (1969) have reported similar effects of legal counsel on mental hospital admission decisions. Most frequently, however, regardless of the caliber of the defense questioning, the court tended to follow psychiatric recommendations with little regard for other testimony.

The other factor appearing to have systematically exerted some influence on the court's decision to agree with a psychiatric evaluation of dangerous was the alleged offense of the defendant. This factor is the same one found related to psychiatric findings of dangerousness. The less serious the alleged offense the greater the likelihood that the court would disagree with a psychiatric finding of dangerousness. Of the defendants charged with a violent crime against person and evaluated as dangerous by the psychiatrists, the court rejected the finding in 13 percent of the cases. This level of disagreement increased to 17 percent for those with offenses potentially violent, to 30 percent for those with property offenses, and to 43 percent for other felonies. Thus, the court was most willing to accept a finding of dangerous for those defendants with the most serious offenses, reinforcing the tendency of psychiatrists to use this criterion in their evaluations.

This finding raises the possibility that the degree of autonomy experienced by the psychiatrists in the courtroom may be less than usually thought. The impression one gets is that the psychiatrists are aware of the court's emphasis on the defendant's current charge in determining dangerousness and, as such, rely heavily on this factor in reaching their findings. At the same time, they provide psychiatric rationales, thus justifying the finding for themselves and for the court on the basis of a supposed expert body of knowledge.

The accuracy of psychiatric predictions

The final and most important question we wished to address with our research was the accuracy of the predictions made by the psychiatrists. Before presenting the data, two points should be made. First, as discussed elsewhere (Cocozza and Steadman, 1976), we were able to avoid many of the problems experienced by earlier works on the psychiatric prediction of dangerousness. Unlike our earlier work (Steadman and Cocozza, 1974) and the work of others (Kozol, Boucher and Garofalo, 1972), this study focuses on explicit determinations of dangerousness made on individual defendants, is based on a clinically relevant cohort, and overcomes many of the methodological weaknesses displayed by earlier studies. Second, despite the intent of the law to provide differential treatment to the dangerous and not dangerous groups, during the period the defendants under study were hospitalized, the two receiving facilities were practically identical.

Rather than distributing those defendants found not dangerous among existing civil psychiatric facilities, New York State's Department of Mental Hygiene decided to establish a new, high security, civil facility for these patients.[3] Even though the dangerous group was to be placed in a correctional hospital and the not dangerous group in a mental hygiene facility, these two were practically one and the same during the first six months of this study. Because of budgetary considerations, DMH initially took over two wards within the correctional facility and used correction officers on an overtime basis. Later, the mental hygiene component moved to a separate building but still on the same campus. Only after fourteen months was the facility staffed completely by mental hygiene employees, and only after sixteen months was the mental hygiene facility on a separate campus. Thus, the two study groups were, for all intents and purposes, in the same facility during their initial detention.[4] Furthermore, the lengths of hospitalization prior to their release to the community or return to court were very similar for the two groups (an average of thirty-seven weeks for the not dangerous and forty-six weeks for the dangerous group). Therefore, the limitations and potentially contaminating factors of differential treatment and lengths of stay were not present, allowing a much more controlled test of the predictive accuracy of the psychiatrists.

In order to determine the accuracy of the psychiatric predictions of dangerousness, we obtained data on the defendants' assaultiveness from several sources including: (1) the maximum security hospitals to which both groups were initially sent; (2) hospital readmission records; (3) inpatient records of all subsequent hospitalizations; and (4) subsequent arrest records.

Our results showed that the patients evaluated as dangerous by the psychiatrists were not more dangerous than those evaluated as not dangerous. As shown in Table 10.4, all of the indicators of dangerous behavior we examined with these data revealed only slight differences between the two groups. None of the differences which did occur were statistically significant and, thus, all could be explained on the basis of chance alone.

It is interesting that on all indicators of inpatient behavior, the psychiatrically predicted dangerous group experienced slightly higher rates. 42 percent of them as compared to 36 percent of the not dangerous group were assaultive during their initial incompetency hospitalization; 3 percent as compared to 2 percent were subsequently rehospitalized for a violent act; and 29 percent as compared to 19 percent were assaultive in the hospitals to which

Table 10.4 Outcome measures for incompetent defendants psychiatrically evaluated as not dangerous and dangerous

Outcome measures of defendants at risk	Psychiatric evaluation	
	Not dangerous	Dangerous
Assaultive during initial incompetency hospitalization[a]	36%	42
Rehospitalized[a]	44%	39%
Rehospitalized for violence[a]	2%	3%
Assaultive during rehospitalization[b]	19%	29%
Rearrested[c]	54%	49%
Rearrested for a violent offense[c]	16%	14%

[a] Percentages based on total study group (N = 257). For rehospitalization measure three cases were omitted since these three defendants were never released from the initial hospitalization and were never at risk for rehospitalization.

[b] Percentages based on defendants rehospitalized (N = 104).

[c] Percentages based on defendants released to the community and therefore at risk of rearrest (N = 166).

they were readmitted. None of these differences are statistically significant. Conversely, all indicators related to behavior once in the community revealed the not dangerous group to experience higher rates, but again only slightly more so than the group predicted to be dangerous by the court psychiatrists.

Perhaps the single most important indicator of the success of the psychiatric predictions is the actual number of these patients subsequently arrested for violent crimes. Yet even here, only a slight difference is revealed by the data. Among patients who had been evaluated as dangerous, 14 percent (thirteen of ninety-six) of those released to the community were subsequently arrested for a violent crime. Among patients who had been evaluated as not dangerous, 16 percent (eleven of seventy) of those released to the community were arrested for a violent crime.

On the basis of these indicators, we conclude that the psychiatric predictions of dangerousness were not at all accurate. There was no significant difference between the two groups on any of the measures examined. Those defendants evaluated by the psychiatrists as dangerous were no more dangerous than those evaluated as not dangerous.

The illusion of expertise

Within American society, psychiatry is seen by the public, by the courts and the legal community, and by legislators as the professional group most rightfully charged with the responsibility to predict the potential danger of individuals. This authority is granted on the basis of the perceived body of expert knowledge available to psychiatrists as a result of their training and experience. The findings presented here seriously question the existence of any such special knowledge. As we have seen, the single factor which appears to have most influenced the psychiatrists in their decisions was the seriousness of the charge on which the defendant was arrested – a factor which any professional, indeed, any lay person could easily employ.

Furthermore, the use of this factor is questionable on at least two grounds. First, these are only alleged offenses. As incompetent-to-stand-trial defendants, these individuals have not been tried and proven guilty. Second, there is little empirical evidence which supports the use of the seriousness of any single crime as an indicator of future dangerous behavior. For example, in their summary work on recidivism over the criminal career the National Commission on the Causes and Prevention of Violence found that 'the more serious the initial crime committed, the lesser the chance it will be repeated' and that those arrested for major violent crimes are 'better parole risks than most others' (Mulvihill and Tumin, 1969: 568).

Even when lack of expertise is acknowledged by a psychiatrist, the pressure to play the role, to meet the expectations of society is difficult to resist. One psychiatrist, just prior to the implementation of the revised statute, commented to us: 'I don't know what dangerousness is. I can't predict it. I'm going to refuse to submit my reports to the courts. I'll take a chance on being held in contempt.' In fact, he did submit reports to the courts, and we know of no psychiatrist in the state who refused to submit recommendations on dangerousness. Even psychiatrists aware of the serious limitations of their expertise pertaining to dangerousness regularly acquiesce to legislative mandates to predict it.

In their predictions, our data suggest, pressure is also felt by the psychiatrists to maintain the illusion of expertise. The psychiatrists, in relying heavily on the alleged charge of the defendant, could have supported their findings of dangerousness with a statement something to the effect of: 'This person is charged with the very serious crime of murder and in order not to risk the possibility of his escaping from a less secure facility, I find him dangerous.' This is not the type of justification they did provide. Rather than focusing on the alleged charge, their explanations referred to the information obtained from their professional psychiatric evaluation and were couched in traditional psychiatric terms.

The existence of such an illusion is not surprising for it has been found by others. Mendel and Rapport (1969), in their study of decisions for psychiatric hospitalization, reported that although the decision makers were greatly influenced by the individual's history of previous hospitalization, they were not aware of this factor's impact. Rather, they saw their decisions as based on the traditional grounds of presenting symptomatology. Similarly, Greenley (1972), in his research on discharges from a mental hospital, found that the desires regarding discharge timing held by the patient's family were strongly and positively related to the actual timing of release. Yet the psychiatrists rarely acknowledged this influence on the discharge process, instead explaining their actions in terms of medical-psychiatric reasons.

Thus, the empirical data from this study and others points to a major gap between the real criteria involved in psychiatric decisions and the ideal ones offered by the psychiatrists themselves for explaining their decisions. Rationales serve not only to hide the importance of non-psychiatric factors and the impact of non-psychiatrists in the decision making process, but also to foster the illusion of the existence of a special psychiatric expertise in such decisions.

Our findings clearly indicate that no such expertise exists and that the attempt to apply this supposed knowledge to predict who will be dangerous results in complete failure. The data suggest that psychiatrists may, in fact, be acting more as seers than as scientists in predicting dangerousness. At least one critic of the profession of psychiatry would not hesitate to agree. Addressing psychiatric practice, in general, Szasz has written, 'The point of this discussion is to re-emphasize that Institutional Psychiatry is largely medical ceremony and magic' (1970: 267). Our data do not extend to the entire practice of psychiatry but in the specific area we have investigated, Szasz's statement would seem to apply. For in predicting dangerousness, psychiatry may be closer to magic than to science.

The definition of magic and the distinction between magic and science are issues which have been under discussion for many years. However, according to Leach (1964), 'The core of the magical act is that it rests on empirically untested belief and that it is an effort at control.' Furthermore, magic is frequently seen as involving secret knowledge of the specialist and, for Malinowski (1948), as utilized primarily for the unpredictable, that is, concerned with the control of the abnormal and uncertain as a mechanism for relieving anxiety. All of these elements of magic can easily be found in the psychiatric prediction of dangerousness as evidenced in our data. There is the presumption of special knowledge as indicated by the legal statutes which mandate psychiatrists to make such predictions. There is the belief that these specialists can accurately predict the future behavior of individuals, a belief shared by many of the psychiatrists and by the judges who, almost without exception, accept the psychiatric recommendations. There is the absence of a perceived need to test out the accuracy of the beliefs and predictions. And finally, there is the unpredictability of the behavior of the mentally ill which is seen as threatening by society and in need of social control.

Whether magic or science, the prediction of dangerousness by psychiatrists represents an excellent example of professionals who have exceeded their areas of expertise and for whom society's confidence in their ability is empirically unjustified.

Notes

1 This section is no longer in effect. It was found unconstitutional in 1974 in *People ex rel. Anonymous v. Waugh*, 76 Misc. 2d 879, 351 N.Y.S. 2d 594 (Sup. Ct. 1974). The court declared that criminal patients who had been indicted and found incompetent to stand trail could not, consistent with equal protection and due process, be detained with convicted criminals in the Correctional Services Facility.

2 Although each defendant was examined and evaluated by two psychiatrists, in almost all cases only one formal report was submitted to the court. The finding as to the defendant's dangerousness given in this report was agreed upon by the two psychiatrists and the report was signed by both of them.

3 The development and evolution of this new facility are described in H. J. Steadman, J. J. Cocozza, and S. Lee (forthcoming).

4 Despite the similarity of staff and setting it is possible that an awareness of the court determination of dangerousness in the two groups influenced the behavior of staff and perhaps of the defendants as well. While our observations over three years at the two facilities suggest no such systematic bias, no data are available

with which to rigorously examine this question. However, since data on these two groups are available not only during hospitalization, but also subsequent to hospitalization this does not appear to constitute a serious problem.

References

Angel, R. B. 1967.
  Explanation and prediction: A plea for reason. *Philosophy of Science* 34 (September): 276–282.
Cocozza, Joseph J. and Henry J. Steadman 1974.
  Some refinements in the measurement and prediction of dangerous behavior. *American Journal of Psychiatry* 131 (September): 1012–1014.
  1976. The failure of psychiatric predictions of dangerousness: Clear and convincing evidence. *Rutgers Law Review* 29 (Summers): 1084–1101.
Deutsch, Albert 1949.
  The Mentally Ill in America. (Second Edition) New York: Columbia University Press.
Deutscher, Irwin 1973.
  What We Say/What We Do: Sentiments and Acts. Glenview, Illinois: Scott, Foresman and Company.
Freidson, Eliot 1970.
  Profession of Medicine: A Study of the Sociology of Applied Knowledge. New York: Dodd, Mead and Company.
Goldstein, Joseph and Jay Katz 1960.
  Dangerousness and mental illness: Some observations on the decision to release persons acquitted by reason of insanity. *Yale Law Review* 70: 225–239.
Greenley, James 1972.
  Alternative views of the psychiatrist's role. *Social Problems* 20 (Fall): 252–262.
Haney, C. Allen and Kent S. Miller 1970.
  Definitional factors in mental incompetency. *Sociology and Social Research* 54 (July): 520–532.
Hempel, C. G. and P. Oppenheim 1948.
  The logic of explanation. *Philosophy of Science* 15: 135–175.
Kozol, H. L., R. J. Boucher and R. F. Garofalo 1972.
  The diagnosis and treatment of dangerousness. *Crime and Delinquency* 18 (October): 371–392.
Leach, E. R. 1964.
  Magic. Pp. 398–99 in Julius Gould and William L. Kolb (eds.), *A Dictionary of the Social Sciences*. New York: The Free Press.
Levinson, Richard M. and M. Zan York 1974.
  The attribution of 'Dangerousness' in mental health evaluation. *Journal of Health and Social Behavior* 15 (December): 328–335.
Malinowski, Bronislaw 1948.
  Magic, Science and Religion, and Other Essays. Chicago: The Free Press.

Mendel, Werner M. and Samuel Rapport 1969.
  Determinants of the decision for psychiatric hospitalizations. *Archives of General Psychiatry* 20 (March): 321–328.
Miller, Dorothy and Michael Schwartz 1966.
  County lunacy commission hearings: Some observations of commitments to a state mental hospital. *Social Problems* 14 (Summer): 26–35.
Mulvihill, D. J. and M. M. Tumin 1969.
  Crimes of Violence. Washington, DC: US Government Printing Office.
Rubin, Bernard 1972.
  The prediction of dangerousness in mentally ill criminals. *Archives of General Psychiatry* 27 (September): 397–407.
Rushing, William A. 1971.
  Individual resources, societal reaction, and hospital commitment. *American Journal of Sociology* 77 (November): 511–526.
Scheff, Thomas J. 1966.
  Being Mentally Ill: A Sociological Theory. Chicago: Aldine Publishing Company.
Sjoberg, Gideon and Roger Nett 1968.
  A Methodology for Social Research. New York: Harper and Row.
Steadman, Henry J. 1972.
  The psychiatrist as a conservative agent of social control. *Social Problems* 20 (Fall): 263–271.
Steadman, Henry J. and Joseph J. Cocozza 1974.
  Careers of the Criminally Insane: Excessive Social Control of Deviance. Lexington, Mass.: D. C. Heath and Company (Lexington Books).
Steadman, Henry J., Joseph J. Cocozza, and Sara Lee, Forthcoming.
  From maximum security to secure treatment: Organizational constraints. *Human Organization*.
Stone, Alan A. 1975.
  Mental Health and Law: A System in Transition. Rockville, Maryland: National Institute of Mental Health.
Szasz, Thomas 1970.
  The Manufacture of Madness. New York: Dell Publishing Co., Inc.
Wegner, Dennis L. and C. Richard Fletcher 1969.
  The effect of legal counsel on admissions to a state mental hospital. *Journal of Health and Social Behavior* 10 (March): 66–72.

CHAPTER 11

Medical dominance: Psychoactive drugs and mental health policy*†

Thomas J. Scheff

The thesis of this article is that present mental health laws, which establish medical dominance in the mental health field, are costly and probably unwise. These laws encourage treatment policies and practices which overemphasize chemotherapy and underemphasize sociopsychological treatment. Some of the scientific evidence relevant to these policies and practices is reviewed. The article ends with suggestions for alternative policies and for research projects which could provide support for legislative change.

Chemotherapy is the treatment of mental disorder that prevails in the US today. Particularly for the more severe disorders, it has been established that tranquilizers and anti-depressants are a quick, cheap, and effective way of stopping symptoms in many cases. Representing the opinion of the majority of psychiatrists is Eisenberg's (1973) statement: 'Tranquilizers and anti-depressants are an effective chemotherapeutic means of managing acute psychotic disorders.'

Chemotherapy has not only had practical results but has also suggested paths toward the theoretical understanding of the mechan-

* John Gai gave helpful advice, and Hally Seerley provided research assistance for the writing of this paper. Leon Eisenberg and J. S. Hughes provided critical comments on an earlier draft.
† Thomas J. Scheff, Medical Dominance: Psychoactive drugs and mental health policy, *American Behavioral Scientist*, vol. 19, no. 3 (January–February, 1976), pp. 299–317. Copyright © 1976 by Sage Publications, Inc. Reprinted by permission of the author and by Sage Publications, Inc.

isms of psychiatric symptoms, such as hallucinations and delusions. Research on the biochemistry of the brain has suggested that symptoms of mental disorder may be caused by metabolic errors in the transmission of neural signals. It is hypothesized that these errors are corrected by the action of the tranquilizing drugs. Although these findings are suggestive, they are still inconclusive (Snyder *et al.*, 1974).

In light of these dramatic developments, the enthusiasm for chemotherapy that exists in the medical profession is understandable. What is more difficult to understand is why this enthusiasm has been allowed to prevail with so little examination of its short- and long-term effects. Although the benefits of the tranquilizers have been demonstrated exhaustively, there have been relatively few studies of the costs and risks associated with their use.

The social value of psychoactive drugs

Although chemotherapy has brought many benefits, it is conceivable, given what we already know, that an examination of the entire structure of the medical use of psychoactive drugs would show that the risks and costs outweigh the benefits. In terms of social policy, it is important not only to establish that chemotherapy is sometimes effective, and that through research it could advance our understanding of some forms of mental illness, but also to establish the ratio of benefits to costs and risks over the whole spectrum of chemotherapeutic practice.[1] In order to make such an assessment, we need to know the answers to the following questions. First, in the entire population that is treated, what is the proportion of cases in which the treatment is effective and necessary? This is the question that controlled longitudinal studies are designed to answer. Second, what are the undesirable side effects of treatment, and in what proportion of the treated patients do they occur?

In assessing the value of a treatment in terms of social policy, these two questions, of efficacy and of side effects, are interrelated. At the one extreme, there are treatments of high value, whose rate of efficacy is high and rate and severity of side effects are low. At the other extreme, there are valueless treatments whose rate of efficacy is low and whose side effects are frequent and severe. As we shall see in the discussion below, the various forms of chemotherapy would appear to fall somewhere between these two extremes, with the phenothiazines (in the treatment of acute psychosis) and lithium carbonate closer to the positive value end of the continuum, the anti-depressants of lesser value, and the phenothiazines in the treatment of chronic psychosis and the anti-anxiety drugs, worse than useless.

The most dramatic changes in the field of mental health in recent years have been brought about in part by the use of thorazine (generic name: chlorpromazine) in the treatment of schizophrenia. Treatment with this drug played a major role in the great reduction of the patient population in mental hospitals that has been occurring since the early 1950s. Thorazine, like the other drugs of its type, the phenothiazines, appears to have distinctly anti-psychotic properties; that is, the phenothiazines do not merely sedate but also interfere with the production of psychotic symptoms, at least in some cases.

It should be clear, however, that these drugs do not cure the disease; they merely stop the symptoms. Eisenberg (1973: 120–121) writes:

> Extensive clinical research has documented the effectiveness of the phenothiazines in terminating an episode of schizophrenia. The natural history of the disorder, however, indicates a substantial risk of recurrence and little residue of benefit from prior treatment.

Furthermore, the studies which show the efficacy of the phenothiazines for some patients also make clear that they are not effective for others. Using the avoidance of rehospitalization within one year as the criteria, controlled studies show that 60 to 70 percent of patients with diagnosis of acute schizophrenia on no drugs, are readmitted within one year, while only 20 to 30 percent of patients receiving drugs are rehospitalized. Clearly some 40 percent of the patients on drugs are helped to stay out of the hospital by the drugs, but 20 to 30 percent are not, and 30 to 40 percent of the patients in the study who did not receive drugs also avoided rehospitalization (Prien and Klett, 1972: 64).

Not all the controlled studies show even this much positive effect. In particular, several studies show that the difference between treated and placebo patients declines with the passage of time, if intervals greater than one year are used. One study indicated that the differences may be as low as 10 to 15 percent after several years (Engelhardt *et al.*, 1967).

In one recent study, the passage of time causes the situation to be reversed. The adjustment of the placebo patients becomes significantly better than those who received the drugs. This study, by Rappaport (1974: 39, 138) concerns 120 first-admission, young, male patients diagnosed as schizophrenic. Comparisons were made on improvement in drug and placebo patients at two points in time, after discharge from the hospital, and at follow-up, which took place up to three years after discharge. Results were as indicated in Table 11.1.

Table 11.1 Evaluation of patients by time and by treatment

Patient's condition	At time of discharge (n = 120)		At follow-up (n = 75)	
	Drug	Placebo	Drug	Placebo
Better	40 (78%)	39 (57%)	21 (57%)	30 (79%)
Worse	11 (22)	30 (43)	16 (43)	8 (21)
Total	51	69	37	38

Source: Adapted from Rappaport (1974).

As can be seen from the table, a substantially larger proportion of the patients on drugs had improved at time of discharge compared with the placebo group. However, by the time of follow-up, within three years, the situation was reversed; it was the placebo group that had a much larger proportion of improved cases. This study suggests, at least for a majority of these types of patients, that phenothiazines are not only ineffective but should not be used. This finding, which is in such stark contrast to existing medical belief and practice, requires some discussion.

Current practice with cases diagnosed as schizophrenia is to routinely administer phenothiazines. Most physicians believe that these drugs are usually effective. One basis for this belief is the large number of studies which suggest that the condition of patients being maintained on phenothiazines deteriorates when the drugs are removed. However, Tobias and MacDonald (1974) in their review of 40 such studies, 25 of which were uncontrolled and 15 controlled, conclude that because of methodological flaws, no inferences can be drawn. It would seem that further long-term studies of the type conducted by Rappaport are urgently needed. In summary, the evidence concerning the phenothiazines suggests that the drugs are effective in some cases, especially in the beginning of treatment, not effective in others, and actually harmful in others. We will now turn to the examination of the ways in which these drugs may do harm.

From the beginning of the use of these tranquilizers, it was known that they sometimes produced detrimental physical side effects:

> sedation and symptoms resembling Parkinson's disease are a problem for some patients and serious toxicity (persistent rhythmical involuntary movements of tongue and face, abnormal pigmentation, low white-cell count and jaundice) afflicts a substantial minority [Eisenberg, 1973: 24].

Eisenberg's estimate of the dangers of the side effects of the phenothiazines, like most psychiatric opinion, is probably understated. It would appear that a new syndrome of central nervous system disorder, tardive dyskinesia, has been created by phenothiazine use. According to Crane (1973: 126–127) its manifestations are:

> slow, rhythmical movements in the region of the mouth, with protrusion of the tongue, smacking of the lips, blowing of the cheeks, and side-to-side movements of the chin, as well as other bizarre muscular activity. More careful examinations of patients on long-term drug therapy revealed that, not only the mouth, but practically all parts of the body could exhibit motor disorders, such as myoclonia, chorea, and athetosis. Overextension of the spine and neck, shifting of weight from foot to foot, and other abnormal postures indicated that the coordination of the various segments of the axial musculature was also affected. Less frequently, the syndrome resembled in every respect known neurological diseases, such as Huntington's disease, dystonia musculorum deformans, and postencephalitic brain damage.

For patients on 'maintenance' doses – i.e., long-term treatment – Baldessarini and Lipinski (1973) estimated that this reaction occurs in from 3 to 40 percent of the cases, with a mean of about 15 percent, a not inconsiderable group.[2] In the more severe reactions, the syndrome continues after the drug is removed. Like lobotomy, the phenothiazines may cause permanent, irreversible brain damage (see Crane, 1973: 127). The manufacturers also warn that these drugs have had many other side effects including 'sudden, unexpected and unexplained death.' This range of severe physical effects suggests that in some instances phenothiazine treatment may be worse than the disease it is supposed to cure.

Of perhaps equal significance are the psychological and social side effects of these drugs. Although it is difficult to make a clear assessment because of inadequate and conflicting evidence, most psychiatrists think that part of the effect of thorazine is sedation. For example, Allan (1975) writes: 'thorazine is often used as a drug of choice because of the sedation it provides. This can be extremely beneficial in calming the patient, and is distinct from the anti-psychotic properties of the drug.'

On the other hand, Crane (1973: 125), who is perhaps the leading authority on the physical side effects of the phenothiazines, seems to disagree:

> Neuroleptics may reduce overactivity and belligerent behavior, but these are secondary effects of a general lessening of psychopathology. Sedation occurs only in the early stages of drug therapy in certain susceptible individuals, or when excessive doses are administered, particularly of chlorpromazine (thorazine).

A review of studies of the effect of thorazine on learning seems to bear out Allan's position rather than Crane's. Hartlage (1965: 235) reports as follows:

> Results of studies involving a number of animals, normal subjects, and psychiatric patients tend to show significant declines in learning on a wide range of tasks, with a linear decline in learning with increased dosage levels.

The social effects of the phenothiazines are virtually unknown. In a pioneering study, which still has not been replicated, Lennard *et al.* (1967) administered a small dose of thorazine to one member of each of seven three-person discussion groups. He found a decrease of initiation of activity by the drugged member, as against the placebos and, significantly, a consistent decrease of communications addressed to that person by the others. These findings are particularly significant because of the low dosage level, only 50 milligrams of thorazine. Since the average dosage of phenothiazines is considerably higher than this (1,600 milligrams per day is not uncommon), and since Hartlage has suggested that decreases in learning are a linear function of increasing dosage, Lennard's findings are extremely important.

For our purposes, perhaps the most significant study of chemotherapeutic practice yet reported was done by Crane (1974) who determined the amount of overdosing and the physical side effects in a group of 160 long-term mental hospital patients. He first established a baseline behavior for each patient at the original drug level, whose drug levels ranged from 21 patients who were not on drugs, to 17 who were getting between 700 and 1,800 milligrams per day, CPZ, eq. (chlorpromazine equivalent: the amount of chlorpromazine that it would take to produce the effect of one of the other phenothiazines). Using this method, he was able to drastically reduce the dosage levels of all of the patients, including 28 patients that he removed from drugs entirely, over the course of one year.

Over the course of a three-year period, he reduced the drug level even more, from an average dose of 336 CPZ eq. to 134. On the basis of this study, it would appear that overdosing is a common occurrence, since all of these patients had been overdosed for years, with a sizeable proportion of them overdosed by extremely large amounts (33% of these patients had been overdosed by 400 or more CPZ eq. a day).

Crane also determined that in this group of 160 patients, 81 (51 percent) had long-lasting physical side effects as a result of the drugs. In this group of 81 patients, he reduced the drugs to below the level that would cause side effects, and still maintained the baseline behavior, in all but 15 percent of the cases. In other words, in 85 percent of the cases, the physical damage which the drugs caused to the patients was completely unnecessary. Since Crane made no assessment of the social and psychological side effects, we cannot obtain a complete picture of damage caused by the drugs. If we think of this study in terms of Lennard's findings, we can see that in Crane's three-year study, the average overdose was 202 CPZ eq., or approximately four times as great as the dose Lennard used. We might therefore conjecture that there was considerable damage done to the social competence of the patients in this study. A similar estimate is possible following from Hartlage's report on the effect of chlorpromazine on learning. Since he suggested that decrement in learning is a linear function of level of overdose, it is not unreasonable to conclude that these patients probably suffered considerable psychological damage from the drugs.

What seems to be needed are long-term controlled studies of the efficacy of phenothiazines, which include consideration of both benefits and costs in the same study – i.e., these studies should include assessment of physical, psychological, and social side effects in both treated and placebo groups. Although there have been some ten thousand papers written on thorazine alone, not a single one of them has considered this issue. Until such studies are done, one is unable to demonstrate that the benefits of phenothiazine treatment outweigh the costs and risks.

Similar comments apply to the other major psychoactive drugs, the anti-depressants, and lithium carbonate, which are used for the treatment of depression, and of manic-depressive psychosis, respectively. As in the case of phenothiazines, existing studies demonstrate that these drugs are effective in some cases, ineffective in others, and harmful in others.[3] Without further studies which include consideration of physical, social, and psychological side effects, one cannot accurately assess their value to society.

In the case of the anti-anxiety drugs, the picture is still less positive. The case of meprobamate is instructive. This drug, known as Miltown, was introduced in the late 1950s as an anti-anxiety tranquilizer. After many years and millions of prescriptions, it became clear in controlled studies that the drug could not be shown to have any more effect than placebos, and clinical experience indicated that the drug was addictive (see Greenblatt and Shader, 1971). For these reasons, meprobamate has been quietly withdrawn from use. In its place have come a number of other anti-anxiety tranquilizers, the best-known of which are Valium and Librium. Once again, however, history may be repeating itself – it now seems possible that Valium and Librium cannot be shown to have any effect greater than a placebo, and that they can be addictive.[4] Nyswander (1975: 152–153) a psychiatrist well known for her studies of addiction, has warned that sustained use of Valium in large doses brings about 'a far worse addiction than heroin, morphine, or demerol.'

The history of the use of meprobamate, Valium, and Librium, when considered in the context of the histories of earlier psychiatric innovations such as lobotomy and electroconvulsive therapy, does not suggest a particularly optimistic outcome. I am not suggesting, of course, that chemotherapy has no value at all. As has already been stated, the effectiveness of phenothiazines and lithium carbonate for some cases of mental illness has been clearly established, as well as the promise of advances in the understanding of the neurological bases of these types of mental illness. But the total costs and risks of chemotherapy, in the context of the medical practice in which it is based, may be unacceptably great, as indicated in the discussion above.

One area where considerably more research on tranquilizer effects is urgently needed concerns dosage levels and psychological and social effects of drugs. Drug manufacturers acknowledge that there is sedation of some patients even at optimum-dosage levels. This problem is greatly magnified in cases where the dosage level is too high. The patient's reaction time, visual and verbal acuity, and social responsiveness are affected. I suspect, however, that there is great temptation for the physician to err toward overdose rather than underdose.

There is wide variation in patients' responses to tranquilizers – so much so that getting exactly the right dosage takes considerable time, observing, and consulting with the patient. In institutional practice, especially, the physician is likely to see an underdose as the more costly error, as the symptoms of the illness often recur as if there were no medication at all. Studies of the dosage levels in actual patient populations, and of the social and psychological costs of the side effects at these levels, would be useful in assessing the long-range social implications of current treatment policies.

Social-psychological therapies

Given the formidable side effects of chemotherapy, why is it there is so much unqualified enthusiasm by physicians? One reason is suggested by the discussion above – the benefits of chemotherapy are often quickly apparent: cessation of the dramatic symptoms of acute psychosis. The costs, however, are less obvious: subtle lowering of competence, the possible masking of significant psychological or social conflict, or physical side effects which may be missed or confused with symptoms of the 'illness.'

Equally important are the weaknesses that physicians attribute to the forms of treatment alternative to chemotherapy, the various forms of sociopsychological therapy. Although there is a very large number of differing approaches, all of these forms of therapy contain, in varying proportions, the following elements (suggested by Mendel and Green, 1967: 30–31):

(1) the development of trust between patient and therapist(s);
(2) reflection of patient's thoughts, perceptions and behaviors by the therapists to the patient: 'This is how we see you'; supportive therapies emphasize this phase;
(3) exploration of the history of the patient's thoughts, perceptions, and behaviors; expressive therapies emphasize this phase;
(4) exploration of alternative ways of handling problems;
(5) trial of alternative ways of handling problems.

Encounter and Rogerian therapies emphasize the second phase, reflection. Psychoanalysis and the cathartic therapies stress the third phase, exploration of the patient's history. Behavior modification focuses almost exclusively on the fourth and fifth phases, trials of new behaviors. (Actually, all sociopsychological therapies, whatever their emphasis, are also dependent on the first phase, the establishment of trust.) Supportive therapies, when used in mental hospitals for prolonged and severe mental disorder, should contain all five elements.

I survey these phases of sociopsychological treatment to underscore the kind of detailed knowledge and understanding the therapist(s) must have of the patient: the minute particulars of the patient's existence and how these particulars are related to the patient's problems. Most physicians, given their extensive caseloads, see sociopsychological methods as impractical. They are seen as impossibly expensive, time-consuming, protracted, and of uncertain effectiveness. Given the choice between chemotherapy, and sociopsychological methods, most physicians rely almost exclusively on chemotherapy.

Because chemotherapy does not remove the source of the disorder, there is a strong temptation for the psychiatrist to resort to continuous drugging, the so-called maintenance therapy. Apparently the majority of patients in mental hospitals, and a sizeable proportion of the elderly in nursing homes, are on high and continuous drug medication. Perhaps the most powerful of the drugs used for this purpose is Prolixin, a phenothiazine derivative. This drug is used in a long-acting form, with injections whose actions last for two weeks. Although commonly called 'the magic elixir' among psychiatrists, it might be serving, at least in some cases, as a chemical straitjacket.

Since certain knowledge of the causation of mental disorder is virtually nil, the most prudent course of action, it seems to me, would be a treatment policy which combines the strengths of both methods, excluding neither. This policy is recommended by Mendel. He acknowledges (1975: 121) that drugs can play a useful part in psychiatric therapy, but has strong reservations about relying on them exclusively and urges restraint in the use of drugs:

> When the therapist delays the administration of drugs until the second outpatient visit or until the second day of crisis intervention, the amount of medication needed may be decreased by as much as 70 percent.
>
> To administer as little medication as possible is not only of value from an economic point of view and from a physiological point of view in terms of avoiding unnecessary side effects; one must also remember that the psychological factors too, can be antitherapeutic. The administration of medication may further reinforce feelings of helplessness and passivity in the patient.

The studies suggested in this article so far have concerned the relative costs and benefits of present treatment policy, which is oriented for the most part to chemotherapy. A much broader question concerns the costs and benefits of sociopsychological treatments, and their relationship to chemotherapy. What are the pressures on therapists which induce them to rely so completely upon chemotherapy, with its risks and uncertainties? Why are the sociopsychological treatments seen as so expensive and unreliable? To begin to answer these questions, it is useful to examine some questions of legal and administrative policy.

Mental health and the law

Present mental health laws and policy establish medical dominance by fiat. Medical dominance is not based on the competitive position of psychiatrists relative to other physicians, mental health professionals, and laymen, in an open market of ideas and practices. The dominance of psychiatrists is largely a result of legal and social definitions. Although the status of mental disorder as a disease is uncertain from a scientific point of view, there is a consensus among most laymen and policy makers that mental disorder is in fact a disease, and that psychiatrists therefore are necessary to control treatment.

Freidson (1970: xi) has argued that administrative and economic dominance of the professions, particularly that of medicine, lies at the root of all health-care problems: 'professional dominance is the analytic key to the present inadequacy of the health services.' For the reasons I will indicate below, Freidson's argument applies especially strongly to the mental health field.

In mental hospitals, clinics, and psychiatric units of general hospitals, the present statutes require that psychiatrists must not only be on the staff, but that they must be in dominant positions. The law invests psychiatrists with authority on the basis of their training, which presumably makes them experts in the treatment of mental illness. However, these legal requirements are costly and wasteful. It is true that some of the tasks involved in therapy, principally the use of drugs, are related to the psychiatrists' training. Most of the tasks are not. That is, much of the function of leadership concerns administrative, psychological, and interpersonal issues. Most of a physician's training not only does not prepare him or her for these tasks, it also interferes in many ways. The bulk of a doctor's training concerns internal bodily states, which deflects interest and attention from the social and psychological concerns which loom so large in a psychiatric unit. Most of the physician's nine years of training is wasted in this context. A social worker with two years of training is much less costly and usually has more training in administrative, psychological, and interpersonal processes.

The scarcity of physicians is another problem, indicated in part by the presence of a quite sizeable group of foreign-trained physicians in US medical practice. About half the physicians licensed in 1975 belong to this group (Mick, 1975). Torrey and Taylor (1972) have argued that foreign-trained psychiatrists tend to be less qualified than those who received their training in this country. Certainly the administrative and interpersonal tasks that psychiatrists face would be crucially affected by differences in competence in the English language and in cultural background. As an example, I might cite the current practice in Texas of employing Cuban psychiatrists whose familiarity with English is, at best, rather weak.

As to the effectiveness of therapy, the legal requirement of medical control is also disruptive. Since psychiatrists are expensive and in short supply, the law guarantees that the therapist with the least contact and knowledge of the patients' condition will be the only staff member with authority for care. In most mental hospitals, the psychiatrist, who is responsible for treatment and vital decisions as to the patient's fate, such as admission and release, is apt to have a very large number of patients under his or her care, in some cases hundreds. The psychiatrist cannot possibly get the extended contact and detailed knowledge that would be involved in high-quality treatment. The law literally forces him or her to become a dispenser of tranquilizers with large numbers of patients. The psychiatrist cannot even do this well since he or she is apt not to obtain the detailed knowledge of the patients' conditions which should govern indications for use, side effects, and dosage regulation.

Furthermore, medical control is disruptive of cooperation among treatment staff. Since psychiatrists are scarce, most of the treatment staff will not be physicians but social workers, psychologists, nurses, and aides. In many cases, the most capable therapist or administrator in the group will not be the psychiatrist but a member of one of the other occupational groups. The arbitrary imposition of medical leadership by legal fiat stifles initiative and creates tensions and resentments which interfere with staff morale and therefore with therapeutic effectiveness.

I have noticed a second consequence of medical control which grows out of social modeling. The psychiatrist is the most prestigious and powerful person on the staff; thus, many of the staff members model their behavior on his or her behavior. Since the psychiatrist is also the person who has the least time for patients, it is not unusual to find many staff members in mental health units acting as if they had virtually no time to give to patients – social workers concentrating on the patients' family, psychologists on tests, nurses on records, and aides on house-cleaning – so the patients are left to their own devices.

The team concept of psychiatric treatment seems to me to be a feasible way out of this morass. A change in legal requirements is all that would be needed. I am not suggesting that psychiatrists be excluded from the treatment of mental illness, but only that they should not arbitrarily be designated as leaders. In the team concept, the leader of the group would be elected. A committee system in which there were representatives of the major groups, the psychiatrists, other professionals, the aides, and the patients would

probably work best. The director of the unit would be elected from
this committee. He or she might or might not be a psychiatrist. In
this arrangement, medical skills would still be available; the
psychiatrist, even if not the leader, would still be a part of the
treatment team. In those cases, psychiatrists could probably use their
best skills to greater advantage. For example, a psychiatrist relieved
of administrative and psychotherapeutic duties might have the time
to do a skillful job of drug therapy, on a consultative basis.

It seems likely that a committee system would result in more
effective leadership, because it would more efficiently utilize all of
the skills present among members of the staff and lead to improvement of staff morale. Under these conditions, it is possible to
envision psychiatric units which would be therapeutic communities:
a realistic treatment plan would be rapidly developed for each
patient, and there would be sufficient staff-patient contact that effective therapy could occur.

The kind of research needed to evaluate the cost-effectiveness of
such team treatment would involve experimental units where medical
control was suspended, so that leadership could be elected on the
basis of skill. Follow-up studies, after a one-year period, would be
needed to compare the cost and effectiveness of such units with
comparable units which had conventional psychiatric leadership. If
such studies demonstrated that team leadership were less expensive
and more effective than psychiatric leadership, these studies would
provide strong incentives for legislative change.

Legal incentive for broad changes in mental health treatment policies are contained in recent court rulings on 'right-to-treatment.' A
recent decision (*Wyatt v. Stickney*) by the US Fifth Circuit Court
contains an extremely detailed listing of the requirements of
'Minimum Constitutional Standards for Adequate Treatment of the
Mentally Ill.' The key item in this list is the requirement of 'individualized treatment and posthospital plans' for each patient, which
must be developed and implemented within five days of admission.
The ruling goes on to list the specific contents of the treatment and
posthospitalization plans: the problems and needs of the patient, the
least restrictive conditions necessary for treatment, long-range and
intermediate goals of treatment with a timetable for their attainment,
a rationale for these goals and their attainment, a specification of
staff responsibility and involvement with the patient, and criteria for
release to less restrictive conditions of treatment, and for discharge.

In my judgment, there is not a single public mental hospital in the US that could adequately implement this one aspect of the court order, even if it were applied to new patients only. The manpower (and womanpower) crisis resulting from having to apply it to the backlog of patients already resident further multiplies the magnitude of the problem.

To make implementation of right-to-treatment real, new directions in policy are needed. Policies are needed which could help realize the therapeutic potential of existing treatment staffs, and locate new sources of recruitment of therapists: new professions, training for laymen, and possibly ways of utilizing patients as treatment resources for each other. Experiments with team therapy may be an important avenue for exploring new policies in mental health treatment.

Summary

This paper questions the wisdom of medical dominance of the mental health field. By examining the costs and benefits of the predominant medical treatment, chemotherapy, I have argued that it is not clear that the overall value has been positive. For this reason, it would seem prudent to undertake a program of research which would compare the long-term costs and benefits of team treatment with existing medical practice as a basis for legislative change.

Notes

1 A valuable discussion of the social implications of psychoactive drugs can be found in Lennard *et al.* (1974).

2 In a recent study, reported below, Crane found 51 percent of the patients in his sample suffering from physical side effects. The wide variation is probably due to variations in dosage levels, duration of treatment, and age of the groups studied.

3 For a review of studies, see Morris and Beck (1974), Prien *et al.* (1974). Physical side effects of lithium are listed in O'Connell (1974). Psychological damage done by lithium is noted in Aminoff *et al.* (1974).

4 For strong doubts expressed about the efficacy of Valium and Librium by a consumer testing organization, see Consumer Reports (1974) and Gordon (1974).

Case

Wyatt v. Stickney (1972) US Dist. Ct. for the Middle Dist. of Ala. F. Supp. 344: 373. [See also *Wyatt v. Aderholt* (1974) US S. Ct., US Law Week (November 19): 2208–2209.]

References

Allan, R. E. (1975).
  Medication in the treatment of chronic patients, in Werner Mendel, *Supportive Care: Theory and Technique*. Los Angeles: Mara.
Aminoff, J. J., J. Marshall, and E. Smith (1974).
  Cognitive function in patients on lithium therapy. *British J. of Psychiatry* 125 (July): 109–110.
Baldessarini, R. J. and J. F. Lipinski (1973).
  Risks vs. benefits of antipsychotic drugs. *New England J. of Medicine* 389 (August 23): 427–428.
Consumer Reports (1974).
  The Medicine Show. Mount Vernon, N.Y.: Consumers Union.
Crane, G. E. (1974).
  Risks of long-term therapy with neuroleptic drugs. Presented at the Wenner Gren Symposium on Antipsychotic Drugs, Stockholm, September 17–19.
  (1973). 'Clinical pharmacology in its twentieth year.' *Science* 181 (July 13): 124–138.
Eisenberg, L. (1973).
  Psychiatric intervention. *Scientific Amer.* 229 (September): 116–127.
Engelhardt, D. M., B. Rosen, N. Freedman (1967).
  Phenothiazines in prevention of psychiatric hospitalization. *Archives of General Psychiatry* 16 (January): 98–101.
Freidson, E. (1970).
  Professional Dominance. New York: Atherton.
Gordon, E. B. (1974).
  Addiction to Diazepam (Valium). *British Medical J.* 1 (January 14): 112.
Greenblatt, D. J. and R. L. Shader (1971).
  Meprobamate: a study of irrational drug use. *Amer. J. of Psychiatry* 127 (April): 33–39.
Hartlage, L. C. (1965).
  Effects of chlorpromazine on learning. *Psych. Bull.* 64 (October): 235–245.
Lennard, H., L. J. Epstein, and B. G. Katzung (1967).
  Psychoative drug action and group interaction process. *J. of Nervous and Mental Disease* 145 (July): 69–77.
Lennard, H., L. J. Epstein, A. Bernstein, and D. C. Ransom (1974).
  Mystification and Drug Misuse: Hazards of Using Psychoactive Drugs. San Francisco: Jossey-Bass.

Mendel, W. (ed.) (1975).
  Supportive Care: Theory and Technique. Los Angeles: Mara.
Mendel, W. and A. Green (1967).
  The Therapeutic Management of Psychological Illness. New York: Basic Books.
Mick, S. (1975).
  The foreign medical graduate. *Scientific Amer.* 232 (February): 14–21.
Morris, J. B. and A. T. Beck (1974).
  The efficacy of antidepressant drugs. *Archives of General Psychiatry* 30 (May):
  667–674.
Nyswander, M. (1975).
  Danger ahead: Valium. *Vogue* 165 (February): 152–153.
O'Connell, R. A. (1974).
  Lithium carbonate: psychiatric indications and medical complications. *New York
  State J. of Medicine* 74 (April): 649–653.
Prien, R. F. and C. J. Klett (1972).
  An appraisal of the long-term use of tranquilizing medication with hospitalized
  chronic schizophrenics: A review of drug discontinuation literature.
  Schizophrenia Bull. 5 (Spring): 64–73.
Prien, R. F. and E. M. Caffey (1974).
  Lithium prophylaxis in recurrent affective illness. *Amer. J. of Psychiatry* 131
  (February): 198–203.
Rappaport, M. (1974).
  Schizophrenics for whom phenothiazines may be contradicted or unnecessary.
  Presented at Western Psychological Association meetings, San Francisco, 1973;
  abstracted in *Psychology Today* (November): 39, 138.
Snyder, S., S. P. Banerjee, H. I. Yamamura, and D. Greenburg (1974).
  Drugs, neurotransmitters, and schizophrenia. *Science* 184 (June): 1243–1253.
Tobias, L. and M. L. MacDonald (1974).
  Withdrawal of maintenance drugs with long-term hospitalized patients. *Psych.
  Bull.* 81 (June): 107–125.
Torrey, E. F. and R. L. Taylor (1972).
  Cheap labor from poor nations. Presented at the meetings of the American
  Psychiatric Association.

CHAPTER 12

Clinical psychopharmacology in its twentieth year*

George E. Crane

The use of neuroleptic drugs (1) for the treatment of mental disorders began in the early 1950s and has increased steadily. According to one estimate (2), 250 million people had received these drugs by the end of 1970. In the last decade, hospital beds have been increasingly phased out, and, to take their place, new community mental health centers have been opened or existing facilities have been expanded throughout the nation. According to the medical profession, this new program for the treatment of the mentally ill would not have been possible without neuroleptics. Psychiatrists, sociologists, and professionals in allied fields have emphasized the advantages of maintaining the mentally ill in the community. On the other hand, it is acknowledged that a large proportion of patients released from hospitals are incapable of meeting the demands of society. Inadequate programs for the management of these mentally handicapped persons have created new and unexpected problems, and, in an effort to solve them, the psychiatric community has become more and more dependent on the use of neuroleptic agents. One of the consequences of this reliance on psychopharmacology has been the tendency to minimize the potential danger of long-term exposure to powerful chemical agents. Thus, permanent neurological disorders have become very common among patients treated with neuroleptics, but little effort has been made to come to grips with this problem.

* Reprinted from *Science*, vol. 181, pp. 124–8, 13 July, 1973. Copyright © 1973 by the American Association for the Advancement of Science. By permission of the author and the AAAS.

Use of neuroleptic agents

Physicians prescribe neuroleptic drugs on a long-term basis for mental disorders such as schizophrenia, psychosis due to mental deficiency, paranoid states of adulthood and senility, chronic brain syndromes, mania, hyperactivity in disturbed children, addiction to narcotics, excessive anxiety as observed in neurosis, and physical illness. The National Research Council of the National Academy of Sciences has recently reviewed the data on the effectiveness of some of the neuroleptics (3), but it has not confirmed claims that such agents are indicated for the treatment of mental conditions other than schizophrenia and related diseases.

There are few schizophrenic patients now living in the United States and Europe who have not received a phenothiazine or a butyrophenone at one time or another. In the last 15 years, neuroleptic agents have replaced most forms of treatment for psychoses and other serious mental ailments. Electric shock therapy and various types of psychotherapy have survived, but the former is seldom used in institutions, and the latter play a subordinate role in the total management of psychotic individuals. The fact that these drugs reduce overt psychopathology without causing excessive sedation, euphoria, or addiction explains, in part, their widespread use in psychiatry. Tranquilization is not a prominent feature of neuroleptic action (4, p. 41) despite the fact that the term 'tranquilizer' is still used in the classification of these drugs. Neuroleptics may reduce overactivity and belligerent behavior, but these are secondary effects of a general lessening of psychopathology. Sedation occurs only in the early stages of drug therapy in certain susceptible individuals or when excessive doses are administered, particularly of chlorpromazine. Animal studies and biochemical research have produced further evidence that the pharmacological effects of neuroleptics are very different from those of hypnotics (barbiturates) and antianxiety agents (meprobamate, chlordiazepoxide).

In the clinical area, large-scale collaborative investigations by the Veterans Administration (5) and the National Institute of Mental Health (6) have proven that neuroleptics are more efficacious in schizophrenia than are inert substances or conventional sedatives. Even though the conclusions of these and other studies are supported by impeccable methodology and highly sophisticated statistics, the questions still remain: How many patients benefit from drug therapy?

How effective are these drugs? Reports on the subject are extensive, complex, and often contradictory, but several reviews permit certain conclusions (7; 8, pp. 70–72). Investigations, with the patient's ability to remain in the community as a criterion of drug effectiveness, reveal that 60 to 70 percent of acute schizophrenics on no drugs are readmitted within 1 year, while only 20 to 30 percent receiving some form of drug therapy require rehospitalization within 1 year. The superiority of drugs over placebo may be somewhat higher when social therapy is provided and when one makes allowances for the failure of certain patients to adhere to the prescribed drug regime (9). However, the difference between those patients treated with drugs and those not treated with drugs decreases over time. According to one study, the difference may be only on the order of 10 to 15 percent after several years (10). As for the quality of the patient's adjustment after he leaves the hospital, the results of drug therapy are even less encouraging: the majority of those who live in the community continue to be unproductive and are often a burden to their families (11). Individuals released to foster homes or other sheltered environments may be as dependent and alienated as those confined to an institution (12).

For patients residing in hospitals, the criterion of drug effectiveness is usually the number of patients requiring a resumption of therapy after the active agent has been replaced by a placebo. The results vary with age, types of symptoms, duration of the disease, methods of assessment, and length of observation. In general, studies reporting a high relapse rate for placebo-treated patients also show a considerable degree of deterioration in the drug group. Major investigations, using standard rating instruments, reveal that fewer than 50 percent of patients hospitalized for several years improve in response to neuroleptics. Yet, according to surveys of medical records, 85 percent of all hospitalized schizophrenics receive medication at any given time (13).

As with other types of chemotherapies, doses depend on a number of factors such as age, severity of symptoms, and duration of illness. Yet there is little uniformity in the dosage of neuroleptics prescribed by physicians, even within reasonably homogeneous classes of patients (14). It is not uncommon to prescribe dosages exceeding those recommended by the manufacturers. Patients who present serious management problems are most likely to receive large quantities of neuroleptics for long periods of time, although the persistence of severe psychoses would suggest that chemotherapy is not effective in such cases. Data on the drugs prescribed for patients attending clinics are not readily available, but there is reason to believe that psychopharmacological therapy is equally extensive in outpatient facilities, since the main function of these centers is to dispense drugs.

There is some justification for the continued administration of drugs to patients who, in the course of treatment, appear to become less psychotic. Therapists, however, fail to take into account the possibility of naturally occurring remissions. Thus, in many instances, the choice of a drug regime is determined more by the severity of a previous episode than by the patient's current status.

Schizophrenia and related mental diseases are often characterized by episodes of violence, self-destructiveness, or utter helplessness. Such episodes may develop suddenly, with no apparent reason, and may last from a few hours to several years. A malfunctioning brain is not the only cause of interpersonal and social difficulties for the schizophrenic patient. The deprivation and stresses of the poverty in which this person is forced to live, whether he resides in a hospital, sheltered living quarters, or his own home, are also, in a great measure, responsible for what is often called unacceptable behavior. Many physicians, nurses, guardians, and family members who resent the patient's behavior and are threatened by potential acts of violence fail to distinguish between manifestations of illness and reactions to frustrations. Hence, drugs are prescribed to solve all types of management problems, and failure to achieve the desired results causes an escalation of dosage, changes of drugs, and polypharmacy. It is often reported that patients refuse to ingest their pills or that relatives fail to supervise the proper administration of medicines (15). Less publicized is the patient's dependence on drugs. The medical staff gains a feeling of accomplishment from the patient's adherence to a prescribed regime, while the nursing personnel and relatives, who are in more direct contact with the patient, derive a spurious feeling of security when the doctor's orders are carried out. Thus, the prescribing of drugs has in many cases become a ritual in which patients, family members, and physicians participate. Mystification, a concept developed by Lennard and associates (16), plays a certain role in the contemporary practice of psychopharmacology, inasmuch as neuroleptics are often used for solving psychological, social, administrative, and other nonmedical problems.

Drugs and community psychiatry

The widespread prescribing of potentially dangerous drugs has been particularly evident in the field of psychopharmacology because of its role in a rapidly expanding and changing program of mental health care. The public and the medical profession consider hospitalization of mental patients a therapeutic failure. Efforts on the part of administrators to improve the image of psychiatric institutes have been largely unsuccessful because of the chronic shortage of trained personnel and spiraling costs of medical care. When psychopharmacological agents were first introduced in the treatment of mental illness, administrators and clinicians hoped that the phasing-out of the old-fashioned state hospitals could be accomplished in a matter of a few years. Indeed, the number of institutional beds has been reduced drastically, and some hospitals have been closed. However, institutional care is still required for chronic schizophrenics and other categories of patients who never leave the hospital and for a substantial proportion of patients who must be readmitted. To meet the demands of patient care with inadequate funds, hospitals keep recently admitted patients for only a short time. For persons requiring more extensive hospitalization, these institutions can provide only substandard psychiatric and nursing care. This situation has generated the feeling that drug therapy is indispensable.

Community mental health centers, which are expected to take over many functions of state institutions, have not always been an unqualified success. Certain well-conducted programs in sparsely populated areas (such as the Saskatchewan Project) have provided excellent low-cost care for patients with chronic mental diseases and thus have practically eliminated the need for prolonged hospitalization (17). Other rapidly expanding mental health programs have created new burdens for the already strained medical facilities of urban areas. Recently, the New York County District Branch of the American Psychiatric Association (18) criticized the state's announced intention of restricting hospitalization of geriatric and chronic schizophrenic patients without making alternative provisions for such persons.

One of the main goals of community-oriented programs is to return hospitalized patients to their homes, but little effort has been made to study the effects that a mentally ill individual has on the psychological climate of his family. At least one study (19) has shown that the presence of such a person at home can be a source of considerable apprehension for members of his family. Physicians practicing in clinics and private offices feel obligated, and sometimes forced, to maintain the patient in the community, despite his precarious state of mind. Under these conditions, it is only natural that community mental health centers, outpatient facilities, and private practices should also rely heavily on drugs.

It has been stated often that, without neuroleptics, modern psychiatric treatment would not be possible. It is also true that the promotion of neuroleptics for the treatment of all types of psychiatric disorders has prevented federal, state, and municipal agencies from providing adequate personnel and better facilities for hospitals and other mental health centers. Mental institutions have benefited little from the expanded support of mental health programs. They continue to be low-morale, underprivileged facilities, compared to the community health centers, which have greater resources and thus attract better trained personnel. Anyone who has had experience with the institutional atmosphere before and after the introduction of drugs knows that the understaffing, insufficient funds, poor housing, marginal food, and improper maintenance of patients' quarters are as great now as they were in the immediate postwar years.

Toxicity

Clinicians feel that the routine administration of neuroleptics is necessary in schizophrenia because responders to drugs cannot be differentiated from nonresponders on clinical grounds. It is equally difficult to predict whether or not a patient will relapse upon withdrawal of the drug. Routine administration would be justified if neuroleptics were low-toxicity agents. While a single dose of any neuroleptic is seldom dangerous, administration over a period of weeks or months causes a variety of side effects and complications (8, pp. 94–116; 20). Parkinsonism is the best known effect of neuroleptics. Often associated with Parkinsonism is akinesia, which, in severe cases, is characterized by physical immobility as well as emotional indifference. This syndrome is poorly understood and often mistaken for psychomotor retardation. Some clinicians may even consider it a desirable effect because it helps control unruly behavior. In the early days of psychopharmacology, psychiatrists were accused of replacing a mechanical straitjacket with a chemical one, a criticism that is still justified when excessive doses of neuroleptics produce severe reduction of motor activity and a general loss of spontaneity.

Hypotension, drowsiness, leukopenia, jaundice, galactorrhea, photosensitivity, impotence, and excessive weight gain occur with a certain frequency. These effects, as well as Parkinsonism, are reversible when the drug is withdrawn, or they may disappear in the course of treatment. The only lethal effect is agranulocytosis, usually caused by chlorpromazine. It seems to be a rare complication, most likely to occur in the elderly during the first few months of therapy. Another serious effect is retinitis, which may result in blindness. It is caused by thioridazine but can be prevented if doses do not exceed those recommended by the manufacturer. In the early 1960s (21), deposits of metabolites of chlorpromazine in the lens and cornea, and less frequently in the skin, became a source of considerable concern, but it soon became apparent that the deposits in the eye were clinically insignificant and that the cosmetically objectionable skin pigmentation could be avoided by early recognition and change to another neuroleptic. More disturbing was the discovery that thioridazine and, less frequently, other phenothiazines may cause abnormalities in electrocardiograms (22). According to clinicians, the abnormalities are of no clinical significance and subside once the drugs are withdrawn. Since most patients are on chemotherapy indefinitely, the changes in their electrocardiograms may also persist indefinitely. Indeed, serious heart complications and cases of sudden death have been attributed to neuroleptics. The role these agents play in cardiac disorders is still uncertain because of diagnostic difficulties and the dearth of good clinical studies.

The variety and number of side effects would suggest that a certain amount of caution and selectivity be exercised in the use of neuroleptics. The fact that the existence of these complications is fairly well known and reasonably well documented in package inserts and in the general literature seems to indicate that clinicians are willing to take a certain amount of risk in prescribing drugs for a serious disease such as schizophrenia. The attitude of the physicians, drug companies, and government agencies toward tardive dyskinesia, however, is more difficult to explain in terms of contemporary medical standards.

Tardive dyskinesia

In the late 1950s, an unusual syndrome was observed in seven patients receiving phenothiazines (23). It consisted of slow, rhythmical movements in the region of the mouth, with protrusion of the tongue, smacking of the lips, blowing of the cheeks, and side-to-side movements of the chin, as well as other bizarre muscular activity. More careful examinations of patients on long-term drug therapy revealed that, not only the mouth, but practically all parts of the body could exhibit motor disorders, such as myoclonia, chorea, and athetosis. Overextension of the spine and neck, shifting of weight from foot to foot, and other abnormal postures indicated that the coordination of the various segments of the axial musculature was also affected. Less frequently, the syndrome resembled in every respect known neurological diseases, such as Huntington's disease, dystonia musculorum deformans, and postencephalitic brain damage (24). In milder cases, particularly when only the distal parts of the extremities are affected, tardive dyskinesia is of little clinical significance, but moderate to severe involvement of the region of the mouth creates considerable embarrassment as well as distress. The condition may be disabling when breathing or motor coordination is seriously impaired, or when it simulates known neurological diseases. The syndrome is called tardive dyskinesia because it manifests itself months or years after the initiation of drug therapy. Some clinicians also refer to it as persistent dyskinesia because it continues unchanged for years after all medication is removed.

The number of patients so afflicted cannot be ascertained. In mental hospitals, 2 or 3 percent of all patients exhibit some motor disorder consistent with tardive dyskinesia, but the percentage may rise to over 50 among patients over age 60 who have been exposed to neuroleptics for 3 years or longer. The frequency with which this disorder occurs in patients receiving neuroleptics in clinics and private offices is less well known. Neurologists claim that it is not uncommon.

Industry, government, and physicians

In 1967, there was a considerable body of evidence to indicate that tardive dyskinesia was caused by neuroleptics, that it occurred in at

least 5 percent of patients exposed to drugs for several years, and
that it could be observed in young adults as well as elderly patients,
regardless of diagnosis. Five years later, many physicians are still
unaware of this problem or seem to be completely unconcerned
about it, although tardive dyskinesia has become a common sight in
all wards of hospitals where drugs are administered routinely for
long periods of time. Lack of clinical information cannot explain this
ignorance of a major health problem – more than 100 papers
reporting 2000 cases of tardive dyskinesia have been published since
1957. The diagnosis offers no major difficulties, nor are special techniques of examining patients or laboratory procedures required.
Tardive dyskinesia becomes more pronounced after drugs are withdrawn, a fact that skeptics have used to question its existence as
a clinical entity. [This seemingly paradoxical phenomenon can be
explained in terms of known mechanisms of synaptic transmission
(25).]

Only recently have drug companies and government agencies
shown some interest in this major health problem. Before 1971,
package inserts devoted one sentence to the description of permanent
neurologic effects of these drugs. This short communication did not
describe the manifestation of tardive dyskinesia, but emphasized,
incorrectly, its rarity and likelihood to occur only in elderly or neuro-
logically predisposed individuals. One company (Squibb, manufacturer of Prolixin) has included a paragraph on persistent neurological
manifestations but, like other drug companies, has avoided using the
term 'tardive dyskinesia.' Like most terms in medical practice, it
leaves much to be desired, but it has been accepted by most clinicians
who are familiar with this drug effect. In 1972, Smith Kline and
French made a number of changes in the package inserts of three
drugs (Thorazine, Stelazine, and Compazine) to include a fairly
detailed description of lasting neurologic effects under the heading
'Persistent Tardive Dyskinesia.' The Food and Drug Administration
held a meeting on 15 May 1972 (26) to discuss means of informing
physicians of the danger of tardive dyskinesia. Since then, it has
urged manufacturers of neuroleptics, other than Smith Kline and
French, to update information on tardive dyskinesia in the package
inserts of their products. Nevertheless, the 1973 edition of the *Physicians' Desk Reference* (27), which is the most popular source of
information on drugs, fails to show any change with regard to neurological effects in 12 of the 17 neuroleptics available for prescription

use. This may give the clinician the false impression that the 12 drugs whose package inserts were not updated are safer than the remaining 5. Drug manufacturers also neglect to include items describing tardive dyskinesia in check lists of the side effects of drugs to be used in research on human beings. Many new drugs are still tested on chronic psychiatric patients with a history of prolonged exposure to neuroleptics.

Physicians and nurses who must deal directly with hospitalized patients are firmly convinced that most patients would become unmanageable if the use of drugs were discontinued. Those employed in noninstitutional mental health centers fear that they may be forced to give up programs responsible for keeping patients in the community. These apprehensions do not seem justified – it was never suggested that the use of neuroleptics should be abandoned. The question is not whether these drugs should be used for specific ailments, the question is whether the current practices of administering these drugs are medically sound. The indiscriminate and excessive use of potentially dangerous drugs for all schizophrenic patients (and for nonpsychotic subjects) is certainly not justified medically. Periodic assessments of therapeutic and unwanted effects are essential. Unquestionably, more selective prescribing of drugs will put new demands on hospitals, outpatient facilities, and private practitioners. Similarly, reduction or discontinuation of drug therapy will create conflicts with families and administrators and may also arouse fears of lawsuits, since the use of chemotherapy is accepted procedure for the treatment of psychosis. [The risk of being sued for not recognizing tardive dyskinesia until it is too late will increase considerably, as demonstrated by recent court cases (28).] Rehospitalization may be necessary in some cases. Since many communities have established centers for the management of psychiatric crises, these facilities may have to expand their services for the management of such emergencies.

Investigators and clinicians claim that knowledge of tardive dyskinesia is inadequate and that much more research is needed in order to deal with this problem effectively. So far, little effort has been made to carry out the necessary long-term studies on the onset and evolution of neurological and other cumulative effects of drugs. During the last 2 years, some 20 papers (29) have been published on the treatment of tardive dyskinesia, even though the majority of clinicians continue to ignore the existence of this complication. It is also revealing that most of the drugs that are responsible for neurologic side effects are being tested for the suppression of tardive dyskinesia. With a few exceptions (2, pp. 297–310; 30), little has been written on the prevention of permanent neurologic effects by a more judicious use of psychoactive agents. This is another indication of how dependent the medical community has become on chemical agents.

Until now, only a few independent investigators have carried out clinical studies on tardive dyskinesia. The problem has become of such a magnitude and complexity that drug companies and certain government agencies will have to take the initiative. A more responsible attitude toward the risks involved in long-term treatment with neuroleptics may necessitate a change in the priorities of drug research and a reallocation of funds. Education of the medical profession and the public by improving package inserts and by mailing informative material to all physicians is essential, but certainly insufficient. The neglect of a serious health problem for so many years has deeper roots than mere ignorance of facts. The problem of tardive dyskinesia should be viewed as another example of large-scale and inefficient application of a potentially useful technical discovery without consideration for its long-term effects on the individual and his environment.

Notes and references

1 The class of neuroleptics (also called major tranquilizers, ataractics, or antipsychotics) includes phenothiazines, butyrophenones, thioxanthenes, reserpine-like substances, and indoles. In the United States, 17 neuroleptics are marketed under different trade names. When I use the term 'drugs,' I refer to these agents.

2 F. J. Ayd, Jr., in *Clinical Handbook of Psychopharmacology*, A. DiMascio and R. I. Shader, Eds. (Science House, New York, 1970), pp. 297–310.

3 Prescribing information for Thorazine (Smith Kline and French, Philadelphia, Pa.).

4 G. L. Klerman, in *Clinical Handbook of Psychopharmacology*, A. DiMascio and R. I. Shader, Eds. (Science House, New York, 1970), pp. 40–56.

5 E. M. Caffey, Jr., L. E. Hollister, S. C. Kaim, A. D. Pokorny, in *ibid.*, pp. 343–386.

6 National Institute of Mental Health, Psychopharmacology Service Center, Collaborative Study Group, *Arch. Gen. Psychiat.* **10**, 246 (1964); R. F. Prien and J. O. Cole, *ibid.* **18**, 482 (1968).

7 R. Gittleman-Klein and D. F. Klein, in *Psychopharmacology*, D. H. Efron, Ed.

(Government Printing Office, Washington, DC, 1968), pp. 1119–1155; R. F. Prien and C. J. Klett, *Schizophrenia Bull.* **5**, 64 (1972).

8 D. F. Klein and J. M. Davis, *Diagnosis and Drug Treatment of Psychiatric Disorders* (Williams & Wilkins, Baltimore, 1969), pp. 70–72.

9 G. E. Hogarty, S. C. Goldberg, and Collaborative Study Group, *Arch. Gen. Psychiat.* **28**, 54 (1973).

10 D. M. Engelhardt, B. Rosen, N. Freedman, N. Margolis, ibid. **16**, 98 (1967).

11 N. R. Schooler, S. C. Goldberg, H. Boothe, J. O. Cole, *Amer. J. Psychiat.* **123**, 986 (1967); *Psychiat. News* (6 December 1972), p. 15.

12 *Psychiat. News* (1 November 1972), p. 1; H. R. Lamb and V. Goertzel, *Arch. Gen. Psychiat.* **26**, 489 (1972).

13 A survey conducted by me on 667 long-term patients at Spring Grove State Hospital revealed the following: 85 percent are currently on drugs; median duration of drug treatment is 6½ years; 33 percent are on drugs more than 90 percent of the time; median current dose is 240 milligrams of chlorpromazine equivalent per day. These data are in agreement with those of Prien and Klett (**7**, p. 2).

14 R. F. Prien, J. O. Cole, N. F. Belkin, *Brit. J. Psychiat.* **115**, 679 (1969). The collaborative group at the National Institute of Mental Health selected 200 patients from 7 typical state institutions for a drug study. The percentage of patients on more than 300 milligrams of chlorpromazine equivalent per day ranged from 37 to 77, even though other criteria for inclusion in the study were identical across the 7 hospitals.

15 H. E. Lehmann, in *Clinical Handbook of Psychopharmacology*, A. DiMascio and R. I. Shader, Eds. (Science House, New York, 1970), pp. 321–341.

16 H. L. Lennard *et al.*, *Mystification and Drug Misuse: Hazards in Using Psychoactive Drugs*, (Harper & Row, New York, 1972), p. 19.

17 A. Stewart, H. G. Lafane, F. Ginsberg, F. Herjanic, *Amer. J. Psychiat.* **125**, 82 (1968).

18 *Psychiat. News* (4 October 1972), p. 1.

19 B. Pasamanick, F. R. Scarpitti, S. Dinitz, *Schizophrenics in the Community* (Appleton-Century-Crofts, New York, 1967), pp. 135–166.

20 Consult Klein and Davis (**8**, pp. 94–116) for other side effects.

21 G. E. Crane, A. W. Johnson, W. J. Buffaloe, *Amer. J. Psychiat.* 117, 1045 (1971).

22 G. E. Crane, *Dis. Nerv. Syst.* **31**, 534 (1970).

23 The literature on tardive dyskinesia (1957 to 1971) is summarized in two review papers by G. E. Crane: *Amer. J. Psychiat.* 124 (Suppl.), 40 (1968) and *Brit. J. Psychiat.* 122, 395 (1973).

24 *Proceedings Centennial Convention on Huntington's Chorea* (Raven, New York, in press).

25 H. L. Klawans, *Amer. J. Psychiat.* **130**, 82 (1973). See references in this paper.

26 *Psychiat. News* (20 September 1972), p. 3.

27 *Physicians' Desk Reference* (Medical Economics Corp., Oradell, N.J., 1973).

28 *Washington Post* (9 April 1972), sect. B, p. 3.

29 H. Kazamatsuri, C. Chien, J. O. Cole, *Arch. Gen. Psychiat.* **27**, 491 (1972).

30 H. L. Hershon, P. F. Kennedy, R. McGuire, *Brit. J. Psychiat.* **120**, 41 (1972); G. E. Crane, *Amer. J. Psychiat.* **129**, 466 (1972).

31 Henry L. Lennard and associates (Family Study Station, San Francisco Medical
   Center, University of California) helped me in the preparation of this article.

Part IV

Alternatives to traditional mental health services

INTRODUCTION

To some degree the entire history of mental health care has been full of experiments and innovations. Community care, family care, group homes, non-psychiatric counseling, and self-help have antecedents throughout the history of mental institutions. Indeed, the CMHCs which began in the 1960s were considered quite a radical departure from tradition, though in fact they are largely integrated into the mainstream psychiatric landscape. As was noted in the first set of readings, change and reform in mental health often retained traditional beliefs and methods. Retention of the status quo may result from intentional conservatism on the part of institutions, providers, and officials. It may also arise from the unintended consequences of a chaotic mental health system lacking in planning and coordination, and mired in the mysteries of third-party reimbursements.

In this final section, we look at a wide variety of alternatives to the traditional mental hospital inpatient service. These models range from methods quite acceptable to the mental health field, to those which challenge the mainstream. Some are found in this country, and others abroad. All address the need to transform the traditional structures of the mental health system which has been handed down to us.

Charles Kiesler begins the section with his review of experimental methods of alternative care. He situates these innovations in the context of the critique of the custodial asylum and in the inability of mental health planning to attain goals which it sets for itself. Despite the dramatic increase in outpatient care as a percentage of all care, Kiesler finds that inpatient care still is on the rise absolutely. This prompts further work on alternatives to traditional treatment. Kiesler reviews a number of such alternatives, including day treatment, outpatient care, independence training, hostel living, and a nonprofessional group home. Apart from the latter, these alternatives all take place within the existing legal, administrative, and professional orbit.

In all cases, alternative care was equal to or better than inpatient care; this judgment was based on outcome measures such as rehospitalization, psychiatric status, school and work performance, social skills, and ability to live on one's own. These findings are quite astounding, especially since alternative care was usually less costly. Remarkably, however, resistance to alternative care comes from such factors as individual institutions' financial incentives to keep beds full, a pressure totally at odds with the overall move to decrease reliance on inpatient care. Other factors are physicians' professionalist notions that they can provide the best treatment, and families' desire to pass on responsibility. Here, as in so many other aspects of psychiatric care, detrimental institutional practices are maintained by a contribution of social forces, despite our knowledge of the self-perpetuating cycle of inpatient hospitalization.

Given the entrenched nature of the mental health system, it is quite easy for innovations to be suppressed or coopted. This is particularly true if the innovations take place within the mainstream. To avoid institutional and professional dominance, and to empower themselves, patients, ex-patients and prospective patients have increasingly developed their own self-help groups and facilities. In a short decade, one-half million such groups have come to serve more than fifteen million people, providing them with more control and participation in their own care. Self-help groups are more personally involving, share skills and knowledge, demystify professional expertise, and provide a reference group which may continue to be useful for the participant long after the initial period of need.

Audrey Gartner and Frank Riessman have been very involved in the self-help movement and provide an account of it in 'Self-help and mental health.' While the authors are very aware of the potential for cooptation, they believe that many self-help groups are capable and strong enough to defeat such attempts. Given that ability to withstand cooptation, they urge that self-help approaches to mental health should not be isolated models, but need to be brought into the mental health services system. This will require regional and national clearinghouses, education about self-help at the undergraduate and graduate levels, and concerted efforts by traditional agencies to cooperate with and help develop such groups.

Some groups will not even take the risk of absorption into the mainstream, as in the case of many mental patients' liberation groups. Many self-help groups have some degree of relationships with professionals, but this is not true of patients movement organizations. In *On Our Own: Patient-Controlled Alternatives to the Mental Health System*, Judi Chamberlin puts forth a model which is both non-professional and anti-professional. A leading patient movement activist, Chamberlin eschews all professional involvement except in the few cases where a professional will assist the patients group according to the group's direct request. Otherwise, mental health providers are guilty of 'mentalism,' the belief that mental illness really exists. Chamberlin would be loath to support the Italian transformation described later in this section, since that reform movement was initiated by psychiatrists.

Such a purist attitude is self-defeating, for there clearly are mentally ill persons in need of assistance, and few of those persons could participate in the marvelous patient-run organization that Chamberlin describes in 'Inside the Mental Patients' Association,' an excerpt from her book. But mental health workers should not dwell on the problems of the 'myth of mental illness' worldview to the exclusion of the great successes of the Mental Patients' Association in Vancouver. Chamberlin offers an important glimpse into the possibilities for self-help, and shows us how even local psychiatric facilities may accept such initiatives.

The selections so far suggest that there is a real gap between professional clinicians' work and the possibility of social change through mental health services. Yet one major alternative of recent years has bridged that gap – feminist therapy. The many-faceted feminist therapy model includes professionals as well as non-professionals, and attempts to reduce the oppressive hierarchical structure so typical of psychiatric agencies. Virginia Donovan and Ronnie Littenberg's 'Psychology of women: Feminist therapy' discusses how that model is 'better defined by the political awareness and social commitment on the part of the therapist than by the particular set of techniques she uses.' The authors, active in feminist therapy practice for over a decade, write that the women's movement critique of therapy was the inevitable result of two factors. First, therapy is concerned with the self and with women's social role as carriers of the culture through relationships and emotions. Second, psychology and psychiatry have been widely used as a justification for women's subordinate role. The first task is unattainable without first correcting the second factor – psychology as social control.

Therefore, Donovan and Littenberg continue, feminist therapy contains an 'analysis of the forms of social, economic, and political oppression that affect women individually as well as as a group. This analysis informs the therapist's understanding of how women develop and function in our society, and how change may occur.' As a result, feminist therapy is much more involved in the outside social world than is most other therapeutic practice. Thus, the feminist therapist deals with social issues which affect her own values and perspectives. Further, she encourages social, rather than only individual change.

In Italy, a professional-political synthesis has achieved a similar involvement of psychiatry with social change. There it has been much more national in scope, and has obtained wider professional support. In 'From confinement to community: The radical transformation of an Italian mental hospital,' Anne Lovell discusses how the Italian reforms have involved professionals shedding much of their professional identity. This results from several factors. First, in the restructuring in Trieste, many problems were defined in social as well as psychiatric terms. This different social level of explanation leads to different interventions, and mental health professionals have no automatic edge in those larger social areas. Second, the Italian alterations broke down traditional staff-patient barriers, and demystified the status of professionals. Third, the staff as well as the patients gravitated to a general social radicalism, thus leading to a redefinition of their own role in the helping fields. For instance, they began to confront the dominate traditionalism in medical and judicial sectors, and realized that radicalizing those sectors was part of overall social politicization. Franco Basaglia's Italian experiments ultimately extended to the level of nationwide legislation, and are perhaps the most radical changes involving professionals, since these reforms break down professional dominance. Further, the new psychiatric radicalism is matched by a deep political radicalism – an example of how both society and psyche may be integrated in social change efforts.

In Italy the Democratic Psychiatry movement had to organize from the ground up to achieve their reforms. But in China, the restructuring of psychiatric services came from the larger society's socialist experiment. Yi-chuang Lu writes in 'The collective approach to psychiatric practice in the People's Republic of China' that Chinese mental health care is more conscientiously planned than are American services. The cohesiveness of Chinese society allows this planning to more accurately set and achieve specific goals. China's 'serve the people' ideology places health services and social services in important positions of respect, and has led to a far more egalitarian treatment system. Key to the whole system is the integration of psychiatric problems with the overall social system. While readers may not agree with China's political structure, they may still find it remarkable to see the extent to which patients are helped by social involvement as described by Lu.

It seems likely that collectivist social structures allow for earlier detection of serious mental illness, and thus for earlier treatment. Chinese psychiatry provides a form of milieu therapy in a highly developed fashion, while American attempts at implementing milieu therapy have not progressed enough. This is partly a result of greater democratization in Chinese hospitals, efforts to diminish professional elitism, and much respect for patients' abilities to help themselves and others.

The various alternatives to traditional mental hospital care which are offered in this last part of the book provide a wide range of possibilities for change. Whatever the problems addressed in earlier readings, it is clear that we possess a vibrant tradition of another sort – reform and innovation to bring better mental health services to more people in more equitable fashion.

CHAPTER 13

Mental hospitals and alternative care: Noninstitutionalization as potential public policy*†

Charles A. Kiesler

The de jure national mental health policy in the United States is deinstitutionalization of hospitalized mental patients and the development of outpatient care through community mental health centers (Kiesler, 1980). Outpatient care has increased dramatically from 379,000 clinical episodes in 1955, to 4,600,000 in 1975, a twelve-fold increase in 20 years. The centerpiece of the legislative effort is the community mental health center system, signed into law in 1963, which in 1975 handled 1.6 million episodes of outpatient care (NIMH, Note 1).

A related effort has been to deinstitutionalize patients, removing them from hospitals and other institutions to alternative care settings. Although this policy has been controversial regarding public opinion, various legal issues, and the lack of appropriate care settings, the clinical outcomes of deinstitutionalization have been viewed more positively, although not uniformly so (Taber, 1980).

As a result of these dual efforts, the proportion of total mental health episodes nationally handled on an outpatient basis has risen from 23 percent in 1955 to 77 percent in 1975 (NIMH, Note 1).

So dramatic has been the increase of outpatient episodes that an

* I thank George Albee, Albert Bandura, Susan Fiske, David Rosenhan, Lee Seehrest, and Hans Strupp for helpful comments on an earlier draft of this article.
† Reprinted from *American Psychologist*, vol. 37, pp. 349–60, 1982. Copyright © 1982 by the American Psychological Association. Reprinted by permission of the publisher and author.

important fact for national mental health policy has been obscured. This is, the number of mental institutional or hospital episodes[1] has actually continued to increase: a 38 percent increase in the period 1955 to 1975 (Vischi, Jones, Shank, and Lima, 1980). In addition to the absolute increase, the episodic rate of hospitalization (per 100,000 population) was greater in 1975 than in 1955.

According to NIMH figures there are currently about 1,800,000 admissions to mental hospitals in the United States during each year.[2] Rubin (1978) estimates the direct costs of inpatient care to be approximately $6 billion (over $10 billion including nursing homes). Of the funds spent on mental health in the United States, 70 percent goes to hospital care (Kiesler, 1980).

Part of this effect is due to 150 years of professional practice in which institutionalization was the treatment of choice. Even the task panel on deinstitutionalization, rehabilitation, and long-term care of the President's Commission on Mental Health (PCMH), while strongly advocating deinstitutionalization of patients, never considered whether the original institutionalization was necessary and clinically efficacious (Platman, 1978).

During these two decades, the site of hospitalization has changed. The number of episodes in state and county mental hospitals fell from 819,000 in 1955 to 599,000 in 1975 (Vischi *et al.*, 1980). These hospitals were the primary target of the deinstitutionalization effort. However, the number of inpatient episodes in all other categories surveyed (general hospital psychiatric units, community mental health centers, VA psychiatric units, and private mental hospitals) has increased from 477,000 to 1.2 million in the same time period. It is noteworthy that state and county mental hospitals still handle more inpatient episodes than any other sites, although they are being rapidly overtaken by general hospital psychiatric units (but see Note 1).

The rate of hospitalization has probably been more affected by the financial support provided by legislative sources than by professional practices per se. While NIMH supports a national *policy* of deinstitutionalization and outpatient care, the Medicaid/Medicare *programs* have incentives favoring hospitalization (as do most other systems of reimbursement for mental health services). Under those programs it is less expensive to the patient to receive care in a hospital than on a continuing outpatient basis. Clinical practice is pragmatically affected by the alternatives open to the patients. The above PCMH task panel says, for example, 'Thus, the level and type of care given to the chronically mentally disabled is frequently based on what services are fundable and not on what services are needed or appropriate' (Platman, 1978, p. 369).

As an example, consider the Medicaid program in greater detail. In fiscal year 1977, $558 million were expended under the Medicaid program for care in state, county, and private mental institutions and psychiatric hospitals, slightly greater than the total federal cost of all 600 community mental health centers in the United States. The national de jure policy of outpatient care, the main original goal of the community mental health centers system, is undercut by a national de facto policy of inpatient care in allocation of funds through the Medicaid system. The total funds spent for mental health services through Medicaid exceeds $4 billion, over half of which goes to nursing homes for mental patients. Quite unintentionally, Medicaid has become the largest single mental health program in the country.

However unintentionally, hospitalizing the mentally infirm is still the national practice. Discussions of deinstitutionalization and attempts to shorten hospital stays still involve the same sequence. Noninstitutionalization is not seriously considered as a policy alternative. The average stay of patients committed to mental hospitals has been reduced. Readmission rates, however, have apparently increased (good national statistics are not available), and the comparative outcomes of noninstitutional modes of care have not been seriously considered.

Clearly, considerable national progress has been made in moving forward the policy of outpatient care and deinstitutionalization. However, one should consider the possibility of a policy of *noninstitutionalization*. This article asks the following questions: (a) What is the scientific evidence regarding the effects of mental hospitalization? (b) What scientific evidence is available concerning the comparative effectiveness and costs of modes of treatment alternative to hospitalization? (c) Are there aspects of hospitalization that suggest it might have negative effects on the individual? The rest of this article considers these questions.

The social psychological effects of institutionalization

Erving Goffman (1961) sees a mental hospital as a total institution sharing certain characteristics with such other total institutions as prisons, the military, and monasteries. He defines a total institution 'as a place of residence and work where a large number of like-situated individuals, cut off from the wider society for an appreciable period of time, together lead an enclosed, formally administered round of life' (p. xiii). His original work was based on a year's field work in St Elizabeth's, a federal mental hospital in Washington, DC.

Since Goffman's seminal essay, a considerable literature has evolved in sociology regarding the potentially debilitating effects of total institutions in general (McEwen, 1980), and mental institutions in particular (Goldstein, 1979). Institutionalization is often seen as: fostering institutional dependency in various ways, leading over time to progressive loss of social and vocational competencies (rendering people less capable of managing their lives on the outside), undercutting one's ability to deal competently and independently with the world outside the institution, and often involving loss of contact with relatives and meaningful others.[3] Mental institutions have additional effects – the stigmatization by others as being mentally diseased, and the self-labeling as mentally ill – that could interfere with the new learning and sense of confidence necessary to produce positive therapeutic change.

A participant-observer study by Rosenhan (1973) is illustrative. In that study, 8 persons posed as patients in various mental hospitals. Rosenhan describes the substantial degree to which the volunteers felt powerless and depersonalized. Among factors contributing to the feeling of depersonalization, Rosenhan found that the staff in mental institutions actually seemed to avoid interacting with mental patients. In 6 of the instances of hospitalization, detailed records were kept, and the total daily contact with psychiatrists, psychologists, residents, and physicians, in any context whatsoever, averaged 7 minutes per patient. If this finding is at all general, such lack of plausible social and professional interaction could potentially have a very negative effect on patients.

In addition to potential lack of quantity care, the quality of care in an institution may be less than that available in other sites. For example, over 50 percent of the psychiatrists who work in state and county mental hospitals received their medical training outside the

United States. Given a potential difference in the quality of medical training, possible language problems, and that a foreign psychiatrist may lack deep understanding of what is normative and deviant in our culture, it is not difficult to imagine the quality of care in such institutions to be less than that available in other places. Further, Lorei and Gurel (1973) found, in a large study of 957 schizophrenic patients discharged from 12 VA hospitals, that the best predictor of readmission to the hospital was the number of times that the patient had been in the hospital before.

If one wished to seriously question whether institutionalization for the mentally disabled is necessary, then essentially none of the data described here are directly relevant. For example, the best predictor of institutionalization is prior institutionalization, but this may simply be due to institutionalized people being the most serious cases. If only the most serious are originally the ones to go into an institution, it is not unreasonable that they be in an institution at any given moment. Further, even though one could document negative effects of mental institutionalization, it does not necessarily follow that there is any simple alternative to institutionalization or that the institutional experience in total was negative. Even though one could have rather negative (and depersonalizing) experience in a mental institution, that experience might still be better than any alternative. A noninstitutionalized control group would be necessary to demonstrate that the negative effects observed are due to institutionalization rather than general progressive deterioration of the patients.

What is really needed are experimental scientific studies of the effects of institutionalization compared to alternative modes of care. One definitional problem is that *alternative care* is a term typically applied to methods of caring for *de*institutionalized patients. That research is not necessarily relevant regarding the possible efficaciousness of alternative modes of care *instead* of the original institutionalization.

What would be the minimum scientific characteristics of a study of modes of care alternative to initial institutionalization? First, all the patients in such a study should be judged as seriously disturbed, so that hospitalization would be the normal method of treatment. Second, the critical scientific element would be random assignment to conditions of treatment, in which some patients by chance would be admitted to the hospital, while other patients would be assigned to some alternative treatment mode, even if only an untreated control condition. Third, one would need to specify the characteristics of the patient population and the details of professional treatment (including psychological testing, clinical judgment, and such behavioral outcomes as employment, school attendance, and the establishment of enduring social relationships). The progress of the patients should be tracked for some time to see if any differences persist over time and to determine how many people in the various samples ended up in an institution.

The most critical element in the list above is random assignment to condition. The art of psychological assessment and diagnosis is nowhere near the level necessary to permit adequate matching as a quasi-experimental technique. Further, the process of professional mental health treatment is sufficiently complex that one cannot point with great precision to those elements of the aid which are critical in the treatment process. The only way to avoid these problems is through random assignment to condition. In searching the literature for studies having these characteristics, I was able to find 10, and these are described in the section below.

True experiments involving random assignment to mental hospitals

Of the 10 studies relevant to these issues, 9 included a true experimental design in which some patients were randomly assigned to a hospital setting (H condition) and others to some alternative method of care (AC condition). The tenth study had a near-experimental design in which all of the patients in one 5-month period were assigned to an inpatient crisis unit, and in the following 5-month period all were assigned to an alternative treatment without hospitalization. The number of subjects in each treatment condition across the 10 studies ranged from 10 to 189, and the total for each condition across all experiments was about 650. The various studies are outlined in Table 13.1.

The intent of each study was originally to test some pet alternative-care project. Although several of the studies are well known, they are individually known for the specific method of alternative care rather than the fact that random assignment to condition allowed a true experimental test of the effects of hospitalization. One piece of evidence that these investigators were primarily interested in a

Table 13.1 Summary of Studies

Study	N	Patients	Excluded	Type of AC treatment	Type of H treatment
Stein *et al.* (1975)	60 each	All	Alcoholism OBS	Coping skills/ independence training	Inpatient mental health institute
Mosher and Menn (1978)	AC = 33 H = 30	Young, first admission, schizophrenia	All other	'Soteria'	'Good inpatient unit'
Brook (1973)	49 each	All	None	'Hostel'	Inpatient unit, mental health clinic
Flomenhaft *et al.* (1969)	150 each	All	None	Family crisis therapy	Psychiatric hospital
Herz *et al.* (1971)	45 each	Not 'too healthy,' not 'too ill'	78%	Day care	Regular inpatient
Pasamanick *et al.* (1967)	57 drug, 41 placebo, 54 H	18–62-year-old schizophrenics; no homicidal or suicidal tendencies; cooperative family	All others	(a) drug/public health visits (b) placebo	Regular inpatient
Levenson *et al.* (1977)	10	Acute schizophrenics	All others	Drug/daily therapy	Regular inpatient
Washburn *et al.* (1976)	H = 30 AC = 29	Females; not suicidal, not homicidal; capable of treatment	58%[b]	Day care	Regular inpatient
Wilder *et al.* (1966)	189 each	All	34%[c]	Day care	Regular inpatient
Krowinski and Fitt (Note 2)	H = 50 AC = 51	Not too healthy/ill, suicidal, violent, disorganized, drug dependent	38%[d]	Day care	Regular inpatient

Note: H = hospital setting. AC = alternative method of care. OBS = organic brain syndrome. U = unknown.
[a] But see Weisbrod *et al.* (1980)
[b] In addition, 27% refused to participate.
[c] 34% of AC patients were transferred immediately to inpatient status.
[d] 12% suicidal; 19% 'too well'; 7% refused assignment.

specific alternative treatment is that they almost uniformly refer to the hospitalized patients as the 'control group.'

The experimental studies

1. The program investigated by Stein, Test, and Marx (1975) was designed to help patients acquire the coping skills and autonomy necessary for reasonable community adjustment. Patients were assigned to either a community living model or to regular inpatient care at Mendota Mental Health Institute; patients were between the ages of 18 and 62 with any diagnosis other than severe organic brain

Initial H stay (days)	% or ratio AC ultimately hospitalized	% or ratio H readmitted	Costs	Outcome/comments
22.9	6/60	14/60	U[a]	No difference in symptoms; greater employment in AC & more time spent in independent settings.
28	53%	67%	$4,400 each	2 years later: AC group had higher occupational level, more living independence. 1-year differences: AC group was more likely to be working, in school, have a long-term friend, less psychopathology.
U	1/49	6/49	$410/mo.	Less remission of symptoms in AC after 6 mo., but more medication given; no differences on 11 other outcome measures.
26.1	14/150	16/150	Less for AC	Approximately same numbers of H readmitted within 6 mo. as AC admitted, but they stayed 3 times as long.
138.8	30%	50%	U	Substantial difference after 4 weeks; less after 2 years.
83	13/57 (drug) 27/41 (placebo)	25/54	U	Drug/public health group better after 2.5 years; erosion of differences after 5 years.
U	U	U	$3,330 (H) $565 (AC)	Remission (not manifestly psychotic): 90% – AC ($M = 12.5$ days); 70% – H ($M = 19.5$ days).
U	U	U	$21,916 (H) $13,824 (AC)	Differences on subjective distress, community functioning, family burden, cost, days of attachment to program, with AC better.
20	40%	45%	U	Patients excluded from AC still included in evaluation sample & data. Few differences between groups.
16	20%	38%	Less for AC	Greater improvement of AC on psychiatric scores; somewhat more AC considered to have improved.

syndrome or primary alcoholism, and they had previously served an average of 14 months in other institutions. The inpatient care involved 'progressive treatment aimed at the preparation for return to the community' and entailed a median length of hospital stay of 17 days. In the community-living approach, which lasted 14 months, the therapeutic staff assisted the patients in their homes and neighborhoods and trained them in such daily living activities as doing laundry, shopping, cooking, grooming, budgeting, and the use of public transportation. Dependent measures included a demographic data form, a short clinical rating scale, a community adjustment form, the family burden scale, and the like. The study tracked the patients for 4 months after their initial interviews. After the 4-month period, there were no differences between conditions in the amount of time patients had spent either in penal institutions or other medical nonpsychiatric institutions. In general, the dependent measures were very similar for both sets of patients. Ultimately, 6 of the 60 AC patients were hospitalized. During the 4-month period, 14 of the 60 H patients had already been readmitted after being discharged once; that is, more hospitalized patients were rehospitalized than those undergoing alternative care were ever hospitalized. There was a highly significant difference between the 2 groups in the amount of time they spent in independent settings during the 4-month observation period (greater time by the AC group). Further, the AC group had a smaller percentage unemployed at the end of 4 months than did the H group, although the difference was mainly in sheltered non-full-time employment. The 6AC patients who ultimately were admitted to the hospital spent a mean of 13.8 days there, whereas the original H group spent a mean of 22.9 days in the hospital during their first admission. No data were given for the length of stay for the 14 H patients who were subsequently readmitted to the hospital. The authors do not describe costs, but a recent economic cost-benefit analysis (Weisbrod, Test, and Stein, 1980) involving a number of assumptions and approximations suggests increased initial costs of the AC group, but a net benefit of $400 per patient per year.

2. Mosher, Menn, and Matthews (1975) compared outcomes in 2 groups of young first-admission schizophrenics: one receiving usual treatment, including drugs, on the wards of a good community mental health center; the other being treated by a nonprofessional staff, usually without drugs, in a small homelike facility called Soteria. Staff and residents share responsibility for the maintenance of the house, preparation of the meals and cleanup, and at least two staff members are on the premises at all times. Residents are discharged when the total group informally reaches a consensus that they are ready to be discharged. The hospital group received a ½-hour of psychotherapy daily, 1½ hours of occupational therapy daily, plus a daily community meeting led by a member of the treatment team. In addition, within the H condition a crisis group met for 1½ hours 5 times per week; a couples group, 2 hours a week; and a women's group, 2 hours a week. Thus the hospital group is clearly an unusual and highly intensive method of inpatient treatment.

Mosher, Menn, and Matthews report various outcome measures

at discharge, 6 months after discharge, and 1 year from admission. Soteria residents had significantly lower scores in psychopathology than the hospitalized patients at all measurement intervals. Substantially more of the Soteria patients were working in full-time or near full-time employment both 6 months after discharge and 1 year after admission. Significantly more Soteria patients were able ultimately to live alone or with peers, whereas hospital patients tended to reside ultimately with their parents or relatives.

Mosher and Menn (1978) report 2-year follow-up. Generally the differences between conditions reported at 1 year continue, but are smaller. Matthews, Roper, Mosher, and Menn (1979), in a more detailed study of relapse, found that AC patients had about a 20 percent better chance of not ever being hospitalizedthan the H patients did of being rehospitalized at any point in time over two years following completion of the program.

3. Brook (1973) describes an opportunistic study that, although not a true random design, is so close as to warrant inclusion in this article. For several months the inpatient unit at the Fort Logan Mental Health Center was closed. All patients who ordinarily would have been hospitalized in this unit were instead put in a 'hostel.' Forty-nine residents who underwent this hostel systems intervention treatment were compared with the last 49 patients admitted to the inpatient unit when it was still open. Since all patients presenting themselves for treatment were included, this comes very close to a true randomized design. Most of the patients were acutely ill: almost half were diagnosed as at moderate to high suicide risk; half were schizophrenic, and half of those, chronic; one fourth were depressive reactive; the remaining fourth involved alcohol or drug abuse, adjustment reaction, marital maladies, or excessive compulsiveness. Of the 49 AC cases, 11 had previously been hospitalized.

The hostel had no residential staffing and neighbors helped with meals and occasional other problems. The overall approach to treatment was intervention by the crisis staff in whatever part of the resident's social system was seen as the source of the crisis, typically the family. Some sessions with patients were held at the hostel, including some with the family; other sessions were held at the patient's home. Individual therapy occasionally supplemented these social systems interventions. When not in evaluation or therapy sessions, patients continued normal activities as far as possible. The mean stay was 5.75 days. Patients were then transferred to outpatient status and scheduled for 6 to 8 more sessions of family or individual therapy.

There were no outcome differences between the two groups on 11 different measures, although the hostel group had less remission of symptoms; on the other hand, the hostel group also received much more medication than did the inpatient group (perhaps reflecting the staff's anxiety about the adequacy of the treatment in the hostel). Of the 49 hospitalized patients, 6 were subsequently readmitted within six months (3 of them twice), whereas only 1 of the 49 patients in the hostel was admitted to hospitalization within 6 months after discharge.

4. Flomenhaft, Kaplan, and Langsley (1969) randomly assigned 150 patients to family crisis therapy and another 150 to regular inpatient care in the Colorado Psychiatric Hospital. The inpatient group stayed an average of 26 days in the hospital; the family crisis therapy group was seen by a team for 2.5 weeks. The typical AC outpatient care consisted of 5 office visits, 1 home visit, and 3 telephone contacts. 'The team's aim is to restore the confidence of the patient and family sufficiently so that they can manage their own problems, cope more adaptively with expected future problems, and perceive less need in the future to exclude a member' (p. 41). The team worked with all members of the patient's immediate family and significant others and was available 24 hours a day. The team took the unusual step of conducting home visits and conducted the first visit at the patient's home within 4 hours after the initial contact. In an analysis of half of the experimental and half of the control subjects 6 months after admission, the AC patients were doing as well as the H patients on 'two measures of functioning, and the experimental (AC) returned to pre-stress functioning much more rapidly than did control (H)' (p. 43).

5. Herz, Endicott, Spitzer, and Mesnikoff (1971) compared daycare treatment with regular inpatient treatment. Their study is unique in that essentially the same treatment occurred for all patients. 'Patients in both groups were treated by the same staff and participated together in the same activities during the day' (p. 108). An initial evaluation and 3 follow-up evaluations of psychopathology and role functioning were made at 2 weeks, 4 weeks, and an average of almost 2 years. The main evaluation instruments were the Psychiatric Status Schedule and the Psychiatric Evaluation Form. Unfortunately the researchers eliminated from consideration patients who were either

'too healthy' or 'too ill' to be included in the study. Thus, 78 percent of the total pool of patients were eliminated from consideration prior to the random assignment to conditions. This design is not inadequate, but the generalizations that can be drawn from it are somewhat more limited.

The average number of days from randomization until the patient was discharged from inpatient or day care and lived in the community full time for at least one week, was 48.5 days for the day patients and 138.8 days for the inpatients (opposite to the usual finding). The data in Table 13.1 of the percentages of people in the H condition readmitted to the hospital, and those in the AC condition ultimately hospitalized, are approximate and are estimated from a figure presented in the original article. The difference between conditions of cumulative percentages of patients discharged from initial hospitalization are consistent and sizable, with more day patients being discharged at all points across a 7.5-month period. Indeed, about 25 percent of the inpatients had never been released after 7.5 months.

At all the outcome points measured in the study, the day patients showed better results on both evaluation forms, although differences between the two groups on these forms persisted only on two subscales at the end of the 2-year measurement period. The authors observed considerable apprehension and resistance among staff members concerning the wisdom of placing acutely ill patients on day care. Even as the study progressed and clear differences were being shown in outcome in favor of day care, 'the antagonism and apprehension lessened but the staff continued to prefer inpatient care' (p. 116).

6. Pasamanick, Scarpitti, and Dinitz (1967) had 3 treatment groups in their study: a regular inpatient group in a state hospital and the psychiatric unit of a general hospital, a group that received only placebos and visits from public health nurses, and a group that combined the public health care with regular medication (AC). Although a psychologist, a psychiatrist, and a social worker were involved in the study, public health nurses were the principal treatment agents, and they regularly visited the patients' homes. There were 4 requirements for a patient to be included in the study: diagnosis of schizophrenia, age between 18 and 62, no evidence of homicidal or suicidal tendencies, and a family willing to provide supervision and information on patient and family at home. Thirty months later, all 3 groups had improved, with very small differences among

conditions on psychiatric evaluations. Comparisons between conditions are reported infrequently, but the authors say that 'in all of the many specific measures, home care (AC) patients were functioning as well or better than the hospital control (H) cases' (p. 251). H patients, however, were much more likely to be rehospitalized than AC patients ever were. Pasamanick *et al.* report a cumulative saving of 4,818 hospital days by the AC group over that experienced by the H group (over 2½ years). Davis, Dinitz, and Pasamanick (1972) report that after a 5-year period, there were small differences among the 3 conditions on problem behaviors, vocational performance, domestic performance, or psychiatric status. If anything, the placebo group tended to be worst on outcome measures, with the drug-public-health condition the best, and the hospital condition intermediate.

7. Levenson, Lord, Sermas, Thornby, Sullender, and Comstock (1977) compared regular inpatient treatment of acute schizophrenics with a specially designed, city-county hospital outpatient clinic. The outpatient group was given a regimen of pharmacotherapy, supportive individual psychotherapy, and family counseling within the context of daily appointments lasting approximately 20 minutes. This intensive treatment continued until the patient entered remission (i.e., was given a global rating of not manifestly psychotic) or was transferred to another less intensive treatment setting. Nine of the 10 clinical patients and 7 of the 10 ward patients successfully attained remission (not a statistically significant difference). As indicated in Table 13.1 the average time to remission was 12.5 days in the clinical group and 19.5 days in the ward group (again, not statistically significant). The authors give no indication of what happened to the patients who did not attain remission. On an expanded brief psychiatric rating scale, both groups improved significantly, but without any significant differences between them. The average cost per remission was $3,330 for the ward and $565 for the special clinic. Although it is clear in this study that the special clinic patients did not do worse than the inpatient group, the *N*s in each condition are so small as to prohibit adequate statistical analysis.

8. Washburn, Vannicelli, Longabaugh, and Scheff (1976) randomly assigned patients to either an inpatient unit or a day-care unit following 2 to 6 weeks of inpatient evaluation (a conservative comparison given that all patients were hospitalized for some period of time prior to randomization). Both groups were treated at McLean

Hospital in Massachusetts, a private nonprofit teaching hospital noted for exceptional service. However, if patients were homicidal, suicidal, or judged by their therapists as absolutely requiring hospitalization, they were not considered candidates for randomized assignment (58 percent). In addition, 27 percent of the total sample refused or were unable to participate. This left 15 percent of the total sample, or 59 patients who were randomly assigned to either an inpatient unit ($n = 30$) or a day-care unit ($n = 29$). The data are very clear and indicate that 'for the range of patients studied, day treatment is, on the whole, superior to inpatient treatment in five distinct areas: subjective distress; community functioning; family burden; total hospital costs; and days of attachment to the hospital program' (p. 665). The differences between conditions, however, lessened over an 18-month to 2-year period of time. The treatment costs for the two groups were quite different. The authors computed totals for 6-month periods across 18 months. Summing these figures, it appears that the average cost of inpatient care for each of the 30 H patients was about $22,000, or a total of over $650,000. The average cost for the day-care patient was less than $14,000, bringing the total for the 29 patients to about $400,000. The difference in cost of treatment between the two groups for the first 18 months of the study was, therefore, more than $250,000. The authors say that the AC group spent significantly fewer hospital days during the second 6 months of the study (and were otherwise similar).

9. Zwerling and Wilder (1964), in an older but well-known study, attempted to ascertain whether psychiatric patients could be assigned in an entirely random fashion from the admitting room of a general hospital to a day hospital. During a 4.5-month period, all patients admitted to the psychiatric service of the Bronx Municipal Hospital Center were randomly assigned either to inpatient treatment or to day care. A total of 189 patients were assigned to each treatment, but staff were allowed to treat the patients however they felt appropriate and the investigators made no attempt to keep the patients in the day hospital.

The principal problem with the study is that it is more an assessment of the attitudes of the staff in that particular hospital than it is a test of whether one can in fact treat all patients with day care. The staff were allowed to reject whomever they wished, and as I have noted, many staff are substantially opposed to treating a majority of the cases in day care.

Wilder, Levin, and Zwerling (1966) followed up on these patients and attempted to assess their status 24 months after their initial admission. One of the difficulties in assessing this follow-up is that the original day-care patients were considered as a statistical group, even though only 39 percent were treated solely in the day-care setting and another 34 percent of the 'day-care' group were treated completely within the inpatient setting. No distinction was made between these subgroups. Most of the data came from an interview with the patient and a member of the patient's family in the home, part of which was conducted with the patient and the family member together.

The day group spent 8 (5-day) weeks in the initial treatment, whereas the inpatient group had a median stay of about 3 (7-day) weeks (the finding reported earlier as typical). However, the day-care group spent a somewhat smaller number of total days in the hospital over the 2-year period than did the inpatient groups. The proportion of AC patients ultimately hospitalized was slightly smaller (40 percent) than inpatients being readmitted (45 percent). The interview data revealed no significant differences between conditions in psychiatric stress. The authors conclude that 'the day hospital was . . . generally as effective as the inpatient service in the treatment of acutely disturbed patients for most or all phases of their hospitalization' (p. 1101).

10. In an unpublished manuscript by Capital Blue Cross, Krowinski and Fitt (Reference Note 2) compared a day-treatment center with inpatient care. Inpatient care included daily visits by a private psychiatrist for therapy and medication. The general inpatient approach was a mixture of medical and milieu models; staff included an occupational therapist, a clinical social worker, and a chief psychiatrist. The day-care center included several modular programs that emphasized helping the individual to function in the community. Staff consisted of 3 MA-level psychologists, 2 clinical social workers, an occupational therapist, a registered nurse, and a part-time psychiatrist.

Patients were eligible if they demonstrated sufficient dysfunction to require inpatient care, but they were excluded prior to randomization if they were suicidal, violent, extremely agitated, disorganized, or drug or alcohol dependent (12 percent); not considered to require hospitalization (19 percent); or refused assignment to the unit (7 percent). Thus 38 percent of the total patient population considered initially were excluded prior to randomization, leaving a net sample of 101 patients.

The day-care patients improved more than the inpatient group on such scales of the psychiatric status schedule as subjective distress, lack of emotion, depressive anxiety, memory disorientation, and parent role (in all, 8 of 28 scales). The inpatient group improved more on one scale, agitation-excitement. Each sample improved on almost all of the 28 measures. On a 'functional baseline system' with categories of impairment, 67 percent of the daycare group were considered to have improved, and 52 percent of the inpatient group also improved.

In a 6-month follow-up, differences between conditions had lessened somewhat. During the 6-month period, 38 percent of the inpatient group had been readmitted to the hospital (for an average of 35 days), while 20 percent of the day-care group had been admitted (for an average of 26.5 days). The Krowinski and Fitt study is unique in its detailed discussion of costs. They compute actual costs of the original inpatient care to be $1,549 per patient and $1,414 for day care (including physician costs, but excluding research costs). Adding the cost of readmission, the total actual cost was $2,742 per inpatient and $1,933 per day-care patient, a difference of 38 percent over the 6 months.

Discussion

All of the studies reported included seriously ill patients. Only 1 study excluded a large proportion of patients prior to randomization, and 3 excluded no one. Hence, neither the exclusion of some patients nor the perceived seriousness of the cases can be considered plausible explanations for the more favorable results seen in the AC conditions. Nor can one assert that the quality of inpatient care in these studies was below the national norm: in most cases, the quality of inpatient care was regarded as very good, probably substantially above average for all institutions.

The results also cannot be accounted for by a specific type of treatment. The type of alternative treatment varied considerably across studies in terms of professional involvement, supervision, and cost. In general, the treatment alternatives did lean heavily, but not exclusively, toward social systems intervention, basic support, and behavioral skill building. However, similar effects were produced by such studies as Brook's, in which patients were left much on their own in a rented house.

Across the 10 studies, an impressive array of outcome measures was assessed, including not only obvious ones, such as psychiatric evaluations, but such policy-relevant variables as subsequent employment, school performance, maintenance of long-term relationships, and independent living arrangements.

It is worth emphasizing that none of these studies showed overall effects on outcome measures that were more positive for hospitalization than for alternative treatment, regardless of specific content, with one limited exception. The possible exception is the Brook study: Less symptom remission occurred in alternative care than in the inpatient crisis unit. However, Brook described substantially different drug levels between the treatments and suggested that as explaining the difference in symptom remission.

Most studies had evidence relating to hospitalization. Some of these effects are quite impressive. For example, the Stein et al. (1975) study, which emphasized the teaching of coping skills and independence, found that 54 of the 60 regular inpatient subjects were initially hospitalized, and 14 were eventually readmitted within 4 months, whereas only 6 of the 60 patients undergoing alternative care were ever hospitalized. In the Pasamanick et al. (1967) study, 13 of the 57 AC patients were ultimately hospitalized within 2.5 years, whereas 25 of the 54 H patients were rehospitalized during that time period.

Further, the costs of these alternative treatments are quite varied. For example, the hostels described in the Brook study cost a total of $410 per month for the whole operation. The studies range all the way up to that of Soteria, described by Mosher, Menn, and Matthews (1975), in which the cost of a patient for the alternative care was essentially the same as the cost for those in the inpatient unit. In no case did the cost of alternative care exceed that of inpatient care (but see Weisbrod et al., 1980).

It seems quite clear from these studies that for the vast majority of patients now being assigned to inpatient units in mental institutions, care of at least equal impact could be otherwise provided. There is not an instance in this array of studies in which hospitalization had any positive impact on the average patient which exceeded that of the alternative care investigated in the study. In almost every case, the alternative care had more positive outcomes. There were significant and powerful effects on such life-related variables as employment, school attendance, and the like. There were significant and important effects on the probability of subsequent readmission: Not only did the patients in the alternative care not undergo the initial hospitalization, but they were less likely to undergo hospitalization later, as well. There is clear evidence here for the causal sequence in the finding alluded to earlier that the best predictor of hospitalization is prior hospitalization. These data across these 10 studies suggest quite clearly that hospitalization of mental patients is self-perpetuating.[4]

However, we can distinguish between which answers these studies provide and which questions they do not address. Further, we can distinguish between basic scientific conclusions and which scientific conclusions have policy implications. Thus, scientifically we can say over 10 studies with random assignment of very disturbed people to regular inpatient care and some form of alternative care, that the alternative care is at least as good as the inpatient care. We can also say scientifically that it does not depend on one specific type of alternative care, since there is some variation among the types of alternative treatment here. We can say scientifically, at least under the conditions investigated across these studies, that hospitalization in mental institutions is self-perpetuating. Scientifically then, these studies taken together seem clear-cut and provocative.

These treatments do emphasize social systems intervention, basic support, and behavioral skill building. However, the fact that other treatment modalities have not received such study does not mean the ones reported here are necessarily the most effective treatment strategies. Further, the consistency of the data across studies does not imply that simply anything would work. All of these AC treatments were active modes of care. Even the Brook (1973) study involved daily professional contact and obviously skilled preparation of the local community to receive the patients acceptingly.

However, the inferential power of these studies lies in the critical variable of random assignment to treatment and to the consistency of the data taken in aggregate across the 10 studies. Individually the studies have other flaws and often do not report such important detail as drug dosages and the like.[5] However, such issues, while potentially damaging in the critic's eye for an individual study, do not provide a reasonable explanation for the consistency of the data across studies. Nonetheless, many hanging questions remain, particularly regarding policy issues. Let us look at some of the unanswered questions that may be critical for patient treatment.

One serious policy drawback is that there is not very good distribution over treatment and diagnosis. For example, schizophrenics are frequently in the populations reported here, but those with organic brain syndrome are essentially absent. It is very difficult to infer from this array of studies whether these effects, however promising, are broadly applicable over the range of problems that now exist in people who are ordinarily admitted to mental institutions.

Put another way, in answer to the policy question, Are we institutionalizing too many people? these studies taken in aggregate indicate a very clear and unqualified yes. As evidenced by these studies, not only is it unnecessary to hospitalize many of the people we are now, it is clear that they could be treated in alternative settings more effectively and less expensively. On the other hand, the policy question, Is it necessary to hospitalize anyone at all? cannot even be addressed by these studies. Few of the studies included all patients prior to random assignment. Indeed, in one study, 78 percent of the potential patient population were excluded in advance of random assignment. Further, we have described group differences. There is little evidence regarding differential effectiveness of specific modalities of alternative care for diagnostic categories or such demographics as age and sex. It seems likely – very likely – that it would not be possible to eliminate inpatient care. On the other hand, although we are left hanging about the degree to which we could reduce inpatient care, it is very clear that it would be reduced dramatically while increasing the effectiveness and quality of care.

I have discussed the need for policy review and change. However, the problems inherent in *implementing* national policy changes in alternative treatment are beyond the scope of this paper. They include general issues of implementing any model programs, including ones in mental health; lack of treatment facilities and personnel for alternative care; lack of coordination among responsible public agencies; issues related to existing chronic cases who have already been in a mental hospital several times; lack of appropriate funding for alternative care both from public agencies and private insurance; lack of organizational attention to the long-term and cyclic nature of some of the diagnostic categories; public resistance to treatment of mental patients in the community; community and personal resistance to closing mental hospitals for economic reasons; lack of knowledge regarding the number of people involved (as opposed to episodes); and other barriers to effective knowledge use in mental health policy (cf. Kiesler, 1981).

The scientific tests involved tend to be quite pure, and perhaps difficult to generalize over a broad array of settings. That is, the individuals concerned are testing some pet alternative care project about which they are enthusiastic, and they compare it to good-to-excellent hospital treatment. To gather more insight about policy implications on a national level would require a variety of more complicated variations in treatment. For example, we have learned little from this array of studies about how to make inpatient treatment more effective than it now is.[6] We have also learned that although there are a variety of potentially effective alternative treatments, we are not much further ahead in considering how to make the alternative treatments even more effective than they appear to be in these scientific tests.

The authors of several of these studies (e.g., Herz *et al.* 1971) have pointed to significant resistance on the part of professional staff to treating serious mental health problems outside an institution. Fink, Longabaugh, and Stout (1970) discuss five different reasons underlying the decision to originally hospitalize a patient: (a) There is financial pressure from hospital administrators to fill beds (a significant problem with the current emphasis on deinstitutionalization). (b) Physicians and other staff members are unclear about who might benefit most from alternative modes of care. (c) Family members often find the subjective cost of maintaining the deviant member in their midst too great. (d) Physicians often feel that separating the patient from the family allows them to learn more about the patient. (e) Physicians feel that hospitalization allows more intensive treatment (although there is no evidence that patients actually get it). It seems clear that such variables as 'professional judgment' lead to excessive hospitalization.

The resistance of staff to these alternative treatments has implications for one possible explanation of AC effects – the so-called 'Hawthorne effect' in which the enthusiasm and interest generated by a new technique or organizational change determine its effectiveness rather than the technique itself. In the studies reported here, however, staff were not enthusiastic, and several studies reported considerable resistance and antagonism. Indeed, such resistance probably makes the differences reported here quite conservative.

One wishes also that there were published national data on different approaches within institutional settings allowing one to look more closely epidemiologically at outcome possibilities as a function of type and frequency of services for mental disorders. NIMH does publish normative data on the number of types of treatment received and types of treatment per episode, but there is no way, given the current state of national data accumulation, to relate those data to outcome variables. Further, the data regarding institutionalization collected by NIMH are not sufficiently thorough to allow even sifting through the data base for post hoc comparisons. Policy concerns demand that we begin to develop some notions of what works in mental health care. The current data base in mental health does not allow that.[7] One could argue that we are currently spending billions for hospitalization, but little or nothing for tests of preventive noninstitutionalization. These studies suggest a change in national funding priorities that would facilitate such studies, including long-term follow-up studies.

I have reviewed studies in which people were randomly assigned to mental institutions or alternative treatment. There is also some evidence on alternative care with random assignment of people already hospitalized (e.g., Fairweather, 1964) that is consistent with the conclusions drawn here. Taken together, these data provide a challenge to current national policy and, hopefully, some impetus to continued policy research in the mental health area.

Notes

1 Episodes are defined as the number of people residing in mental hospitals at the beginning of the year plus all admissions during the year. The number of people is somewhat less, although good reports are kept only of episodes. For some years, NIMH has estimated the number of people hospitalized by multiplying episodes by .83, a constant originally derived for the state of Maryland during the early 1960s.

2 This figure (1975) includes people already resident at the beginning of the year, but excludes 978,000 discharges of people with a primary diagnosis of mental disorder from general hospitals without a psychiatric unit.

3 Whether the changing site of mental hospitalization and the decreased length of patient episode make the concept of total institution no longer applicable to

mental hospitals is unknown. The relevant data do not exist. My interchangeable use of the terms *mental hospital* and *mental institution* is not meant to imply a theoretical stance; rather I regard it as an empirical question.

4 In each of the eight studies reporting this statistic, the difference is consistently in favor of the AC condition. The difference in proportion across the eight studies is highly significant ($p < .001$) by my calculations. Thus H patients are more likely to be readmitted to the hospital than AC patients are ever to be admitted.

5 This article was originally submitted for publication in November 1980. In June 1981, Braun, Kochansky, Shapiro, Greenberg, Gudeman, Johnson, and Shore reported a review of the literature on 'de-institutionalization,' which they defined as including alternative care. Of the 10 studies reported here, they defined four as 'alternatives to hospitalization' and two as 'modifications of traditional hospitalization' (day care); they did not report the other four. They criticized individual studies in detail, but concluded, 'experimental alternatives to hospital care of patients have led to psychiatric outcomes not different from and occasionally superior to those patients in control groups . . . best supported for alternatives to admission and for modifications of conventional hospitalization.' Their inclusion of studies without random assignment, the arbitrary distinction between day care and other forms of alternative care leading to a smaller number of studies within categories, and the lesser number of true experiments reviewed led them to somewhat more conservative but still similar conclusions.

6 However, it is interesting that Glick, Hargreaves, Drues, and Showstack (1976) report that patients randomly assigned to a short (4-week) hospitalization period function as well on discharge as long-term (90–120 days) patients did when they were ultimately discharged.

7 I should add in this context that all of the discussions above exclude such mental-health-related problem areas as drugs, alcoholism, teenage runaways, and the like. This article is intended as a low-level first cut toward a tough-minded scientific approach to outcome research in mental health care that has policy implications. Taken in isolation, these data could easily be overinterpreted; perhaps it is important to say what I have not done here. For example, this article in no way can be applied to such possible questions as different methods of treatment, the effects of drugs versus other kinds of treatment, unimodal versus multimodal treatment, the effectiveness of psychotherapy per se, professional versus nonprofessional care, and the like. All of these areas involve important policy-related questions; however, this article is in no way addressed to them.

Reference notes

1 National Institute of Mental Health. *The financing, utilization, and quality of mental health care in the United States*. Rockville, Md.: Author, 1976. (Draft report)

2 Krowinski, W. J., and Fitt, D. X. *On the clinical efficacy and cost effectiveness*

of psychiatric partial hospitalization versus traditional inpatient care with six month follow-up data. Report to Capital Blue Cross, Reading Hospital and Medical Center, Day Treatment Center, 1978.

References

Braun, P., Kochansky, G., Shapiro, R., Greenberg, S., Gudeman, J. E., Johnson, S., and Shore, M. F.
Overview: Deinstitutionalization of psychiatric patients, a critical review of outcome studies. *American Journal of Psychiatry*, 1981, *138*, 736–749.

Brook, B. D.
An alternative to psychiatric hospitalization for emergency patients. *Hospital and Community Psychiatry*, 1973, *24*, 621–624.

Davis, A. E., Dinitz, S., and Pasamanick, B.
The prevention of hospitalization in schizophrenia: Five years after an experimental program. *American Journal of Orthopsychiatry*, 1972, *43*, 375–388.

Fairweather, G. W.
Social psychology in treating mental illness. New York: Wiley, 1964.

Fink, E. B., Longabaugh, R., and Stout, R.
The paradoxical underutilization of partial hospitalization. *American Journal of Psychology*, 1970, *135*, 713–716.

Flomenhaft, K., Kaplan, D. M., and Langsley, D. G.
Avoiding psychiatric hospitalization. *Social Work*, 1969, *16*, 38–45.

Glick, I. R., Hargreaves, W. A., Drues, J., and Showstack, J. A.
Short vs. long hospitalization: A controlled study: III. Inpatient results for non-schizophrenics. *Archives of General Psychiatry*, 1976, *33*, 78–83.

Goffman, E.
Asylums: Essays on the social situation of mental patients and other inmates. Garden City, N.Y.: Doubleday, 1961.

Goldstein, M. S.
The sociology of mental health and illness. *Annual Review of Sociology*, 1979, *5*, 381–409.

Herz, M. I., Endicott, J., Spitzer, R. L., and Mesnikoff, A.
Day versus inpatient hospitalization: A controlled study. *American Journal of Psychology*, 1971, *127*(10), 107–117.

Kiesler, C. A.
Mental health policy as a field of inquiry for psychology. *American Psychologist*, 1980, *35*, 1066–1080.

Kiesler, C. A.
Barriers to effective knowledge use in national mental health policy. *Health Policy Quarterly*, 1981, *1*, 201–215.

Levenson, A. J., Lord, C. J., Sermas, C. E., Thornby, J. I., Sullender, W., and Comstock, B. A.
Acute schizophrenia: An efficacious outpatient treatment approach as an alternative to full-time hospitalization. *Diseases of the Nervous System*, April 1977, pp. 242–245.

Lorei, T. W., and Gurel, J.
Demographic characteristics as predictors of post-hospital employment and readmission. *Journal of Consulting and Clinical Psychology*, 1973, *40*, 426–430.

Matthews, S. M., Roper, M. T., Mosher, L. R., and Menn, A. Z.
A non-neuroleptic treatment for schizophrenia: Analysis of the two-year post-discharge risk of relapse. *Schizophrenia Bulletin*, 1979, *5*, 322–333.

McEwen, C. A.
Continuities in the study of total and nontotal institutions. *Annual Review of Sociology*, 1980, *6*, 143–185.

Mosher, L. R., and Menn, A. Z.
Community residential treatment for schizophrenia: Two year follow-up. *Hospital and Community Psychiatry*, 1978, *29*, 715–723.

Mosher, L. R., Menn, A. Z., and Matthews, S. M.
Soteria: Evaluation of a home-based treatment for schizophrenia. *American Journal of Orthopsychiatry*, 1975, *45*, 455–467.

Pasamanick, B., Scarpitti, F. R. and Dinitz, S.
Schizophrenics and the community. New York: Appleton-Century-Crofts, 1967.

Platman, S. R. (Coordinator).
Report of the Task Panel on Deinstitutionalization, Rehabilitation, and Long-Term Care (President's Commission on Mental Health, Vol. 2). Washington, DC: US Government Printing Office, 1978.

Rosenhan, D. L.
On being sane in insane places. *Science*. 1973, *179*, 250–258.

Rubin, J.
Economics, mental health, and the law. Lexington, Mass.: D. C. Heath, 1978.

Stein, L. I., Test, M. A., and Marx, A. J.
Alternative to the hospital: A controlled study. *American Journal of Psychiatry*, 1975, *132*, 517–521.

Taber, M. A.
The social context of helping: A review of the literature on alternative care for the physically and mentally handicapped. Washington, DC: National Institute of Mental Health, 1980.

Vischi, T. R., Jones, K. R., Shank, E. L., and Lima, L. H.
The alcohol, drug abuse, and mental health national data book. Washington, DC: US Department of Health, Education, and Welfare, 1980.

Washburn, S., Vannicelli, M., Longabaugh, R., and Scheff, B. J.
A controlled comparison of psychiatric day treatment and inpatient hospitalization. *Journal of Consulting and Clinical Psychology*, 1976, *44*, 665–675.

Weisbrod, B. A., Test, M. A., and Stein, L. I.
Alternatives to mental hospital treatment: II. Economic benefit-cost analysis. *Archives of General Psychiatry*, 1980, *37*, 400–405.

Wilder, J. F., Levin, G., and Zwerling, I.
A two-year follow-up evaluation of acute psychotic patients treated in a day hospital. *American Journal of Psychiatry*, 1966, *122*, 1095–1111.

Zwerling, I., and Wilder, J. F.
An evaluation of the applicability of the day hospital in treatment of acutely disturbed patients. *The Israel Annals of Psychiatry and Related Disciplines*, 1964, *2*, 162–185.

CHAPTER 14

Self-help and mental health*

Audrey J. Gartner and Frank Riessman

Over the past ten years, self-help groups (also called mutual-aid groups or mutual-support groups) have spread from coast to coast and have ballooned to a total of about 500,000; they now involve more than 15 million people[1]. The US Department of Health and Human Services predicts that the number of persons reached by mutual-support or self-help groups should double by 1990 to reduce the gap in mental health services[2].

Not only has there been growth in numbers, but also in the range of problems addressed by the groups. There are self-help groups for nearly every disease category listed by the World Health Organization as well as groups concerned with a wide variety of psychosocial problems. Self-help groups have arisen to help people through literally the whole range of life crises, from birth to death. Groups have developed for couples who are infertile, parents of newborns, parents whose child has died, single parents, divorced persons, adolescents and their parents, older persons having difficulties with their children, and the widowed. There are groups for parents who abuse their children, for isolated older people, the handicapped, drug abusers, suicide-prone people, smokers, drinkers, overeaters, and patients discharged from mental institutions.

Self-help groups are also developing among those with caretaking responsibilities for others – parents of children with handicaps, parents or relatives of individuals who have been institutionalized,

* Reprinted from *Hospital and Community Psychiatry*, vol. 33, no. 8, pp. 631–5, 1982, by permission of the authors and the American Psychiatric Association.

those taking care of sick or older parents, and spouses of those who have had strokes or other disabling conditions. There are also self-help food cooperatives, job-finding groups, energy conservation groups, and housing and community groups. Extensive lists of self-help groups are available in the literature[1, 3].

What is a self-help group?

Self-help groups have been defined as 'voluntary small group structures for mutual aid in the accomplishment of a specific purpose. They are usually formed by peers who have come together for mutual assistance in satisfying a common need, overcoming a common handicap or life-disrupting problem, and bringing about desired social and/or personal change'[4].

The following can be added to this description:

- Self-help groups always involve face-to-face interactions.
- Personal participation is extremely important, since bureaucratization is the enemy of the self-help organization.
- The members agree on and engage in some actions.
- Typically the groups start from a condition of powerlessness.
- The groups fill needs for a reference group, a point of connection and identification with others, a base for activity, and a source of ego reinforcement.

There are groups addressed to particular mental health conditions, such as Depressives Anonymous, Manic-Depressives Anonymous, Neurotics Anonymous, and Schizophrenics Anonymous. Recovery, Inc., begun as an ex-patient group, is now the largest group for persons with nervous disorders, including former inpatients and those who have never been hospitalized.

Other groups have formed to deal with the various forms of addiction. Here self-help groups have played an important role and frequently are recommended as the treatment of choice by traditional mental health agencies: for alcoholics, Alcoholics Anonymous, of course, but also more specialized groups such as the Calix Society for Catholics, the National Association of Recovered Alcoholics in the Professions, and Women for Sobriety; for the drug-dependent, the Delancy Street Foundation, Narcotics Anonymous, and Pills Anonymous.

There are also groups addressed to the mental health needs of various populations: for children who have problems with an alcoholic parent, Alateen; for abusive parents, Parents Anonymous, or for the consequences of parents' sexual molestation of their children, Daughters and Sons United; for minority group members, Sisterhood of Black Single Mothers; for the mentally retarded, National Association for Retarded Citizens; for the chronically disabled, Center for Independent Living; for older persons, Senior Actualization and Growth Encounter; and for women, thousands of groups ranging from local organizations such as Abused Women's Aid in Crisis and the long-established national La Leche League to those focusing on particular life crises such as divorce or widowhood.

Indeed, one of the most important expressions of self-help is found in the feminist perspective. The feminist focus on health and body issues, fostered by the shared experiences of consciousness-raising groups, has broadened until today it encompasses self-help and know-your-body courses, alternative health care services, women's centers and clinics, and a distinguished body of literature, including books (*Our Bodies, Ourselves*[5] is the best-known example), pamphlets, and movies[6]. Among the self-help groups dealing with specific health issues are DES-Action, Reach to Recovery (for women who have had mastectomies), and Womanpause.

The specific goals of any woman's self-help group vary, but two are always central. One is to provide health education for women; the second is to aid a woman in self-fulfillment. A study examining alternative self-help support systems[7] documents the existence of many women-to-women mental health and related services that are meeting a vast array of emotional and physical needs which many women feel are best understood by other women.

Prevention and self-help

The role of prevention in human services has taken on new relevance recently, since Richard Schweiker, Secretary of the Department of Health and Human Services, singled out prevention as a major concern. Self-help groups have two unique preventive features: they provide social support to their members through the creation of a caring community, and they increase members' coping skills through the provision of information and the sharing of experiences and solutions to problems.

The importance of social support in preventing mental illness is seen in a prevention equation, adapted from George Albee[8], former chair of the task force on prevention of the President's Commission on Mental Health:

$$\text{Incidence of dysfunction} = \frac{\text{Stress + Constitutional vulnerabilities}}{\text{Social supports + Coping skills + Competence}}$$

The equation suggests two major strategies for preventing dysfunction: decreasing stress, constitutional vulnerabilities, or both, or increasing social supports, coping skills, and competence. While stress appears to be a major factor contributing to the development of dysfunction, we cannot always control the stressors in our lives. Many stressors – illness or death of a loved one, accidents, and economic setbacks – cannot be eliminated or reduced by the individual. It is difficult, then, to have an impact on the numerator of the prevention equation. The bottom line, literally, lies in strengthening social supports, coping skills, and competence.

The scientific community and popular culture have both hailed social support as a vital component in health and survival. Research data from psychiatric, psychological, and sociological studies point to the effectiveness of social-support groups in protecting their members from the emotionally and physically deleterious effects of illness and in improving the quality of their lives.

One such study assessed the relationship between social and community ties and the mortality rates of a sample of 4,725 residents in the San Francisco Bay area over a nine-year period[9]. The authors examined the impact of various social ties – marriage, family and friends, membership in a religious group, and informal and formal group associations – on mortality from all causes. The findings showed that people with the most social ties had lower mortality rates over the period than those without such ties, even taking into consideration self-reported physical status, socioeconomic status, health practices, and use of preventive health services. It was only in the presence of mounting social disconnection, when individuals failed to have links in several different spheres of interaction, that mortality rates rose sharply.

Self-help groups have developed to replace the natural support networks that have been lost or have become disconnected as society has changed. Disintegration of the traditional extended kinship system and the isolation of mobile nuclear families have made families particularly vulnerable to stress. While the stresses placed on new mothers or on the newly widowed once were addressed in the family setting, in contemporary America support groups have come to play an important role in the lives of many.

A study of factors in postpartum emotional adjustment sheds light on the effectiveness of mutual aid in helping new mothers improve their coping skills[10]. A total of 298 new mothers who belonged to mutual-support education groups experienced less emotional distress in the six months after childbirth than did 362 control subjects, and their infants were healthier. Follow-up studies four to six years later showed that, compared with the control subjects, the new mothers in the experimental self-help group had maintained their emotional gains, had subsequently given birth to greater numbers of healthier children, and had suffered fewer physical illnesses, marital conflicts, sexual problems, and divorces. The data showed that although preparing for problems of postpartum adjustment is helpful to new mothers, developing a network of supportive friends and family is more important.

Programs for widows involve a variety of relationships between those who have successfully adapted to their widowhood and the newly widowed, through individual widow-to-widow programs, mutual-support groups, and services such as 'widow hotlines' staffed by the widowed. A two-year study of postbereavement adaptation by 162 widows showed that although participants in an experimental widow-to-widow program followed the same course of adjustment to bereavement as those in a control group, those receiving intervention adjusted more rapidly[11]. Lieberman and Borman reported that active participation in THEOS, a self-help group for the widowed, positively affects the mental health status of the members[12]. Both current and former THEOS members who helped each other through their social network consistently showed better outcome on seven variables: depression, anxiety, somatic symptoms, use of psychotropic drugs, self-esteem, coping mastery, and well-being.

Despite the benefits shown in these and other studies, the great majority of widowed persons do not participate in self-help groups. And, as a recent report shows, the need for social support may be particularly great among widowers[13]. Researchers at the Johns

Hopkins University School of Hygiene and Public Health conducted a twelve-year survey of more than 4,000 widowed persons age eighteen and over. They found that the death of a spouse appears to be much more devastating to men. Very little difference in death rates was found between persons who had lost a husband or wife in the past year and married persons of the same age, sex, and background. In the ensuing years, however, the survey found that widowed men as a group had a mortality rate 28 percent higher than that of their married counterparts. Moreover, widowed men between the ages of fifty-five and sixty-five, who made up more than one-fourth of the people in the study, had a mortality rate 60 percent higher than that of married men of the same age.

Many more people might join a self-help group if one suitable to their needs existed, if they were made aware of the group, and if they were encouraged to join by mental health practitioners, physicians, funeral directors, friends, or others familiar with their needs.

Deinstitutionalization

While the preceding studies have dealt with acute mental health needs, the following project demonstrates a self-help approach to a chronic condition. With the growth of deinstitutionalization, self-help groups are bridging the gap between hospitalization and community living for ex-patients.

The Community Network Development Project at the Florida Mental Health Institute illustrates how the creation of a mutual-aid network can be an effective method for reducing hospital recidivism among mental health clients[14]. The project's development was guided by the belief that a self-help program for aftercare clients should strengthen the members' abilities to take an active part not only in their own rehabilitation, but in the rehabilitation of their peers as well.

The project consisted of the establishment of a mutual-aid network of self-help groups for aftercare clients. Members of the support groups were trained in leadership and given responsibilities ranging from teaching some psychoeducational classes to telephoning members to remind them of the next group meeting, driving members to meetings, baking cakes for the group, and arranging outings. Not only did this program help individuals improve their personal functioning, but it also contributed to the survival of the groups.

Eighty patients who were being discharged from a nine-week intensive treatment unit were randomly assigned to the project or to a control group for traditional aftercare services. Both groups received equivalent discharge planning, including appropriate referrals to a local mental health center for follow-up treatment if necessary. The groups did not differ significantly according to age, sex, race, marital status, diagnosis, previous hospitalization, or length of follow-up time. At an average follow-up interval of ten months, only half as many project members as control subjects had required rehospitalization (17.5 percent to 35 percent), and their average length of stay was less than a third as long as that of the controls (7 days versus 24.6 days). Finally, twice as many project members were able to function without any contact with a mental health system (52.5 percent versus 26 percent).

How do groups work?

The power of self-help groups derives from their combining a number of very important properties – the helper-therapy principle, group reinforcement, continuous intervention, an ideological perspective, and the implicit demand that the individual do something for himself. They enable their members to feel and use their own strengths and power and to exert control over their own lives.

The helper-therapy principle, in its simplest form, states that those who help are helped most[15]. Thus, an alcoholic in AA who is providing help and support to another AA member may be the one who benefits most. Since all members of the group play this giving role at one time or another, they all benefit from the helping process. While all help-givers themselves may be helped in a nonspecific way by playing the helping role, people who have a particular problem may be helped in much more specific ways by providing help to others who have the same problem, whether it be alcoholism, drug addiction, smoking, or underachieving.

Dewar[16] said, 'It feels good to be the helper. It increases our sense of control, of being valued, of being capable.' Part of this feeling comes from the self-persuasion and positive role-playing that occurs. In the process of influencing others with the same problem, the helper must play the 'well' role – the sober alcoholic, the coping single parent, the controlled schizophrenic – and, in doing so, persuades or influences himself. Further, playing the helper role achieves special benefits. In helping another struggle with a similar problem, the helper has a chance to observe how the other addresses the problem, and may gain insight and a feeling of social usefulness.

Of course, in self-help the participant is not an isolated individual, but part of a group that provides support, reinforcement, a safe haven, feedback, sanctions, and norms. Many of the groups also provide an ideology – a perspective on one's problems, other's attitudes, and the ways one may respond.

While the range of self-help groups is broad, and the particular factors involved vary, Durman[17] identifies as common themes their response to the 'need for human interaction, available quickly in crisis, at all hours, for potentially long periods of time, in which the focus is not basic change in the outlook or personality, but in sustaining the ability to cope with a difficult situation.'

Self-help and professionals

The new models of service delivery to be developed in the 1980s will incorporate an increasingly strong relationship between professionals and self-help groups. An ongoing concern in the self-help movement has been the nature and extent of professionals' involvement in the functioning of the groups. Alternative self-help models of practice stress mutual aid, intimacy with others, and personal caring and involvement, while professional caregiving has been seen by some critics as more detached and distant. Independence from professional intervention has been part of the self-help rhetoric from the beginning of the movement, and concern has often been expressed about the potential hazards of involving professionals, such as their usurping control of the group.

Controversy over professional involvement with self-help groups should not obscure the fact that professionals have been involved for a long time with many self-help activities. Professional participation has ranged from following a relative hands-off policy through facilitating the establishment of groups or intervening for a limited time and then ending involvement (as in the case of many widows' groups) to maintaining an ongoing leadership role.

However, professionals typically have not been trained to perceive a need, help establish a self-help group to fill the need, and then disengage from the group. Special training is required to overcome some of these 'trained incapacities.' The professional could be trained to help lay individuals who want to start a self-help group or who need assistance in relating to groups that already exist. Training would reduce the danger of the professional usurping control, developing or maintaining member dependence, or professionalizing a nonprofessional movement.

The kind of assistance provided could range from instilling group development and process skills to developing public relations skills. The professional might help the group acquire needed resources and improve linkages with the formal caregiving system. Direct consultation to the group might be provided occasionally, as needed. Professional practitioners can bring to self-help groups the values of a systematic approach, particular skills, and access to resources. In return, there is much that self-help groups can bring to traditional human service practice – vitality, a new perspective, an energy and involvement too often lacking, and a potential constituency.

We do not hold the view that self-help is so precious and tenuous an arrangement that involvement with professionals will co-opt or corrupt it. At the least, there can be a complementary relationship. Sometimes, as with postsurgical groups, one can follow the other, or, as with Recovery, Inc., individuals can be involved simultaneously with both a self-help group and professional care. Beyond this, we envision the potential for a new synthesis that relates self-help approaches to professional practice and vice-versa.

Self-help and health

In the new health-related self-help groups, professionals may play a role that differs somewhat from their roles in other support groups. In most self-help groups, the professional generally is peripheral. However, in the health-related self-help groups, the professional may become somewhat more involved because the members recognize that relevant medical information and advice are essential. Thus, in arthritis self-help groups, members typically want professional information on the latest developments in treatment, on current research findings, and on new approaches to ameliorating the effects of the illness. They also want advice on ideas and interventions that they hear about through sources such as the media and their friends. Often the professional can play an important role in correcting misinformation.

Hypertension groups, multiple sclerosis groups, and other such groups follow a similar pattern. Sometimes group members will be interested in using approaches that have a professional technical basis such as biofeedback, meditation, and other relaxation techniques, and here again the professional may advise about these approaches and facilitate their use.

In some ways the professional's role in health groups is similar to that of the sponsor in Parents Anonymous. In the latter case the professional, usually a social worker, contributes to the understanding of the group's process and other group-related issues, but in no way leads the group, or makes decisions for the group. The basic autonomy of the group prevails, but there is a special role for the professional that the group recognizes and typically requests.

The basic experiential effect of the self-help group, particularly as it functions to help members deal with problems of living related to the illness or health problem, should not be overlooked. In the case of most chronic illnesses, the basic issue is care rather than cure, and the mutual-support group can play a powerful role in helping individuals cope with their illness and with life problems related to family, job, and life style. The group can also reduce the isolation that often accompanies the illness and can provide the basic support that a large body of research has shown to be critical in reducing the effects of illness and stress.

In essence, then, this 'mixed' type of self-help group maintains the two fundamental characteristics of all mutual-support groups – the group's autonomy and decision-making power, and its experiential input in dealing with problems or needs – while adding professional expertise.

Converting needs into resources

The human service needs of contemporary society are great, but the realities of the present are such that there will not be sufficient professional resources to meet them. In the United States, there are 32 million arthritics, 20 million people with high blood pressure, 5 million diabetics, 10 million alcoholics, 4 million drug addicts, and millions suffering from other physical and mental ailments. It is impossible for the professional caregiving system to provide all the services needed by these people. Thus the self-help strategy takes on enormous meaning. Self-help converts problems or needs into resources. Instead of seeing 32 million people with arthritis as a problem, it is possible to see them as resources and caregivers who will be active in dealing with the everyday concerns of the arthritic.

Mutual-aid groups are inexpensive, highly responsive, and accessible to the consumer, who himself is a caregiver as well as receiver. They can expand infinitely to deal with the ever-expanding need; as the need arises, so does the potential for response. What we see now is only the tip of a very large iceberg. An extensive study by the California Department of Mental Health's Office of Prevention shows that although 75 percent of those queried felt that getting together with persons with similar health and mental health problems was a good idea, only 9 percent had done so[18]. There is, it seems, a considerable market for further growth of self-help activities. Few developments in recent years have as far-reaching potential for mental health services as does the self-help phenomenon. The mental health services network is strained by growing and more diverse demands for services at a time of limited fiscal resources. Now, too, there is increasing questioning of the nature and efficacy of traditional professional services. Self-help becomes a way to expand human services quantitatively by reaching more people, and qualitatively by making people more independent and interdependent. At the same time, self-help groups provide a personalized and energetic approach to human services.

References

1 Evans, G.: *The Family Circle Guide to Self-Help*. New York, Ballantine Books, 1979.
2 Promoting Health, Preventing Disease: Objectives for the Nation. Washington, DC, US Department of Health and Human Services, 1980.
3 Gartner, A., Riessman, F.: *Help: A Working Guide to Self-Help Groups*. New York, New Viewpoints – Vision Books, 1980.
4 Katz, A., Bender, F. (eds): *The Strength in Us: Self-Help Groups in the Modern World*. New York, Franklin Watts, 1976.
5 The Boston Women's Health Book Collective: *Our Bodies, Ourselves*. New York, Simon & Schuster, 1971.

6 Marieskind, H. I., Ehrenreich, B.: Toward socialist medicine: The women's health movement. *Social Policy* 6: 34–42, 1975.

7 The women and mental health project: Women to women services. *Social Policy* 7: 21–27, 1976.

8 Remarks made at conference: An ounce of prevention: reorienting mental health priorities, January 16, 1981. *Self-Help Reporter* 5: 1–2, 1981.

9 Berkman, L. F., Syms, S. L.: Social networks, host resistance, and mortality: A nine-year follow-up study of Alameda County residents. *American Journal of Epidemiology* 109: 186–204, 1979.

10 Gordon, R. D., Kapostins, E. E., Gordon, K. K.: Factors in postpartum emotional adjustment. *Obstetrical Gynecology* 25: 156–166, 1965.

11 Vachon, M. L. S., Lyall, W. A. L., Rogers, J., *et al.*: A controlled study of self-help intervention for widows. *American Journal of Psychiatry* 137: 1380–1384, 1980.

12 Lieberman, M. A., Borman, L. D.: The impact of self-help groups on widows' mental health. *National Reporter* 4: 2–6, 1981.

13 Greenberg, J.: Researchers find widowers die earlier than widows do. *New York Times*, July 30, 1981, p. 1.

14 Gordon, R. E., Edmunson, E., Bedell, J., *et al.*: Reducing rehospitalization of state mental patients: peer management and support. *Community Mental Health*. Edited by Yaeger A., Slotkin R., New York, Plenum, 1982.

15 Riessman, F.: The 'helper-therapy' principle. *Social Work* 10: 27–32, 1965.

16 Dewar, T.: Professionalized Clients as Self-Helpers: Self-Help and Health: A Report. New York, City University of New York, Queens College, New Human Services Institute, 1976.

17 Durman, E. C.: The role of self-help in service provision. *Journal of Applied Behavioral Science* 12: 433–443, 1976.

18 Office of Prevention, California Department of Mental Health: A study of Californian public attitudes and beliefs regarding mental health and physical health. *Pursuit of Wellness* 1: 1–65, 1979.

CHAPTER 15

Inside the Mental Patients' Association*

Judi Chamberlin

People do not have to be in a life-crisis situation to need help and support. Most people need help at some point in their lives. Seeking help with one's problems, however, can be regarded as a stigmatizing act, an admission of weakness. The present system, in which the givers of help derive status and financial rewards, while those who seek help are seen as needy or sick, perpetuates the rigid separation between the helper and the helped. Detachment and impartiality, which mental health professionals believe are the proper therapeutic attitudes, become, in practice, either cold formality or the shallow pretense of friendliness. Alternative services replace medical and bureaucratic distance with real friendliness – not the bland, impartial 'friendliness' of a person behind a desk but the open give-and-take of a relationship between equals. Having problems is seen as a normal component of living in a sometimes difficult and threatening world and not as part of an illness existing only in some unfortunate people.

Former mental patients need many special kinds of help, not because they are sick but because in addition to experiencing personal crises, they have been through the often debilitating experience of psychiatric institutionalization. Ex-patients may need special help with places to live, with dealing with bureaucracies, and with finding jobs. Most services offered to ex-patients continue to place

* From *On Our Own: Patient-controlled Alternatives to the Mental Health System*. Copyright © 1978 by Judi Chamberlin. A Hawthorn Book. Reprinted by permission of the author and E. P. Dutton, Inc.

them in the category of needy, incompetent individuals who couldn't possibly help themselves or one another without outside intervention.

Mental patients are taught to think of their difficulties as 'symptoms,' which require professional expertise to treat. Even practical problems, such as finding a job or a place to live, tend to be handled by social workers within the overall psychiatric framework. And within this framework, every difficulty the patient or ex-patient experiences may be viewed as an indication of mental illness.

Patient-run alternatives break down these barriers. When ex-patients work together, without professional supervision or control, no one is seen as inferior. Humiliating features of professionally run services (closed files and meetings, for example) are eliminated. Patients are able to turn to one another and to find that a relationship of equals provides help in a warm and supportive way. A model for a good alternative service for ex-patients must include the following elements:

1 The service must provide help with needs as defined by the clients.

2 Participation in the service must be completely voluntary.

3 Clients must be able to choose to participate in some aspects of the service without being required to participate in others.

4 Help is provided by the clients of the service to one another and may also be provided by others selected by the clients. The ability to give help is seen as a human attribute and not as something acquired by education or professional degree.

5 Overall direction of the service, including responsibility for financial and policy decisions, is in the hands of service recipients.

6 Clients of the service must determine whether participation is limited to ex-patients or is to be open to all. If an open policy is decided upon, special care must be taken that the nonpatients do not act oppressively toward the ex-patients. In other words, such a service must be particularly sensitive to issues of mentalism (as previously defined).

7 The responsibility of the service is to the client, and not to relatives, treatment institutions, or the government. Information about the client must not be transmitted to any other party without the consent of the client, and such information must be available to the client.

In the detailed examination that follows of the operations of the Mental Patients' Association (MPA) in Vancouver, particular attention is paid to how closely this model is followed. While MPA does not follow the model in every respect, it is the largest and most successful organization that approaches the model.

Today, six years after it was founded, MPA operates a drop-in center and five cooperative residences. The drop-in center is open seven days a week from 8.00 a.m. to midnight, and provides social and recreational activities. Members are free to come at any time for coffee, to use the arts and crafts room or the photography darkroom, to sit, talk to others, sleep, watch TV or listen to the radio, to use the phone, or for any other reason. Drop-in center coordinators, elected by the membership and placed on salary for six-month terms, are always available to members, to teach a skill or just to talk.

At the weekly drop-in center meeting, coordinators and members resolve questions or problems in connection with the running of the drop-in center. All questions are decided by majority vote, coordinators and members together. The meeting determines the allocation of the center's budget, plans activities, and resolves any disputes among the membership.

MPA also runs five cooperative residences, which altogether have a capacity of forty-nine. Each house is responsible for the running of its own affairs, including the election of two coordinators, who are placed on salary by MPA for six-month terms. The coordinators (who do not live in the house, although they may be residents of another MPA house) are available as resource people to the residents of the house.

The entire organization is run by the membership. Day-to-day administrative matters are handled by the office and research coordinators, also elected by the membership for six-month terms. During the weekly business meeting coordinators and members make decisions about overall MPA policy. Every third week there is a general meeting, which is the main decision-making body of MPA. During 1976 the general meeting voted the board of directors out of existence and legally became the governing body of the organization, 'to conform to the practice of a society which is based on power reversal and self-help.'[1]

The organization defines a member of MPA as anyone who has come to the drop-in center more than once or who lives in an MPA residence. (Many residents don't come to the drop-in center.) There is no requirement that a member be a former mental patient, although most are. Coordinators are members of the organization who have been selected by the membership for additional responsibilities.

Funding for MPA has been obtained from a number of Canadian government sources, local, provincial, and federal, over the years. While it is difficult to make direct comparisons between Canadian and US government programs, most of the funding could be broadly compared to US antipoverty grants.

MPA serves several hundred members through its various facilities and activities. There are no membership dues, no applications, no formalities. It is truly an open door. An informative and entertaining newsletter, *In a Nutshell*, is written, illustrated, and produced by MPA's membership.

The drop-in center is located in a storefront building in a residential section of Vancouver. The present center, which was acquired by MPA in 1974, was renovated by the membership. Three former stores were combined to provide a large living room, an office, a kitchen, a crafts room, a darkroom, a workshop, a TV room, quarters for the caretaker, two small bathrooms, and a storage area. The living room is a large open area with attractive built-in furniture providing seating for about twenty people. Fish swim in an aquarium, provided by a hobbyist member. An upright piano against the wall provides the opportunity for frequent impromptu concerts. A ping-pong table gets heavy use.

The best way to understand MPA is to spend a typical day at the drop-in center. It is 8.00 a.m. and the caretaker has just unlocked the door. The coordinator on the 8.00 a.m. to 1.00 p.m. shift has arrived, as have several early-morning regulars. Someone sets up the large percolator and soon the fragrant aroma of coffee begins to drift from the kitchen to the living room. The morning regulars are mostly quiet sorts who sip coffee, read the paper, or nap on the couches. The day starts slowly.

By midmorning, the office, which adjoins the living room, is busy. The phone has begun to ring regularly. Members walk freely in and out of the office, chatting with the office coordinators. Everyone is on a first-name basis. Small groups of people are conversing in areas throughout the center – topics range from the weather to intimate personal problems, and everything in-between. The ping-pong table is in use. A member brings some food from the grocery store across the street and cooks himself breakfast. Some members live in furnished rooms without cooking facilities. Clean Up After Yourself, warns a sign above the sink, mostly observed.

Shortly after eleven o'clock, the weekly drop-in center meeting is called to order. The five drop-in coordinators, the workshop coordinator, the transportation coordinator, the caretaker, and perhaps eight members are present. The meeting takes place in the living room, and not all members present choose to participate in the meeting. A list is passed around so that the coordinators can sign up for their shifts. The first item of discussion is planning the activities for the forthcoming week. The transportation coordinator lists the times he is available to drive the MPA van, which is used for grocery shopping for the residences as well as for drop-in center activities. Everyone suggests activities, and those eliciting the most enthusiasm are scheduled. There will be a trip to a local movie theater, a bowling night, and an afternoon at a public swimming pool.

Discussion then turns to problems created by Richard, a member who has been violating one of the drop-in center rules; specifically, he has been refusing to leave at the midnight closing time. Richard has been asked to be present at the meeting in order to try to resolve the problem. The caretaker explains the rule to Richard again and details several incidents when he has had great difficulty persuading Richard to leave. Several other complaints against Richard also come up. Richard tries to explain his difficulties, but finally agrees that they are irrelevant to the question at hand. He agrees to cooperate with closing time in the future. Several people indicate to him that they would like to get to know him better – perhaps he will come to them the next time he is upset.

Noon – the time of the weekly business meeting – is approaching, and the drop-in center meeting is brought to a close. By this time about twenty-five people are gathered in the living room. Since it is a larger group, the business meeting operates slightly more formally. A chairperson is selected – first volunteers are asked for, and if none are forthcoming, individuals are asked if they want to chair. An effort is made to find someone who has not chaired a meeting for a while. A secretary is selected by the same method. An agenda is prepared – some items are carried over from previous meetings, others have been placed there by people who have specific questions to raise. Several additional items are added to the agenda as the meeting starts. Last week's minutes are read. A member, Larry, asks that the meeting consider the subject of lifting a ban that has been in force against him for the past six months. It is decided to consider this item first.

Larry had been banned from the drop-in center for six months (bans are instituted by a vote of the membership) for breaking one of the large plate-glass windows. Many people present remember the incident and have strong feelings about it. The chairperson makes sure each person who wants to speak is recognized. A number of people ask Larry to pay for the window he broke, and a payment schedule is worked out with him. Larry explains that he had been using illegal drugs at the time of the incident and is now determined to stay clean. A motion is made that Larry be allowed back to the drop-in center on the conditions that he pay for the window and refrain from using illegal drugs. Larry indicates that the motion is acceptable to him, and it is then put to a vote and passed.

The usual first agenda item, 'the roundabout,' then begins, during which each person present is able to speak on his or her activities during the past week. Since MPA is a large organization, this gives everyone a chance to be kept up to date on everything that is happening. A number of interesting things are mentioned. One of the office coordinators has received a request for several speakers to do a presentation about MPA to a college class, and volunteers are found. Gerry, who has been handling MPA's books and financial affairs since the organization began, mentions a problem he has had recently in placing fire insurance coverage for the residences. The insurance agent has asked him whether the houses were for sick people. Gerry tells the meeting, 'I tried to give him a short course in what MPA was all about, and I think it helped.' He is expecting to hear shortly about the insurance.

The meeting continues until about 2.30, covering a diversity of items – vacancies in the MPA residences, requests for more volunteers to work on the *Nutshell*, plans for a series of Saturday night dances. The major item of the day's meeting is a discussion of the budget for the forthcoming fiscal year. A large chart is displayed showing how much money the organization has been getting from the various funding sources and how the money is spent. The focus of the discussion is what areas should be expanded if additional funding is secured. Several alternative proposed budgets have been prepared by the office coordinators, and the meeting votes on which one to adopt. The final decision will be made at the next general membership meeting.

The drop-in center empties out for a while after the meeting ends. The coordinator on the afternoon shift sits around talking with some of the people who remain, and gradually the room begins to fill again. Friendly groups chat in different parts of the room. Another pot of coffee is made. The phone rings continually. Constant cries of 'Is Joanne here?' 'Has anyone seen Fred?' 'When will Anne be back?' No distinction is made between personal calls and 'official' ones. Occasionally, a person unfamiliar with MPA calls and asks to speak to 'the director' – it can take awhile to explain that there is none and to find out who can best help the caller.

By midevening, the drop-in center is fairly noisy. Many people are old friends who obviously enjoy being together. Although there is a constant influx of new members, some have been coming to MPA for years. Occasionally, as with any large group of people, there are disagreements, and voices are raised. MPA is a free and easy place, but violations of the four rules, the four basic MPA principles, are immediately dealt with. The rules, posted prominently on the wall, read:

1 No alcohol
2 No nonprescription drugs
3 No violence
4 No disturbing the peaceful enjoyment of others

To return to our typical day . . . it is now late evening, and the day's activities are coming to an end. A small group is gathered quietly in the TV room. A few people are reading or napping in the living room. Several people are emptying ashtrays, washing the coffeemaker, and sweeping up. The evening coordinator and the caretaker start reminding people that midnight is approaching. One by one, people say goodnight and depart.

The drop-in center is one major component of the Mental Patients' Association; the residences are the other. The residence program grew out of needs that became obvious in the early months of the drop-in center's existence. Some members asked to be allowed to sleep in the drop-in center – they literally had no other place to go. Others lived in isolated furnished rooms so depressing that they simply could not bear to go back to them after spending stimulating hours at MPA. The needs of members who wanted MPA as a place to live were in conflict with those who wanted it as a social center. It became obvious that the two functions would have to exist in physically separate locations.

The first residence was started in a rented house after MPA had been in existence for about six months. The basic operating principles are radically different from halfway houses or boarding homes, the two main types of living arrangements available to recently discharged patients. Decision making is in the hands of the residents. This includes not only trivial day-to-day decisions – what should be served for dinner, for example – but also major ones. Prospective new residents are accepted into the house by the vote of current residents. In order to provide practical and emotional support for residents, two residence coordinators are elected by the residents of each house. Over the years the residence program has grown so that there are now five residences, each conducting its own affairs, yet each a component part of MPA.

The MPA residences are located in residential neighborhoods in Vancouver and are indistinguishable from the houses around them. MPA believes that a residence is a group of people living together as a family and thus should be able to locate in single-family areas. After years of effort, MPA has been successful in getting the Vancouver City Council to agree to a special zoning designation of 'Community Residential Facility' for its houses, as well as for any similar group-living arrangements. Community Residential Facilities are legally able to locate in any neighborhood. Previously, the city had tried to classify the houses as boarding houses, which have to make elaborate and expensive physical alterations and are limited to certain zones. It was MPA's successful argument that since their residents live together in a family manner, they should be considered families for zoning purposes. Similar zoning regulations are being introduced in a number of cities, making it easier to establish similar family-style residences there.[2]

There is no official wake-up time. As each resident gets up, he or she prepares breakfast and washes the dishes. A schedule pinned to the wall shows the day each resident is scheduled to cook dinner; another schedule sets out the various housekeeping responsibilities. The jobs rotate each week. A bulletin board shows a schedule of MPA activities. House members are free to come and go. A few have jobs, many are on welfare, some of whom are registered for a part-time work program (often performed at MPA) that gives them an additional fifty dollars a month. While some residents prefer to spend most of the day at home, others spend time at the drop-in center, visiting friends, going to school, or participating in training sessions. How residents spend their time is up to them.

The two house coordinators stop by frequently. Their function is to serve the needs of the residents. This can take the form of refereeing interpersonal disputes, helping a resident to deal with welfare or other bureaucracies, and being available for informal discussion and advice. The coordinators influence the running of the house, but decision-making power lies in the collective hands of the residents, expressed at the weekly house meeting. Often a resident new to the house and freshly out of a mental hospital will try to cast the coordinator in the role of director, and it may take a long time to convince him or her that there is no director.

Some residents are under psychiatric outpatient care. Whether or not to get psychiatric treatment is the decision of each resident. Occasionally, a resident may be legally required by the terms of his or her discharge to go for outpatient treatment, but even in these situations it is the responsibility of the resident to arrange it. Residents who are taking psychiatric medication are responsible for taking and safeguarding their own pills.

A study of the residence program, which was tabulated by a long-time MPA resident, clearly shows the effectiveness of the MPA houses. Over a ten-month period, 118 people lived in the five houses. Only 10 percent returned to the hospital; 42 percent went on to other living arrangements in the community; the rest continued to live at MPA. In the opinion of the coordinators and other residents, 66 percent of the residents improved during their stay in the house. The average length of stay in an MPA residence is seven months.[3]

Now that MPA has been described, I will examine it in conjunction with the model for a good alternative service that I proposed earlier.

1. *The service must provide help with needs as defined by the clients.* MPA clearly fits this description. MPA was organized by ex-patients who recognized that their needs were not being met by the existing mental health system. I believe that only in a service founded by clients can this criterion be met. When the service is formulated without input from clients, needs will be predefined, and clients will have to fit that structure in order to use or benefit from the service. At MPA, new needs are continually presented and the organization

has grown in response to these needs. The group has been free to change in response to needs because there was no master plan to fulfill. Flaws can be recognized and dealt with because there is no bureaucracy to defend an unsuccessful plan. Ideas fail or succeed based only on whether or not they work.

MPA's nonbureaucratic, nonhierarchical structure is an essential element in fulfilling the model. Participatory democracy works to ensure that needs are articulated and plans are made to deal with them. Of course, the model does not always work exactly as it is supposed to. From time to time, people with strong and compelling personalities have managed to attain a degree of personal power. There are times when indifference among the membership has been a serious problem. But it is impressive that MPA tries to deal with these problems. The structure of the organization encourages open discussion. Agendas of all meetings are open to any item any member wants dealt with. All meetings (of which MPA has many) are open for any member of the organization to attend. This structure helps the organization to rebound from situations where membership control has temporarily lapsed.

2. *Participation in the service must be completely voluntary*. MPA meets this standard completely. Usually, the initial contact with the drop-in center is made by the prospective member. In the residences it is sometimes a hospital social worker who makes the first inquiry, but the prospective resident makes all the arrangements. No one can 'place' a person at MPA. I believe that complete voluntariness is one of the keys to MPA's success. People who have been in mental hospitals are accustomed to plans being made for them in which they have little say, and their attitude toward their 'placements' (whether in hospitals, outpatient clinics, halfway houses, or the like) reflects this lack of control over their lives. Voluntariness and membership control are directly linked. People who are involved in a compulsory activity know that they do not control it, no matter what they may be told.

3. *Clients must be able to choose to participate in some aspects of the service without being required to participate in others*. No one at MPA has a 'program.' Each member chooses for him or herself what aspect of the organization to participate in. Some members partake only of the 'service' aspects without getting involved in decision making. Many residents never go to the drop-in center. Some

members wouldn't dream of missing a business or general meeting, others attend infrequently. A few people are seldom seen except at the free Wednesday night dinners and Saturday morning breakfasts. *MPA does not keep records on members.* No one keeps track of a member's utilization of activities and services. Members are seen as responsible people who do not have to be compelled to do things 'for their own good.'

Requiring people to do things 'for their own good' means there must be an authority figure, a person who decides what other people do. When a person is required to do something and then told that it is what he or she 'really' wants, the power of the authority figure is mystified. This is what commonly happens to people in mental institutions and other kinds of institutions that control people's lives.

4. *Help is provided by the clients to one another and may also be provided by others selected by the clients. The ability to give help is seen as a human attribute and not as something acquired by education or professional degree.* MPA was started as a self-help organization, one in which people turned to one another and everyone was equal. An important and significant difference between MPA and many other 'self-help' organizations is that MPA did not develop under professional sponsorship, nor did it employ or consult outside 'experts.' The people who founded MPA were largely skeptical about the abilities of mental health professionals. Decisions about whether or not to consult professionals were felt to be purely personal ones. MPA *as an organization* takes neither a propsychiatry or an antipsychiatry position. Some members trust psychiatrists and hospitals, others turn to them reluctantly in situations of extreme distress, and others want nothing to do with them. Some members feel a strong commitment to self-help principles, while others think professional expertise is usually necessary. When a member becomes extremely distressed, there is a tendency to encourage that person to seek professional help, *even if such help has proved unhelpful to that person in the past.* Ideally, a client-run alternative service would pay more attention than has been done in MPA to the development of self-help, by holding ongoing consciousness-raising meetings, for example.

5. *Overall direction of the service, including responsibility for financial and policy decisions, is in the hands of service recipients.* MPA has avoided splitting off certain kinds of decision making to a

small group within the organization. This is one of its greatest strengths. Membership control is meaningless if policy decisions come from above.

6. *Clients of the service must determine whether participation is limited to ex-patients or is to be open to all. If an open policy is decided upon, special care must be taken that the nonpatients do not act oppressively toward the ex-patients. In other words, such a service must be particularly sensitive to issues of mentalism.* MPA has, since its beginning, been open to anyone who wants to join. This position has significant strengths and weaknesses. A positive effect of open membership is that MPA does not define the needs of ex-patients and nonpatients differently. Everyone is seen as benefiting from participation. Although the open membership policy was not set up with this result in mind, what has evolved is that most of the nonpatients in MPA are coordinators – people put on salary by the organization. One of the unintentional results is that nonpatients are seen as more competent, less needy people, since their role in MPA is largely giving help to others rather than getting it for themselves. Ideally, open membership should lead to the recognition that *all* people, not just those who have been labeled mentally ill, benefit from caring and emotional support, but, in order to reach this ideal, there must be an ongoing consciousness-raising process. This has not happened at MPA.

7. *The responsibility of the service is to the client, and not to relatives, treatment institutions, or the government. Information about the client must not be transmitted to any other party without the consent of the client, and such information must be available to the client.* MPA's policy of keeping no individual records is significant. The keeping of records by an alternative service creates problems both of confidentiality (for outside parties) and of access (of members to their own records) that are probably insurmountable. Record-keeping implies that some people need to keep track of other people; and a two-class system is created. In MPA, when utilization reports are necessary for government agencies (for funding purposes), surveys of the membership are made. This is another example of the importance of down-valuing efficiency. While it might be easier to write a report if attendance records were kept for each member, it would destroy the character of the organization.

Clearly, while MPA does not fit the proposed model completely, it provides a good example of a functioning, successful alternative service for former mental patients. It stands in strong contrast to professionally oriented 'alternative' services.

MPA recently began making an effort to reach another kind of long-term patient – those still in the hospital. In late 1976 MPA established a branch of the drop-in center at Riverview Hospital, near Vancouver, which is the only public mental hospital in the province of British Columbia. Many of the patients making use of the drop-in center are people who have been in the hospital for years and have become quite institutionalized. The MPA drop-in center is the only place in the institution where patients can go and not be under the surveillance and control of hospital staff. The five project staff members are elected by the membership of MPA and placed on salary; four of them are former Riverview patients. The MPA Riverview Extension Program is set up to develop relationships with patients classified as 'chronic,' patients in locked wards and those with grounds privileges and day passes, in order to aid in the process of reintegration into the community. Project staff will be available to accompany patients off grounds as requested. We will provide liaison between patients and appropriate local community service personnel. We will help patients about to be discharged from hospital to obtain suitable living accommodation within the community and attempt to provide transportation for this purpose when necessary.

We will provide a drop-in centre at the hospital for patients to socialize, develop new relationships, secure assistance in legal matters, and obtain advocacy in hospital-related affairs.

We will encourage patient use of services currently available both at Riverview and in the community. Also, we will provide necessary services not presently existent such as an adequately developed housing registry, familiarizing patients with the Lower Mainland transit system, and attempting to provide or secure necessary and suitable short-term accommodation to enable patients to make use of overnight or weekend passes. In addition, an attempt will be made to supply any other services within our means that are deemed necessary but not available during the life of the project.[4]

The MPA Riverview drop-in center quickly became a popular gathering place for patients. Coffee was always available, and the patients recognized that the center provided a free space where there was no pressure and where they could be comfortable. In the first few weeks of its existence, the drop-in center found five patients who were ready for discharge and assisted them in finding accommodations in boarding homes.

The project is not run completely along MPA principles, although there are plans to convert to participatory democracy as soon as possible. Working with patients who are still in the hospital is quite different from being with ex-patients. One project staff member, himself a Riverview ex-patient, told of realizing just how institutionalized people could become when he found that many of the patients addressed him as 'sir.'[5] Undoing patients' reliance on authority figures is difficult with institutionalized patients, who must, in fact, defer to authority figures all day long. For the present, patients are excluded from the daily project staff meeting. An exciting innovation introduced by the MPA Riverview Extension Program is a weekly meeting among Riverview staff, project staff, and patients. In the meeting I observed, patients had a chance to question the clinical director of the hospital in a democratic setting that was not available anywhere else in the institution.

The MPA Riverview Extension Program raises a number of questions about the relationship between a self-help group and an authoritarian mental hospital. The program wants to establish a patients' council, in which current and former patients would meet regularly with hospital staff to discuss patients' rights issues. Members of the program's staff believe that incidents of patient abuse and other rights violations are high. The hospital has made it difficult for MPA to visit the long-stay wards, where many abuses are believed to occur. During one meeting between the program's staff and Riverview administrators, a hospital official asserted that hospitals are not democratic places.[6] The interests of the hospital would obviously not be served by an independent patients' council, and it is doubtful that a council will be set up on the model proposed by MPA. Since the interests of the hospital and MPA are so different, it is questionable that negotiations could produce any meaningful compromise, and the possibility of cooptation is great. It would be advantageous to the hospital for the MPA program to become comfortable with the concessions they have been granted and decide not to push for more at the risk of losing the drop-in center. At present, the program's staff is determined to resist cooptation.

Notes

1 MPA Constitution, *In a Nutshell: Mental Patients' Association Newsletter* 4, no. 3 (July 1976): 1.

2 Fran Phillips, Housing designation, *In a Nutshell* 4, no. 4 (October 1976): 10.

3 Residence program – A history of residents at the Mental Patients' Association, November 1976, provided by MPA.

4 Funding application, quoted in Dave Beamish, MPA Riverview Extension Program, *In a Nutshell* 4, no. 4 (October 1976): 5.

5 Personal interview with Dave Beamish, December 16, 1976.

6 Meeting at Riverview Hospital, December 17, 1976.

CHAPTER 16

Psychology of women: Feminist therapy*

Virginia K. Donovan† and Ronnie Littenberg

Feminist therapy in 1981 grew, though its growth was disorderly and diverse. There was no center, no leading exponent, no single theory, and few articles or books. In part this has to do with the origins of feminist therapy. Born in the women's movement, it retains much of the quality of a social movement, and is better defined by the political awareness and social commitment on the part of the therapist than by the particular set of techniques she uses. Therefore, it is important to describe the history and politics of feminist therapy.

The critical examination of therapy (and psychological theory) by the women's movement of the 1960s was inevitable both because of the nature of therapy and because of its use as an ideological weapon against women. On one hand, therapy concerned itself with those areas of experience assigned to and 'carried' by women in our culture – primarily relationships and feelings (Miller 1976). On the other hand, psychological theories about women's nature were used to justify women's place in the home and their 'appropriate' roles in relation to men and children. Therapists treated women for their failure to adjust to a world of increasing contradictions for women.

* Reprinted from Barbara Haber, ed. *The Women's Annual: 1981*, pp. 211–35, Boston: G. K. Hall & Co, by permission of the authors and publisher.
† Both authors contributed equally to this paper. Order of authorship was determined by a flip of the coin.

Historical background

Since World War II women's lives have been changing rapidly. Women were drawn into the work force at record levels during the war, when they assumed jobs previously reserved for men. They were later pushed out of these jobs by returning soldiers. Women's participation in the work force never returned to prewar levels and a powerful ideology emerged (or reemerged in new forms) (Ehrenreich and English, 1978) that helped justify their return to the home and acceptance of work at low pay. Psychology, advanced as a neutral, objective science of behavior, was central to this ideological effort. Behavioral scientists joined child-rearing experts in promoting the theory of maternal instinct; women would fulfill themselves by caring for their children. Less than total mothering would lead to deprived children; children needed constant attention by one caretaker or they became apathetic and hopeless. Penis envy and its resultant rejection of femininity was considered the cause of women's desire for other kinds of fulfillment. Similarly, female masochism was offered as an explanation of why self-abnegation was really gratification. Perhaps most cruelly, women were blamed for any problems with their children (mothers must have been overprotective or rejecting or both) (Ehrenreich and English, 1978) and for their own inability to find contentment (they were neurotic).

Women who were full-time housewives found themselves increasingly isolated, sometimes from the extended families and communities they had moved away from expressly to benefit the children. In general these women were isolated from adult company, especially from other women, and from the social relations that being part of the work force promotes. Housework was devalued (domestic skills bought in the marketplace yielded very low wages), invisible, repetitious, lonely, without boundaries, and often empty. Women who felt forced to sacrifice their own needs by an ideology that taught that serving others was their only legitimate role logically felt an increasing loss of self-hood.

Other changes in women's lives increased the tension between idealized domestic life and actual possibilities. Women's lives could not make up for the contradictions in the whole society between human needs and the social inequalities of race, class, and sex. They continued to enter the labor force (in 1960, 40 percent of all American women held jobs), and more of those who did were married with children. They juggled the demands of work and home without the support of day care, flexible work arrangements, or collectivized (or even shared) household responsibilities. They were likely to continue to look for jobs that were part-time, flexible, and easy to enter and exit, that is, low-paying jobs. At the same time, larger numbers of women were graduating from college than ever before and facing the choice of pure domesticity or women's low-paid work, since college degrees often brought them no gain in the job market.

Betty Friedan (1963) named the barrage of propaganda that blamed women for their unhappiness in the face of these increasing contradictions and changing expectations, 'the feminine mystique.' A general critique of women's relationship to society emerged and was consolidated in the formation of the National Organization for Women in 1964. Militant middle-class feminists revived liberal feminism and demanded equality for women. Although this movement did not challenge the larger social structure, it did push beyond the demand for formal equality in civil and political spheres to recognition of women's oppression in the 'private' areas of life – including sexuality and reproduction.

At the same time, a political movement was growing that did begin to question capitalism. The civil rights movement of the early 1960s exposed the underside of the prosperous 1950s: racism and poverty. The rise of black consciousness at home and of Third World liberation movements abroad expanded ideas of freedom and liberation. The Vietnam War brought home an awareness of the workings of the United States political economic system overseas. These movements helped clarify how, in this economic system, many people paid a high price so that some fewer members could make a profit.

In the social movements accompanying these events women worked side by side with men, expanding their analysis of the oppression of others, and gradually recognized the direct impact of oppression on their own lives. A women's liberation movement burst forth in the late 1960s that went further than any had before, both in its social criticism and in its understanding of the penetration of capitalism into personal life. Women discovered that their intimate oppression forced a redefinition of political and personal life and captured this insight in the phrase, 'the personal is political.'

Consciousness raising was a main method women used to break through previous perceptions of the world and themselves. Central to this process were the connections drawn between personal experiences and feelings and social reality; the recognition that many problems formerly seen as purely personal were now seen as shared by many women and thus were part of their social experience.

As women questioned all aspects of personal life, attention necessarily turned to psychological theories and therapy. Therapy was one area outside the home that dealt with private life – the world of family relationships and feelings. With exploration of people's intimate experiences in the family, a route was provided to understand how social reality is internalized. For example, therapy reveals how society's relations of domination and submission are reproduced by a hierarchical family (men are heads of household) in which children first learn to accept inequality as natural and are socialized into sex roles and relations of power.

Women took some of the lessons of consciousness raising and tried to refashion therapy so it would be more useful and less oppressive. Therapy could be, it was hoped, a place for a more thorough exploration of one's situation as a woman, focusing on the particular ways women learned about human relations and themselves and examining their (often hidden) needs and desires. Therapy could also be a method of changing the sometimes indirect or self-defeating ways women tried to get their needs met (directness by women in trying to meet their own needs had always been accompanied by the threat of isolation). To do this, however, certain aspects of therapy had to be changed.

Feminist therapy defined

Szasz (1961), Chesler (1972), Tennov (1976), Johnson (1980), and others have written of how traditional psychotherapy has been used as a means of social control and as such is harmful to women and other oppressed groups. Among the criticisms made by feminists are that the structure of the therapeutic relationships is based on authoritarian, patriarchal roles and reinforces women's sense of dependency and inadequacy; that a medical model treats unhappiness as pathology or as an illness; that the goal of treatment becomes adjustment not change; and that social problems are often treated as though they were the responsibility of the individual.

During the past decade several books and papers on feminist therapy have been published (Mandler and Rush, 1974; du Bois,

1976; Williams, 1976; Rawlings and Carter, 1977; Brodsky, 1980; Gilbert, 1980; Kaschak, 1981; Ernst and Goodison, 1981). These describe therapists' attempts to reconceptualize the goals of therapy and the nature and function of the therapeutic process, and how to adjust the role of the therapist to be more compatible with newly developed theory on the psychology of women as well as with the overall goals of the women's movement. Beyond agreement that feminist therapy is not based on a particular theory of psychological development or on specific therapeutic techniques, definitions differ widely. In fact, a recent paper by Kaschak (1981) provides a detailed comparison *among* feminist therapies. She divides them into radical grassroots, radical professional, and liberal professional approaches and compares these to nonsexist and traditional psychoanalytic therapy.

This discussion does not attempt to review all that is currently being said or written, but rather describes one approach or way of thinking about women and therapy, and identifies some of the major issues being addressed by therapists of similar orientation.

To begin, feminist therapy must be distinguished from other kinds of services or experiences often provided by feminist organizations (even though some of these may have a therapeutic effect or be used in conjunction with therapy), and from nonsexist therapy. Therapy is a voluntary consulting or counseling relationship in which the therapist has formal training or acquired skills in the helper or facilitator role. The problems to be worked on are defined by the client and, at least initially, perceived by her to be partly personal in nature. Usually the client is also seeking relief from some kind of subjectively experienced psychic discomfort or pain. Therapy as described here is not a counseling relationship characterized as primarily educational or information-sharing (job counseling, referral networks, etc.), or which only teaches a particular skill (assertiveness training, relaxation techniques, etc.), or which is a leaderless activity (consciousness raising, support, or self-help groups).

A therapist who is not overtly authoritarian or oppressive and who espouses egalitarian values with respect to sex roles is not necessarily a feminist therapist, although she may share values and attitudes with feminist therapists (Rawlings and Carter, 1977; Kaschak, 1981). With a nonsexist, humanistic approach sex-role behaviors are not prescribed and may even be openly questioned. A client is assumed to be a person with strengths; these are identified and allied with by the therapist to promote the client's development as a competent and autonomous person. The therapy relationship is characterized by trust, mutuality, and respect.

Feminist therapy becomes distinct from nonsexist therapy in the therapist's analysis of the forms of social, economic, and political oppression that affect women individually as well as as a group. This analysis informs the therapist's understanding of how women develop and function in our society, and of how change may occur. (Without this analysis a therapist is not a feminist therapist even if she identifies herself as one.) The feminist therapist's belief that the personal is political, that for fundamental changes to occur in the emotional lives of women basic social structures must change, has two direct implications for her work. The first is that she actively struggles with the manifestation of sexism, racism, and class oppression that affect her own attitudes and values. She believes that therapy is *not* value free and that she must understand her own values and make them explicit. The second is that she believes that there are no individual solutions for social, moral, and political problems; however, she recognizes that joining with others to work for change can be a major source of validation and empowerment.

Concretely, these implications mean that a feminist therapist cannot be working in an isolated way. She must be informed of and involved in working with women and other groups for social change. She must be aware of the social and political work going on in her community so that she is able to share her understanding and resources with her clients.

A crucial aspect of her work is in helping her clients to distinguish the things in their lives or situations for which they are personally responsible, to identify self-defeating behaviors, and to differentiate both from attitudes and circumstances that reflect broader social problems. With respect to the former, the therapist helps her clients set goals and develop skills so they are able to make effective and appropriate changes in behavior. With respect to the latter she tries to validate the clients' experiences of frustration or powerlessness, and encourages them to meet and join with others who have similar problems.

Feminist critiques of theory

Since feminist therapy is not grounded in a separate coherent theory of psychological development and change, feminist therapists have examined traditional theories for their usefulness in conceptualization and practice of therapy. These examinations take different forms depending on the nature of the theory. In the case of family therapy, recent focus has been on integrating feminist therapy principles with a family systems approach. Feminist therapists have assessed gestalt, encounter, and humanist therapies and described techniques they found useful. They have tried to deepen, revise, and reformulate psychoanalytic theory according to feminist insights. Current thinking in each of these areas is briefly described.

Family systems therapy

The practice of family therapy usually involves techniques based on major concepts about family systems (Chasin and Grunebaum, 1980). These concepts are sometimes organized into particular systems approaches (structural theory, communications theory, Bowen theory), but writers have also tried to integrate these approaches or provide transcendent concepts (Framo, 1972; Chasin and Grunebaum, 1980). The most general theme is that the unit of understanding or treatment is the family or the system. Family therapists believe that individual behavior can best be understood as part of an interacting system. In a family or closely related unit, members 'reciprocally carry part of each other's psychology and form a feedback system which in turn regulates and patterns their individual behaviors' (Framo, 1972: 271).

Many therapists are drawn to family systems therapy as an effective and realistic approach that helps people deal with interpersonal relationships. It allows therapists to work with all members of a system, for example, children and parents, without becoming an advocate for either (as was often the case in traditional child-guidance clinics); they can work with both people in a couple or with an extended family.

Family therapy theory includes a number of underlying assumptions attractive to many therapists. It emphasizes the importance of social context in determining behavior, viewing symptoms as manifestations of system difficulties. It moves away from victim-blaming and medical models of individual pathology; all behavior is seen as adaptive in its context, and thus traditional concepts of etiology and diagnosis are eschewed.

Although many family therapists would describe themselves as adherents of equality between men and women, there has been a stunning absence of discussion of sexism and feminism in the literature. This makes it likely that most family therapists in fact hold unexamined values and biases about women's role in the family (Hare-Mustin, 1978), about definitions of power and reality in the family, and about what constitutes mental health for women (Broverman *et al.*, 1970; American Psychological Association, 1975). Without consciousness-raising about sexism, therapists are unaware of ways they may subtly (or not so subtly) reinforce traditional roles and behaviors that are damaging to women. Only very recently have writings appeared about family systems approaches and feminism (Hare-Mustin, 1978; Gurman and Klein, 1980; Caust, Libow, and Raskin, 1981; Libow *et al.*, 1981).

They have pointed to cases in which the model of family therapy is biased against women, as in the Bowen model that explicitly values intellectual processes over emotional processes, and the Boszor-menyi-Nagy model that supports sex-stereotyped roles (Hare-Mustin, 1978). Even when the model is thought to be value-free, sexism often exists in the therapist's assumptions about what behavior is expected from each. For example, family therapists may see themselves as models for appropriate sex-role behavior and sex-role relations in which men dominate. Hare-Mustin (1978) points out how 'Minuchin sees himself as modeling the male executive functions, forming alliances, most typically with the father, and through competition, rule-setting, and direction, demanding that the father assume control of the family and exert leadership, much as Minuchin leads and controls the session' (p. 184). Similarly, women therapists are often taught to use their feminine traits of warmth and wisdom (parallel to women's traditional roles in the family) to appeal to the masculine instincts of male clients (Hare-Mustin, 1978).

Accompanying a lack of analysis of sexism, family therapists often adopt a morally neutral stance that can lead to their defining behavior only as a 'couples interaction,' even when the behavior may assault a woman's sense of reality or, in some cases, actually physically harm her. In contrast, feminists believe that some behavior is wrong and unacceptable (such as physical abuse) and disagree with the tendency in a systems approach to see oppression as a 'mutually regulated dance.'

Marriage is viewed as a closed system by family therapy models, with little attention given to members' relationships with the outside world (Gurman and Klein, 1980). This conceptualization results in tremendous distortion of power relationships within the family by ignoring women's lack of power, limited economic opportunities, and experiences of sexism in the rest of the world. The power aspects of sex roles in the family are largely ignored by family therapists unless it is the women who appear to have power. Then the power (real or apparent) is seen as the basis for psychological dysfunction (Hare-Mustin, 1978).

In the closed-model system a woman is defined primarily in relational terms and implicitly expected to derive her identity and satisfactions within the family unit (Gurman and Klein, 1980). This reproduces the way in which women are defined in our culture and allows little space for the kind of self-exploration so often denied to women and so much needed by them. Although some family therapy models stress the need for a balance between separation and closeness, for a woman to balance out a lifetime of living through and for others, she may need the context of individual or group therapy to begin to see herself as a separate person.

Libow and associates (1981) describe how issues of power and insight are the major sources of differences in approach between family and feminist therapy. In their structural approach, family therapists rely on 'expert' power, power based on the knowledge and skills of the therapist as owned by her and needed by the family. The expert role is strategic, and is used to exert pressure to effect change. She may use a variety of techniques that are active, directive, and whose purposes are not necessarily made explicit to the family. Insight is not a goal in itself.

In contrast, feminist therapists rely on 'referent power,' based on using the self as a point of identification and emphasizing the commonality of women's experience. The feminist therapist is seen as a partner in a collaborative venture; she stresses respect in the relationship between client and therapist in order to move away from the paternalistic models of expert doctor and dependent patient, and to respect the client's capacity for self-knowledge and self-direction. She thus tries to demystify the therapy process, and stresses open and direct communication between herself and her client. Insight, consciousness-raising, and education are viewed as necessary to an understanding of one's personal history and social and political realities.

Family and feminist therapy differ as well in their approach to sex, class, and ethnic differences. Some family therapists feel that ethnic and class characteristics must be noted to understand the family, but not necessarily challenged (Pearce, 1980; Libow *et al.*, 1981). They argue that to do so might drive families away. Feminist therapists directly explore and confront sex-role-related stereotyped behavior as well as the influence of class and ethnic behavior. They believe that in a society that is sexist, racist, and stratified by class, it is impossible to know who you are and where you stand without understanding how those stratifications affect your history and possibilities. Not to explore these dimensions is to return women's problems to the realm of being 'only internal.'

Not all feminist family therapists agree that power and insight must be handled differently. (This is partly the result of different schools of family therapy.) Hare-Mustin (1978) argues that it is possible for a family therapist to equalize the relationship by demystifying therapy and by using consciousness-raising, education, and insight. She also provides examples of how issues such as sex, race, and class could be explored in the context of family therapy.

Family systems theory and practice have been developed on a model of the heterosexual nuclear family. Although theorists would claim that this approach can be applied to any system, for example lesbian couples or single-mother families, this has yet to be demonstrated. Examination of family therapy by feminists is only beginning. To what extent it can be used with nontraditional families or in nonsexist ways, or integrated with principles of feminism is still controversial. Discussion is tentative, and much more is needed: on the different kinds of family therapy and their relationship to feminist therapy; on description of the populations, problems, and goals brought to therapy; and on the sexual politics of family therapy.

Human potential movement or growth movement therapy

Very little has been written by feminist therapists on the human potential movement (sometimes called third-force psychology or growth movement therapy). Human potential therapies emphasize the importance and validity of feelings and individual entitlement. They consist of strategies to help people bypass some defenses and resistances against directly experiencing feelings. Ideally, this is attempted in a context in which the client feels safe and trusting.

In their book, *In our own hands: a woman's book of self-help therapy*, Ernst and Goodison (1981) describe why they and other feminists might be drawn to this approach. Growth movement therapies promote self-awareness, self-assertiveness, and acceptance of one's feelings and one's body. As with some other therapies, to emphasize feelings is to enter and validate the realm of experience assigned to women. However, growth movement therapies make a public credo out of knowing and attending to one's own feelings. For women, this has a liberating aspect. By training, women are more likely to recognize others' needs than their own. They are also more likely to be punished if they try to meet their own needs in direct or open ways (Miller, 1976). Growth movement therapies provide techniques that help identify feelings, and that give permission for the expression of taboo or unacceptable feelings. For example, gestalt techniques aid in the discovery of feelings that have been denied by examining projections of one's own feelings onto parts of dreams and onto behaviors and attitudes disliked in other people, or by uncovering unconscious conflicts between needs and obligations.

These therapies also encourage and train people in the direct expression of their feelings. Female socialization usually prohibits women from being directly angry, competitive, or even dependent (dependency is both sanctioned and condemned). Encounter techniques permit and teach more direct assertive behaviors to substitute for the indirect and sometimes manipulative ones on which women have learned to depend.

Feminist therapists have found the growth movement's emphasis on body awareness and acceptance to be useful. Women have been kept ignorant of their bodies' workings, taught to be scared or disgusted by their bodies' sexual and other physical functions, and alienated from their bodies by mass media stereotypes of beauty (Barbach, 1975; Orbach, 1978; Ernst and Goodison, 1981). Growth movement techniques include direct work with the body to loosen blocks against feelings (Reichian therapy) and strategies for becoming aware of feelings and attitudes about one's body.

The liberating aspect of this focus on feelings and entitlement is accompanied by a philosophy (and often practice) that is deeply oppressive to women as well. This approach implicitly and explicitly emphasizes feelings to the exclusion of intellect and values and fails to take into account the individual's social context. Feminist writers (Ehrenreich and English, 1978; Ernst and Goodison, 1981) have criticized the human potential movement for its lack of analysis of sexism and the social conditions that affect and constrain experience and opportunity. Without such an analysis the human potential movement disregards the sources of pain, suffering, and oppression that exist in society and shape contemporary life.

By positing unlimited potential for individual transformation and growth, the human potential movement assumes an isolated human being, free to restructure her life situation. This atomized person has within her her own reality, which is largely independent of social structures and interpersonal relations. In this view something is real only if it is felt to be real. This promise of total control may be particularly seductive at a time when a woman is experiencing less control over her life and less possibility for fulfillment.

The human potential movement's ideal individuals are completely self-centered and free to seek their own gain at whatever cost to others. It leaves out consideration of social embeddedness and the process through which needs are satisfied in a social context. Human bonds and responsibility are also denied by this model that both encourages women to practice an aggressive individualistic male model of living and perpetuates their sense of aloneness.

Self-awareness is emphasized to the exclusion of other types of awareness. The lack of race, class, and sex analysis allows participants to forget these 'troublesome' aspects of life. Women are offered a false egalitarianism that denies the discrimination and unequal treatment they actually receive in daily life. These more universal values such as racial, sexual, and social equality are ignored, since human potential therapies consider values to be excess baggage that detract from individual achievement.

Without an understanding of sexism, in practice these therapies reproduce sexist and authoritarian modes within the therapeutic relationship (Ernst and Goodison, 1981). Issues of leadership are rarely addressed. In some instances cult leaders and showmen such as Fritz Perls and Werner Erhard offer a patriarchal model of domination as they refuse to deal with power and authority in the therapy relationship. In other forms of growth movement therapy the therapist may identify himself as a humanist and claim that therapy can be without any power relationship. (Feminists believe therapy always involves a power relationship that should be recognized and explored.)

Instant trust and uncritical openness, which are particularly difficult for women, are often goals of human potential therapies. While no one should be expected to offer such blind faith, women often have been pressured to do so even though this repeats their unquestioning submission to men. Women simply do not have the freedom to be openly angry and assertive and, in fact, male society would not accept this kind of intimacy coming from women's own perspectives and initiatives. In general, values concerning desirable behavior are formulated without regard to their particular meaning to women. Physical touching, for example, is uncritically encouraged without consideration of its associations for women with sexual possession and male exertions of power.

The same blindness to sexism is manifested in humanistic psychology's blindness to racism and class stratification. By not even trying to grasp these central structures of society, humanists reinforce their own variant of the status quo. Thus they do not question capitalism or patriarchy, and they tailor techniques to contain and manage discontent. For example, they run sensitivity groups for large corporations, conduct transactional analysis groups in prisons, and operate encounter sessions between police and ghetto residents (Ehrenreich and English, 1978).

Feminist therapists have taken from the human potential movement techniques for uncovering feelings, and have applied them in settings that can become safe places for women to share feelings and values (Ernst and Goodison, 1981). They have rejected the underlying assumptions of the human potential movement that individual improvement and liberation are possible or sufficient.

Psychoanalysis

Psychoanalysis is both a theory of development, of society, and of civilization, and a form of therapy. Both exist within Freud, but the tension between them is complex and often contradicted. The pressure on the individual practitioner to focus on the individual and attempt to help find particular solutions to her problems has led to revisions in theory that continue to be disputed (Schneider, 1975; Jacoby, 1975). The relationship between psychoanalytic theory and psychoanalytic therapy has not been clarified by feminists who criticized Freud's theory of female development for its male supremacist view; that is, acceptance of the authority of patriarchal society, of the biological inferiority of women, and of the superiority of vaginal orgasm. They have also criticized his cultural theory that transforms historical phenomena into universal, biological instincts and they have documented Freudian concepts never substantiated by research (Millett, 1970; Chesler, 1972; Brown, 1973; Schneider, 1975; Rohrbaugh, 1981). Recently, some feminists have attempted to use the psychoanalytic methodology to develop new insights on female psychology (Chodorow, 1978; Miller, 1976). These attempts will be described briefly. Our focus, however, is primarily on feminist *therapy*, not theories of development or the psychology of women.

Very little has been written by feminists on psychoanalytic treatment and still less on the relationship of theory to practice. Ernst and Goodison (1981) describe how psychoanalysts' training, because it is expensive and selection is highly controlled, tends to eliminate all but financially well-off white men. Training is hierarchical and conservative, discouraging questioning and alternative points of view. Treatment is costly, further removing analysts from contact with anyone unlike themselves. Psychoanalysts bring to the therapy situation the values and attitudes of the dominant patriarchal society, and although they may examine the way their feelings affect the therapy (countertransference), they are less likely to examine the way their values do. Transference in therapy involves a power relationship within which the client ('patient' in psychoanalytic terms) is encouraged to reexperience childhood feelings. New emotional experiences with authority figures may be constructive, but if the reality of the relationship is denied and not explored they can also be harmful. Psychoanalysis locates the source of current feelings in early childhood experiences and this is similarly double-edged. It may be helpful to recognize the origins of assumptions about interpersonal relationships and to find earlier bases for feelings, but this can also invalidate a woman's sense of her objective social and economic realities if these are not also identified.

Despite these problems and dangers, many feminist therapists incorporate some concepts from psychoanalysis into a psychodynamic approach. These include concepts of the unconscious, transference, conflict, and a general understanding developed by Freud of how social reality takes root in personality through early childhood experiences. While there are some articles written from a feminist perspective by psychoanalysts or with a psychoanalytic approach (Miller 1973; Strouse 1974), we have seen nothing by feminist therapists explicitly about the usefulness of psychoanalysis as a therapy.

Two recent books by feminists working within the psychoanalytic tradition have attempted to comment on, use, and revise psychoanalytic theory toward new understandings of female development. Jean Baker Miller, in *Toward a new psychology of women* (1976), offers a fascinating account of how a shift in perspective from a male point of view to a feminist one alters our understanding of female psychological dynamics. Beginning with an analysis of women's subordinate status to men, she examines how this social role defines the personality characteristics that women develop and determines their activities, roles, and emotional experiences. Men (or dominants, as she calls them, thus extending the analysis to power relationships among other groups as well) hold power and create social structures and ideology that justify their power and 'scientifically' demonstrate how *their* nature is *human* nature. Women are assigned to parts of human experience and human nature that are unacknowledged and denied by men, such as feelings of 'vulnerability, weakness, helplessness, dependency, and the basic emotional connections between an individual and other people' (p. 22). Issues women deal with – human development and human ends (how to care for people, how to organize society to serve people – concern basic questions of our culture and need to be reintegrated into the whole society to be solved. Miller's analysis generates new understandings of women's strengths and weaknesses and of their search for creativity and affiliation. She argues that psychoanalysis has been mainly concerned with these crucial areas of experience, but at the same time she shows how a perspective that begins with an analysis of social roles allows and requires reformulations of psychoanalytic concepts, psychological terminology, and theories of development and female nature.

Nancy Chodorow, in *The reproduction of mothering* (1978), uses object relations theory to explain how women's role as primary, and at times exclusive, child-rearer creates sex differences and leads to the social organization of gender inequality. Chodorow offers the most elaborate view to date of the mother-daughter relationship and how it affects our sense of ourselves as independent persons and our relationships to others. Unlike Miller's book, however, sexuality and early emotional experiences are emphasized over social and historical factors, and some feminists believe that psychoanalytic assumptions previously challenged by feminists as invalid, remain (Rich, 1980; Rohrbaugh, 1981). Rohrbaugh (1981) argues that Chodorow accepts Freud's theory of penis envy and castration anxiety despite the fact that these have not been verified in research, that she assumes all women are heterosexual, and that she uses sexuality as an explanation for mothers' differential treatment of boys and girls, but leaves out social explanations, in effect blaming women for female oppression. Rohrbaugh points out how Chodorow maintains that women define themselves in relational terms as a result of emotional and personal experience rather than as part of a social role.

The resurgence of interest in psychoanalysis has been noted by many feminist therapists. At the 1981 conference of the Association for Women in Psychology (AWP), papers on this topic drew overflowing crowds. Because feminist therapy has not grown from a theoretical base in psychological theory and because its development is still in the early stages, feminists are drawn to possible sources of new insight and theory. Whether or not psychoanalysis can provide them remains highly controversial.

Problems addressed by feminist therapists

A feminist perspective has enabled therapists to 'see' problems that previously have been ignored, thought to be insignificant, or have been looked at incorrectly. Some of the issues recently addressed have been: violence toward women – rape, battering, incest, and sexual harassment; substance abuse – alcohol and drug addiction, compulsive eating and dieting; and sexuality.

Although these issues influence the lives of most women, they have been avoided by therapists (including women) for several reasons. First, most therapists have been trained in traditional (male) psychological theory, which as Naomi Weisstein (1971) put it '. . . has nothing to say about what women are really like, what they need and what they want . . .' (p. 209).

Second, therapists have had to struggle with personal reluctance to involve themselves with problems that may evoke their own deep fears (a common reaction to battering and incest), that arouse feelings of contempt or revulsion toward their clients' unacceptable, non-sex-role stereotypic behavior (e.g., the alcoholic mother who neglects her children), or that make them feel frustrated and angry at their clients' powerlessness and victimization.

Third, many women clients experience a deep sense of shame and guilt about their problems, blaming themselves and perceiving (often accurately) that they will also be blamed by others. Out of a sense of self-protection they often deny, minimize, or communicate only indirectly the existence of their 'unacceptable' problems.

In response to these three obstacles, feminists have tried to educate themselves and the general public by documenting the existence, incidence, and manifestations of problems affecting women, their causal factors and psychological consequences. They have also worked to develop treatment and support services and to coordinate their work with other community (often nonprofessional) groups.

Violence toward women

Feminists writing about violence toward women (Brownmiller, 1975; Walker, 1979, 1980; Herman, 1981; Leidig, 1981) have attempted to dispel several popular myths: namely, that victims of violence 'asked for it' or provoked it, that violence typically occurs between two disturbed individuals, or that violence occurs mainly among nonwhite or poor people. Whether it takes the form of rape, battering, incest, sexual harassment, or pornography, a feminist analysis holds that violence against women is pervasive and is the product of a patriarchal culture in which men control the form of social institutions and women's bodies.

The *threat* of violence affects all women and benefits all men, and as such is a potent source of social control that keeps women isolated, frightened, subservient, and dependent. Typically, when women do report incidents they are disbelieved or blamed. The greater the intimacy between perpetrator and victim the less the incidence of reporting and the greater the tendency to blame the victim (Leidig, 1981). Thus acts such as marital or date rape, spouse battering, or incest are often kept hidden and many times are not identified by the victim as violent.

Walker (1979), writing about battered wives, and Herman (1981), about father-daughter incest, report that victims of domestic violence often feel confused about whether they identify themselves as victims and that this confusion in part reflects guilt or shame about their experiencing feelings of pleasure, closeness, or power in the relationship with the abusive man. A similar confusion is often experienced by victims of sexual harassment (e.g., the young female worker being pressured to be sexually involved with a male boss) or rape (e.g., forcible sex occurring after a date or when the woman has been drinking, or sex between therapist and client).

While media coverage, educational campaigns, and the establishment of local hotlines, crisis centers, and shelters have helped to break down the isolation of some women victims, many others continue to live with a sense of deep shame and guilt, holding themselves responsible for what has been done to them. Feminist therapists have attempted to deal with this problem by learning about the form and consequences of violence, particularly domestic violence, so they can recognize symptoms and indirect clues that violence has occurred and help their clients to share their painful secrets.

While traditional psychotherapeutic approaches might use a model of intrapsychic pathology (e.g., the woman is masochistic, the man psychopathic) or a family systems perspective of shared responsibility (each party has responsibility for the events between them), a feminist approach would emphasize labeling events for what they are: sex under circumstances of coercion is rape, pushing and hitting even if no medical attention is needed is battering, any form of secret sexual contact between a parent or parent figure and a child is incest, and so forth. The therapist would share her belief that although the victim is not to blame, she might need to take major steps to protect herself in the future. The therapist would also work to educate her client about healthy intimacy and sexuality, since many women have had little experience with sexual relationships that are caring and mutually satisfying.

A feminist therapist assumes that a working therapeutic alliance is not possible if a woman's health and safety are in danger and may involve herself in some kind of direct legal intervention or in helping her client get money and shelter; in any case, the therapist works concretely with the woman to develop escape or conditions of safety for herself and her children. The assumption that the client's safety is primary also determines the form of therapy. For example, Walker

(1979, 1980) concluded that it is almost impossible to make couple therapy safe for a battered woman – that a woman's need to please combined with her fear of the batterer massively interferes with her being able openly to express her feelings in therapy. Walker therefore recommends individual or group treatment for the woman and separate treatment for the man. Herman (1981), in contrast, reports that some family therapy programs for victims of father-daughter incest have been effective, but she notes that in these programs the offenders have been ordered by the courts to participate and that nonparticipation would mean jail sentences.

Because the privacy of the individual therapy relationship may in effect reinforce a woman's isolation and need for secrecy, most feminist therapists at some point encourage clients who are victims of violence to involve themselves in community-based programs or groups. In most major cities there are networks of shelters and hotlines for rape victims and battered women. Typically, these provide shelter, legal, economic, and medical advocacy, and some kind of counseling. Individual and group counseling for rape victims emphasizes women giving comfort and support to each other about the trauma experienced with its accompanying fear, rage, and sense of powerlessness and invasion.

Assertiveness training and gestalt techniques are often used in counseling programs for battered women; the former to teach appropriate, effective ways of expressing their needs and protecting themselves; the latter to help evoke, in a safe setting, feelings (particularly those of anger) that previously have been expressed only indirectly or repressed altogether. Counseling usually takes place in a group and often the counselors themselves are former victims. This structure provides a direct way for women who have been isolated, dependent, and powerless to see that they can support and protect each other and together find effective ways of confronting their oppression and reconstructing their lives.

In many areas groups for incest victims have been formed, some led by therapists, some by other victims, and some established on a leaderless self-help basis. These groups provide a supportive context for victims to share their secret, to express the feelings of rage and sadness felt toward parents for abusing or failing to protect them, and usually to plan some kind of direct steps to confront or to share with other family members what has occurred. The breakdown of secrecy both within the group and within the family helps free victims from the paralyzing sense of shame and guilt with which most of them have lived for many years.

Substance abuse

Although addiction to drugs and alcohol tends to be more profoundly disruptive to women's lives and functioning than compulsive eating and dieting, feminist analyses have shown that women with these problems have much in common. Feminists interpret women's addictions as being both a symbolic protest against the pressures and demands placed on them in our society and as attempts to reconcile or escape these pressures. Up to a point, use of alcohol or drugs or concern with dieting and thinness is culturally supported: women must strive to be sexier, funnier, calmer, and more beautiful for men. Furthermore, several billion-dollar industries are involved – the drug industry, the medical establishment, food, entertainment, and clothing industries. When women's involvement with food or drugs gets out of control, that is, when they can no longer fulfill their caretaking, nurturing, and sexual functions, they are judged harshly as being repulsive, weak, self-destructive, and crazy. It is with both the widespread existence of addictions and the condemnation of women who 'go public' with their problem that feminists have concerned themselves.

Drug and alcohol addiction

From one-third to one-half of the alcoholics in this country are women, making a conservative figure of 3.3 million women with serious drinking problems (Sandmaier, 1980). 60 to 80 percent of psychoptropic drugs prescribed (depending on classification as tranquilizer, sedative, or stimulant) are prescribed to women (Nellis, 1980). An estimated one to two million women have prescribed-drug dependencies and many are cross-addicted to alcohol (Fidell, 1981). Addictions cross class, race, and ethnic lines. Despite these statistics, drug and alcohol addiction are generally viewed as male or lower-class phenomena; research and treatment efforts have been almost exclusively directed toward men (Nellis, 1980; Sandmaier, 1980; Gomberg, 1981; Fidell, 1981).

As with violence against women, the erroneous view of addictions as sex-linked or class-linked partially reflects how women hide the problems out of shame and guilt. This distortion also serves a function in our sexist society. The double standard where men's excessive drinking is tolerated but women's is not maintains male power by punishing and condemning women for deviating from the 'true' female role. This serves as a warning to other women to hide or deny their commonality with the 'fallen women' (Sandmaier, 1980). When drugs are involved (since for women most drugs are legally obtained by prescription) pressure to hide the scope of the problem is strong, for to not do so would implicate the government, drug companies, and the medical profession (Nellis, 1980).

Most drug and alcohol treatment programs and techniques have been developed for men and have been singularly ineffective for women. First, these programs almost never accommodate the realities of women's lives – that most are poor or economically dependent and have almost exclusive responsibility for raising their children. Unless a program can help free a woman from at least some of her work and family responsibilities, she cannot participate in treatment *at all*. Programs developed by women for addicted women have begun to incorporate child care and job training components but progress has been slow due to lack of funding and nonsupportive social attitudes. (For the women who have already lost their families and homes – the 'bag ladies' – there are seldom available shelters or legal or medical help that they need to survive.)

Many male-oriented drug and alcohol programs use aggressive confrontation techniques to challenge the men's perceptions of control, power, and self-sufficiency. These are highly inappropriate for women and serve to reinforce their already low self-esteem, sense of powerlessness, and dependency. Even supportive self-help treatment approaches (such as Alcoholics Anonymous) are often male-dominated and as such encourage women to give up their addiction so that they may return to their homes and their nurturing roles as wives and mothers, thus reinforcing their guilt that they have failed as women (Nellis, 1980; Sandmaier, 1980).

Feminists and therapists try to intervene in the cycle of powerlessness, anger, and guilt by providing (usually in a group context) support and analysis that the women's 'failures' as wives, mothers, and women reflect their attempts to live up to impossible societal standards, and that their guilt and self-hatred only compound the problems. Practical needs are addressed and self-control is urged.

Typically, the focus is on here-and-now aspects of the women's lives; they are encouraged to develop friendships and to learn to advocate for and support each other in times of stress and crisis.

Recognizing the high rate of alcoholism in the lesbian and gay communities (several studies show an incidence of about 35 percent) (Sandmaier, 1980) and the heavily heterosexual orientation of most traditional treatment programs and self-help groups, feminist therapists have begun to do outreach and develop services to meet the special needs of these clients. These therapists interpret the high rate of alcoholism as a function of gay bars being the *only* safe and available social context in which lesbians can socialize. Also, living in society where they are so openly feared and hated creates tremendous pressure and many lesbians turn to alcohol and drugs to anesthetize their feelings of anger, guilt, and self-hate. Through lesbian alcoholic groups, education in the gay community, sponsorship of drug and alcohol-free coffee houses and cultural events, and through support groups for friends and lovers of alcoholics, progress has been made in providing support and encouragement for lesbian women to gain better control over their drinking and drug use.

Eating disorders

Societal preoccupation with thinness is the basis of several major industries: fashion, health clubs, diet books and foods, drugs, weight loss programs, and so on, and these are aimed at and paid for primarily by women. Weight and dieting are the foci of many women's lives no matter how little their actual weight deviates from population norms, for there is the widespread belief that being thin makes you beautiful, happy, and desirable to men.

Bruch (1973), in her pioneering work, notes that many people misuse eating functions in an effort to solve or hide problems of living. She views eating disorders as being on a continuum with the extremes of obesity and anorexia nervosa having much in common: the experience of not owning one's sensations and body, distorted and unrealistic body images, and the misperception of body functions so that food intake becomes associated with power and control. She says that an essential aspect of anorexia nervosa is a pervasive sense of ineffectiveness. 'The main issue is a struggle for control, for a sense of identity, competence, and effectiveness' (p. 25).

Bruch locates the source of eating disorders in a culture that overemphasizes thinness and in disturbed family interactions. Feminists, however, have taken her analysis a step further by pointing out that the central features of anorexia nervosa – the sense of powerlessness and the symbolic attempts to gain control – describe the conditions of life *for most women*. Chronic patterns of misusing food and dieting are seen as both a symptom of women's sense of futility in trying to cope with contradictory role demands, and as problems in and of themselves (Boskind-Lodhal, 1976; Orbach, 1978; Wooley and Wooley, 1980).

As with other issues addressed by feminist therapists, the treatment of choice for eating disorders is group therapy. Early groups for compulsive eaters and dieters emphasized fat and overweight (Orbach, 1978). Therapists discovered, however, that more and more women attending groups were not overweight but showed other symptoms: anorexics – women who had dieted to the point of starvation; 'fat thin people' – women who maintained a normal weight level only through constant dietary vigilance; and bulimics – women who compulsively and regularly binge and then purge food by vomiting or using laxatives. What these women had in common with overweight women were distorted body images, guilt, and self-hate about their eating behaviors, and unrealistic ideas about what food and weight control would give to them. Accordingly, the focus of feminists' treatment groups broadened to include those women.

Orbach (1978) in her work with compulsive eaters and Boskind-Lodhal and Sirhan (1977) in their work with bulimics describe similar approaches to therapy groups. They use a combination of behavioral and gestalt techniques to help members explore meanings attributed to fat and thin to understand ways they use eating or dieting to avoid anxiety-provoking situations, to develop greater body and sensory awareness, and to reclaim aspects of themselves previously denied or attributed to weight, for example, competence, power, anger. Emphasis is not on weight or dieting but on members relearning to recognize hunger and to use food to satisfy that need. At the same time, they examine how their socialization as women has contributed to their conflicts and problems, and discuss how in their daily lives they may begin to assume more autonomy and control.

Sexuality

In the consciousness-raising groups of the late 1960s and early 1970s, as women shared with each other their most personal and intimate experiences they came to realize that as long as men took an active, dominant, autonomous role, and women a passive, receptive, reactive role, sexual relations became another area of male dominance and control. Following the principle that the personal is political, feminists developed an analysis of sexuality that held that major support for male dominance and patriarchy lay in men's control over the reproductive and sexual uses of women's bodies. Women do not have reproductive freedom; they lack control over contraception, abortion, sterilization, childbirth, and child care, and the sexual division of labor places the burden and responsibility for child rearing solely on women. Neither do women have freedom of sexual expression – the right to control the choice of a partner and to determine when sexual relations are to take place. There is the cultural requirement that legitimate female sexual expression be only within heterosexual marriage; women who fail to abide by this standard are denied the financial and political protection of men. Feminists concluded that there can be no sexual liberation without women's liberation – that until women had control over their bodies and access to the political, social, and economic privileges allowed men, the so-called sexual liberation movement served only men.

A feminist analysis of sexuality has had a major impact on the work of therapists. Most sex research and psychological theories assume a patriarchal male model sexuality with an emphasis on activity, autonomy, and achievement of orgasm and dissociated from the interpersonal and emotional aspects of relationships (Miller and Fowlkes, 1980; Person, 1980). Feminists believe the forms of expression of sexuality are not innate but reflect political and cultural institutions that affect the conditions of one's life and one's consciousness (Rich, 1980). A feminist therapist would not assume heterosexuality or hold it to be the only standard of health, but rather would believe that other forms of sexual expression (lesbian relationships, celibacy, and having and raising children outside of marriage and the nuclear family) are not the only valid but may be the only viable options for some women. Sexuality would not be considered to be a matter of lifestyle or limited to what happens in bed. The feminist therapist would move the focus away from genital sexuality to issues of identity, expression of intimacy, and the capacity for the experience of sensual pleasure.

Lesbians and therapy

Many lesbians seek therapy from feminist therapists or lesbian feminist therapists. Most lesbians are not in therapy because of problems with sexuality per se, but because of the stresses of living in a society that assumes heterosexuality and severely sanctions homosexuality. Abbott and Love (1971) state, 'Lesbianism is the one response to male domination that is unforgiveable' (p. 610). The lesbian suffers the oppression of all women and, in addition, is denied the benefits of a sexist system: financial security, protection, and the reflected status and power of men.

Some of the particular problems dealt with in therapy are social isolation and feelings of shame and guilt about being lesbian. In addition, lesbian adolescents, mothers, and couples have special problems and are particularly vulnerable to legal and political harassment. Much of the shame and guilt experienced by lesbians derives from the discrepancy between the societal and family values with which they were raised, and their choice to be openly lesbian (Litwok *et al.*, 1979). The feminist therapist can help her lesbian clients by emphasizing and validating the affirming, strengthening aspects of a woman's decision to live independently of men.

Since a major problem of many lesbians seeking therapy is isolation, a feminist therapist *at a minimum* must be familiar with the activities, problems, and resources of the lesbian and gay community to help her client join and get support from that community (Sang, 1977; Litwok *et al.*, 1978). Escamilla-Mondanaro (1977) argues that only a lesbian therapist is equipped to help a lesbian client. While others do not feel this is absolutely necessary for good therapy, it is clear than an important factor is the extent to which the therapist can serve as a role model and the setting of therapy validates and affirms a lesbian and gay lifestyle.

Inhibition of sexuality

Person (1980) writes that traditionally the two problematic areas of female sexuality have been those of masochism and inhibition of sexuality: problems of assertion in the interpersonal context, inhibition of sex per se (that is, desire, arousal or orgasm), and low sex drive. The problem of female masochism has long been reinterpreted as being about power relationships in a patriarchal culture (Horney, 1967; Person, 1974; Miller, 1976). Women's 'low sex drive' is regarded by feminists to reflect both differences in male and female socialization and male sexual expression being held to be the norm of health (Person, 1980; Miller and Fowlkes, 1980; Tiefer, 1981).

Assuming, then, that a woman has adequate information about physiology, anatomy, and arousal, problems of sexuality may lie in the interpersonal realm, for example, not insisting on adequate stimulation, faking orgasms, attending to her partner's needs at the expense of her own; or they may reflect psychological fears or conflicts so that she is not able to experience desire, arousal, or orgasm. While a feminist therapist may work with a client individually to help her sort out in which areas her perceived sexual problems lie, an increasingly popular and effective form of treatment has been time-limited groups modeled on those described by Barbach (1975) for preorgasmic women.

Preorgasmic groups differ from traditional approaches to sex therapy in that the emphasis is on the woman's own needs, a partner is not necessary, and the approach and techniques are not limited to heterosexual women. The structure of the groups is typically six to eight members who meet twice a week with two coleaders for a period of about five weeks. In addition, members do one hour daily homework exercises that emphasize getting in touch with their bodies and sexual feelings and learning how consistently to achieve orgasm alone. Group discussions are combinations of education about physiology and anatomy and members' sharing experiences and using each other as sources of validation, permission, and support. As with so many other forms of group treatment for women, members usually experience a sense of relief and strength in sharing with other women both their pain and despair and their sense of exhilaration and liberation at being able to feel more autonomous and in control of their lives.

Clinical practice of feminist therapists

One outcome of the women's movement in the 1970s was the development of alternative feminist services that would be responsive to the needs of women: crisis centers, hotlines, shelters, counseling centers, women's schools, and therapy collectives. Many feminist therapists have chosen to work in these settings. From an analysis of the oppressive aspects of a hierarchical work structure and professionalism (Tennov, 1976), from community organizing and political work, and from their personal experience in consciousness-raising groups of sharing resources, power, and responsibility (Kravetz, 1980), some feminists have organized their service agencies on collective decision making, authority and financial bases. Decision making is by discussion and consensus, tasks and leadership roles are shared or rotated, and salary levels are based on need or the principle of equal pay for equal work rather than on the therapist's degree or level of advanced training. Although therapists must often sacrifice the status, pay, and security of jobs in mainstream mental health settings, working in collectives gives them far greater control over their working conditions and a way to integrate their feminist analysis, social and political activism, and practice on a day-to-day basis.

Feminist therapists who cannot or have chosen not to work in alternative settings have focused on educating and organizing around sexism in their workplaces. This may take the form of identifying institutional policies that support or encourage sexism or other forms of oppressive social relations, demanding and running different treatment services for women, confronting sexist or racist attitudes among colleagues, and organizing staff training and education programs. Schultz (1977) gives a good personal description of working to combat sexism and racism in a drug-treatment program.

Through participation in professional organizations and coalitions, feminist therapists, regardless of work setting, come together to share and coordinate resources. Training, supervision, and study groups allow them to raise consciousness about biases in their attitude and work, to keep abreast of theory development and research on the psychology of women, and to develop ways of incorporating these insights and new information into clinical practice.

Future directions

For the most part, feminist therapy has been oriented to women in their 20s, 30s, and 40s. The different needs of adolescents, older women, women in institutions (mental hospitals or prisons), and of the physically disabled need to be acknowledged and taken into account.

Although most feminist therapists have been in consciousness-raising and political groups and found the group experience itself to be invaluable to their personal and political development, little has been written on all-women therapy groups: how they develop and function, what concepts and techniques from traditional theory and research might be useful (or harmful), and when group or individual therapy is indicated. These topics need to be considered and explored.

While some feminist criticisms of therapy and psychological theory have noted heterosexist biases (Rich, 1980; Rohrbaugh, 1981), in feminist therapists' revisions this critical point has been for the most part ignored. Similarly, although feminists stress the importance of awareness of race and class, their importance in the practice of feminist therapy is virtually never discussed in published papers. These issues need to be integrated at the level of theory development for the implications they have on how therapy is practiced.

Feminist therapy is more developed in practice than in theory. Earlier we said this is because of its origins in social movement and its vital continuing connections with the reality of women's lives today. Feminists need to construct theory that maintains the dialectic between the individual and society (in contrast to most psychological theories of development that attend primarily to the individual), and that can bridge the gap.

References

Abbott, S., and Love, B. 1971.
    Is women's liberation a lesbian plot? In *Woman in Sexist Society*, eds. V. Garnick and B. K. Moran, pp. 601–21. New York: Basic Books.
American Psychological Association. 1975.
    Report of the task force on sex bias and sex-role stereotyping in therapeutic practice. *American Psychologist* 30: 1169–75.
Barbach, L. 1975.
    For Yourself: The Fulfillment of Female Sexuality. New York: Doubleday.
Boskind-Lodahl, M. 1976.
    Cinderella's stepsisters: A feminist perspective on anorexia nervosa and bulimia. *Signs: Journal of Women in Culture and Society* 2 (1976): 341–56.

Boskind-Lodahl, M., and Sirhan, J. 1977.
  The gorging-purging syndrome. *Psychology Today* 10, no. 10: 50–52.
Brodsky, A. M. 1980.
  A decade of feminist influence on psychotherapy. *Psychology of Women Quarterly* 4: 331–44.
Broverman, I. K., Broverman, D. M., Clarkson, F. E., Rosenkrantz, P. S., and Vogel, S. R. 1970.
  Sex role stereotypes and clinical judgments of mental health. *Journal of Consulting and Clinical Psychology* 34: 1–7.
Brown, P. 1973.
  Radical Psychology. New York: Harper Colophon Books.
Brownmiller, S. 1975.
  Against Our Will. New York: Simon & Schuster.
Bruch, H. 1973.
  Eating Disorders. New York: Basic Books.
Caust, B. L., Libow, J. A., and Raskin, P. A. 1981.
  Challenges and promises of training women as family systems therapists. *Family Process* 20: 439–47.
Chasin, R., and Grunebaum, H. 1980.
  A brief synopsis of current concepts and practices in family therapy. In *Family Therapy*, eds. J. Pearce and L. Friedman, pp. 1–15. New York: Grune & Stratton.
Chesler, P. 1972.
  Women and Madness. Garden City, N.Y.: Doubleday.
Chodorow, N. 1978.
  The Reproduction of Mothering: Psychoanalysis and the Sociology of Gender. Berkeley: University of California Press.
Chodorow, N. 1981.
  Oedipal asymmetries and heterosexual knots. In *Female Psychology: The Emerging Self*, ed. S. Cox, pp. 228–47. New York: St. Martin's.
du Bois, B. R. 1976.
  Feminist perspectives on psychotherapy and the psychology of women: An exploratory study in the development of clinical theory. Unpublished doctoral dissertation, Harvard University.
Ehrenreich, B., and English D. 1978.
  For Her Own Good: 150 Years of the Experts' Advice to Women. Garden City, N.Y.: Anchor.
Ernst, S., and Goodison, L. 1981.
  In Our Own Hands. Los Angeles: J. T. Parcher. Distributed by Houghton Mifflin, Boston.
Escamilla-Mondanaro, J. 1977.
  Lesbians and therapy. In *Psychotherapy for Women*, eds. E. I. Rawlings and D. K. Carter, pp. 256–65. Springfield, Ill.: Charles C. Thomas.
Fidell, L. S. 1981.
  Sex differences in psychotropic drug use. *Professional Psychology* 12: 156–62.
Framo, J. L. 1972.
  Symptoms from a family transactional viewpoint. In *Progress in Group and Family*

Therapy, eds. C. Sager and H. S. Kaplan, pp. 271–308. New York: Brunner/ Mazel.

Friedan, B. 1963.
The Feminine Mystique. New York: Norton.

Gilbert, L. A. 1980.
Feminist therapy. In *Women and Psychotherapy*, eds. A. M. Brodsky and R. T. Hare-Mustin, pp. 245–65. New York: Guilford.

Gomberg, E. S. 1981.
Women, sex roles and alcohol problems. *Professional Psychology* 12: 146–55.

Gurman, A. S., and Klein, M. H. 1980.
Marital and family conflicts. in *Women and Psychotherapy*, eds. A. M. Brodsky and R. T. Hare-Mustin, pp. 159–84. New York: Guilford.

Hare-Mustin, R. T. 1978.
A feminist approach to family therapy. *Family Process* 17: 181–94.

Herman, J. L. 1981.
Father-daughter Incest. Cambridge: Harvard University Press.

Horney, K. 1967.
Feminine Psychology. New York: Norton.

Jacoby, R. 1975.
Social Amnesia. Boston: Beacon.

Johnson, M. 1980.
Mental illness and psychiatric treatment among women: A response. *Psychology of Women Quarterly* 4: 363–71.

Kaschak, E. 1981.
Feminist psychotherapy: The first decade. In *Female Psychology: The Emerging Self*, ed. S. Cox, pp. 387–401. New York: St. Martin's.

Kravetz, D. 1980.
Consciousness-raising and self-help. In *Women and Psychotherapy*, eds. A. M. Brodsky and R. T. Hare-Mustin, pp. 267–83. New York: Guilford.

Leidig, M. W. 1981.
Violence against women: A feminist-psychological analysis. In *Female Psychology: The Emerging Self*, ed. S. Cox, pp. 190–205. New York: St. Martin's.

Libow, J. A., Raskin, P. A., Caust, B. L., and Ferree, E. F. 1981.
Feminist therapy and family systems therapy: Reconcilable or irreconcilable differences? Submitted for publication.

Litwok, E., Weber, R., Ruox, J., DeForest, J., and Davies, R. 1979.
Considerations in Therapy with Lesbian Clients. Philadelphia: Women's Resources.

Mandler, A. V., and Rush, A. K. 1974.
Feminism as Therapy. New York: Random House.

Miller, J. B. 1973.
Psychoanalysis and Women. New York: Brunner/Mazel.

Miller, J. B. 1976.
Toward a New Psychology of Women. Boston: Beacon.

Miller, P. Y., and Fowlkes, M. R. 1980.
Social and behavioral constructions of female sexuality. *Signs: Journal of Women in Culture and Society* 5: 783–800.

Millett, K. 1970.
Sexual Politics. Garden City, N.Y.: Doubleday.

Nellis, M. 1980.
The Female Fix. Boston: Houghton Mifflin.

Orbach, S. 1978.
Fat is a Feminist Issue. New York: Berkeley Medallion.

Pearce, J. K. 1980.
Ethnicity and family therapy: an introduction. In *Family Therapy: Combining Psychodynamic and Family Systems Approaches*, eds. J. K. Pearce and L. J. Friedman, pp. 93–116. New York: Grune & Stratton.

Person, E. S. 1974.
Some new observations on the origins of femininity. In *Women and Analysis*, ed. J. Strouse, pp. 289–302. New York: Grossman.

Person, E. S. 1980.
Sexuality as the mainstay of identity: Psychoanalytic perspectives. *Signs: Journal of Women in Culture and Society* 5: 605–30.

Rawlings, E. I., and Carter, D. K. 1977.
Psychotherapy for Women. Springfield, Ill.: Charles C Thomas.

Rich. A. 1980.
Compulsory heterosexuality and lesbian existence. *Signs: Journal of Women in Culture and Society* 5: 631–60.

Rohrbaugh, J. B. 1981.
The psychology of women, 1980. In *The Women's Annual, 1980 – The Year in Review*, ed. B. Haber, pp. 200–230. Boston: G. K. Hall and Co.

Sandmaier, M. 1980.
The Invisible Alcoholics: Women and Alcohol Abuse in America. New York: McGraw-Hill.

Sang, B. E. 1977.
Psychotherapy with lesbians: Some observations and tentative generalizations. In *Psychotherapy for Women*, eds. E. I. Rawlings and D. K. Carter, pp. 266–78. Springfield, Ill.: Charles C. Thomas.

Schneider, M. 1975.
Neurosis and Civilization. New York: Seabury.

Schultz, A. P. 1977.
Radical feminism: a treatment modality for addicted women. In *Psychotherapy for women*, eds. E. I. Rawlings and D. K. Carter, pp. 350–69. Springfield, Ill.: Charles C. Thomas.

Strouse, J. 1974.
Women and analysis: Dialogues on Psychoanalytic Views of Femininity. New York: Dell.

Szasz, T. 1961.
The Myth of Mental Illness. New York: Harper & Row.

Tennov, D. 1976.
Psychotherapy: The Hazardous Cure. Garden City, N.Y.: Anchor/Doubleday.

Tiefer, L. 1981.
Contemporary sex research. In *Female Psychology*, ed. S. Cox, pp. 23–41. New York: St. Martin's.

Walker, L. E. 1979.
  The Battered Woman. New York: Harper & Row.
Walker, L. E. 1980.
  Battered women. In *Women and Psychotherapy*, eds. A. M. Brodsky and R. T.
  Hare-Mustin, pp. 339–63. New York: Guilford.
Weisstein, N. 1971.
  Psychology constructs the female. In *Woman in Sexist Society*, eds. V. Gornick
  and B. K. Moran, pp. 207–84. New York: Basic Books.
Williams, E. F. 1976.
  Notes of a Feminist Therapist. New York: Praeger.
Wooley, S. C., and Wooley, O. W. 1980.
  Eating disorders: obesity and anorexia. In *Women and Psychotherapy*, eds. A.
  M. Brodsky and R. T. Hare-Mustin, pp. 135–58. New York: Guilford.

CHAPTER 17

From confinement to community: The radical transformation of an Italian mental hospital*

Anne M. Lovell

No possible alternative to the institution exists unless it is a constant
and practical critique of every form of institution: from the mental
hospital to the mental health system, from the center to the
neighborhood.[1]

In January 1977 the residents of Trieste, Italy, a seaside town near
the Yugoslavian border, learned that their local mental hospital, San
Giovanni, would be closed within the year. Visiting the hospital the
following summer, I was struck by the signs of an institution in
transformation. Going through the main gate, which is now always
open, I passed many empty buildings. Some residents were on their
way to work; older ones were walking up the hill to the hospital
cafe. A young woman in blue jeans stopped to ask directions, for it
is easy to get lost. Built in 1904 by the Austro-Hungarian empire,
the hospital consists of several buildings sprawled throughout a tree
and bush covered area, with a church and cemetery near the top.
The woman, so I later found out, was one of several 'hippies' (called
friccatone in Italian, from 'freak') left over from a music festival held
on the hospital grounds the week before, and sponsored by the local
alternative 'free' radio station. I soon developed a system for finding
my way to the ward where I was staying: walk past the mural that

* Originally published in *State and Mind*, vol. 6, no. 3, 1978, pp. 7–11. Reprinted
by permission of the author.

reads 'For Women Obedience Is No Longer A Virtue – We Want Bread and Roses,' take a left at 'Freedom Is Therapeutic', and finally turn right at 'Come And Get Your Electroshocks With Us. Signed: Pinochet.' Even the ward itself symbolized changes at the hospital. Upstairs a group of Southern Italian volunteers shared space with a community mental health team from France. Downstairs, in one of the last vestiges of the old institution, lived eight or so severely retarded men. Until recently some conscientious objectors had been teaching them basic skills to combat years of institutionalization.

The story of how Trieste's mental hospital was closed is but one chapter in an ongoing struggle against what was then defined as psychiatric oppression. It begins in the early 1960s, when Franco Basaglia, a Venetian psychiatrist, took over the direction of the Gorizia mental hospital in Northern Italy. The facts about Trieste will only take on real meaning if they are placed within the context of this anti-institutional movement in Italy. Let's briefly backtrack.

The work of opening up[2] the hospital at Gorizia[3] – what Basaglia considered a typical 'violent total institution'[4] housing Italian and Slavic patients from rural and working class backgrounds – represented a crisis in both the institution of Italian psychiatry and its body of knowledge. Little by little, over a seven-year period, Basaglia's team exposed the strictly custodial functions of the hospital, which they saw as being masked by an ideology of treatment. They created a type of therapeutic community, which differed markedly from its Anglo-Saxon counterparts. For example, the hierarchical and power relationships within the hospital were constantly challenged and linked to the class and power contradictions outside the hospital. (In American and British therapeutic communities the tendency is to mystify such relationships through the false assumption of consensus in decision-making and by blocking the dialectic between the inside and outside of the institution.) Indeed, to the Gorizians, the overturning and opening up of the mental hospital could only be understood as part of a broader class struggle in Italy as a whole. As a later evaluation of the Gorizia experiment stated, the separating out of custody and treatment

were not the *product of historical backwardness*, but an *element inherent to psychiatry*, and thus explainable only by bringing 'society' into the analysis and denunciation of the hospital. Both society as an organization of the state (given the function carried out by psychiatry in separating normal from abnormal, so as to control a rigidly prefabricated norm) and society as divided into classes (because of the fact that hospital inmates came from proletarian or subproletarian backgrounds).[5]

In 1968, *L'istituzione negata* ('The Institution Denied'),[6] edited by Franco Basaglia, was published. Widely read throughout Italy, not only did it document and analyze the changes at Gorizia; it also carried the anti-institutional debate into other areas: schools, universities, factories. By this time the local (Christian-Democrat) government in Gorizia was beginning to react against the psychiatric experiment. Partly as a result of this attack, a 'diaspora' followed, with mental health workers from Gorizia moving on to meet the challenge of mental hospitals in Perugia, Parma, Reggio Emilia, Arezzo and other cities. From this loose movement of psychiatric 'technicians,'[7] who linked their work to the strong Italian working class movement, developed a formal organization, Psichiatria Democratica. The technicians' alliances with unions and progressive political parties were also beginning to form the base from which Basaglia and his colleagues would eventually be able to influence national, as well as local, mental health reforms.

In 1971, Basaglia took over as the director of Trieste's psychiatric hospital. He had been invited by the local left-center government in a period when Italy was implementing nationwide health reforms. The nature of the general struggles had evolved since the Gorizia experiment. Economic and social marginalization was becoming a mass phenomenon; institutions and their relationships to production had been challenged by workers and students. The labor movement had moved from a focus on wage demands to challenging virtually all aspects of everyday life.

But there were administrative, judicial and ideological blocks to dismantling the hospital. Furthermore, the problem of transformation – of how to avoid changing a custodial-repressive institution into new apparatuses that would continue transmitting the dominant ideology, in perhaps more subtle and efficient ways – was monumental.

In July 1971 the hospital consisted of some 1,100 patients, most of whom had been involuntarily committed. There were nineteen wards, for whom nine doctors and almost 300 nurses were responsible. The hospital itself exerted traditional forms of control over the patients. With the threat of electro- and insulin shock therapy always in the background, such types of physical restraint as tying patients down to their beds, enclosure in a special cage consisting of wire netting around a bed, and isolation in a small unfurnished room, were used. The main gate to the hospital was always closed and any patient passing it had to show his or her documents. Doors on the wards were locked as much as possible, thus limiting the spaces in which inmates could move about. Outdoor areas were enclosed by walls and chicken wire.

Activities included primarily ergotherapy (occupational therapy): about 280 patients worked in hospital maintenance (carpentry, potato peeling, garbage collection) for about 600 lire (about $1.00 then) and three to four packs of cigarettes a month. Four times a year parties were held. One included a lottery; the prize was a cake baked in the hospital kitchen.

The first changes in the hospital were complex. Because it is impossible in one article to describe or analyze five years' work, I am forced to omit the many obstacles to the transformation, which included pressure from the courts, attacks by members of the neo-fascist political parties, and strikes. The nurses' strikes began around wage demands; but as nurses began to receive the brunt of the violent consequences of unlocking a ward that had been closed for years, they eventually struck to once again close the newly opened hospital. Nevertheless, it was easier to first overturn the hospital from within, where the people who desired the change were part of the institutional fabric.

Dismantling a hospital and rebuilding identities

The first step in destroying the mechanism of a total institution is to restore an identity to those persons who have been depersonalized, segregated, excluded, their histories wrested from them. Taking advantage of a provision in the 1968 mental health reform law, the Trieste team developed an administrative-judicial category known as *ospite* (guest). These were people who were formally discharged from the hospital but who, because of difficulties in finding lodging and a job (especially given Italy's economic crisis), slept on hospital grounds in autonomous living situations. (The architecture of the hospital, with its scattered buildings, is conducive to such a conversion into independent living spaces). The status of *ospite*, though, was given not as a reward for becoming 'rehabilitated,' but as a starting point from which to re-enter the material world. This status, along with a subsidy which the local (provincial) government eventually provided, gave ex-patients *contractual* power with which to re-enter the social realm, rather than maintaining them under some sort of guardianship. By the end of 1973, 300 people had become *ospite*.[8]

The old ergotherapy was replaced by a cooperative (Cooperative Lavorativa Unita), incorporated as such. Ex-patients and unemployed Triestini, who had never come into contact with psychiatry previously, but had heard of the cooperative through word of mouth, ran the organization, independently of the hospital. About sixty people work at least four hours a day, earning from 130,000 to 160,000 lire a month, about $148–182. (This figure can only be compared with salaries in Italy. A metal-mechanical worker, for example, earns 320,000 to 350,000 lire a month).[9]

The Trieste team believes that it is necessary to totally eliminate the mental hospital. In their view, people are psychiatrized – and indeed may develop symptoms interpreted as 'paranoid,' 'psychotic,' etc. – when their basic needs cannot be met. The mental hospital itself creates the 'illness' for those who, because of the seriousness of their disturbance and economic hardships, are expelled from society and relegated to an institution. The hospital is indeed viewed as a sickness factory: it identifies, codifies and expropriates suffering, crystallizing it into 'illness.' The work at Trieste was directed at progressively demystifying the role of the patient and his or her illness. The needs that lie behind the illness (for affection, food, decent housing, etc.) then become the focus that further work must address.[10]

From the beginning, electroconvulsive therapy was eliminated. Then, as the wards were opened up, more and more meetings were held among patients, personnel and outsiders. The object of meetings was to resolve the contradictions that existed at the origins of each patient's supposed 'illness.' If resolving the initial contradictions was not possible, a new mode of being with the patient would have to develop. One doctor described what this might mean: 'The most immediate, urgent responses were given to patients in crisis. A nurse might stay with a desperate patient for several hours, with a willingness to share his or her anguish, when it was impossible to give a concrete response.'[11] While the above example involves a nurse, it could apply as well to a psychiatrist or the volunteer or another patient.

The same doctor illustrates how patients are 'dialectized,' their history reconstructed. The patient is no longer seen as a series of characteristics in a psychiatric ward, but as a person with an understandable and very human story. I have summarized two of his examples:

> Victor broke a plate of noodles and gravy at lunch time, messing the patients around him, the walls, and the floor. The nurse said that he did this a couple of times a week, with no motive. Other staff agreed with their colleague, and Victor refused to answer the doctor's query. During a visit by Victor's sister, the doctor learned that Victor thought he had an ulcer and that he repeatedly asked for broth; but the nurse would answer that she did not have time to change his plate.
>
> Fedora, who was usually very quiet, suddenly broke into a state of physical and motor agitation one day, without apparent reason. The nurses confirmed that she was a 'cyclical case', and that that kind of behavior repeated itself from time to time. Despite medicine and attempts to understand her anxiety, nothing worked. She stayed awake all night, bothering everyone else on the ward. The next day, a Wednesday, she was talking calmly to her cousin who explained that the day before, she had gone to a funeral rather than visit Fedora as she had done every Tuesday for four years.[12]

The ward from which these examples are taken was one of the last vestiges of the old asylum to change at Trieste. After incidents such as the above, the nurses began to hold meetings with others on the ward team. Little by little, through the exchange of information, patients reappropriated their own history. For example, when patients themselves began to have meetings, they talked about their lives before institutionalization. This process, along with the cooperative and the creation of *ospite* status, began to build an identity for the patients.

As the wards were emptying out, more outsiders were coming into the hospital. For example, many well-known musicians, actors, and artists would perform on hospital grounds, attracting the townspeople of Trieste. On the other hand, patients would leave the institution, staying in regular hotels during their vacations, and a villa in a country village was opened for them. A group of artists worked for weeks with the patients, painting murals and building the famous blue horse, *Marco Cavallo*, which was to become a symbol of freedom not only for them, but for progressive mental health workers all over Europe. At one point, dozens of patients paraded into the streets of Trieste, with the huge papier mâché horse and 'outsiders' following them.

The setting up of a day care center in one of the former wards is a story worth noting. Someone who worked there wrote:

> The significance of the presence of children in a mental hospital lies . . . in the illusion that one day we'll stop building mental hospitals in and on the heads of children. The contradiction, the unacceptability, lies in the fact that 'normal' children are in a place for 'crazy' people. If this space, this reality, were not being used by the 'normal' adult to teach the child to be and become normal, then it could be used by the adult to learn to live with children, for a pedagogy that will serve the normal adult, bound to measure him or herself within the limits of his or her (negative) reason.[13]

Another outside presence consisted of the over 900 persons who visited or worked at the hospital in the early 1970s. They came from all over Italy; some had scholarships from the Trieste provincial government. The influence of the Trieste experience on other psychiatric institutions both in Italy and in other countries (France, Belgium, Mexico, Brazil, to name a few) is beyond measure.

From psychiatry to political struggle

Clearly the hospital could not be emptied out without creating external services. But the decision to work in the community was based on the idea that 'rehabilitation' must take place in the social spaces of the city, cradle of the original contradictions – and not in new mini-institutions. One danger of going into the community is that the culture and logic of the mental hospital extends itself, part of the content of an individual's suffering is identified and codified, and the person is directed into 'appropriate' institutional channels. New services become new tools for control. The question was whether or not situations would be created which would allow people to express their own needs in such a way as to find real and adequate responses that would not come from psychiatry, but ultimately from their social and political struggles.

In 1972 the hospital was divided into five areas corresponding to districts of about 60,000 people each, in and around the city. Unlike community mental health centers in the US, the staff for the sector (catchment area) had worked in the hospital and/or was the same as that in the corresponding hospital ward. Staff began community work before the centers were created, discharging patients, connecting with the political and social forces in the community, especially around health issues.

Today there are six such community centers, each very different from the others, having been developed in different times and situations. The Barcola Center, for example, is located on the seafront in an old but newly-painted two-story building. There is no rigid organization of work at the center except for a general meeting once a day. There are nine beds where people in crisis can stay overnight with no mandatory supervision or questions asked. Many elderly people who are not ex-patients come to Barcola simply to have lunch and meet with others. Most problems at Barcola are defined as social, not psychiatric. Women's groups are held weekly. The women at the center prepared a booklet, in which they drew up three composite case histories, based on women who had come to the center for help. The booklet explains how psychiatric 'symptoms' arose from oppression in the women's lives, specifically sexism. It urges women to struggle together rather than to turn to psychiatry.

One psychologist at the Barcola Center recounted the following anecdote to explain how its technicians work to help people solve real problems, rather than to create new ones. A man came to Barcola who appeared to be hallucinating. He claimed to see dark insects, and was very upset that he could not get rid of the sight of these bugs. Rather than interpret the 'case' as might be likely in an American mental health practice, a group of workers accompanied the man to his house – which they found to be in terrible disarray (he was too old to clean for himself very well) and filled with little black insects. 'Treatment' thus became a collective effort to clean the man's house, disinfect it and set up a system whereby someone would come weekly to help him with such chores. Not surprisingly, his 'hallucinations' disappeared.

As the changes described in the past few pages have given an identity to the patient, they have also meant a loss of the old identity for the technicians (doctors, nurses, social workers, psychologists). The roles change as the scientific ideology of psychiatry, and the hierarchical practice based upon it, are negated. The distance between roles (for example, nurse and doctor) is shortened and a certain interchangeability takes place. In the community, the nurse goes on call when the doctor isn't available and makes a decision regarding the dosage of a medicine. The sociologist stops research to go out and look for apartments. The doctor goes to lunch at a patient's house, or accompanies a group to the beach. Several Trieste technicians have explained that as the 'illness' is demystified, the work may seem to become simple, even 'banal.' The new spaces of intervention become the family, the workplace, the progressive political groups. Just as the ex-patient has now entered a social realm with the same crises everyone else in the city is facing, the patients' crises are no longer seen to lie within themselves. There are conflicts between different levels of power, different interests, different institutions. The Trieste technicians have written that, for them, the problem is how to proceed in a search for the possibility of acting as technicians within the class struggle.

Work in the community has also changed the mental hospital's relationship with other institutions. There is the continual struggle to oppose medical ideology and practice outside the circle of the Trieste group. For example, 90 percent of the emergency commitments to the hospital used to come from the emergency room of the general hospital. The mental hospital had been – as most are – a receptacle for contradictions that the other institutions could not handle; elderly people, for example, were sent there because other social services for them did not exist. The Trieste psychiatrists set up a 24-hour emergency service, in the emergency room. They refused to normalize situations by simply agreeing to commit someone, but instead called into question the expropriation of power from the potential patient. This caused everyone involved, including the doctors from the general hospital, to look for solutions other than the separation or exclusion of the suffering person. It also broke that alliance between the judiciary and psychiatry. The magistrate would prepare an order, the police would take the patient to the emergency room, expecting the doctor to make out a certificate for commitment. Even before the 24-hour emergency service was set up, the psychiatrists would 'free' the patients when they arrived by ambulance at the mental hospital. At one point, the district attorney even called a meeting with the local political forces, to patch the alliance back up.

Today twenty-two psychiatrists work at Trieste. Four work on an admissions ward, which they want to do away with eventually. The actual hospital population is down to 102. The crisis-intervention at the general hospital, which was not set up without problems (from outside the Trieste group), has reduced hospitalization by two-thirds.

The work of Trieste is far from finished. Each transformation opens up a new contradiction. For example, closing the hospital has caused many citizens to articulate their fears and wishes for control of patients, which some have hoped the centers would do. The centers are careful to refuse this role whenever its possibility crops up. They now work towards self-management of health rather than for its expropriation by technicians and their science. For ultimately, as Basaglia wrote:

> When a person is freed (from the institution), he or she once again gains rights (money, retirement, pension, etc.), begins to manage money, exits from a relationship of guardianship, enters once again into the 'social contract.' The person suffers but has the possibility of a social contract, is no longer disinherited, excluded, 'crazy.' The marginalized person thereby enters, however, the world of competition. Reality.[14]

Suffering has to be validated by *not* relegating it to a special place. The experience of Trieste is not a model to be replicated; that would be impossible. What we can learn from it are its messages and the questions it raises: How do we break with the systems of control and the logic of the institution without creating new mechanisms that institutionalize illness? How do we link the transformation of psychiatry to the larger social and political struggles against a system which by necessity, in its very existence, must create suffering?[15]

Notes

1 From a document, 'Alternative alle istituzioni' ('Alternatives to institutions'), prepared by Barcola Mental Health Center, 1977 (mimeographed).

2 Throughout this article 'opening up' refers to a process of both eliminating all forms of confinement within the institution and re-establishing a relationship with the external community.

3 Little exists in English on the Gorizia experience. See Donata Mebane-Francescato and Susan Jones, 'Radical psychiatry in Italy: Love is not enough,' in *Rough Times*, produced by Jerome Agel and the *Rough Times* Staff, 1973.

For a contextualization of Gorizia within a more recent overview of the radical psychiatry movement in Italy, see Paolo Crepet and Giovanni de Plato, 'Psychiatry without asylums: Origins and prospects in Italy,' *International Journal of Health Services*, Volume 13, Number 1, pp. 119–129, 1983.

4 Le istituzione de violenza, in *L'Istituzione Negata*, Franco Basaglia (editor), Turin: Einaudi, 1968.

5 Report of the Trieste Operators, compiled by Maria Grazia Giannichedda, 1977 (mimeographed), p. 4. This is the only official paper of the Trieste group publicly distributed before the end of 1977. The other articles and papers referred to in this article were written by individuals. For more on the ideas of the Trieste group during this time period, see Franco Basaglia, 'Breaking the circuit of control,' in *Critical Psychiatry*, David Ingleby, editor, New York: Pantheon, 1980.

6 This book was never translated into English. Selections will appear in the English language anthology of selected writings by Franco Basaglia Ongaro, edited by Nancy Scheper-Hughes and Anne Lovell, to be published by Columbia University Press in 1985.

7 Basaglia differentiates the technician, who works with practical knowledge, from the intellectual, whose realm is theoretical knowledge. Hence all mental health workers are technicians. Their role in refusing the dominant ideology which they are supposed to transmit, through their work is discussed in 'Peacetime Crimes,' by Franco Basaglia and Franca Basaglia-Ongaro, in Scheper-Hughes and Lovell, *op. cit.*

8 Much of the information on the old hospital and the statistics are taken from the above-mentioned Report of the Trieste Operators. Other information is based on two personal visits by the author, one in August 1972, the other in June 1977.

9 Robert Maggiori, 'Fermer l'asile: Un entretien avec Franco Basaglia,' ('Closing the asylum: A conversation with Franco Basaglia'), *Libération*, April 14, 1977, p. 4.

10   The hypothesis of our (mental health) center tends to create a discussion around radical needs, which are the need for community, for authentic interpersonal relationships, for structuring one's own identity and corporeal image. With the concept of radical, we are indicating needs that cannot be in the social market, which objectify themselves in exchanges not defined in an alienated way (in the long run, even the need for a home can become radical in a certain historical/economic context). [These needs] are closely linked to the man-nature dialectic, and induced in social development.

Edgardo Battiston and Mario Reali, 'Esperienze di trasformazione dall'ospedale al centro,' ('Experiences in the transformation from hospital to center') Cooperative Libraria, Centro Culturale Via Gambini, April 1977 (mimeographed), p. 10.

11 Renato Piccione and Tommsio Losavio, 'Cronicita e lungo degenza,' Cooperativa

Libraria, Centro Culturale Via Gambini, September 1977 (mimeographed), p. 5.

12 *Ibid*, p. 4.

13 Quoted by Franco Rotelli in 'Note ed appunti sulla pratica psichiatrica Triestes' ('Notes and precisions on psychiatric practice at Trieste'), Cooperativa Libraria, Centro Culturale Via Gambini, September 1977 (mimeographed), p. 4.

14 'Fermer l'asile . . .,' *op. cit.*

15 This article was written before the untimely death of Franco Basaglia in August of 1980. Many of his ideas and of the demands of Psichiatria Democratica were incorporated into the Law 180, passed in 1978. Considered the most radical mental health law in the Western World, the legislation prohibits new admissions to psychiatric hospitals, prohibits the construction of new hospitals, and encourages community care by what is essentially the criterion of the 'least restrictive alternative.' For more on the law, see Scheper-Hughes and Lovell, op. cit. Also, Paolo Tranchina, Guiliana Archi, and Maurizio Ferrara, 'The New Legislation in Italian Psychiatry: An Advanced Law Originating from Alternative Practice,' *International Journal of Law and Psychiatry*, Volume 4, pp. 181–190, 1981; Loren Mosher, 'Italy's revolutionary mental health law: An assessment,' *American Journal of Psychiatry*, Volume 139, pp. 199–203, February 1982.

CHAPTER 18

The collective approach to psychiatric practice in the People's Republic of China*†

Yi-chuang Lu

The striking changes created by the Chinese revolution are nowhere more apparent than in the treatment of the mentally ill. To understand these changes, how they came about, how effective or successful they are in the treatment of mental illness, one must understand how they are embedded in an overall, collective approach to overcoming obstacles and solving problems. Empirical analysis of the new approach to psychiatric practice in a society with a set of vastly different cultural values from those held previously – as well as from those held in Western society – may provide new perspectives on our established patterns of psychiatric treatment, as well as fresh views on formulating hypotheses and theoretical models of social and individual change. Elsewhere (Lu, 1977) I discussed how individuals in Chinese society at large are encouraged to work together for the common weal; how the energies of the entire society are directed through ideological statements, dramatic display and practical enforcement to concentrate on certain social values. Here, I focus on social values relevant to the treatment of mental illness: collective

* I am grateful to Arlene Kaplan Daniels and Rachel Kahn-Hut for their encouragements, critical comments, and generous and invaluable help in revising this paper. Acknowledgement is also made to Daniel X. Freedman, MD, Chair of the Department of Psychiatry of the University of Chicago for his support over the years.
† Reprinted from *Social Problems*, vol. 26, pp. 2–14, 1978, with permission of the Society for the Study of Social Problems and the Author.

responsibility; 'serving the people' and sharing; the minimization of elitism; and reaffirmation of faith in the human ability to transcend difficulties.

After the United States and China resumed cultural contacts in 1972, reports were published on psychiatry in China, such as those by Sidel and Sidel (March/April 1972); Sidel (June 1972); Ratnavale (1973); Kagan (1972); Kety (1976); and Lowinger (1976). While these describe observations made during short visits to one or more mental hospitals in China, none treat the dramatic changes of social values and their impact on Chinese psychiatric practice in a larger conceptual context. One way to explore the impact of social change on psychiatric practice is to analyze the working assumptions about the social self used in practice. It is generally recognized that a significant element in mental health or illness is the level of self-esteem an individual possesses (Sullivan, 1962; 1956). In any society, humans work to establish and maintain self-esteem and a consistent conception of themselves as well as a congruent view in the minds of others (Dai, 1963; Blumer, 1969; Schwartz and Stryker, 1970; Mead, 1934; Shitbutani, 1961; Rose, 1962). The interplay of social values and life careers plays an important role in establishing and maintaining this sense of self-esteem. This paper presents a study of an innovative, collective approach to promoting mental health which has emerged in a society with a relatively coherent, overall ideology which can be understood by us in terms of the concept of social self.

Method

This report of the impact of change of social values on the current practice of psychiatry in the People's Republic of China (PRC) is based on observations, interviews, and personal experience during my two visits to the PRC, the first for about a month in 1974 and the second for forty days in the fall of 1975. These materials are further supplemented by the data and insights acquired during a two-month stay in the fall of 1977. Moreover, this paper draws upon published and unpublished reports, informal interviews with visitors to China, as well as my own observations and interviews on pre-1949 Chinese society. In addition to general observations of social, interpersonal and emotional relationships of people in the society, I visited the Psychiatry Department and its wards of the Third Hospital of Peking University Medical School during all three China trips. I also visited the Tientsin Hospital for the Prevention and Treatment of Mental Illness (hereafter called Tientsin Mental Hospital) in 1974 and 1975; and the Shanghai Hospital for the Prevention and Treatment of Mental Illness (hereafter called Shanghai Mental Hospital) in 1975 and 1977. In addition to observing the social interactions among all people in these hospitals and current methods of therapy, including physical treatments such as acupuncture and traditional Chinese herbal medicine to relieve mental symptoms, I also interviewed patients, ex-patients and their families. Becoming a participant observer in various types of small group 'study sessions' in the mental hospitals afforded an unusual opportunity to learn about the collective approach to the treatment, rehabilitation and prevention of mental illness. It should be pointed out that both individual and collective approaches are used in China today. However, the present paper is concerned with only the collective approach, for it is a prominent feature in contemporary Chinese psychiatric practice that involves people at all levels of society.[1]

Social values and innovations in psychiatric practice
1. Collective responsibility as reflected in the integration between the mental hospital and the community

Collective or social responsibility in mental health means that lay people and medical personnel work together to help psychiatrists to identify early symptoms, prevent and treat mental illness. Before 1949, the facilities for psychiatric services were fragmentary, limited, and quite negligible relative to the needs of the huge population of the society. Psychotic patients received custodial care, though such care was only available to a small number of people in big coastal cities. The relation between patients and doctors or staff was hierarchical, patients being passive, dependent receivers of care. Any treatment available was rendered on an individual and isolated basis. There were very few trained psychiatrists or mental health workers.[2] However, during recent visits to Chinese mental hospitals, I found programs systematically organized according to new basic principles. An analysis of these principles shows that they have a foundation in new social values in the society.

One of the major new social values in China is collective or social responsibility. This is reflected in the implementation of a program to integrate the mental hospital with the community. In this program, instead of waiting for patients to come to the hospital, the psychiatrists and other mental health workers go out to the community for mental health education, early detection of mental symptoms, treatment and rehabilitation. They work closely with the family, the work unit, the school and the neighborhood committee. This practice is called 'the open-door hospital.' The services of 'bare-foot doctors' reach a wide population, especially in rural areas. The involvement of the society is also indicated by the practice whereby patients continue to receive their wages or salary during the period of hospitalization. Their jobs are held for their return. There also appears to be less division between the mental hospital and the outside world or between the life of the sick and the well. For example, the patients participate in the same political and social movements, such as 'struggle-criticism-transformation' as does everyone else in society. One of my visits to China coincided with a period of political-ideological movement taking place in the entire country. In the mental hospitals, I saw patients, as other people in society, holding small group sessions studying and discussing the traditional novel 'Water Margin' used in that movement, and branding it a negative example. The patients in the group pointed out that they should not surrender to their 'enemy,' their mental illness, like the people in the novel, who surrendered after a long and complicated struggle. Here traditional cultural resources were used to give the patients new interpretations applicable for solution of new problems in mental health. Hospitals do not separate the individual patients from the social groups and places where they had been unable to function. The rationale is that after discharge from the hospital patients will have to return to these groups to continue their lives; further, the support of the people outside is greatly needed to ensure the successful return of the patients. In addition, the social groups where the patients originally functioned are considered reliable reality-testing sources and are used to help patients to restore their health (and to realign patients with the consensus about reality). The patients' continued interactions with family members, co-workers, and neighbors are assumed to provide patients with opportunities to learn consensual reality. These figures are considered important, especially since the patients' perceptions of the motives of their significant others may be a source of difficulty in relationships. Significant others who were a source of the patients' difficulties are thus expected to play a significant role in assisting patients to learn consensual reality.

Psychiatrists in mental hospitals explained how members of these social groups, such as patients' co-workers, were invited to reassure paranoid patients about motives that were misinterpreted and ultimately incorporated into the patients' delusions. To this end it is common for those people who are important in the life of a patient to come to the hospital to participate in study sessions with patients and staff. At the same time, the hospital staff also helps those from the outside to understand the patients' illnesses and how to manage them. Ex-patients of the hospital, as liaison persons between the life outside and inside the hospital, also return to the hospital and tell new patients about their experiences during their previous hospitalizations and after discharge. Those returning also serve as models for hospitalized patients to follow in their path back to health. This integration between the hospital and society is considered an important means of helping patients to learn how to manage their objective situation in life and develop a sense of reality.

In order to see how involving the community in prevention, treatment and rehabilitation of mental illness operates, an example of a specific program in an urban community and one in a rural area will be described. The program in the city of Tientsin is called 'The Link Between Mental Hospital and the Community.' It is the policy of the Tientsin Mental Hospital to work closely and regularly with all institutions in the city where there are large numbers of workers. A team composed of psychiatrists, a nurse, a worker and the chief administrator from the Tientsin Mental Hospital showed me how the hospital coordinated its work with a factory by taking me to a textile factory of four thousand workers of which six workers had become patients at this hospital. I interviewed the factory's administrator, a general physician from the factory's clinic, the section head, the supervisor of an ex-patient, this patient's co-worker, and finally the patient, Mr C. himself. All those mentioned had been involved in Mr C.'s rehabilitation and the prevention of a relapse. Together with the psychiatric team from the mental hospital, the factory team described to me the close coordination between these two institutions in working with ex-patients, as well as in the detection and prevention of mental illness among the factory personnel. The following is an outline of the kind of cooperation these two institutions were said to enjoy:

(1) Before 1969, that is before the establishment of the new program initiated at the time of the Cultural Revolution, workers who became mentally ill were simply sent to mental hospitals for treatment. Beginning in 1969, instead of waiting for factory workers to become so ill that they had to be admitted to the hospital, doctors and mental health workers began to come to the factory for preventive work.

(2) The major role of the psychiatric team in the factory is to educate members of the factory about psychiatry, on how to observe the onset of symptoms and then to deal with them.

(3) During earlier years of this program, the psychiatrists visited the factory regularly once a week to teach psychiatry as well as to treat patients. As time passed, and as the factory personnel learned about the detection of symptoms and management of emotional problems, the psychiatrists come less frequently. However, they do come to the factory any time they are asked, including holidays. Furthermore, they make follow-up visits to the homes of ex-patient-workers from time to time.

(4) The factory and the hospital routinely communicate with each other about current problems and the condition of ex-patient-workers. As soon as there is a relapse, psychiatrists as well as the ex-patients' supervisors and co-workers visit the ex-patient at home. In addition to insuring that former patients take the prescribed medicine, a major objective of these visits is to provide the patients with social and emotional support. Ex-patients also return to the hospital once a month to attend recovery-group meetings, some of which I had also observed.

The program, in extending mental health care to the rural areas, relies even more heavily on the involvement of the people in the community who are peasants. It emphasizes both prevention and home delivery services. From the descriptions provided, a glimpse of such a program administered by the Department of Psychiatry of the Third Hospital of Peking University Medical School (a training center) will illustrate this type of program, now implemented with varying degrees of success in different parts of the country. The psychiatrists of this hospital informed me that the program was launched in June 1974. It covered twelve communes in the Hai Tien area with a population of 189,915 persons. The hospital provided three to four months psychiatric training to the general physicians of the health stations in all the communes. But the most important target of the training program was the large number of 'barefoot doctors' who were themselves peasants in the local community. All the staff, including the psychiatrists and even the chief of the Psychiatry Department, took turns going down to the countryside to 'labor together' with peasants. In the health stations of their communities, the 'barefoot doctors' were given lectures on psychiatry, especially on how to detect emotional and mental symptoms and to provide preventive and positive mental health measures. They were also taken to this hospital in Peking periodically for clinical training on mental examinations, diagnosis, and treatment by the psychiatrists. Since these 'barefoot doctors' work regularly on the farms, know the families well and enjoy their trust, they were considered among the most effective mental health workers. After the 'barefoot doctors' had furnished the psychiatrists with information on peasants seen to need psychiatric attention, the psychiatrists, accompanied by the former, went to the patients' homes and the community to conduct mental examinations and diagnoses. Then a mental health-illness census was taken in each of the twelve communes. Out of the total population of 189,915 surveyed in these communes, 1166 people, as of June, 1976, have been found to be suffering from some mental health problems. Treatment was given to these patients as far as conditions permitted. For example, of the 300 schizophrenic patients, a systematic treatment lasting four months was given to 211 cases. Most of them (64 percent) were reported recovered or showed marked improvement and functioned well in the community. On the basis of experience gained from this program, a method known as 'Hospital Bed at Home' was developed. Under this method, as many patients as possible were treated by the psychiatrists and staff in the patients' homes rather than in the hospital. The injection of a tranquilizer said to be effective for a period of two weeks had helped a great deal in the care and therapy at home. (I was told that detailed findings are to be published in the future.) This program has gained strong support from the peasants. It is not only economical, but seems to generate a feeling that others are concerned for them, and so the peasants experience an increased sense of self-esteem.

2. The application of 'serving the people' and sharing to psychiatric practice

While the notion of collective or social responsibility emphasizes how the hospital and community are integrated and work together, the value of 'serving the people' stresses the notions of sharing weal and woe and of subordinating individual interests for the common good. This value finds its expression most visibly in the interpersonal relationships among people in mental hospitals that I visited. The dedication of hospital personnel to 'serving the people' is reflected in their patience and sacrifice in the 'heart-to-heart talk' with patients. This term refers to the very intimate, warm, personal, and trusting conversations and relationships between a patient and a psychiatrist or a hospital worker. In cases of extremely withdrawn patients who are not very responsive to others, the psychiatrists are said even to move into the patients' ward, to sleep there, eat there, and focus on the task of helping patients emerge from that mental state. In addition to other methods of treatment, this 'heart-to-heart talk' is also used with paranoid patients who refuse to eat.

The notion of 'serving the people' is injected into the Chinese understanding of psychiatric problems and behaviors related to these problems. An example is the emergence of a new attitude toward suicide. It is said that suicide for personal reasons is considered an act of betrayal to the revolution or welfare of others, the common goal of the society. Positive efforts are made to integrate patients into affiliative social groups which give a sense of importance and usefulness (Taipale, 1973). In addition to the acupuncture and medical therapies they receive, patients are organized into groups to study Chairman Mao's article 'Serving the People,' and to help each other to see the importance of serving others rather than brooding about one's own needs. Patients are also encouraged to help each other to see how much they are needed in common efforts to build a new society.

We do not know how effective this method of treatment is. But it is reasonable to suggest, following Durkheim (1951), that this approach does provide patients with a sense of participation, belonging and mutual support in a group setting. It is at least an attempt to break down the patients' sense of isolation or egoism, to show others' concern for them and to restore their sense of self-worth. Equally important, it seeks to redirect the attention of patients away from themselves and towards others, and to replace self obsession with a commitment to a common objective greater than self. Personal problems which seem insoluble are made to look insignificant beside larger problems of the society which have been solved by determination and common effort – as the patients and all other Chinese are assured. Instead of directing their hostility toward self-destruction, the patients are urged to direct their energy into constructive endeavors which give them new hope. For this agreed objective of the society is meaningful to the patient. The feeling of being able to contribute to the welfare of others evokes a sense of importance and self-esteem.

The application of the value of sharing and mutual help to the hospital life finds expression in the organization of patients into various study groups. In every small group of eight to ten patients, leaders are elected to conduct such meetings. In all the mental hospitals I visited I observed a high degree of social interaction between patients and staff, and among patients themselves. The strong emphasis on sharing and mutual help among patients themselves for therapy can be seen in the following example of a small group discussion I attended, part of what is known as 'Collective Psychotherapy,' conducted on the psychiatric wards of the Third Hospital of Peking University Medical School. In the meeting room, a big blackboard sign, 'The Study Session to Raise the Level of Therapeutic Effectiveness,' hung on the wall. There were twelve male paranoid schizophrenic patients with three therapists who played a 'supporting-leading role,' sitting among the patients around a table. Each patient in this meeting reported to the group his own symptoms and problems. Then these symptoms and problems were commented on and analyzed by other patients in this group. From time to time, when the situation required, the therapists helped patients to lead the discussion or commented on the patients' statements; but discussion was mainly carried by patients themselves. At the beginning of the group meeting, I was surprised to hear patients casually using psychiatric terms and concepts such as visual and auditory hallucinations, delusions and ideas of reference. Later I learned that before a small group of discussion took place, patients were given lectures on psychiatry. This process is called 'transmitting psychiatric knowledge to patients.' The existence of such classes is an indication that patients are considered to have an important role in their own treatment. In this study group, I found the patients articulate, frank, and ready to speak their minds. After the rest of the patients analyzed a patient's symptoms and problems, or offered 'criticisms,' the patient defended his own position vigorously. This back-and-forth debate on one patient's problem continued for a while before turning to the next patient. Occasionally, the positions of some patients were somewhat modified after the debates, but they generally tried hard to defend themselves. I was amazed at how easily patients handled the criticisms of others. When they did not agree with others' statements they did not appear offended. This imperturbability may come from the training the Chinese receive from childhood on criticisms, self-criticism and transformation sessions.

While patients in the small group discussion might be blind to evidence of their own delusions and problems, their analysis of their fellow patients' problems and delusions seemed quite reasonable. After attending this session and other group meetings such as rehabilitation sessions, I could understand why this type of group discussion, when used repeatedly, is effective in treatment and rehabilitation (Lowinger, 1976). Patients value the opinions of peers who share similar experiences with them. The relative objectivity possible in looking at somebody else's problems, and the frankness encouraged in expressing opinions about them as well as the informal and subtle pressures interactants may exert on each other, all may eventually contribute to the modification of and change in individual delusions. While milieu therapy is a common concept in American psychiatry, it is not systematically practiced. This coordinated stress on the patients themselves for the treatment of mental illness, as distinguished from major reliance on professional psychiatric services, is a unique feature of psychiatric practice in present-day China.

3. The 'minimization of elitism' as observed in the interpersonal relationships in mental hospitals

The rigid hierarchy of medical-psychiatric practice is one of the major barriers to any patient-oriented therapy. The traditional concept of the doctor-patient relationship as well as the traditional hierarchical social roles between members of different categories in Chinese mental hospitals have undergone great change (Ratnavale 1973: 1083). After the Cultural Revolution, intensive efforts were made to minimize the differential social roles between doctors and staff, between doctors and patients and between staff and patients. Nurses and workers have been given greater influence and importance and they play a more active role in the management of the hospital. Although the major responsibility of the maintenance work of the hospital wards rests on the workers, to narrow the social distance between doctors, nurses, workers and patients, people in all these categories share some maintenance activities from time to time, as people from all professions in the society engage in manual labor at one time or another.

The traditional doctor-patient role relationship in which the doctor is treated as the powerful active person and the patient the powerless, passive receiver has been greatly modified. Instead of relying heavily on the individual psychiatrist's responsibility in treatment (as in traditional psychiatric care), the patients are encouraged to investigate their own illness and symptoms, and to understand their treatment. In the mental hospitals I visited, the psychiatrists said to me: 'Now the physicians and patients are comrades and therefore they are equal. They work together to find out the best ways to help patients get well.' While such statements of ideology are only to be expected, the striving for egalitarian role relationships between doctors, staff, workers and patients can be seen in action in the mental hospitals. For example, in a large recreation room of the Shanghai Mental Hospital, there were recreational activities occurring at one end of the auditorium while psychiatrists and nurses in white medical gowns performed side by side with patients on the stage at the other end. They sang, played various kinds of musical instruments, and danced for an audience of about one hundred plus a few medical staff and workers. At the right corner under the stage, there was an orchestra of eight persons accompanying the singing and dancing or playing a solo piece. Again, this orchestra included medical staff, nurses and workers, as well as patients, with a recreational therapist as the conductor. A patient served as the Master of Ceremonies of the performances on the stage. From time to time, a patient from the audience stood up, announcing that he or she represented certain patient groups, and requested that certain doctors or patients from a particular male or female ward perform. Generally, those requests were met. The psychiatrist who guided me said that such a practice promoted positive relationships between patients and doctors and staff and it increased the patients'

confidence in doctors and the hospital, one of the most basic requirements in the process of the treatment of mental illness.

4. Faith in human ability, social roles and the mental hospital

How does strong faith in human beings and in human ability to
change human behavior through education and changing social roles
affect psychiatric practice? In mental hospitals, the therapeutic
process concentrates on the conscious mind rather than on changing
unconscious motivations. Freudian theory is not considered applicable to Chinese cultural and social conditions. In answering my
questions about the significance of the unconscious, the psychiatrists
stated that they had not done research on this subject. But they held
the view that the conscious and unconscious should not be separated,
and that human behaviors are not so dominated by the unconscious
as some believe. Consequently, conscious human efforts are very
important in modifying human motivations and behavior. In the
mental hospitals, therefore, the stress is on will power and determination. Patients are encouraged to have 'revolutionary optimism'
and confidence in the human ability to achieve the objective of
regaining health. In the discussion groups, patients are therefore
urged to study an article by Chairman Mao entitled: 'The Foolish
Old Man Who Removed the Mountains.' This is a story of an old
man who had two mountain peaks on his property. With great determination, he led his children in digging up these mountains. When
his neighbors laughed at him, he replied that when he died his
children would carry on; when they died, there would be his grand-
children, and so on. He was unshaken in his conviction. Finally God
was moved by this determination and sent two angels to carry away
the mountains. Then the late Mao Tse-Tung said: 'Our God is none
other than the masses of the Chinese people. If the people dig
together, why can't that be done?' (Mao, 1972). The patient-leaders
in the discussion groups exhort the patients to learn this optimistic
spirit and determination and put them into practice.

   This inculcation in the patients of faith in conscious human efforts
to regain health is coupled with another practice which seems very
effective in changing the low self-concepts of patients. This practice
involves the recognition of the importance and the use of what we
may call social role and role model in the treatment of mental illness.
My observations of this practice in Chinese mental hospitals show

how hospital personnel can shift (at what is deemed the appropriate time) the patients' social role from that of passive recipient to that of active participant. The opportunity to become active increased self-esteem and created models for other patients to follow. For example, in the wards of the Tientsin Mental Hospital, I noticed some patients, called 'Red Sentries,' who wore red arm bands and actively worked with and helped other patients. After talking to them and the psychiatrists, I learned that as hospitalized patients improved, they were selected to help in the care of sicker or newly arrived patients. These 'Red Sentries' were identified by the psychiatrists and hospital personnel as the backbone of the hospital. They were considered important members in the therapeutic team because they served as good models for sicker patients to follow and helped them to have determination to get well. Their arm bands are symbols of prestige among other patients. The importance of having 'model-patients' to promote the morale of other patients is supported by my observations of American patients in a chronic schizophrenic research unit of a United States state hospital. Although no systematic use was made of the event, patients there were very much encouraged and seemed more hopeful after noticing a chronically catatonic, stuporous patient emerging from that state (Lu, 1970). In Chinese mental hospitals, another role assigned to the improved patients is the role of promoter of mental health education, that is, they are organized into publicity teams to promote mental health education in the general population and to lessen the stigma traditionally attached to the mentally ill. The patients are also encouraged to serve as guides to members of the patients' families or to clinic patients in the hospitals, in explaining hospital rules, routines and procedures. Whenever feasible, everyone in the hospital is given a meaningful role and is made to feel useful to others.

The implications of Chinese psychiatric practice: New perspectives on treatment and on theoretical formulations

In this paper, an attempt has been made to discuss the effect of social values in the present Chinese society on the methods and approaches to psychiatric treatment. The common goal to promote mental health by hospital staff, by the community, by the rest of the society, and (most important) by the patients may provide all those concerned with a sense of group participation and group belonging which may broaden individuals' self-identity and enhance their strength and feeling of self-esteem. This sense of national community is a strong driving force in promoting the mental health program in China. In the Chinese psychiatric community, a supportive and therapeutic system has been established parallel to the supportive culture of the society. Instead of depending completely on mental health professionals, the system uses a social network approach which relies heavily on the communities, on others significant to the patients in all areas of their lives, as well as on the patients themselves for support in modifying and changing attitudes and behavior. The provision of social roles to furnish a sense of usefulness and to offer role-models for other patients, the reduction of formerly wide differences in social roles among members of different categories in the mental hospitals, the emphasis on the positive aspects of human nature, the attempts to promote optimistic attitudes toward life – all may increase the patients' confidence in themselves and in others, decrease their sense of isolation, and enhance their self-esteem and feeling of security. Finally, in the mental hospitals, the use of education in the form of lectures and small group discussions, as well as persuasion and moralistic reasoning to modify and change patients' views of life and behavior, is another characteristic feature of the collective approach to psychiatric practice in China.

To examine the implications of this approach for psychiatric practice and to broaden our views on our current assumptions underlying psychiatric treatment in the United States, the case of an ex-schizophrenic patient of the Tientsin Mental Hospital, whom I interviewed, is presented. Mr C., a custodian of machinery tools in the textile factory that I visited, was described by the psychiatrists and personnel of the factory as an extremely ambitious, narrow-minded man greatly concerned with his 'self-regard.' He worked very hard and always wanted to do more and better than others. By February 1975, when the time approached for colleagues in his section to vote for the 1974 award to the one who had contributed most to the *collective achievement* of this section, he began to work extraordinarily hard, and became extremely competitive with others in the section. He quarrelled with his fellow workers, suspecting them of gossiping about and laughing at him behind his back. He worried that his work would not be better than that of others in his section and would prevent him from getting the award. The section head and the patient's supervisor noticed that Mr C. could no longer concentrate on his work and often stared into space. At the same time, he was very anxious and said he suffered from insomnia. To prevent his condition from deteriorating, in addition to calming him with traditional Chinese herbal medicine, a psychiatrist and the patient's supervisor went to talk and reason with him. The supervisor who had always appreciated his work and considered him one of the 'backbones' of his section assured him that others in the factory were well aware of his hard work. He also praised him for his enthusiasm. At the same time, the supervisor reduced the patient's work load and advised him to take it easy. Both the supervisor and the psychiatrist also explained to the patient that to achieve the common objective to build a new society, one should not be so extremely concerned with one's own fame or work only for one's gain, but should devote oneself to serving other people, in this case by promoting collective achievement in the factory. Mr C. was urged to study Chairman Mao's writings 'Serve the People' and 'On Contradiction.' Furthermore, to curb Mr C.'s tendency to drift away from people, and to become obsessed with autistic thoughts, they also encouraged his fellow workers to talk to him and involve him in their social activities. Co-workers who were the patient's objects of suspicion showed their understanding by praising his contribution to production, while assuring him that they were not gossiping about him. The psychiatrist, the supervisor and colleagues visited the patient's home to show their concern and give further support. After a few days, the patient's anxiety diminished and he was able to continue his work and to function normally. Instead of worrying about his personal success and being obsessed with a fierce drive to compete with co-workers, he became concerned with the achievement of the group. It was reported that his distrust of his co-workers gradually subsided, his relationship with them was greatly improved, and he could sleep well. When I interviewed him, we had a very cheerful and friendly conversation.

An examination of this case suggests that the major strain leading to the patient's mental symptoms is related to problems of work performance. The Chinese psychiatrists also reported that instead of stresses relating to problems prevalent in pre-1949 society, such as unemployment, economic difficulties, prostitution, venereal diseases, family difficulties especially involving in-laws in the patriarchal family, the major strains leading to mental symptoms in present day Chinese society tend to consist more of problems involving performance in school and in work. This new tendency, it seems to me, has parallels in American society. My findings on American schizophrenic patients indicate that their major role strains center on their inability to cope with the demands or high social expectations for achievement, independence and work performance (Lu, 1970). While the major strains of both these groups are shown to center on their inability to cope with situations related to work performance, a closer analysis of the problems of the patients from these two very different cultures suggests that the dynamics of stress point in opposite directions. In the American individualistic and achievement-oriented society, schizophrenic patients find themselves unable to cope with demands for independence, for fulfilling personal ambition and achievement. Conversely, in present Chinese society where collective achievement, mutual dependence, public service and group responsibility are valued, the dynamics of stress seem to stem from the patient's failure to cope with cultural demands to minimize the individual competition with others for personal gain and recognition and the related failure to subordinate private to public interest. In other words, different cultural values in the two societies may produce different conflicts around which the patients' difficulties arise. Disparate values may also affect the differences in the psychiatric treatments used in these societies.

An examination of the case of Mr C. suggests how different are treatments prescribed in China from those used in the United States. While Chinese psychiatrists do counsel their patients on how to strike a proper balance between public and personal interest, the patients are generally directed to identify with the interest of the group. Therefore, instead of supporting the patient's efforts to achieve private ambition and promote personal growth as American therapists might do, Chinese doctors discourage private ambition and desire for personal gain, while urging identification with the collectivity and its common goals. While American therapists in Western society, which strongly emphasizes personal strength, might perceive the support provided the patient by the Chinese psychiatrists, the supervisor, the patient's colleagues and others as too protective, inhibiting independence, it appears that the enormous support this Chinese patient received helped him to abandon his symptoms and resume former functioning. Even though he did not win the prize, Mr C. continued to work satisfactorily.

As fundamentally different as are Chinese and American societies and their methods of treating psychiatric illnesses, the common objective of therapy in both societies is to enable the patient to live, to work, to function and to think as effectively as possible in terms of each society's values, norms, expectations and demands. In the process of treatment, the doctors, social workers, nurses, psychologists, other therapists and personnel inevitably transmit their social values, norms, expectations and demands to the patient. This obvious point has been underscored in China by explicitly social and 'political' methods of treatment, whereas it is obscured in the United States by preoccupation with professional techniques in therapy.

Once we are aware of this inevitably value-laden aspect of therapy, we recognize that if cultural norms of independence, personal achievement and success are pushed too far, a basic aspect of human need – the interdependence of human beings on each other – may be neglected. In his work *The Pursuit of Loneliness*, Slater contends that the human need for interdependence is suppressed in American society out of commitment to individualism (independence). But the more people have succeeded in denying the reality of human interdependence, the more they 'have felt disconnected, bored, lonely, unprotected, unnecessary and unsafe.' Consequently, people don't know who they are and what they need. For, he points out, 'Part of the individual is after all committed to the group. Part of him wants what the group wants; part does not.' And any group sentiment expresses some part of our being (Slater, 1976). A consequence of this denial of the reality of human interdependence is demonstrated in the findings of my research on the major role strains of the American schizophrenic patients, as noted earlier.[3] Viewed from a cross-cultural perspective, for effective functioning of a society and the emotional health of its members, certain measures of both independence and social (collective or group) support are essential. These two human needs are not mutually exclusive, but the emphasis on one or the other depends on the cultural value-orientation of the society.

The examination of the Chinese collective approach to mental health care also suggests that before breakthroughs in etiology of major psychoses are achieved, and more effective theoretical models are developed on which to base therapies, we need to explore other etiological assumptions to help develop new theories in psychiatric practice. For example, in his hypotheses on mental illness, Kohn has suggested that schizophrenia is produced not just by genetic vulnerability, but by its interaction with stress and with one's conceptions of the external world and of self that define one's stance toward reality (Kohn, 1976). This hypothesis points out the need to consider the role of social self and social organization and their interactions with genetic vulnerability for an understanding of schizophrenia. In our search for effective psychiatric practice, it is therefore all the more necessary to explore these two concepts further (whatever the genetic vulnerability) so that new theoretical models on psychiatric practice may develop.

Concluding remarks

In this paper, a description and analysis of the collective approach to promoting mental health in China has been presented. A review of the Chinese collective approach from a comparative cultural perspective reveals: (1) disparate cultural values in different societies may produce different conflicts giving rise to patients' difficulties. They may affect differences in the psychiatric therapies used as well as in the effectiveness of treatment; (2) the values, norms, and expectations of different societies are transmitted to the patients by the therapists and other psychiatric personnel in the process of treatment in the respective societies.

The Chinese society, polity and specific policies in various areas have been undergoing rapid change and will continue to do so. Whatever the future may bring, the Chinese experiment in the collective approach to the treatment of mental illness and its results as reported in this paper remain a significant part of our experience in the perennial search for solutions to one of human beings' most intractable problems. The reported results of the Chinese approach to psychiatric treatment may owe much to the opportunity to develop a therapeutic policy which is consistent with the larger coherent goals of the society. As Chinese society, both in the past and at the present time, rests on a fundamentally different order of values and principles from American society, the costs and benefits, problems and achievements of the two systems of treatment may well be the opposite of each other. But from a cross-cultural perspective, what some Western analysts see as the restriction of individuals' autonomy and independence may offer the Chinese an opportunity to establish, restore and increase self-esteem as well as to acquire meaning in life through rewards accompanying services to the common goal (Record and Record, 1976).

Notes

1 In Chinese society, psychiatric practice, like other aspects of life today, has been undergoing rapid changes. The social movement to achieve 'The Four Modernizations,' particularly the new programs to emphasize science and technology, to develop basic scientific research and to overhaul the educational system launched in late 1977 and 1978, can be expected to affect psychiatric practice in some way. Although the basic principles in psychiatric practice are expected to continue, we must remember that this report describes practices which obtained in the years I visited China. Furthermore, it deals mainly with treatment relating to psychoses and is not intended to be a comprehensive discussion of less severe forms of illness such as neurosis. In spite of the obvious limitations of these data, the description and analysis contained in this paper represent efforts to understand Chinese practices at this stage of China's cultural contacts with other parts of the world, by a person who had conducted research on psychiatric patients in both pre-1949 China and thereafter in the USA.

2 These descriptions come from personal observations and experiences while working at the Peking Municipal Psychopathic Hospital as well as in the Peking Union Medical College Hospital in pre-1949 China (see also Ho, 1974).

3 The need of mental patients for group support and a sense of belonging is also reflected in the serious problems arising out of the program implemented in the United States in recent years to return mental patients to communities which do not provide them with adequate support. It was reported that consequently patients were left on their own in the community and 'lost their only real community, the hospital' (Robert, 1978). An example of the strong rejection of mental patients by the community can be seen in the recent protest of a Chicago neighborhood where the Illinois Department of Mental Health and Developmental Disabilities plans to transfer some patients to a community center (Stevens, 1978).

References

Blumer, Herbert 1969.
  Symbolic Interaction. New Jersey: Prentice-Hall.
Dai, Bingham 1963.
  Failure in psychotherapy: Persons and Process: A sociopsychiatric approach. Pp. 7–14 in *Annals of Psychotherapy*. Vol. 4, no. 2, monograph 6, New York: The American Academy of Psychotherapies.

Dunham, H. Warren 1976.
Social Realities and Community Psychiatry. New York: Human Sciences Press.
Durkheim, Emile 1951.
Suicide. Chicago: Free Press.
[1897]
Ho, D. Y. F. 1974.
Prevention and treatment of mental illness in the People's Republic of China.
American Journal of Psychiatry, July.
Kagan, Leigh 1972.
Report from a visit to the Tientsin Psychiatric Hospital. New York, China Notes,
National Council of Churches 10 (Fall): 37–39.
Kety, Seymour S. 1976.
Psychiatric concepts and treatment in the People's Republic of China. Pp. 36–45
in Robert Cancro (ed.), *Annual Review of the Schizophrenic Syndrome,* 1974–75.
New York: Brunner/Mazel Publishers.
Kohn, Melvin 1976.
Social class and schizophrenia: A critical review and a reformulation. Pp. 311–340
in Robert Cancro (ed.), *Annual Review of the Schizophrenic Syndrome,*
1974–1975. New York: Brunner/Mazel Publishers.
Lowinger, Paul 1976.
Psychiatry in China: A Revolutionary optimism. Medical Dimensions 5, 11: 25–31.
Lu, Yi-chuang 1961.
Mother-child role relations in schizophrenia: A comparison of schizophrenic
patients with non-schizophrenic siblings. *Psychiatry* 24 (May): 133–142.
1962. Contradictory parental expectations in schizophrenia. *AMA Archives of
General Psychiatry* 6 (March): 219–234.
1970. Schizophrenia and social self. Unpublished manuscript.
1977. The Chinese experiment: Changing social values. Unpublished manuscript.
Mao, Tse-tung 1972.
The foolish old man who removed the mountain. Concluding speech at the
Seventh National Congress, Peking, China (in Chinese).
Mead, George H. 1934.
Mind, Self and Society. Part III. Chicago: University of Chicago Press.
Ratnavale, David N. 1973.
Psychiatry in Shanghai, China: Observations in 1973. *American Journal of
Psychiatry* 130, 10 (October): 1082–1087.
Record, Jane Cassels and Wilson Record 1976.
Totalist and pluralist views of women's liberation: Some reflections on the Chinese
and American settings. *Social Problems* 23, 4: 402–414.
Roberts, Steven V. 1978.
Mentally ill: What about the half-way home idea? The *New York Times,* March
19: 10E.
Rose, Arnold 1962.
Human Behavior and Social Processes: An Interactionist Approach. Boston:
Houghton Mifflin.
Schwartz, Michael and Sheldon Stryker 1970.
Deviance, selves and others. *American Sociological Association.*

Shibutani, Tamotsu 1961.
Society and Personality, An Interactionist Approach to Social Psychology. Boston: Prentice Hall.

Sidel, Ruth and Victor Sidel 1972.
The human services in China. *Social Policy*: 25–30.

Sidel, Ruth 1972.
Mental diseases and their treatment. Pp. 289–305 in Joseph R. Quinn (ed.), *Medicine and Public Health in the People's Republic of China.* US National Institute of Health.

Slater, Philip 1976.
The Pursuit of Loneliness. Boston: Beacon Press.

Stevens, Michelle 1978.
Near west siders protest move of mental patients. *Chicago Sun-Times*, May 2: 28.

Sullivan, Harry S. 1956.
Clinical Studies in Psychiatry. New York: Norton.
1962. *Schizophrenia as a Human Process.* New York: Norton. (Especially pp. 198–199; 125, 223.)

Taipale, Vappu and Likka Taipale 1973.
Chinese psychiatry: A visit to a Chinese mental hospital. *AMA Archives of General Psychiatry* 29, 3 (Sept.): 313–316.

Weinberg, S. Kirson (ed.) 1967.
The Sociology of Mental Disorders. Chicago: Aldine.

ABOUT THE AUTHORS

Leona L. Bachrach holds a Ph.D. in sociology from the University of Connecticut. She is currently Research Professor of Psychiatry at the Maryland Psychiatric Research Center, University of Maryland School of Medicine. She is also Senior Consultant to the Maryland Mental Hygiene Administration in Deinstitutionalization Planning. In 1977 she was invited to serve on the staff of the President's Commission on Mental Health at the White House, where she held staff responsibility for the Task Panels on Deinstitutionalization, Rehabilitation and Long-Term Care, and Rural Mental Health. Dr Bachrach is the author of numerous articles and books dealing with service planning for mental patients, particularly the chronically disabled. She has also written extensively on issues of service delivery in rural communities. She holds membership in a variety of professional organizations including the American Sociological Association, the Rural Sociological Society, and the American Public Health Association. In December 1982 she was elected to Honorary Fellowship in the American Psychiatric Association.

Ellen L. Bassuk MD is Associate Professor of Psychiatry at Harvard Medical School. She was recently a Fellow at the Mary Ingraham Bunting Institute at Radcliffe College. Her research has included the impact of chronic mental patients on general hospital emergency wards.

Phil Brown is Assistant Professor of Sociology at Brown University. His Ph.D. is from Brandeis University. He has written *The Transfer of Care: Psychiatric Deinstitutionalization and its Aftermath* and *Toward a Marxist Psychology*, and edited the collection *Radical Psychology*. His research on mental health policy and mental patients' rights has appeared in *Social Science and Medicine*, *International Journal of Health Services*, *Journal of Health Policy, Politics, and Law*, *Journal of Community Psychology*, and *Mental Disability Law Reporter*. He is also Research Fellow in the Harvard Medical School Department of Psychiatry at the Massachusetts Mental Health Center.

Judi Chamberlin is a former mental patient and a long-time activist in the psychiatric inmates' liberation movement. She is a member of the Mental Patients' Liberation Front of Boston. She lectures widely on the subjects of patients' rights and patient-controlled alternatives to the mental health system. She has represented the patients' point of view on numerous boards and committees, including the Task Panel on Legal and Ethical Issues of the President's Commission on Mental Health and the Blue Ribbon Commission on the Future of Public In-Patient Mental Health Services in Massachusetts.

Joseph Cocozza J. received his Ph.D. from Case Western Reserve University. He was Chairman of the Department of Sociology at Ursuline College (Cleveland, Ohio) 1970–73 before joining New York State Office of Mental Health as a Research Scientist in 1973. Subsequently, he was the first Director of Research and Evaluation for the NYS Council on Children and Families (1978 to 1981) and most recently the Executive Deputy Director of that agency. In this role he has had responsibility for the overall supervision, administration and coordination of all five policy and research units. Throughout his involvement with the Council, he has maintained primary responsibility for research grant development and contact with funding agencies. He has worked closely with staff at all levels of the thirteen state agencies associated with the Council as well as the Governor's office and Division of the Budget regarding the resolution of issues and the development of policy for children and family services within New York State.

George E. Crane received his medical degree at the University of Milano in 1936. Following work in bacteriology and service in the US Army in World War II, he was trained in psychiatry at Pilgrim State Hospital. As a psychiatric consultant at Montefiore Hospital in New York, he discovered antidepressant properties of tuberculosis medications. This work, along with the growing use of neuroleptic drugs, led Dr Crane to devote most of his work to psychopharmacology. He held positions at the Brockton, Massachusetts VA Hospital, St. Elizabeth's Hospital in Washington, DC, Spring Grove Hospital and North Dakota State Hospital. Dr Crane also directed the Early Clinical Drug Evaluation Unit of the National Institute of Mental Health for a period in the 1960s. Presently retired, Dr Crane continues his research in tardive dyskinesia and other side effects of neuroleptics, and consults to state and federal agencies.

Virginia K. Donovan received a Ph.D. in psychology from the State University of New York at Buffalo. Since 1971 she has been a psychotherapist and member of the Women's Mental Health Collective, a private, non-profit clinic in Somerville, Massachusetts. She currently teaches a seminar on a feminist approach to therapy.

Audrey J. Gartner has an MA in history from Wellesley College. She is Associate Director of the National Self-Help Clearinghouse and editor of its newsletter, the *Self-Help Reporter*. She is also managing editor of *Social Policy* magazine, where some of her writing on self-help groups has appeared.

Samuel Gerson received his Ph.D. in clinical psychology from the University of Texas at Austin in 1979. He is currently Director of the Adult Outpatient Clinic, Department of Psychiatry, Cambridge Hospital, Cambridge, Massachusetts. He is also Instructor in Psychology in the Department of Psychiatry, Harvard Medical School.

Irving D. Goldberg, a biostatistician, was Chief of the Applied Biometrics Research Branch of the National Institute of Mental Health until his retirement from Federal Service in 1982. Between 1957 and 1967 he served as the Assistant Chief of the Biometrics Branch of the National Institute of Neurological Diseases and Blindness of the National Institutes of Health, and until 1957 was a Senior Biostatistician with the New York State Department of Health. Mr Goldberg has authored or co-authored numerous articles on epidemiologic and health services research in the fields of health and mental health. He is the co-editor of two books and his works appear in various medical, psychiatric, psychological and public health journals, and as chapters in books. Mr Goldberg holds a BS degree from the City College of New York, and an MPH from the University of Michigan.

Howard H. Goldman MD, Ph.D. is a psychiatrist and mental health services researcher. Currently he is Assistant Director for Mental Health Financing at the National Institute of Mental Health – on leave from his position as Associate Professor of Psychiatry, Langley Porter Institute, University of California, San Francisco. Dr Goldman has been involved in policy-related research on various aspects of deinstitutionalization and the care of the chronically mentally ill. His most recent work is on financing mental health services. He trained at Harvard, Brandeis, and Worcester State Hospital where he did the work included in this anthology.

Charles A. Kiesler is Dean of the College of Humanities and Social Sciences and Walter VanDyke Bingham Professor of Psychology at Carnegie-Mellon University. He was Head of the Department of Psychology at Carnegie-Mellon University from 1980–1983; and acting Dean of the College of Humanities and Social Sciences during 1981–1982. He was formerly Executive Officer at the American Psychological Association (1975–1979) and editor of the *American Psychologist* (1975–1981). His books include *Attitude Change: A Critical Analysis of Theoretical Approaches* (with B. E. Collins and N. Miller), *Conformity* (with S. Kiesler), *The Psychology of Commitment*, and an edited collection *Psychology and National Health Insurance: A Sourcebook* (with N. Cummings and G. VandenBos). His current professional interests are in the development of research issues in national mental health policy; he is presently writing a book on that topic.

Lorraine V. Klerman, DrPH, is a Professor of Public Health at the Florence Heller Graduate School for Advanced Studies in social Welfare, Brandeis University, Waltham, Massachusetts. Her interest in the problems of children and youth have led her to study a variety of socially disfavored adolescent behaviors including pregnancy, excessive absenteeism, and aggressive or acting-out behavior. She was principal investigator of the Brandeis-Worcester Training Program in Social Research and Psychiatry, a National Institute of Mental Health-funded training program whose goal was to provide psychiatrists with the necessary skills to do social research. The work on that project led to co-authorship of the book *The Enduring Asylum: Cycles of Institutional Reform at Worcester State Hospital*.

Donald W. Light is Professor of Sociology in the Graduate Program at Rutgers University and director of behavioral and social medicine at the NJSOM unit of the University of Medicine and Dentistry of

New Jersey. He holds graduate degrees from the University of Chicago and Brandeis University. He is author of *Becoming Psychiatrists*. His current work includes comparative and historical studies of the professions.

Ronnie Littenberg received her Ph.D. in clinical psychology from Harvard University. She is a feminist therapist and founding member of the Women's Mental Health Collective, a private, non-profit clinic in Somerville, Massachusetts in existence since 1970. She has taught courses in Women and Psychology at Wellesley College and at the Cambridge Goddard Graduate School for Social Change. She currently teaches a seminar for therapists on feminist approaches to therapy and is an activist in the Women's Reproductive Rights movement.

Anne M. Lovell is a Fellow in the Psychiatric Epidemiology Program at Columbia University. She is co-author of *The Psychiatric Society* (with Robert Castel and Françoise Castel, Columbia University Press, 1982) and is editing, with Nancy Scheper-Hughes, a collection of writings by Franco Basaglia and Franca Ongaro Basaglia, to be published by Columbia University Press.

Yi-chuang Lu received her Ph.D. in sociology from the University of Chicago. She is presently Research Associate in Psychiatric Sociology at the Department of Psychiatry, University of Chicago. She has been a researcher and a psychiatric social worker in her native China, has taught sociology at the University of Utah, and was a researcher at Manteno (Illinois) State Hospital. Professor Lu's research has been published in the *Archives of General Psychiatry*, *Psychiatry*, *American Journal of Sociology*, *American Sociological Review*, *Social Problems*, *Marriage and Family Living*, and *Sociology and Social Research*.

Joseph P. Morrissey is Senior Research Scientist with the Bureau of Evaluation Research, New York State Office of Mental Health in Albany, and Adjunct Professor of Sociology, SUNY-Albany. His graduate degrees are from Clark University and the University of North Carolina-Chapel Hill. He formerly held positions at the National Institute of Mental Health and the Florence Heller School for Advanced Studies in Social Welfare at Brandeis University. He is author or co-author of numerous publications on the sociology of mental hospitalization, the delivery of mental health services, and interfaces between law and psychiatry. These include *The Enduring Asylum* (1981) and *Interorganizational Relations: A Sourcebook of Measures for Mental Health Programs* (1982). His current research focuses on community support systems for chronic mental patients and assessments of insanity defense reforms.

Alberta J. Nassi, Ph.D. is an Assistant Clinical Professor of Psychiatry and Clinical Director of Adult Day Treatment at the University of California, Davis School of Medicine. Her research interests include political psychology, adult development and the clinical application of object relations theory. She received her doctorate in clinical psychology from the University of California, Davis and completed an internship at Yale University.

Darrel A. Regier is Director of the Division of Biometry and Epidemiology, National Institute of Mental Health. He came to NIMH in 1975 as a Research Psychiatrist in the Applied Biometrics Research Branch, where he developed the Primary Care Research Section. In 1977, he was appointed as Director of the Division of Biometry and Epidemiology which conducts and supports a wide range of epidemiological, mental health services, and statistical research activities. Dr Regier has authored numerous articles in the fields of mental health epidemiology, services research, and statistics, with a particular focus on the primary health care sector. He has served as a guest lecturer at several medical schools and is on the editorial advisory board of the *Health Policy Quarterly* and the NIMH Health Science Reports Series. Dr Regier holds a BS degree from Wheaton College, Wheaton, Illinois, an MD from Indiana University School of Medicine, and an MPH from Harvard University School of Public Health. Clinical training included a straight medical internship at Montefiore Hospital and Medical Center, Bronx, New York, and a psychiatry residency and social psychiatry fellowship from Massachusetts General Hospital and Harvard University, Boston, Massachusetts.

Frank Riessman, Ph.D. is Professor of Sociology at the Graduate School of the City University of New York and Professor of Education at Queens College. He is director of the National Self-

Help Clearinghouse, editor of *Social Policy* magazine, and editor of *Ideas for Action* newsletter. Professor Riessman is author of numerous articles in professional journals and national magazines, as well as fifteen books including: *What Reagan is Doing to Us, Self-Help and the Human Services, The Inner-City Child, The Service Society and the Consumer Vanguard, Children Teach Children, Strategies Against Poverty, Social Class and Social Policy, Mental Health of the Poor* and *The Culturally Deprived Child.*

David Rothman, a member of the History faculty at Columbia University since 1964, has recently been appointed the first Bernard Schoenberg Professor of Social Medicine at the Medical School and Director of the Center for the Study of Society and Medicine. Professor Rothman graduated from Columbia College in 1958 and completed his Ph.D. in history at Harvard in 1964. He has written extensively on the evolution and social significance of mental hospitals, penitentiaries, and juvenile institutions; he has also been concerned with social policy in such areas as deinstitutionalization, treatment of the poor and children's rights. His book, *The Discovery of the Asylum*, won the Albert J. Beveridge Prize in 1971 for the outstanding work in American history. *Conscience and Convenience* (1980) traces the history of institutions and their alternatives through World War II. *Doing Good: The Limits of Benevolence*, (1978) co-authored with Willard Gaylin, Steven Marcus and Ira Glasser, examines the concept of paternalism in the helping professions. With Stanton Wheeler, he brought together historians and policy analysts to examine *Social History and Social Policy* (1980). His most recent research, in collaboration with Sheila Rothman, concerns the legal, political and social consequences of court-initiated reform. The results of this analysis, *The Willowbrook Wars*, will appear in the spring of 1984. Professor Rothman is a Fellow of the Hastings Institute of Society, Ethics, and the Life Sciences, and is on the boards of a number of public interest law organizations. He and Sheila Rothman recently returned from three-month Fulbright-Hayes Professorships in India, where they lectured on American social history and social policy.

Thomas J. Scheff is a Professor of Sociology at the University of California, Santa Barbara. He edited *Mental Illness and Social Processes* and *Labeling Madness*, and wrote *Being Mentally Ill: A*

Sociological Theory and *Catharsis in Healing, Ritual, and Drama*. His articles have appeared in numerous professional journals, including *Journal of Health and Social Behavior*, *Social Problems*, *American Journal of Psychiatry*, and *American Behavioral Scientist*.

Andrew Scull is an Associate Professor of Sociology at the University of California, San Diego. He was educated at Oxford and Princeton Universities. His books include: *Decarceration, Museums of Madness, Madhouses, Mad-doctors and Madmen: The Social History of Psychiatry in the Victorian Era, Social Control and the Modern State* (with Stanley Cohen), and *Durkheim and the Law* (with Steven Lukes). His articles have appeared in such journals as: *European Journal of Sociology, Politics and Society, Economy and Society, Social Problems, Social Science and Medicine, Psychological Medicine, Medical History, Victorian Studies, Stanford Law Review*, and *Michigan Law Review*, and in numerous anthologies.

Henry J. Steadman received his Ph.D. from the University of North Carolina. Since 1970 he has been a Research Scientist in the Special Projects Research Unit (SPRU) (now the Bureau of Evaluation Research) of the New York State Office of Mental Health, serving as its Director since 1974. In the latter capacity, he has been responsible for the organization and direction of a twenty-member social science research program oriented both to short-term policy analyses and longer-term research studies focused on the interface between the mental health and criminal justice systems, manpower issues, and the utilization of mental health services. His own research has produced four monographs and over forty-five articles in sociological, criminological, psychiatric and legal journals. Currently he serves on the Criminal Justice Mental Health Standards Task Force of the American Bar Association; the National Academy of Science's Committee on the Application of Behavioral Sciences to the Mission of the Secret Service; and on the editorial boards of the *International Journal of Law and Psychiatry, Law and Human Behavior*, and *Behavioral Sciences and the Law*.

Carl A. Taube is Acting Chief, Mental Health Economics Branch, Division of Biometry and Epidemiology, National Institute of Mental Health. He holds a Ph.D. in sociology from American University. His main interests are health services research and health economics.

His many publications appear in such journals as the *American Journal of Psychiatry*, *American Journal of Public Health*, *Archives of General Psychiatry*, and *Hospital and Community Psychiatry*, as well as in many anthologies.